# DECONSTRUCTING THE HERO

This book sets out to explore the structure and meaning of one of the most popular literary genres – the adventure story. It offers analytical readings of some of the most widely read adventure stories such as *Treasure Island*, *Robinson Crusoe* and the *James Bond* stories, and describes how these stories are influential in shaping children's perceptions and establishing values.

When many of these stories define non-white, non-European people as inferior, marginalize women and exploit the natural environment, we should be worried about what they are teaching our children to think. Moreover, since these stories are enormously popular, they help such values to survive despite efforts to the contrary.

Margery Hourihan shows how teaching children to read books critically can help to prevent the establishment of negative attitudes, discourage aggression and promote more positive values.

**Margery Hourihan** currently lectures part time in the School of Teacher Education at the University of Technology, Sydney, where she was formerly a senior lecturer and co-ordinator of the MA in Children's Literature and Literacy.

# DECONSTRUCTING THE HERO

## Literary theory and children's literature

*Margery Hourihan*

London and New York

First published 1997
by Routledge
2 Park Square, Milton Park, Abingdon, Oxon, OX14 4RN

Transferred to Digital Printing 2005

Simultaneously published in the USA and Canada
by Routledge
270 Madison Ave, New York NY 10016



Typeset in Garamond by M Rules



*British Library Cataloguing in Publication Data*
A catalogue record for this book is available from the British Library

*Library of Congress Cataloguing in Publication Data*
Hourihan, Margery, 1935–
Deconstructing the hero: literary theory and children's literature / Margery Hourihan.
p. cm.
1. Children's literature—History and criticism. 2. Heroes in literature. 3. Values in literature. 4. Prejudices. I. Title.
PN1009.A1H67 1997
810.9'352—dc21 97–10958
CIP

ISBN 0–415–14419–1
0–415–14186–9 (pbk)

*For Catherine, Madeline and Michael*

# CONTENTS

# ACKNOWLEDGEMENTS

Permission is gratefully acknowledged to reproduce the following copyright material:

Excerpt from 'The Waste Land' in COLLECTED POEMS 1909–1962, copyright 1936 by Harcourt Brace & Company, copyright 1964, 1963 by T.S. Eliot.
Reproduced by permission of Faber and Faber Ltd and Harcourt Brace & Company

Excerpt from 'The Highwayman' by Alfred Noyes, reproduced by permission of John Murray (Publishers) Ltd

Excerpts from *The Argonautica* by Apollonius of Rhodes, translated by Richard Hunter, by permission of Oxford University Press

Excerpt from *The Republic* by Plato, translated by F.M. Cornforth, by permission of Oxford University Press

Every effort has been made to obtain permission to reproduce copyright material. If any acknowledgement has not been made, we would invite copyright holders to inform us of the oversight.

# INTRODUCTION

Stories are important in all cultures. People have always used stories to render the vast heterogeneity of experience meaningful, to explain the behaviour of the physical universe and to describe human nature and society. They are the most potent means by which perceptions, values and attitudes are transmitted from one generation to the next. All teachers know the power of stories as educational tools. They are vivid, enjoyable, easily understood, memorable and compelling. They appeal to people of all ages, but for children who have not yet achieved the ability to reason abstractly they provide images to think with. Our most basic concepts, such as time and causation, are embedded in the stories told to children from infancy onwards, and for this reason we feel there is truth in the shape of stories even when we know their content is fantasy. A story which begins with 'once upon a time' and ends with 'and they lived happily ever after' implies things about time and change, about cause and effect, and human relationships, regardless of where it is set or who the characters are, and it asserts an essential optimism: problems can be solved, things will turn out well, happiness is achievable. That many, perhaps most, people in our society cling stubbornly to a belief in the shape of this tale, despite the disappointments and uncertainties of life as it is lived, attests to the power of stories.

In Western culture there is a story which has been told over and over again, in innumerable versions, from the earliest times. It is a story about superiority, dominance and success. It tells how white European men are the natural masters of the world because they are strong, brave, skilful, rational and dedicated. It tells how they overcome the dangers of nature, how other 'inferior' races have been subdued by them, and how they spread civilization and order wherever they go. It tells how women are designed to serve them, and how those women who refuse to do so are threats to the natural order and must be controlled. It tells how their persistence means that they always eventually win the glittering prizes, the golden treasures, and how the gods – or the government – approve of their enterprises. It is our favourite story and it has been told so many times that we have come to believe that what it says about the world is true.

Only in the last few decades have people begun to question its message, to argue that those with different coloured skins are not inherently inferior, that women are not naturally subordinate, that the relentless conquest of nature may have appalling consequences, that logic alone will not satisfactorily answer all our questions, that the achievement of power and success will not necessarily lead to contentment. But the story is deeply entrenched, belief in its general outlines underlies most of the ways in which Western society functions – especially competitive, free-market capitalism – and it is relinquished reluctantly. So as social reform movements make tentative headway various kinds of backlash emerge. Racism assumes subtler and more elusive forms; imperialism is replaced by economic domination; feminism is attacked in the name of family values; governments officially support the preservation of the environment but because of economic demands forests continue to be felled, national parks are mined, more freeways are constructed, more species expire. For the European/American patriarchy, power remains the central political concern. And the story continues to be told.

The story of the hero and his quest, the adventure story, is always essentially the same. It is the story of Odysseus, of Jason and the Golden Fleece, of Beowulf, of Saint George, of the Knights of the Round Table, of Jack and the Beanstalk, of Robinson Crusoe, of Peter Rabbit, of James Bond, of Luke Skywalker, of Batman, of Indiana Jones, of the latest sci-fi adventure and the latest game in the computer shop. It appears in countless legends, folk tales, children's stories and adult thrillers. It is ubiquitous. Northrop Frye has argued that the quest myth is the basic myth of all literature, deriving its meanings from the cycle of the seasons and 'the central expression of human energy [which transformed] the amorphous natural environment into the pastoral, cultivated, civilized world of human shape and meaning . . . the hero is the reviving power of spring and the monster and old king the outgrown forces of apathy and impotence in a symbolic winter' (Frye 1983: 187–8). Whether we accept this or not, the centrality of the hero story in our culture is unarguable.

Not only is it everywhere about us, it inscribes the set of related concepts, the fundamental dualisms, which have shaped Western thought and values. Plato and Aristotle articulated the basic dualisms when they asserted the superiority of humans to animals, free men to slaves, men to women, reason to passion and soul (or mind) to body. Christian thought largely mirrors these values, and links them to the concepts of good and evil. The hero always embodies the superior terms of these dualisms as he adventures forth on his quest and encounters evil monsters, dragons, witches and their like. Later hero tales contain the ancient dualisms as a substratum of values and add new ones to them. So Robinson Crusoe, a disciple of Cartesian reason, sees the black savages who visit his island as depraved and brutish, and Defoe's story thus links the dualism of white and black to the traditional pairs. Following the success of *Crusoe* the age of imperialism produced a flood of adventure stories in which intrepid British lads struggled against dark-skinned opponents to bring enlightenment to the distant reaches of the empire. In post-imperial stories, James Bond and his like defend democracy against communism and these concepts are likewise added to the pattern and defined as, respectively, good and evil. In 'realistic' hero tales the identity of the enemy, of 'them', changes to reflect political circumstances but fantasy and science fiction are free to invent images of the 'others' which emphasize our qualities by the force of contrast. Thus, for instance, the Daleks, Doctor Who's main opponents, are depicted as lacking the compassion and respect for life which make us human, and viewers are able to feel a comfortable sense of superiority. By drawing a distinction between us and them in this way, and defining our civilization in contradistinction to our opponents, real and imaginary, the hero story asserts the 'natural' superiority of the West.

This adversarial way of perceiving the world means that conflict is seen as natural and inevitable. The hero is constantly confronted by enemies which he must overcome, so he is above all things a man of action. He is good at fighting, and he uses his club, or sword or gun to telling effect. His victory is celebrated by the people he saves from the dragon, the outlaws, the aliens or the communists. Thus the story glorifies violence and defines manhood within this context. There is a level of psychological allegory in the story which is concerned with the transition from boyhood to manhood, and at this level the monsters represent fears and self-doubts which must be overcome, and in some cases the actual ceremonies of initiation which must be endured, before the boy can call himself a real man. At this level the phallic symbolism of the weapon which he wields is only too apparent. This level of psychological meaning reinforces the literal significance of the story, defining the essential qualities of true manhood as prowess, courage, aggression, determination, dominance. Sexual dominance is conflated with physical and political dominance, and women in hero stories appear only in relation to the hero. They are part of the way his manhood is defined: some are his devoted assistants, dedicated to his cause, some are trophy brides, and some are dangerous opponents who seek to steal his potency – witches and vampires who must be destroyed. In this way the story also defines good and bad femininity and inscribes the subordinate place of women. Like the dragons, the wild animals, the ogres, the savages, the aliens, they are essentially 'other'. They cannot share the role of the master for it is his destiny to be master – over all others.

The hero story has dominated children's and young adult literature, passing on the traditional values to each new generation. Most authorities on children's literature assume that hero tales are unequivocally good for children, as morally and mentally nutritious as apples and wholemeal bread. Charlotte Huck says that a knowledge of these stories 'gives children an understanding of a particular culture; but more importantly it provides them with models of greatness through the ages' (Huck *et al.* 1987: 314). Bernice Cullinan in *Literature and the Child* says:

> children absorb quest tales 'into the bloodstream', assimilating the values of human society past and present. Values inherent in quest tales, shaped by generations of human experience, emerge consistently and are widely accepted. Because most children unconsciously learn from experience that goodness is generally rewarded and wickedness punished, quest tales affirm their knowledge.
>
> (Cullinan 1989: 306)

Such statements recognize the power of these stories as agents of cultural transmission but fail to examine the nature of the values inherent in them. What does the 'greatness' they model consist of? What kind of goodness is rewarded in them? What kinds of behaviour do they endorse? What do they suggest about the roles and relationships of men and women? What attitudes do they encourage towards people of other cultures? In short, what meanings does the quest myth impose upon readers?

If Western society is to become less violent, less destructive of nature, more genuinely equitable, we need to tell different stories, especially to children, but we also need to understand the hero story and its appeal, to deconstruct it and see how it functions, for its meanings inhere in its structure as well as its content. Literary theory provides tools for this task. Perhaps the central insight of structuralist and poststructuralist theory is that no text is innocent: all stories are ideological. The ideology may not be overt; indeed, as Peter Hollindale points out (1988: 19) obviously ideological stories risk being dismissed as didactic. But a writer's own values are inevitably implicit in the text, seeming simply part of the texture of reality. The countless nineteenth-century children's stories which restrict girls and women to limited domestic roles are products of their writers' unexamined assumptions about gender, and they carry a powerful, though passive, ideological message. More generally, stories are the products of the time and the social group which gave rise to them, and the values of that time and that group will inform the language in which they are written. As Hollindale says: 'A large part of any book is written not by its author but by the world its author lives in' (1988: 23). So stories inevitably transmit many of the values of their time to succeeding generations even though, as time passes, interpretations are modified.

We can begin to unpack the ideology of hero stories by examining the binary oppositions which are central to them. The qualities ascribed to the hero and his opponents reveal much about what has been valued and what has been regarded as inferior or evil in Western culture. A consideration of what is foregrounded, what is backgrounded and what is simply omitted from these stories throws further light on the hierarchy of values which they construct. Analysis of narrative point of view, focalization and narrative voice can show how the reader's sympathies and perceptions are manipulated. The shape of the story and the nature of its closure are also significant. The language, imagery and symbolism of particular stories function within the context of these structural features. As John Stephens points out (1992: 120) narrative consists of three interlocked components: the discourse, or surface of the text, the story, and a significance derived by readers from the first two. It is the significance readers are likely to derive from hero tales that is of central concern, but it is also necessary to consider why the stories are so popular, what is it about their structure that attracts and satisfies so many readers and viewers.

Ancient hero myths and fairy tales have been analysed by scholars in a number of disciplines, notably anthropology, mythology and psychology. However, this book is not concerned with the meanings which the ancient myths or the later folk tales held for the people who produced them. It is the meanings young readers might make from the stories available to them today that are of concern here. Scholarly analyses of myths and traditional stories are interesting in their own right and they heighten our responsiveness to the kinds of significance which may still inhere in the tales, but contemporary readers, especially young readers, will construct meanings related to their own lives and to the society they live in. A child reading a modern version of 'Little Red Riding Hood' in which the wolf is killed and Red Riding Hood rescued by a hunter will not know that the 1697 Perrault version of the story did not include the hunter and ended with both the grandmother and Red Riding Hood still inside the wolf (Perrault [1697] 1969: 25–9). Nor will he or she know that there was an earlier oral French version in which Red Riding Hood had not yet acquired the red hood, and escaped from the wolf in an enterprising manner by asking to be allowed to go outside to relieve herself (Darnton 1984: 46). Today's child readers will not be concerned with the possible meanings of these earlier versions for the people of the time, but will construct meanings from the version of the story presented to them, including the intervention of the hunter, and the interesting questions are what this motif might signify to children and why the addition of the hunter, which transforms the story into a version of the hero myth, has become so firmly established in our time.

The hero stories discussed in this book are all popular and influential. They include traditional tales which are still widely known and often retold for young readers, classic and present-day works of children's and young adult literature, works intended for adults but often read by younger audiences, and popular formulaic literature such as science fiction and detective stories. Other works which are particularly influential or illuminating, such as Shakespeare's *The Tempest*, are discussed at various points. Children's literature does not exist in isolation and its significance cannot be properly appreciated unless it is explored in the broader cultural context. Children's literature is a thriving industry today. Among the vast numbers of new titles that appear each year there are many which simply retell the old story with present-day trappings. A number of non-traditional works conscientiously foreground reformist values – and often win prizes although they may fail to win many readers. But there are some that manage to take the hero story with its compelling narrative power and infuse it with new meanings, and the final chapter of this book is devoted to a discussion of some of these.

All texts are ideological and all have a point of view from which their subject matter is perceived. This book, of course, is no exception. It does not seek to be neutral, but rather to analyse the meanings and impact of hero tales from a different perspective from that which sees them as depictions of human greatness and expressions of the noblest ideals. As a woman I am one of those whom the hero tale confines to the margins. Hero stories are not my story, but when I was young I learnt, like all female readers of Western literature, to read as a male, to share the perspective of the protagonist, and in doing so I internalized the view that the male was the norm and the female something less. The belief that great literature was 'universal' and so could not focus primarily on the doings of women seemed unarguable. If I found books exclusively concerned with the doings of men somewhat alienating I believed that was a failure of appreciation on my part. As a young teacher in the 1960s I did not find it strange that *Treasure Island* was often the prescribed novel for classes consisting entirely of Australian girls, and for a long time I accepted the views of male critics who believed *Jane Eyre* to be of limited value. I read and think differently now. One of the aims of this book is to show how the hero story looks if one reads it as a woman, how, instead of providing 'models of greatness', it teaches confusion, timidity and self-hatred.

Although of English background I am Australian and so I grew up knowing what it is like to be out of the mainstream of Western culture. As an avid childhood reader of English stories I came to feel that I lived in an inherently inferior part of the world where nothing that happened could be of real significance. As I read I dreamed of going to the northern hemisphere which was the site of real culture, and that is exactly what many Australians of my generation did as soon as they could afford it, saving for years to amass the fare for the month-long sea voyage to London, fleeing to centrality and significance. It is only since the flowering of Australian culture that began with the election of the Whitlam government in 1972 that I have come to see this perception of Australia as something constructed by what I read, and to believe that it may be more exciting to be part of the formative stage of an emerging culture than a participant in the latter years of an established one. More recently still I have begun to acquire some small understanding of what the enaction of the hero story by the white settlers in Australia meant to the indigenous people. Not having suffered their fate I cannot share their perspective but I now realize its validity. Another aim of this book is to show how the point of view of the hero story is always that of the victor and the colonizer, and how it suppresses the perspective of the conquered and the colonized.

The hero story celebrates the conquest of nature as well as of 'savages'. The earliest extant version, the *Epic of Gilgamesh*, tells how Gilgamesh and his friend Enkidu ventured into the cedar forest, bravely confronted the giant who guarded it, and cut down the trees. Once, as Northrop Frye suggests, this may have been the essential human endeavour, the transformation of nature into 'shape and meaning', but today the urgent requirement is the salvation of the natural environment, and we need to reassess the ideas of achievement and progress which are inherent in the hero story. The connections between the exploitation of nature, the oppression of subject peoples and the subordination of women is a major focus of eco-feminist theory. The Australian eco-feminist philosopher, Val Plumwood, whose work I have found particularly helpful, says:

> The concept of reason provides the unifying and defining contrast for the concept of nature, much as the concept of husband does for that of wife, as master for slave. Reason in the western tradition has been constructed as the privileged domain of the master, who has conceived nature as a wife or subordinate other encompassing and representing the sphere of materiality, subsistence and the feminine which the master has split off and constructed as beneath him. The continual and cumulative overcoming of the domain of nature by reason engenders the western concept of progress and development.
>
> (Plumwood 1993: 3)

Progress and development have led to the exhaustion and pollution of many of the planet's resources, and the continuation of the process at anything like the present rate can only lead to disaster. This is another reason for considering the hero story from a non-traditional perspective, for questioning the values it inscribes.

There is no single, correct way of viewing any issue, event or text. All the truths which we perceive are partial and relative, all interpretations are to some extent misinterpretations. To assert this is not to suggest that the attempt to understand is pointless, or that 'anything goes', for all misinterpretations are also partly interpretations. What is important is to recognize the plurality of human 'truth'. As Jonathan Culler puts it in *On Deconstruction*:

> According to the paleonymic strategy urged by Derrida, 'misreading' retains the trace of truth, because noteworthy readings involve claims to truth and because interpretation is structured by the attempt to catch what other readings have missed and misconstrued. Since no reading can escape correction, all readings are misreadings; but this leaves not a monism but a double movement. Against the claim that, if there are only misreadings, then anything goes, one affirms that misreadings are errors; but against the positivist claim that they are errors because they strive toward but fail to attain a true reading, one maintains that true readings are only particular misreadings: readings whose misses have been missed. This account of misreading is not, perhaps, a coherent, consistent position, but, its advocates would claim, it resists metaphysical idealizations and captures the temporal dynamic of our interpretive situation.
>
> (Culler 1983: 178)

There are, then, many ways of reading hero stories, and all are to some extent misreadings. This book deliberately brings particular and partial perspectives to bear upon them, not in an attempt to provide final, correct interpretations, but to challenge the traditional readings which see in them only expressions of 'greatness', models of ideal human behaviour. These conventional monocular interpretations affirm the values and behaviour patterns which have perpetrated and justified a wide range of oppressions and led to a complex of environmental problems that threaten the very civilization they have created. It is time to tell new stories and read the old ones differently.

# 1

# THE STORY

Though infinitely varied in detail the hero story is always the same. Exciting and suspenseful, it keeps the reader turning the pages to find out what happens next as one peril, predicament, terror, mystery and struggle follows another, but the hero's ultimate triumph is always assured. Most readers enjoy these stories, they are the basis of some of the most popular films ever made, and children often nominate 'adventure' as their favourite kind of reading (Lodge 1987: 151). One reason for their appeal is their very predictability: the formula to which they conform is so familiar that they present no challenge to the reader's interpretive or critical skills. Further, their series of banal thrills reinforce the standard perceptions and prejudices of our culture, assuring the young Western male reader of his innate superiority.

Whether it is *The Odyssey*, *Jack and the Beanstalk*, *Treasure Island*, *Doctor Who*, *Star Wars*, the latest James Bond thriller, or *Where the Wild Things Are*, the hero story takes the form of a journey and follows an invariable pattern:

- The hero is white, male, British, American or European, and usually young. He may be accompanied by a single male companion or he may be the leader of a group of adventurers.
- He leaves the civilized order of home to venture into the wilderness in pursuit of his goal.
- The wilderness may be a forest, a fantasy land, another planet, Africa or some other non-European part of the world, the mean streets of London or New York, a tropical island, et cetera. It lacks the order and safety of home. Dangerous and magical things happen there.
- The hero encounters a series of difficulties and is threatened by dangerous opponents. These may include dragons or other fantastic creatures, wild animals, witches, giants, savages, pirates, criminals, spies, aliens.
- The hero overcomes these opponents because he is strong, brave, resourceful, rational and determined to succeed. He may receive assistance from wise and benevolent beings who recognize him for what he is.
- He achieves his goal which may be golden riches, a treasure with spiritual significance like the Holy Grail, the rescue of a virtuous (usually female)

prisoner, or the destruction of the enemies which threaten the safety of home.

- He returns home, perhaps overcoming other threats on the way, and is gratefully welcomed.
- He is rewarded. Sometimes this reward is a virtuous and beautiful woman.

Some of the meanings of the story, especially the inscription of white European dominance, the marginalization of women and the privileging of action and extroversion over imagination and feeling, are already apparent from such a summary.

## THE POWER OF THE MYTH

> . . . myth has in fact a double function: it points out and it notifies, it makes us understand something and it imposes it on us.
>
> (Roland Barthes, *Mythologies* [1957] (1973): 117)

The hero story has been with us since the emergence of Western culture. The oldest extant written version is *The Epic of Gilgamesh* which, according to its English translator, probably belongs to the third millennium BC (Sandars 1960: 13). The written version, discovered on clay tablets in cuneiform script during the nineteenth-century excavations of Nineveh, belongs to the seventh century BC and was probably the work of Assurbanipal, the last Assyrian king, but fragments which have turned up amongst the Hittite archives and in Palestine suggest the tale was already widespread in the second millennium BC. Sandars speculates (pp. 44–5) that it would have been possible for the poet of *The Odyssey* to have heard the story of Gilgamesh direct because ships from the Greek islands and Ionia traded on the Syrian coast during the second millennium BC. Homer's *Odyssey*, which is generally agreed to be about three thousand years old, and is still regularly retold for children in beautifully illustrated versions, may be regarded as the paradigmatic version. It tells of the homeward journey of Odysseus, or Ulysses, who left his kingdom in Ithaca to fight with the Greeks at Troy where he acquitted himself nobly, being clever as well as brave. The actual text of Homer's poem is quite complex for the tale of Odysseus's wanderings is embedded within an account of the troubles in Ithaca during his absence, where his faithful wife, Penelope, is besieged by a horde of suitors competing for the opportunity to take his place as king. But Odysseus's journey is the heart of the poem, and in retellings for young readers his adventures are usually related in simple sequential order. After the sacking of Troy, Odysseus and his followers set out for home. However, the gods send storms which drive his ship off course. They are blown into unknown waters and visit wild and magical places including the land of the Lotus-eaters, the savage Cyclopes' island, the island of Aeaea, which is ruled by the beautiful enchantress, Circe, and the underworld itself. They encounter the sirens who would lure their ship to destruction, and the terrifying rocks and whirlpool, Scylla and Charybdis. Here the ship is finally wrecked and all Odysseus's followers drowned. Odysseus himself survives and is cast up on the island ruled by Calypso, another beautiful enchantress, who is so charmed by him that she invites him to share her bed and offers him immortality if he will stay with her; Odysseus, however, is not to be deterred from his purpose:

> The divine Calypso certainly did her best to keep me yonder in her cavern home because she wished to be my wife, and with the same object Circe, the Aeaean witch, detained me in her castle, but never for a moment did they win my heart. So true it is that his motherland and his parents are what a man holds sweetest.
>
> (Homer 1946: 141–2)

Zeus intervenes to persuade Calypso to release him and he presses on, reaching the Phaecian kingdom where the virtuous Princess Nausicca comes to his aid. She conducts him to her father, Alcinous, who assists him to return to Ithaca. There, with the help of his son, Telemachus, and the goddess, Athene, he slays the suitors, proves his identity by stringing the great bow which no other could bend, and reclaims his kingdom and his wife. The outlines of Homer's story are so familiar to us, the series of magical adventures so compelling and charged with latent symbolism, that they seduce our attention from the fact that it is a story about mastery.

The persistence of this pattern which inscribes the myth of Western patriarchal superiority is apparent when we see that Maurice Sendak's celebrated children's picture book, *Where the Wild Things Are* [1963], tells a story which is in essence exactly the same as the story of Odysseus. A small boy called Max, dressed in his wolf suit, misbehaves and threatens his mother, so he is sent to bed without his supper. Once in his room he embarks on an imaginary journey, through a forest and across an ocean, to the land where the wild things are. Despite their ferocious appearance Max tames them by saying 'Be still!' and looking into their eyes without blinking, whereupon they make him their king. He is given a crown and a sceptre and they obey him. Max and the wild things indulge in a joyous and anarchic rumpus which stretches across six pages of illustrations, but finally, lonely for love, Max stops the rumpus and departs despite the wild things' plea: 'Oh please don't go – we'll eat you up – we love you so!' (Sendak [1963] 1967). He sails home, into his own room where he finds that a hot supper is waiting for him.

Like Odysseus and all the other heroes of antiquity, Max is the primary force in his story. His goal, like Odysseus's, is to regain his kingdom (his position as a loved child with the freedom of his whole home). Like the ancient heroes he shows no fear in the face of the wild things he encounters and he subdues them by the exercise of his will. Though they linger in the magical wilderness for a time, neither Max nor Odysseus can be persuaded to stay there despite appeals and blandishments; they remain dedicated to their purpose. Each achieves a successful return to home and normality and is rewarded by the love of a faithful kinswoman. They regain their kingdoms.

*Where the Wild Things Are* is justly admired for its exquisite illustrations, its psychological acuity and the polysemic nature of the simple story. Some of the meanings which readers might make from the text and the pictures are that in his dream Max realizes he has the power to control his 'wild' emotions, understands that when he threatened his mother he had not ceased to love her. The wild things' appeal to Max: 'Oh please don't go – we'll eat you up – we love you so!' echoes the earlier threat he made to her: 'I'll eat you up!' and shows his awareness that the intensity of his anger was a function of the intensity of his love. The hot supper which his mother has left for him shows that she realizes this too. The possibility of such personal meanings constitutes a potent appeal for child readers. But part of the story's enormous and enduring popularity is attributable to Max's role as a hero who undertakes a successful quest and masters the wild things – and from that other, socially significant meanings emerge. Although he is no more than 4 years old, Max has learnt the trick of domination and is clearly a potential member of the patriarchy.

The hero story is a myth in both the traditional sense and the sense in which Roland Barthes uses the term in *Mythologies* to describe the way certain stories and images function to shape our perceptions of reality. For Barthes, myths are omnipresent signs which impose upon us the belief that something simply 'goes without saying'; they create a perception of the 'falsely obvious' (Barthes [1957] 1973: 11). He argues that the very principle of myth, in this sense, is that 'it transforms history into nature' (p. 129). It makes contingent events and behaviour seem inevitable, part of the nature of things. As an example of a myth in operation he cites a magazine photograph of a French Negro soldier saluting the French flag. The photograph, he says, signifies that France is a great empire, without any colour discrimination, and that all her sons gladly serve under her flag with no desire to be free from so-called colonialism. The picture is of an actual soldier, with a personal history, photographed at a particular moment in time, but its mythic power distracts the observer's attention from these specifics and encourages the reading of the photograph as a *natural* expression of the grandeur and multiculturalism of imperial France. At the same time the fact that the photograph depicts a real person seems to provide empirical evidence of the truth of the myth. The hero story has become a myth in this sense, all the more powerful because of its ancient origins.

To explain how myth works Barthes ([1957] 1973: 113–15) uses the linguist Saussure's concept of the sign. Saussure calls an acoustic or written symbol (e.g. 'wolf') a signifier; the signifier evokes a concept, the signified (the speaker's or listener's mental idea of a wolf). The word, or sign, consists of the signifier and the signified. The crucial point is that the signifier does not relate to anything in the physical world (any actual animal); it relates to a mental concept which may involve any number of emotional associations. In the case of 'wolf' these associations might include 'dangerous', 'slavering', 'predatory', 'shaggy', 'huge fangs', 'blood-thirsty' and so on – all the ascriptions which have led to the persecution and extermination of the wolf in many parts of the world, despite the extreme rarity of actual wolf attacks on humans. Barthes describes myth as a second-order semiological system: just as words act as signifiers in linguistic systems, so a myth evoked by a particular story, or perhaps a painting, photograph or ritual, signifies a range of meanings. When we encounter any version of the myth it imposes the meanings of the pattern as a whole upon us whether or not this accords with lived experience. So a picture of a knight on horseback spearing a dragon, or the simple phrase 'Saint George and the dragon' immediately calls up ideas of a chivalric tradition in which courage, prowess and a determination to triumph over an evil enemy are the paramount values. The meanings of the hero story are invoked. A Sydney football team called Saint George uses the dragon as its logo, knowing these symbols will suggest that the team is brave, strong and aggressive. Beyond this, the evocation of the myth also implies that football is a noble pursuit, that it is somehow an expression of the highest qualities of manhood.

A related idea is the concept of intertextuality which stresses the extent to which all texts are necessarily derived from pre-existing texts and discourses, and will themselves form part of the context from which subsequent texts are derived. Likewise the reader's interpretation of any particular text will be determined in part by his or her prior experience of other texts. Values and perceptions implied by frequently encountered motifs come to seem simply 'true', to go without saying. Story patterns which are re-used and reworked in one text after another are one of the most obvious examples of inter-textuality, and of these patterns the hero/quest story is the most frequently encountered. Some reworkings, such as Joyce's *Ulysses* and Eliot's *The Waste Land* allude deliberately and self-consciously to earlier versions of the story. In other cases it is difficult to tell whether particular echoes are intended or not: Tolkien's account of Frodo's and Sam's journey through the rocky wastes of Mordor in *The Return of the King* recalls phrases from Section Five of *The Waste Land*, but both call upon traditional Christian symbolism and descriptions of difficult pilgrimages. In yet other cases the story structure is used without any obvious references to particular pre-texts, but the general resonances of the genre are inevitably invoked; this is the case with straightforward adventure stories like Rider Haggard's *King Solomon's Mines*, and, of course, *Where the Wild Things Are*.

Because of its omnipresence the hero story lends itself to parody. George Lucas' 1977 film *Star Wars*, one of the most famous modern manifestations of the myth, raids the clichés of earlier hero films: the young hero, Luke Skywalker, swings across a chasm on a rope with Princess Leia in his arms, recalling a host of swashbuckling adventurers such as Douglas Fairbanks and Errol Flynn; his adviser Obi Wan Kenobi (Alec Guinness), dressed in a brown monk's cloak and hood, and the dark lord, Darth Vader, in black metallic armour, fight to the death with laser-swords in a pastiche of mediaeval romance. The most amusing of these parodic allusions is the final aerial fight in which the good rebels attack in small, two-man spacecraft with the pilots wearing flak-jackets, goggles and airforce moustaches while phrases from old films about the Battle of Britain crackle from their radios. But such parodies do not question the values implicit in the story, they merely revisit them with affectionate amusement.

In Western culture the hero story has come to seem simply a reflection of the way things are. The perception of those who are different as actual or potential enemies who must be opposed has assumed the status of self-evident truth. The assumption that the West ought to dominate the rest of the world because of its natural fitness to do so has come to seem equally natural. This is not necessarily a matter of crude racism; many who would reject suggestions of inherent racial superiority nevertheless accept Western cultural superiority without question. Edward Said, whose perspective derives from his membership of both the European and Arabic cultures argues, in *Orientalism*, that an idea of the non-European, and specifically of the Oriental, has been constructed in Western thought on the basis of European theories of race, civilization and language; in this conception the Oriental is defined as inherently subordinate to the European and the Orient is designated as a field of European study, conceptualization and colonization. The Europeans who study are necessarily seen as superior to the non-Europeans, the objects of study:

> Orientalism is never far from what Denys Hay has called the idea of Europe, a collective notion identifying 'us' Europeans against all 'those' non-Europeans, and indeed it can be argued that the major component in European culture is precisely what made that culture hegemonic both in and outside Europe: the idea of European identity as a superior one in comparison with all the non-European peoples and cultures. There is in addition the hegemony of European ideas about the Orient, themselves reiterating European superiority over Oriental backwardness.
> (Said [1978] 1995: 7)

The need to struggle for 'success' has come to seem equally axiomatic, and we have structured many of our social and political institutions as sites of this struggle. International relations are largely based on the assumption that 'they' are potential or actual enemies and the process of demonization reinforces the perception; only the identity of the demons changes. Recently Muslim fundamentalists have come to replace 'Communists' as the most popular demons. In Western democracies parliaments and law courts operate adversarially. Competition for promotion and power is endemic in most large organizations. But it is probably in sport that the struggle to win is most intense and victory most celebrated.

Sport is one of the major means by which values and attitudes are shaped in Western culture. Governments spend large amounts of money in the pursuit of national sporting success, successful sportsmen are idolized and imitated, and televised sport is avidly watched by millions. Those sporting activities which arouse the most passion are constructed as ritual re-enactments of the myth: 'our' team, or 'our' Olympic representatives go forth to do symbolic battle with their opponents. They are expected to be strong, brave and dedicated to the cause. They are expected to win. If they succeed they are awarded a glittering trophy and we welcome them home as national heroes. Significantly most of the sport which is widely promoted through the media is male sport. In a paper delivered at the University of Technology, Sydney, in 1995 Gay Mason argued that sport, in general, plays a central role in the development of masculinity and that 'sporting discourse offers a prime site for the construction of "maleness"' (1995: 6). According to Mason the images of male bodies engaged in sporting activities constitute one of the main ways in which the superiority of men becomes 'naturalised', and the media, in their reporting of sport, 'conspire in naturalising hegemonic masculinity' (1995: 6). The notions of male physical strength, force, potency and skill constructed by sport are translated into social concepts of masculine authority and power.

Men's ongoing domination of politics and sport, despite some significant gains by women in other fields, means that public positions of real and symbolic power are still overwhelmingly occupied by males, and suggests the continuance of an underlying belief in the natural inferiority of women. These concepts are inscribed in the hero story in which women play subordinate roles, in which their relative insignificance seems to 'go without saying'.

## DUALISM AND BINARY OPPOSITIONS

The conceptual centre of a hero story consists of a set of binary oppositions: the qualities ascribed to the hero on the one hand and to his 'wild' opponents on the other. So in Stevenson's *Treasure Island* [1883], for example, the hero, Jim Hawkins, and his friends, consistently referred to as 'gentlemen', are opposed to the pirates who, apart from Long John Silver himself, are described as dirty, drunken, irrational, deceitful and violent, whereas the gentlemen are neat, sober, rational, honest and self-controlled. The gentlemen are presented as upright citizens and the pirates as criminals. The gentlemen are associated with civilized England and the pirates with the 'wild' island. Thus we could construct two balanced lists:

| | | |
|---|---|---|
| gentlemen | – | pirates |
| neat | – | dirty |
| sober | – | drunken |
| rational | – | irrational |
| honest | – | deceitful |
| self-controlled | – | violent |
| law-abiding | – | criminal |
| England | – | island |

Because the story is narrated in the first person by Jim and Doctor Livesey, we see the pirates only through their eyes, and they are perceived as evil; 'good' and 'evil' could therefore be added to the respective lists. The signifiers in each column form a cluster with each term supported by the others, so that, as we read, it seems self-evident that the gentlemen are good and the pirates evil. The reader constructs this meaning from the text although, when the motives and deeds of each group are examined closely, there is little to choose between them. Both are driven by the desire to have the gold for themselves and both kill members of the opposing group in the struggle to secure it. (*Treasure Island* is discussed in more detail in the following chapters.)

The linguist, Saussure's, description of language as a system of differences (de Saussure [1915] 1974: 111–21) has enabled the perception that, in any particular text, the meanings of the signifiers are functions of their relationships to each other within that text. That is, the text is a system which constructs a pattern of meaning, more or less consistent within itself, but only problematically related to external reality. So the meaning of 'pirate' in *Treasure Island* is the opposite of 'gentleman' and is different from the meaning of 'pirate' in, for instance, John Ryan's Captain Pugwash stories where the pirates are innocent, comic, slightly anarchic figures who behave like members of a gang of small boys, or Margaret Mahy's picture book *The Man Whose Mother was a Pirate* where 'pirate' means 'fun-loving free spirit' as opposed to timid and conformist office-workers. Likewise 'good' in *Treasure Island* means little more than 'belonging to the establishment' while 'evil' means being outside it. The meanings of hero stories depend upon these related pairs of signifiers which express the dualistic structure inherent in Western thought, a pattern of values which naturalizes the dominance of the European patriarchal elite and the subordination of other cultural groups, other social classes, women and nature.

The dualism of Western culture has been explored from both poststructuralist and feminist perspectives, and is lucidly analysed by the eco-feminist writer Val Plumwood in *Feminism and the Mastery of Nature* (1993). A dualism is more than a dichotomy, for in a dualism one of the two contrasting terms is constructed as superior and the other as inherently inferior in relation to it. The inferiorized 'other' is treated in a variety of ways: It may be backgrounded, that is simply regarded as not worthy of notice, as is the case with females in boys' adventure stories like *Treasure Island*. It may be defined as radically different, distinct in as many ways as possible from the superior norm, thus underlining its inferiority; this occurs, for example, in the polarization of gender roles in fairy tales. The inferiorized group tends to be treated as homogeneous in order to emphasize its distinctness from the dominant norm; thus, for instance, the cannibals in *Robinson Crusoe* [1719] are depicted as homogeneous in their savagery, and radically different from the civilized Crusoe. Further, the inferior group is defined only in relation to the superior; its members' lack of the superior qualities is presented as the essence of their identity. No attempt is made to elucidate their own qualities from their own perspective, or to show them as significant in their own right. As Said shows ([1978] 1995: 31–92) this has been fundamental to the development of the concept of the 'Oriental'. As an example of this concept in operation he cites (p. 46–7) Henry Kissinger's observation that Western thinking is more accurate than Oriental thinking about the world because the Newtonian revolution, which emphasizes the recording and classifying of data, did not take place in the East; thus Oriental modes of thought are evaluated not in terms of the insights they have achieved but in terms of their deficiency as compared with Western thought, their lack of scientific method.

The effect of dualistic thinking is to naturalize domination, for it becomes part of the identities of both the dominant and subordinate groups. Plumwood identifies a number of crucial, interrelated dualisms which effectively reinforce each other forming a fracture that runs through our culture (Plumwood 1993: 42–3). The set, suggested by Plumwood, includes:

| | | |
|---|---|---|
| reason | – | emotion |
| civilization | – | wilderness |
| reason | – | nature |
| order | – | chaos |
| mind (soul) | – | body |
| male | – | female |
| human | – | non-human |
| master | – | slave |

In hero tales of the Christian era 'good' is frequently attached to the 'reason . . . master' side of these dualities and 'evil' to their opposites, thus powerfully reinforcing the sense of the innate superiority of civilized, rational, male order as against wild, emotional, female chaos.

The development of these dualisms has been a historical process. The primary civilization/wilderness opposition is central to *The Epic of Gilgamesh*, but it is in classical Greek thought that the interlocking pattern becomes established. Its basis is inherent in the very word 'barbaros' (barbarian) which meant a person who could not speak Greek, but made sounds like 'bar-bar'; for the Greeks humanity was divided into Greeks and non-Greeks (or barbarians) and the division implied the natural superiority of Greek culture and language. Plumwood connects this way of perceiving reality to aspects of classical logic which, of course, has been fundamentally influential in Western thinking across the disciplines. In particular she notes (p. 56–7) the concept of logical opposition, or negation, which divides the universe conceptually into X and non-X (e.g. human and non-human, Greek and non-Greek) thus foregrounding X and defining the rest simply by the lack of the qualities which go to make up X. This pattern of thought is apparent in Greek hero tales which tell how representatives of the Greek patriarchy, aided by the gods, overcome a variety of inferior, uncivilized, irrational creatures.

In *The Odyssey* the ordered, properly governed world of Ithaca with its assembly of citizens is opposed to the chaotic and savage places Odysseus visits on his homeward journey, just as Odysseus himself, whose courage and prowess is matched by his power of reason, is opposed to the various magical and savage beings he encounters. One of these is the Cyclops, Polyphemus, a one-eyed giant who lives in a cave with the sheep and the goats which he herds. When he describes the race of Cyclopes to King Alcinous, Odysseus says they are:

> a fierce uncivilized people, who never lift a hand to plant or plough but put their trust in Providence. . . . The Cyclopes have no assemblies for making laws, nor any settled customs, but live in hollow caverns in the mountain heights, where each man is lawgiver to his children and his wives, and nobody cares a jot for his neighbours.
>
> (Homer 1946: 144)

It is the lack of an ordered agricultural way of life and of community laws and customs, rather than his use of violence, which makes the Cyclops monstrous in Odysseus's eyes, and accords with his uncouth appearance. Odysseus himself is perfectly capable of violence; he sharpens a stake, heats it in the fire and drives it into the Cyclops's single eye while he lies in a drunken sleep, but he regards Polyphemus's devouring of his men, who are his 'guests', as savagery. In this section of the narrative Odysseus's superior powers of reason are demonstrated by the schemes he devises to deceive the Cyclops and escape from his cave. He ensures that the other Cyclopes will not come to Polyphemus's aid by telling him that his name is Nobody, so that when Polyphemus cries out in pain after his eye has been put out and they ask who has harmed him they go away when he answers 'Nobody'. Having blinded the Cyclops, Odysseus lashes himself and his men to the underbellies of the rams so that, although he guards the entrance to the cave, Polyphemus cannot detect the escaping men. While the philosophical concepts of good and evil are only uncertainly present in *The Odyssey*, which belongs to a time several hundred years before Plato attempted to define the nature of the good, the story nevertheless invites the audience's approval for Greek civilization and the dominance of reason as against the savagery and folly of people who have neglected to develop a proper political system.

It was in Greek thought that the privileging of reason as against emotion and 'nature' became established. Plato identified reason as the highest faculty and the essence of human identity. He regarded the soul as tripartite, consisting of reason, spirit and appetite, reason being concerned with the pursuit of wisdom and truth, spirit seeking honour, and appetite pursuing physical pleasure. It was the role of reason to control the other two (*Republic* IX 580, 1941: 300–2). Reason is thus opposed to the lower faculties and especially to appetite which is related to the body, which in its turn is related to nature.

Although for both Plato and Aristotle reason is what distinguishes human beings from the rest of animate nature neither regards it as inhering equally in all human beings. In particular slaves and women are regarded as deficient in reason. In a passage in the *Politics* justifying slavery Aristotle asserts that duality is inherent in 'the constitution of the universe' and links the various dualisms so as to demonstrate the 'natural' dominance of elite males:

> such a duality exists in living creatures, but not in them only; it originates in the constitution of the universe; even in things which have no life, there is a ruling principle, as in musical harmony. But we are wandering from the subject. We will, therefore, restrict ourselves to the living creature which, in the first place, consists of soul and body: and of these two, the one is by nature the ruler, and the other the subject. . . . And it is clear that the rule of the soul over the body, and of the mind and the rational element over the passionate is natural and expedient; whereas the equality of the two or the rule of the inferior is always hurtful. The same holds good of animals as of men; for tame animals have a better nature than wild, and all tame animals are better off when they are ruled by man; for then they are preserved. Again the male is by nature superior, and the female inferior; and the one rules, and the other is ruled; this principle, of necessity, extends to all mankind. Where then there is such a difference as that between soul and body, or between men and animals (as in the case of those whose business it is to use their body, and who can do nothing better), the lower sort are by nature slaves, and it is better for them as for all inferiors that they should be under the rule of a master. For he who can be, and therefore is another's, and he who participates in reason enough to apprehend, but not to have reason, is by nature a slave.
>
> (Aristotle 1905: 33–4)

A little further on he explains that this elite male superiority is moral as well as 'natural' and intellectual:

> For the slave has no deliberative faculty at all; the woman has but it is without authority, and the child has but it is immature. So it must necessarily be with the moral virtues also; all may be supposed to partake of them, but only in such manner and degree as is required by each for the fulfilment of his duty.
>
> (Aristotle 1905: 51)

Thus the good/evil opposition is added to the complex of dualisms.

The intersection of the Greek tradition with Hebraic thought can be seen in the mediaeval Christian conception of human nature in which reason is again regarded as the highest human faculty; below it is the will, and, subordinate to both, the senses which may tempt the soul to sin, and which it is the task of reason to control. In this tradition it was reason that separated human beings from the beasts and allied them to god and the angels.

'O God, a beast that wants discourse of reason/Would have mourned longer' (I, II, 150–1) Hamlet says when he wishes to condemn his mother's hasty remarriage as a matter of mere appetite. Because of their association with copulation and reproduction, women were consistently associated by Christian thinkers with the senses and the body, and hence with nature, rather than with the higher faculty of reason. And, for Christian thinkers, nature itself, the material world, was 'fallen', corrupt and inferior to the pure realm of the spirit.

All these dualisms are implicit in chivalric hero stories such as the legend of Saint George and the dragon in which pure, knightly representatives of the Church and of the dominant aristocracy do battle against inferior, evil creatures. The story of Saint George is a development of the Greek tale of Perseus whose rescue of Andromeda from a dragon highlighted his courage and prowess. Saint George is qualified to rescue the sacrificial maiden because of his Christian purity. This version of the myth was brought back to England by Crusaders who claimed to have been inspired by a vision of George at the Battle of Antioch in 1309 and Saint George was adopted as patron saint of England. The dragon in this legend is both a creature of the darkness, of chaos and wilderness, and the embodiment of evil as it is conceived in Christian belief. In a recent [1989] children's picture-book version of the story by Geraldine McCaughrean the good/evil dualism achieves a Manichean absoluteness. The dragon, a hideous and foul emanation of nature, is overtly defined as wicked: 'Its father was Evil, its mother Darkness, and its name was Wickedness.' Conversely when Saint George appears to challenge the dragon he asserts his virtue: 'Hear this, beast, that I am George of Lydda, and a pure man!' (McCaughrean [1989] 1990). The male/female dualism is present in a similarly extreme form. The princess Sabra who is left for the dragon to devour is beautiful, pure and passive. She accepts her fate limply: 'The girl cast one imploring look towards the town. But the windows of her father's palace were empty. Her head fell forward in despair.' George, on the other hand, appears riding a noble horse, armed with a lance and a sword, and ready for action. He confronts the dragon without hesitation and struggles against it determinedly while the bound and helpless girl is able only to look on. When he is victorious the King offers him marriage to the princess as a reward, but George declines, explaining that he 'has other dragons to vanquish', and he rides onward. The story defines 'good' as the activist struggle against 'evil'.

From the Renaissance onwards another related dualism was constructed in the self-definition of European civilization as against the 'inferior' cultures of the 'other' non-Europeans of Asia, Africa and, as Europeans 'discovered' it, the rest of the globe. This dualism is at the heart of the hero stories which emerge from, and justify, European imperialism. The rest of the globe was regarded as a natural site for European expansion and domination and this perception was reinforced by Cartesian theories of nature. Descartes conceived of nature, including animals, as a vast mechanism which could be understood by the application of mathematical principles. He argued that the mechanistic material world of nature, although constructed by God, was radically separate from the reasoning mind. In this model the reason/nature dualism is complete. The body is part of nature, a machine, and hence separate from, and subordinate to, the mind whose function is to know itself; feelings are rejected as irrational intrusions and imagination is distrusted. Descartes' theory necessarily dispenses with distinctions between various classes of human beings for all human minds are conceived of as seats of reason. However, the older patterns of thought in which some human groups, such as women, slaves and 'savages', were closer to nature and less endowed with reason, remained influential. During the period of imperialist expansion these concepts naturalized the exploitation of the resources of non-European parts of the globe and the domination of non-European peoples, and in our own time they have, *inter alia*, facilitated legalized discrimination against non-white people in the United States and South Africa, the persecution of the Jews and other 'inferior' groups in Nazi Germany, and the inferiorization and demonization of wartime and Cold War enemies.

The hero story which is, in essence, the dramatic depiction of these dualisms has evolved over time as the patterns of thought developed, with the hero and his opponents mutating to fit the changing conceptual and political environment but always demonstrating the 'natural' superiority of the Western patriarchy. During the period of imperialist expansion tales like *Robinson Crusoe* and the innumerable adventure stories spawned by its success constructed images of unenlightened savages and dangerous wildernesses in need of development by civilized Europeans. The European conflicts of the early and middle years of this century saw the emergence in English children's literature of heroes such as W.E. Johns' intrepid Captain James Bigglesworth who symbolized British decency as opposed to the 'evil' of the 'Huns' and other inferior foreigners. In the Cold War world of the second half of the twentieth century new forms of the story emerged to inscribe the mutant form of the dualism which defined the Communist bloc and the 'free' world in oppositional terms, and James Bond evolved as a representative of civilization, reason, order and freedom – and of the new consumerism of the West. With the disintegration of Communism and the postmodern fragmentation of the clearly demarcated camps emphasis seems to be shifting to 'the enemy within': serial killers, drug dealers and criminal syndicates, symbols of the irrational, the dark side of the psyche, are the wild things of many contemporary hero stories. But the story does not merely adapt, mothlike, to the environment; because of its omnipresence in our culture it is a powerful agent in shaping social and political attitudes, and its influence is always conservative. It suggests that existing power relationships are both inevitable and right, that, as Barthes says, they simply 'go without saying', and thus it makes the envisionment of different relationships, and different social values, difficult.

## Civilization and wilderness

The hero's departure from home to venture into the wilderness is the basic component of the hero tale: Odysseus' journey takes him into terrifying and magical places, qualitatively different from the orderly city-state of Ithaca. Theseus journeys from Athens into the darkness of the Minotaur's labyrinthine lair. Jason sails from Greece to the distant and magical kingdom of Colchis. The Arthurian knights leave Camelot, its orderly perfection symbolized by the mystic circle of the Round Table, to pursue their quests in dark forests and the realms of evil sorcerers. The heroes of European and English fairy tales leave their homes to enter the wider, dangerous, world, or the even more dangerous forest. Prospero, driven from the civilized world of Milan, is washed ashore on Caliban's island. Robinson Crusoe leaves England and is wrecked on another island which turns out to be frequented by cannibals. Other nineteenth century British adventurers, like Gordon Stables' Stanley Grahame and Rider Haggard's Allan Quartermain, face wild animals and dark savages in the distant reaches of the Empire. Sherlock Holmes leaves the domestic comforts of 221B Baker Street to venture into the dark places of the criminal underworld. Peter Pan has left Kensington for the Never Land, and Peter Rabbit disobediently enters Mr McGregor's garden. Both Bilbo Baggins and Frodo Baggins leave the homely confines of the Shire to travel into Mirkwood and beyond, in Frodo's case penetrating into the dark land of Mordor itself. James Bond leaves the bureaucratic world of Whitehall to pursue the enemies of the free world in a variety of exotic locations. The heroes of science fiction battle evil threats in the wider reaches of the galaxy. And Max leaves his bedroom to travel to the place where the wild things are.

Even in the simplest versions of the story, this structural pattern is resonant with a range of meanings. In his psychoanalytical account of hero tales, *The Hero With a Thousand Faces* [1949], a seminal work on the topic, Joseph Campbell stresses the role of the wilderness as symbolic of the unconscious:

> The regions of the unknown (desert, jungle, deep sea, alien land, etc.) are free fields for the projection of unconscious content. Incestuous *libido* and patricidal *destrudo* are thence reflected back against the individual and his society in forms suggesting threats of violence and fancied dangerous delight – not only as ogres but also as sirens of mysteriously seductive, nostalgic beauty.
>
> (Campbell [1949] 1968: 79)

Campbell reads the story as a universally beneficent narrative of the progress of the psyche towards maturity, wholeness and enlightenment. As the quotation above demonstrates he recognizes that it is concerned with male development, that females appear only as figures in the male hero's story, but he does not see this as a limitation. Precisely which secondary meanings a particular reader will construct from the civilization/wilderness opposition depends upon his or her own psychological and social experiences and experience of other texts, but the primary meaning – the valuing of home as the site of order and reason and the perception of what is 'out there' as wild and threatening – is imposed by the very shape of the story.

*The Epic of Gilgamesh* contains a powerful inscription of the opposition between the ordered place, the civilized city of Uruk, and the surrounding forest wilderness. In the section of the epic which Sandars calls 'The Journey into the Forest', Gilgamesh, prince of the city of Uruk, determines to venture into the great cedar forest with his companion and servant, the wild man, Enkidu. His motives are to slay the ferocious giant, Humbaba, who guards the cedar, to make the cedar available to Uruk for building, and to win enduring fame for himself. Enkidu tries to dissuade him by describing the fearfulness of Humbaba, and the counsellors of Uruk likewise say that he is young and rash to think of opposing Humbaba whose breath is like fire and whose jaws are death itself. But Gilgamesh says that he would prefer fame and an early death to sitting at home all the rest of his days (thus anticipating Achilles' choice in *The Iliad*). He asks the god Shamash for his protection, and requests his mother, Ninsun, to pray for him to Shamash. After initially attempting to dissuade him she does as he wishes, arraying herself in her jewels and climbing to the roof of the temple to intercede for him. Gilgamesh and Enkidu are then armed with swords in golden scabbards, axes, and a bow and quiver which the armourers of Uruk have made for them.

They traverse many leagues in a few days and so reach the gate of the towering forest. They sleep there that night and Gilgamesh has a dream in which he is assisted in his enterprise by a being of great brightness and grace. Interpreting this as a favourable omen they continue on their way. The next night Enkidu has a more ominous dream, but Gilgamesh is undeterred; he seizes an axe and cuts down a cedar tree, whereupon the god Shamash tells him to go forward without fear. Humbaba, however, is enraged at the violation of his woods and emerges from his house of cedar, menacing Gilgamesh. Weeping, Gilgamesh again appeals to Shamash who sends eight winds to help him. The winds beat against Humbaba so that he is unable to move despite his great strength; he gives up the contest and appeals to Gilgamesh for mercy, promising to yield the trees to him and to be his servant if he is allowed to live. Although Gilgamesh would have spared him Enkidu insists that Humbaba must die and they kill him with their swords. Then the world changes:

> Now the mountains were moved, the ranges of the hills were moved, for the guardian of the cedar lay dead.
>
> Enkidu had struck him, and the cedar was dashed to pieces. Enkidu did it; he uncovered the dwellings of the Great Ones. So Gilgamesh felled the trees of the forest and Enkidu cleared their roots as far as the banks of the Euphrates.
>
> (Sandars 1960: 82)

The central opposition here is clearly not between reason and nature or reason and emotion for the heroes are guided by dreams and supernatural advice, not by logic, and they are moved by emotions which they do not hesitate to express. The Greek awareness of mind and reverence for reason, the concept of *logos*, is far in the future; Athene, the bright goddess of wisdom, has yet to be born from the head of her father, Zeus, and Plato is almost as far distant from Gilgamesh as we are from him. The dualism in this earliest version of the story is the primary opposition between civilization and wilderness. Gilgamesh serves civilization and order both in his determination to clear the land and cut down the cedars so that they might be used for building, and in his bid to subdue the giant Humbaba who is the guardian of the forest. In Western culture this is the primal task. Just so did the European settlers in America and Australia clear the land in order to establish civilized settlements and subdue the 'wild' indigenous tribes who were the guardians of the forests, invoking divine support for their efforts.

It is only in recent decades that some groups in the West have broken free from the power of this aspect of the myth, emerging as defenders of the forests against the loggers who continue to fell them in the cause of 'development'. The environmental movement, like feminism, represents a profound challenge to some aspects of the myth of the hero, and it is significant that in contemporary texts concerned with a woman's search for self, the experience of deep empathy with the natural world is often an important stage in that process of discovery. In Margaret Atwood's *Surfacing* [1973], for instance, the troubled protagonist returns to her remote childhood home in northern Quebec and surrenders to the elemental power of the wild as she seeks for understanding:

> The forest leaps upward, enormous, the way it was before they cut it, columns of sunlight frozen; the boulders float, melt, everything is made of water, even the rocks. In one of the languages there are no nouns, only verbs held for a longer moment.
>
> The animals have no need for speech, why talk when you are a word
> I lean against a tree, I am a tree leaning
>
> (Atwood [1973] 1979: 181)

Unlike Gilgamesh her concern is to achieve connection with the wilderness, not separation and dominance.

Sandars suggests (1960: 31) that Gilgamesh's forest is simultaneously an actual forest, probably in Syria or south-west Persia, the home of uncanny powers, and 'the dark forest of the soul', and he comments that the work can be read on several levels like a mediaeval allegory. But at a time in human history when there seemed no clear distinction between outer and inner darkness, and when the lands beyond the known world were as mysterious as the underworld and the magical realms inhabited by the gods, there is no need to think of it as allegory. Much later the Greeks believed that the home of the gods was literally on the top of Mount Olympus, and Homer had Odysseus sail to Hades' kingdom in just the same way as he sails anywhere else. The forest simply *is* all three things simultaneously. Northrop Frye suggests (Frye 1983: 187–8) that in early myths the wilderness is the wild, unpredictable forces of nature while the devouring dragon or monster is death and primeval chaos, so that to kill it is to bestow life and establish human order.

As Plumwood points out (Plumwood 1993: 43) this symbolism survives as a residue in much later works, reshaped and redeployed according to the context of the times. We can recognize it in fairy tales which emphasize the dangers of the forest where wolves lurk; the powerful appeal of 'Little Red Riding Hood' is due in part to its dramatic use of these ancient motifs. The opening lines of Dante's *Inferno* employ the same symbolism in a more sophisticated manner, evoking the dark forest of the soul:

> Midway this way of life we're bound upon,
> I woke to find myself in a dark wood,
> Where the right road was wholly lost and gone.
>
> Ay me! how hard to speak of it – that rude
> And rough and stubborn forest! the mere breath
> Of memory stirs the old fear in the blood;
> (Dante 1949: 71)

So the ancient opposition is modified by the Christian context.

This primary opposition between the wilderness and the orderly world of home is at the heart of all hero tales. It is central to Sendak's picture book, *Where the Wild Things Are*, in which the wilderness of Max's dream is symbolic of his psychological state and of the disruption caused by his actions. Having been sent to bed without his supper as a punishment for his wild behaviour Max conjures the primeval forest from his imagination:

> That very night in Max's room a forest grew
> and grew –
> and grew until his ceiling hung with vines
> and the walls became the world all around
> (Sendak 1967)

The illustration shows the trees towering around him as the cedars towered around Gilgamesh and Enkidu. Although Max is neither afraid nor repelled by the creatures of the wilderness he establishes mastery over them. He enjoys the 'wild rumpus' he shares with them but it begins and ends at his command, and when he has had enough he resumes his self-control and returns righteously to the good order of home. Though the story suggests a benign attitude to wilderness, and emotional 'wildness', the superior value of ordered civilization is asserted as absolutely as in the oldest tales.

The symbolism of the forest and its guardian monsters has flourished in the literature of Australia, where white settlement is very recent and where the settlers confronted a continent which appeared to them to be as much a wilderness as the cedar forest which Gilgamesh and Enkidu entered. The primary theme of white Australian writing, at least until the last few decades, has been the alienating and terrifying encounter with the land, but many Australian stories conclude on a far less confident note than Gilgamesh's adventure. The bush has evoked ambivalent responses from white Australians, but on the whole fear and uncertainty has outweighed delight. The white child lost in the bush is an iconic image in Australian art, and tales, such as the story of Eliza Frazer, in which lost Europeans are adopted by Aboriginal tribes and absorbed into their culture, grip white imaginations. David Malouf's internationally acclaimed novel, *Remembering Babylon* (1993) is the latest work of literature to employ the motif. It is as though white Australians have always doubted their ability to maintain their cultural identity against the physical and psychological encroachment of the land.

Probably the most famous of all Australian short stories, Henry Lawson's 'The Drover's Wife' [1892], is a simple, emblematic hero tale which evokes a sense of the vastness of the bush and its indifference to the fragile impact of white civilization. In this story a woman alone in a bush hut with her four small children is threatened by a poisonous snake lurking under the shaky floor boards of the main room. She sits up all night waiting for it to emerge so she can kill it with a stick. As she waits she recalls other threats which she has struggled against in the bush while her husband was absent droving – a bushfire, a flood, a mad bullock and a villainous-looking tramp. At last, near morning, the snake emerges and she manages to kill it – as Gilgamesh killed Humbaba – so that she and her children are safe again for the time being. Although she is a woman she has displayed true heroism and has temporarily subdued the wilderness to defend her small space of order.

The civilization/wilderness opposition is central in Patrick White's *Voss* [1957] but there is no triumph for civilization and the work suggests the impossibility of such an outcome. Modelled on the explorer, Ludwig Leichardt who disappeared in the Australian desert in 1848, Voss is a visionary who travels into the interior of the continent intent upon mastering its mystery, achieving some ultimate and transforming knowledge. But the expedition is doomed and after the deaths of the other white members of the group Voss is killed by Aborigines. Thus the guardians of the wilderness prevail and the arrogant interloper is absorbed by the land which he sought to master: 'His dreams fled into the air, his blood ran out upon the dry earth, which drank it up immediately. Whether dreams breed, or the earth responds to a pint of blood, the instant of death does not tell' (White [1957] 1960: 394). Whether he achieves any final insight remains uncertain, but civilization continues to be confined to the fringes of the continent, ultimately unable to penetrate its vastness.

The conclusion of *Voss* gains force from the contrast it represents to the normal outcome of the hero tale. Hero stories are essentially optimistic for they assert, against all the evidence, that victory is possible. The hero triumphs over the wilderness, and therefore over chaos, nature, evil, death itself. Perhaps it is the daunting size and aridity of the Australian continent which has made that optimism rare in Australian hero stories, even those written for children. In the nineteenth century there were some undistinguished attempts to transplant the British imperialist boys' adventure story, with its triumphant finale, into the Australian context. In these tales, such as E.B. Kennedy's *Blacks and Bushrangers: Adventures in Queensland* (1889), a youth, usually fresh from England, is the intrepid hero, and the local fauna and 'savage' Aborigines, guardians of the wilderness, are the foes he must overcome. Maurice Saxby describes the general mediocrity of these pastiches (Saxby 1969: 30–42). Later Australian children's books which are the products of genuine experience eschew this facile and derivative posturing. As in 'The Drover's Wife' the land is never finally subdued; at best an uneasy truce is achieved.

This is the case in Ivan Southall's *To the Wild Sky* which won the Australian Children's Book of the Year Award in 1968. In this story a group of 12- to 13-year-old children are in a small plane on their way to an outback holiday when the pilot dies of a heart attack. One of the boys takes over the controls and manages to crash land, somewhere in the centre of the continent. With no means of summoning assistance the children must confront the wilderness where only the skills of the Aboriginal people, the guardians of the land, are of use to them; the wealth, technology, education and civilized mores of white Australia are irrelevant there. It is possible they will survive, but the reader's final impression is of the fragility of that possibility. Although Southall seems primarily concerned with the relationships between the children – their insecurities, jealousies and class differences – it is the elemental confrontation with the land, the invocation of the primary civilization/wilderness dualism, that gives the tale its power.

Patricia Wrightson's *The Nargun and the Stars* [1973], one of the outstanding works of Australian children's literature, makes sensitive use of material from Aboriginal mythology to dramatize an encounter between a white child and the ancient land. The narrative point of view positions white Australians as interlopers who must forge a relationship with the indigenous people by learning to understand their Dreaming before they can find their own identity. Simon, the protagonist, who comes to the Hunter Valley to live with elderly relatives, is a white child who has been emotionally damaged by the deaths of his parents. His quest is to rediscover meaning in his suddenly empty universe. During his lonely wanderings he encounters some of the creatures of the Dreamtime, emanations of the land itself: the frog-swift golden Potkorook who lives in the swamp, the tree-dwelling Turongs and the earthy Nyols. Unlike the giant Humbaba and the dragons and ogres of European legends, and even unlike the snake in 'The Drover's Wife', these creatures are not constructed as threats which must be overcome and Simon does not seek to master them. He accepts their presence, and as he does so the land gradually becomes alive and meaningful for him. However, not all the Dreamtime creatures are harmless. He also encounters the Nargun, an ancient and destructive creature of living rock. It cannot be killed like the giant Humbaba or the dragons which were destroyed by Perseus and St George. Implicit in its endurance is the recognition that, when the civilization of the white settlers is over, the land will still be there. In these Australian stories the shape of the traditional hero tale has been modified to express some of the changing values of our time.

## Reason and Irrationality

In the pattern of linked dualisms which have shaped Western culture it is the privileging of reason that naturalizes and justifies dominance by the Western patriarchy. If, as Aristotle put it, 'it is clear that the rule of the soul over the body, and of the mind and the rational element over the passionate is natural and expedient,' then likewise the rule of rational beings over irrational creatures is 'natural and expedient' (Aristotle 1905: 33). Thus the mastery of animals, women and 'savages' was naturalized, for all three of these groups were regarded as closer to nature, less endowed with reason than Western men.

This privileging of reason, established in classical Greek thought, was intensified during the Enlightenment which saw the emergence of modern science and a belief in scientific rationalism as the means of arriving at social and philosophical, as well as scientific, truth. At the same time industrial development changed living patterns in the West, leading to the emergence of patriarchal capitalism as the primary shaping force of society. Finally, and perhaps most significantly for the spread of the hero story, it was the period when the later phase of English and European imperialism began in earnest. As a result of these interdependent social changes there were new worlds for white men to conquer, new fortunes to be made, and new fields of knowledge from which new kinds of power could be derived. (Women, on the other hand, may well have lost some of the little status and autonomy they once possessed as the spheres of work and home became more distinct and they were increasingly relegated to the domestic world.) Hero stories in which British and European adventurers established mastery over less rational, 'inferior' non-Europeans flourished during this period.

Imperialism can be justified only if it is seen as bestowing a superior way of life upon the conquered peoples; that is, it depends upon a belief in the superiority of Western culture and the altruism of the conquerors. The hero tales of the period constructed such images of the impact of European settlement and dominance. Exotic, that is non-European, places were defined as the wilderness – moral, and in many cases physical – into which the hero ventured, confronting and overcoming a variety of colourful dangers by reason of both his ancient qualities of courage and prowess and his superior powers of reason, his European knowledge, and his European technological expertise. His successful dominance of these 'wild' places is always depicted as bestowing benefits upon them. In Defoe's *Robinson Crusoe* the natives who visit the island upon which Crusoe is cast up are cannibals whose barbarity fills him with horror; he regards them as lacking full humanity, unredeemed by reason. Crusoe plants European crops and imposes a regime of European order on the island which, from his point of view, was simply 'wild' before his coming. Likewise he regards Friday as an unredeemed savage who must be taught to live according to European religion and reason, and Friday is depicted as learning eagerly and joyfully. The implication is that the culture Crusoe teaches him is self-evidently superior to his own so that he accepts it without question.

This pattern of binary oppositions in which reason is especially privileged reappears with little modification in Western hero tales throughout the eighteenth and nineteenth centuries. Rider Haggard's *King Solomon's Mines* [1885], written 160 years or so after *Crusoe* presents a somewhat more informed and appreciative picture of African tribal culture than Defoe's account of the cannibals, but European rationality is still shown as innately superior to tribal ways of thought, leading to natural dominance. In this tale three British adventurers, the narrator, Allan Quartermain, Sir Henry Curtis, and Captain Good, venture into the unexplored heart of Africa in search of Sir Henry's missing brother and the legendary diamond mines which he attempted to reach. The heroes are depicted as educated gentlemen, with a rational understanding of reality that is superior to the Africans' superstitious and inductive interpretation of things. They use their superior knowledge and powers of deduction to impose their will on the natives. The most spectacular instance occurs when they use their knowledge of a predicted lunar eclipse to convince the natives that they have the power to control nature (Haggard [1885] 1958: 149–52). The narrative justifies their ruse because it enables them to overthrow a cruel tribal tyrant and install their protégé, a 'good' native and the rightful king. Such incidents are significant not only because they demonstrate the superiority of the rational approach in achieving practical results, but because they imply that it is 'natural and expedient' for the British heroes to use their knowledge and logic to manipulate and master the Africans.

The right of the heroes to kill the wild animals of Africa for gain is also assumed throughout this story as in many others of the period. As well as killing for food they hunt elephants for ivory. Quartermain is a professional hunter, and this is depicted as a manly vocation. The male/female opposition forms an additional, minor strand in the story reinforcing the other dualisms. European women are completely excluded from the world of the text while African women are depicted as subordinate participants in the military culture of the natives and as the source of evil. The cruel tyrant is inspired by Gagool, an ancient witch and prophetess who makes sibylline pronouncements while in a trance-like state, and uses her influence to direct his wrath towards any who challenge her power. The new, good king condemns her as 'the evil genius of the land' (p. 197). Thus female power is shown as an aspect of nature's darkness and mystery, and of subterranean emotions, finding expression in manipulative evil because it is excluded from the sphere of manly action. Reason, courage and leadership are shown as aspects of the masculine.

Another enormously popular work of imperialist fiction, Kipling's *Kim* [1901], chronicles a different phase of imperialism and depicts the natural mastery of rational Europeans in a more absolute way than either *Robinson Crusoe* or *King Solomon's Mines* which deal only with the penetration of the wilderness and the initial assertion of reason over the dark and the irrational. In *Kim*, mastery has been achieved and a system of rational order successfully established. The British administration of India is presented as a necessary and benevolent domination of a potentially chaotic mixture of lesser races, religions and cultures. The instrument by which order is maintained within and threats from without averted is the Secret Service and the effectiveness of the Secret Service is the result of the careful collection and categorization of information combined with the ability to make deductions from this information and act upon them. It is rationality in action, the Great Game which the British play and win. Colonel Creighton, the spy-master who inducts Kim into the Service, says to him that: 'There is no sin so great as ignorance' (Kipling [1901] 1946: 125).

Creighton, the embodiment of British rationality, is depicted as a subtle, intelligent and learned man who respects the ancient cultures of India, but he nevertheless believes that the Indians are incapable of orderly self-government, and the image of India constructed in this work bears out his belief. Kim, who has learned Indian ways directly, delights in the rich variety of life in the streets and bazaars, and the text conveys this colourfulness to the reader while implying that it is the variety of disorder. The Indian characters are vividly drawn, especially the Secret Service agents, the wily horse trader Mahbub Ali and the learned Hurree Babu who longs to be made a fellow of the Royal Society, along with the holy Lama from Tibet whose *chela* (disciple) Kim becomes and who wanders the land seeking the river of enlightenment. But these characters share no common qualities or beliefs which link them together and define them as 'Indian'. They are vivid but distinct like the jewels in the memory game which forms part of Kim's training. The tray of sapphires, black veined turquoises, flawed emeralds, pipe amber, rubies, ivory and crystals, is an image of India's rich multifariousness: its profusion, its beauty and its contrasts. But the tray of jewels has no natural coherence or pattern; it is only the act of categorization which imposes a conceptual order upon its randomness. Likewise, the text implies, the cultural richness of India is incoherent, likely to disintegrate into civil disorder without the controlling intelligence of the British rulers, and the Indians themselves are depicted as recognizing and accepting this. The dominance described in this work is not dominance over simple savages, but mastery of a confluence of ancient cultures and philosophies which nevertheless are 'naturally' subordinate to British rationality. Edward Said says of *Kim*:

> its author is writing not just from the dominating viewpoint of a white man in a colonial possession but from the perspective of a massive colonial system whose economy, functioning, and history had acquired the status of a virtual fact of nature. Kipling assumes a basically uncontested empire. On one side of the colonial divide was a white Christian Europe whose various countries, principally Britain and France, but also Holland, Belgium, Germany, Italy, Russia, Portugal and Spain, controlled most of the earth's surface. On the other side of the divide, there was an immense array of territories and races, all of them considered lesser, inferior, dependent, subject.
>
> (Said [1993] 1994: 162)

At the time *Kim* was being written there was growing internal dissent in India. The Young India movement had begun towards the end of the century and the Indian National Congress had been established in 1885, but Kipling allows no shadow of this discontent to fall upon the picture of India which he constructs in the text.

In the post-colonial world the assumption of Western cultural superiority endures as is evident from the widespread acceptance of the role of the West, and especially of the United States, as international peace-keeper and moral guardian, and it is the rational and scientific basis of western culture which is seen as accounting for both its economic and its supposed moral pre-eminence. The racism, inequity and violence which disfigure American life, the ruthless consumerism and the moral deficiencies of the economic rationalism which drives Western policies are perceived as merely external sores upon an inner purity, the pure superiority which the hero myth inscribes. And the myth dominates contemporary popular culture in the West, for both children and adults.

Western rationality and technological superiority are repeatedly shown prevailing over alien irrationality and wildness in spy stories, war stories, stories of international intrigue, thrillers and science fiction tales. Crime stories show the hero, whether policeman or subtle private detective, using his powers of deduction to root out the sources of violence within society. American superheroes like Batman and Superman are symbolic embodiments of rational and moral superiority. When they change from their mundane identities they leave human complexity behind with their civilian clothes and become streamlined incarnations of the American way of life, motivated only to preserve it. And they are invincible; the stories suggest that success is inherent in the very nature of rational superiority. Even in books for very small children, such as Jean De Brunhoff's popular Babar stories, rationality is shown as inevitably and beneficently ascendant over the irrational and the 'wild': Babar, a young elephant educated in Paris, returns to the jungle and becomes king of the elephants, offering them reason and progress. They embrace his gifts gladly and learn to live with French elegance. The motif of the good animal, the natural leader who brings reason and order to his fellows in the wilderness, saving them from evil dangers, reappears in the 1995 Walt Disney movie and best-selling home video, *The Lion King*. The summary on the jacket of the video asserts its significance. The lion cub Simba:

> must struggle to find his place in nature's great 'circle of life'. Befriended by a host of warmhearted characters, Simba experiences some of life's most glorious moments and toughest challenges. But before he can take his rightful place as the ruler of the Pride Lands, Simba must overcome great fear and adversity – climaxed by a blazing battle with his evil and greedy uncle, Scar!

The use of animals as the characters in such children's stories implies that the dominance of reason and those who bestow it is a universal principle, a 'law of nature', part of the process of evolution, not merely a matter of human politics.

## Good and Evil

The most simplistic of the dualisms implicit in popular hero stories is the good/evil opposition. Often these terms mean little more than 'us and them': the hero who represents the Western patriarchy is 'good' by definition and his opponents are necessarily 'evil' because they *are* his opponents. This is the case in many 'realistic' adventure stories such as *Treasure Island* where almost no moral analysis of the hero's actions or those of his opponents is provided. These stories do not claim to offer more than action and suspense; they are simply images of the commonplace values of their time in action. But many fantasy tales have a symbolic structure which foregrounds 'the struggle of good against evil' and high claims are made for some of these works. Ursula Le Guin speaks of *War and Peace* and *The Lord of the Rings* as though they were of equal value (Le Guin 1975: 88). Patricia Meyer Spacks says that the 'moral and theological scheme' of *The Lord of the Rings* has 'force and complexity' (Spacks 1968: 82). Charlotte Huck claims the quality of 'truth' for fantasy as a genre:

> Adults may find, in these and similar stories, many of the collective images or shared symbols called archetypes by the great psychologist Carl Jung. Children will simply recognize that such a fantasy is 'true'. All our best fantasies, from the briefest modern fairy tale to the most complex novel of high adventure, share this quality of truth.
>
> (Huck *et al.* 1987: 339)

Tolkien himself, in *Tree and Leaf* (1964) suggests that the happy ending, which he regards as an essential feature of fairy stories and fantasy, 'may be a far-off gleam or echo of *evangelium* in the real world' (p. 62), a sign, that is, of the joy of the resurrection.

Do fantasy versions of the hero story offer an exploration of the nature of good and evil that is more than a restatement of the traditional dualisms? In particular, does Tolkien's enormously influential trilogy do so? The world of Middle-earth is marvellously rich in imaginative detail; Tolkien draws on his knowledge of several mythologies and languages as well as his inventive powers to create a range of colourful and often memorable creatures. Some, like the ringwraiths, the faceless Dark Riders whose substance has been destroyed by their addiction to the ring of power, have real poetic and symbolic force. The story, the heroic journey to destroy the evil ring, is interesting because of the variety of places and creatures the heroes encounter, and the symbolic apparatus has a Wagnerian expansiveness, but as a vision of good and evil it is ultimately less illuminating than fairy tales like 'Bluebeard' or 'Little Red Riding Hood' which do convey something of the psycho-sexual darkness from which human evil arises.

It is not only in comparison with such traditional material that Tolkien's work seems deficient as moral analysis. William Golding's *Lord of the Flies* was published in the same year [1954] as the first volume of Tolkien's trilogy and written in part as a response to the horrors of World War II (Davis 1963: 30), and, it must be assumed, despite Tolkien's disclaimer in the foreword to later editions of his work, *The Lord of the Rings* was also in part a response to what the two world wars revealed of the capacity for human evil. Not only does the trilogy directly address the issue of evil, it evokes images of twentieth century battlefields to provide evil with substance (see below). Like *The Lord of the Rings*, Golding's fable is an essentially allegorical work which draws on traditional Christian symbolism, but in contrast to the length and variety of the trilogy it restricts itself to the smallest of canvases – a group of schoolboys on a tropical island. Within these self-imposed limits it explores the nature and psychological wellsprings of human evil, probing the arrogant, hierarchical and anti-intellectual ethos of the elite school attended by the upper class boy, Jack, and his followers. Their conviction of innate superiority, nurtured in that environment, permits them to establish a brutal tribal totalitarianism and indulge in a series of sadistic cruelties which are crude assertions of sexual potency and political power. The reader is able to observe the results of unmodified and unexamined egocentricity as the taboos imposed by adult society fall away. Jack and his schoolfellows have developed no sense of responsibility with which to replace those taboos, unlike middle-class Ralph and lower-class Piggy whose more democratic education has provided them with a sense of community which they struggle to enact.

*Lord of the Flies* shows how it is possible for ordinary boys to perpetrate horrors, given certain experiences and conditions, but *The Lord of the Rings* makes an absolute division between the good heroes and the evil beings who are their enemies. It attempts to construct an image of hell itself, the kingdom of Mordor, domain of the dark lord, Sauron, who lusts for power over the whole of Middle-earth, but this structure remains a formal pattern, a mere paradigm of evil: the Dark Land is barren and colourless; volcanic smoke hovers over it; it resembles both a battlefield and an industrial waste land, 'pocked with great holes, as if, while it was still a waste of soft mud, it had been smitten with a shower of bolts and huge slingstones' (Tolkien 1955: 211). And, of course, it recalls *The Waste Land*. As the hero, Frodo, and Sam, his retainer, struggle through the stony desert towards Mount Doom they suffer from thirst. Sam mutters 'Water, water!' and we are told that he had last been able to fill his water bottle from one of the 'highway cisterns' (p. 213) but there was no hope of more. This is recognizably the place of 'empty cisterns and exhausted wells'; they are on

> The road winding among the mountains
> Which are mountains of rock without water . . .
> (Eliot (1992): lines 333–4)

But the desert of *The Waste Land* is an expression of the spiritual desolation of the West, present in the poem in the fragmentary glimpses of the arid relationships, sexual exploitation and meaningless rituals of modern life. There is nothing of this in *The Lord of the Rings* and the intertextual echoes do not make up the deficiency. Evil, in Tolkien, is external to the heroes, reaching out for them, but not originating from them or from any human beings.

Nor is Sauron himself more than a cipher. He has no discernible motivation, not even the envy which Marlowe's Mephistophilis attributes to Lucifer, the desire to 'enlarge his kingdom' (Marlowe [*c.* 1604] 1909: 132) by destroying for others the possibility of the bliss he has himself lost. The problem is not the work's Christian schema but the failure to invest that schema with any but the most formal and conventional significance. Neither Sauron nor his servants the Orcs provide any insights into the nature of institutionalized or individual evil; they do not help us to understand how the horror of the Holocaust could have occurred, how torture can remain commonplace in the late twentieth century, or how a young man could have walked into the tourist resort of Port Arthur in Tasmania one afternoon in the autumn of 1996 and shot thirty-five people. The chief qualities displayed by the Orcs are lower-class crudity, physical ugliness and 'darkness', while the good characters are physically attractive, well-mannered, articulate, and white. 'Good' and 'evil' in this work are as much a matter of class and aesthetics as anything else. Finally, for all its variety, *The Lord of the Rings* simply reasserts the traditional dualisms and the superiority of the Western patriarchal elite.

This is readily apparent if we compare the language used to describe the good characters with descriptions of the Orcs. Here is Frodo's, and the reader's, first sight of the elf lord, Glorfindel:

> Suddenly into the view below came a white horse, gleaming in the shadows, running swiftly. In the dusk its bit and bridle flickered and flashed, as if it were studded with gems like living stars. The rider's cloak streamed behind him, and his hood was thrown back; his golden hair flowed shimmering in the wind of his speed. To Frodo it appeared that a white light was shining through the form and raiment of the rider, as if through a thin veil.
>
> (Tolkien 1954: 221)

The indicators of the elf-lord's goodness are all to do with status, wealth, beauty and blondness. The same devices are used throughout to define other 'good' characters. In contrast the evil beings are dark and forbidding in a similarly conventional way. The Orc Lieutenant of the Tower of Barad-dûr is:

> a tall and evil shape, mounted upon a black horse, if horse it was; for it was huge and hideous, and its face was a frightful mask, more like a skull than a living head, and in the sockets of its eyes and in its nostrils there burned a flame. The rider was robed all in black, and black was his lofty helm.
>
> (Tolkien 1955: 164)

When we glimpse the Orcs in close-up we realize that their grammar and their manners are both proletarian, while their names and the descriptive language align them with animals:

> 'Hola! Gorbag! What are you doing up here? Had enough of war already?'
>
> 'Orders, you lubber. And what are you doing, Shagrat? Tired of lurking up there? Thinking of coming down to fight?'
>
> 'Orders to you. I'm in command of this pass. So speak civil. What's your report?'
>
> 'Nothing.'
>
> 'Hai! Hai! Yoi!' A yell broke into the exchanges of the leaders. The Orcs lower down had suddenly seen something. They began to run. So did the others.
>
> 'Hai! Hola! Here's something! Lying right in the road. A spy, a spy!' there was a hoot of snarling horns, and a babel of baying voices.
>
> (Tolkien [1954] 1981: 432)

It is interesting to note that similar indications of ordinariness mark Piggy, in *Lord of the Flies*, as a lower-class child, and his nickname is also an animal term. In Tolkien these characteristics function as signs of the Orcs' evil natures but in Golding's work they are used as evidence of the human experiences, including experiences of discrimination and suffering, that have allowed Piggy to develop wisdom and compassion, qualities the privileged Jack has signally failed to achieve.

It is true that Tolkien's good characters are not necessarily incorruptible. The man, Boromir, becomes a traitor because of his desire to rule. The great wizard, Saruman the White, destroys himself by a Faustian ambition. And even Frodo, at the last moment, is seized by a desire to keep the ring. This recognition of human frailty gives the work poignancy but there is nothing of the moral ambivalence of real life and none of the agony of conflicting passions and reason. Part of the problem, perhaps, is that Tolkien's creatures are peculiarly sexless so that their motivations seem one-dimensional and transparent and goodness is entirely conventional. The 'good' societies of Middle-earth are male-dominated and aristocratic. Women are restricted to circumscribed roles. Order of a traditional, pre-industrial, hierarchical kind is valued and control over one's emotions is admired. The only relationships which do not seem constrained and difficult are the boyish friendships between male comrades, yet even those are undercut by a sense of class to the point where, in their moments of supreme peril, on the slopes of Mount Doom, Sam, who had been Frodo's gardener, continues to call him 'Master' (1955: 221).

The fundamental opposition in *The Lord of the Rings* is not between good and evil in any meaningful sense, but between an idealized and highly conservative vision of an essentially British world and that which is alien to it. The hobbits are English country gentry. The Riders of Rohan with their braided flaxen hair, long swords and painted shields come from an Anglo-Saxon past. Gondor, where the young hobbit, Pippin, acquires a hauberk and a coat of arms, comes out of a dream of mediaeval chivalry. The elves belong to Celtic legend, refracted through the mind of Malory and other romancers. Against these gentlemanly and aesthetically appealing persons stand the Orcs and the other servants of Sauron who are 'foul' and black, alien and lower-class. The work is a long testament to the natural superiority of the European, and especially the British, patriarchy.

Other works of fantasy, influenced by Tolkien, construct similar definitions of good and evil. One of the best known, most praised, and most indebted to Tolkien, is Susan Cooper's *The Dark is Rising* sequence [1973–7] which draws heavily on Arthurian and other Celtic legend to enrich its metaphysical theme. Unlike Tolkien, Cooper does not invent a secondary world; her struggle of the Light against the Dark is played out in southern England and Wales across a range of fifteen centuries or so. The hero of the sequence is Will Stanton, the youngest child of a large middle-class family, who lives in a modern village in Buckinghamshire. On his eleventh birthday he learns that he is one of the 'Old Ones' with an important part to play in their ongoing battle against the Dark. The Old Ones seem to be akin to Christian angels who assume human form from time to time, and the most prominent of them is Merriman Lyon whose name, in an earlier incarnation, was Merlin. This fusion of Arthurian and Christian material derives from Malory, but Cooper's attempt to achieve an additional fusion with modern English life is less successful.

Like Tolkien's Sauron, the chief incarnation of evil in this work is a symbol without substance, the dark Rider, to whom infinite but non-specific and seemingly unmotivated malice is attributed. His role is limited to threatening manifestations at moments of crisis, and the onslaughts of the other powers of darkness are similarly insubstantial. Early in the second work in the series Will is attacked by dark clouds (Cooper [1973] 1976: 40–1) and the full force of their malevolence achieves only the onset of bad weather – heavy snow and freezing temperatures over Christmas and New Year. The depression and inconvenience this occasions is quite effectively realized, but as a demonstration of the nature of evil it is less than adequate. History is called upon to provide further evidence of the reality of evil at work in the world – in the form of assaults on English shores:

> He saw one race after another come attacking his island country, bringing each time the malevolence of the Dark with them, wave after wave of ships rushing inexorably at the shores. Each wave of men in turn grew peaceful as it grew to know and love the land, so that the Light flourished again. But always the Dark was there, swelling and waning, gaining a new Lord of the Dark whenever a man deliberately chose to be changed into something more dread and powerful than his fellows.
>
> (Cooper [1973] 1976: 121)

The major problem with this is the determined insularity of its perspective and its equation of 'the Light' with settled English life. A modern instance of English virtue is provided by the description of the happy life of the middle-class Stanton family and their comfortable Christmas rituals. Thus, as with *The Lord of the Rings*, 'good' comes to be defined as that which is manifested by the British establishment, and 'evil' as anything which opposes it.

The final volume of the sequence, *Silver on the Tree*, contains a vivid incident which does throw light on the way deliberate ignorance and unexamined bigotry facilitate the infliction of cruelty by one human being on another. The Stanton children witness a small boy of Indian background being bullied by a group of mindless white boys and they intervene to cut it short. Later the father of one of the white boys calls on the Stantons to 'discuss' the incident (Cooper [1977] 1979: 60–4) and reveals a smug, self-serving racism which allows him to regard all 'Pakkies' as natural inferiors who do not merit the same standards of treatment as whites. This incident seems to belong to a different genre from the fantasy sections with their supermarket of New Age symbols (a crystal sword, spinning mandalas, rainbows, mistletoe and so on), romantic Arthurian material and the repeated perception of English history as a series of assaults by the Dark upon the Light. Finally the unsatisfactoriness of these sometimes quite poetic stories inheres not in the Blytonesque absurdity of a group of children engaged in a struggle against demonic powers which obligingly wait until the school holidays to attack, but in their cosiness, their definition of 'good' as simply a matter of traditional English decency and their reduction of 'evil' to anti-English behaviour dressed up with some polite symbolism. Like Tolkien's trilogy and most of its numerous progeny they reiterate the traditional dualisms but provide no real insights into human nature or the human condition.

## THE HERO'S POINT OF VIEW

Perhaps the most obvious feature of the hero story is that it is *his* story. Other characters are included only insofar as they impact upon him. The reader perceives the world of the text and the events which occur in it from the hero's point of view, or the point of view of a narrator who admires him and places him in the foreground, so that the story imposes his perspective and his evaluations. Therefore one of the overriding meanings which readers construct from these stories is that it is the hero who is of primary importance and the activities of such men that matter in the world: others exist only to assist their enterprises, and those who oppose them are wicked, or at least misguided.

Narrative point of view is the most powerful means by which the reader's perceptions and sympathies are manipulated. In first-person narratives the character telling the story filters the events through his or her own consciousness. A first-person narrator may be naive or limited in understanding so that the reader will be sceptical of his or her judgements as, for instance, we are sceptical of the superficial, pedantic Lockwood's judgement of Heathcliff in *Wuthering Heights*, but even so the narrator's perspective cannot be ignored. More usually, especially in children's literature, a first-person narrative invites the reader's acceptance of the narrator's values and judgements.

In third-person narratives the point of view is less obvious and consistent. The events may be focalized through the consciousness of one or more of the characters. The reader's opinions about the other characters and events will, therefore, be influenced by the attitudes of the focalizing character. The structuralist critic Gérard Genette (Genette [1972] 1980: 161–211) usefully distinguishes between focalization and narrative voice. Narrative voice is the anonymous voice which tells the story. It is not the voice of the author (although it may express some of the author's views) since even an omniscient narrator 'assumes' that the events are true, whereas the author knows that he or she is imagining them. The narrative voice influences the responses of the reader in various ways – for example, by the selection and ordering of information, and by the use of language. Most obviously an anonymous narrator may intrude comments to guide the reader's responses. This was common in nineteenth- and early twentieth-century children's books. In *The Tale of Peter Rabbit*, for instance, the anonymous narrator points out that Flopsy, Mopsy and Cottontail 'were good little bunnies' (Potter 1902: 17), whereas Peter 'was very naughty' (p. 18).

Ismay Barwell in her essay 'Feminist perspectives and narrative points of view' (Barwell 1993) argues that every text is gendered since every act of narration, even where the narrative voice is apparently objective and omniscient, involves a process of selection – since it would be impossible to provide every piece of information about every incident in a sequence of events – and the nature of that selection implies certain values: 'Even where the point of view is "impersonal," the narrative events and states of affairs reveal selections made on the basis of preferences which in their turn reveal judgements about what is interesting' (p. 99). The 'desires, attitudes and interests which guide the choices made' (p. 98) must be either male or female. She goes on to say: 'A text may be intended for women and may be about women, but it may still have a masculine point of view because the beliefs in the hypothetical narrator point of view about women are masculine' (p. 101). An example of such a text would be a conventional romance which depicts women behaving and feeling about men in the way men believe them to do.

The selections made in a particular act of narrating also constitute an ethnic and class perspective. The totality of the selections carries implications about what is interesting and important and about what is of no account, or so uninteresting that it is omitted or mentioned only when it impinges upon significant events. To take an obvious example: in *The Odyssey* the reader is given information about the men who accompanied Odysseus on his voyage only when their actions are relevant to the fortunes of Odysseus himself, as, for instance, when he plugs their ears with wax so they will not hear the sirens singing and so drive the ship on to the rocks in an ecstasy of delight (Homer 1946: 199). The implication is that it is Odysseus the king who is important in the scheme of things; the men are neither significant nor interesting in their own right. Likewise in many nineteenth- and early twentieth-century children's stories servants have a shadowy presence, but they are rarely mentioned because from the narrator's middle-class point of view they are of no significance.

Similarly the selections involved in a particular narrative stance imply views about the relative worth and significance of various kinds of human activities. So the overwhelming concentration, in hero tales, upon physical action and conflict, relegates not only domestic activities and relations, but also creativity, imagination and emotion to the margins.

Because hero tales are narrated from the hero's point of view, and because he occupies the foreground of the story, the reader is invited to share his values and admire his actions, although many heroes do things which most present-day readers would find questionable if they were presented differently. In the English fairy story 'Jack and the Beanstalk' the narrative point of view requires the reader to approve, or at least condone, criminal and extremely selfish behaviour on the part of the hero. The 1807 Tabart version of the story (Opie and Opie 1974: 164–75), from which later retellings derive, is an omniscient third-person narrative in which the narrator provides information only as it relates to Jack and in which sections of the story are focalized through Jack himself. We see both home, the world on the ground, and the magical world in the sky from his point of view. He is the initiator of the action: it is his decision to swap the cow for the magic beans; he climbs the beanstalk of his own volition on each occasion; he persuades the giant's wife to admit him, and he decides to steal the hen, the money bags and the harp. The other characters exist only as actors in his story: the two benevolent assistants, the fairy and the giant's wife, the monstrous giant whom he must overcome, and his mother who is there to welcome him home and reward him with her approval at the end, are all insignificant compared to Jack. Jack not only steals the giant's possessions, he manipulates and deceives the giant's kindly wife, who several times saves his life, and finally he abandons her, perhaps to her death, when he cuts down the beanstalk. It requires conscious critical detachment to focus on the sufferings of the giant's wife for, while reading the story, we are swept along by its strong forward momentum and controlled by Jack's perception of things. So it is his initiative, cleverness and success which are foregrounded. It could be argued, following Jack Zipes's views about the inherent radicalism of folk tales, that Jack's destruction of the giant is an imaginative depiction of the possibility of overthrowing unjust authority:

> the basic nature of the folk tale was connected to the objective ontological situation and dreams of the narrators and their audiences in all age groups . . . these narratives, even though marked by bourgeois stylization, all retain hope for improving conditions of life and . . . the fantastic elements (miracles, magic) function to bring about a *real* fulfilment of the desires of the protagonists who were often underdogs or victims of social injustice.
>
> (Zipes 1979: 28)

But if the story does involve an envisioning of successful revolution the image of the new regime which would replace the brutal injustices of aristocratic power is one of ruthlessly *laissez-faire* opportunism, a restructured patriarchy in which power passes to enterprising entrepreneurs motivated by self-interest, ready to snatch the money and the hen that lays the golden eggs as soon as an opportunity appears.

*The Odyssey* likewise requires approval for Odysseus's wholesale slaughter of the suitors and brutal execution of the women of his household who had provided them with sexual favours. The anonymous narrator focuses attention upon Odysseus's concern for his honour which is always of paramount importance to him, and these bloody deeds are presented as required by honour and thus as heroic. This is underlined in the text by the introduction of the goddess Athena who urges him to action, and by the reaction of his faithful old nurse, Eurycleia:

> She found Odysseus amongst the corpses of the fallen, spattered with blood and filth, like a lion when he comes from feeding on some

farmer's bullock, with the blood dripping from his breast and jaws on either side, a fearsome spectacle. That was how Odysseus looked, with the gore thick on his legs and arms. But when Eurycleia saw the dead men and that sea of blood her instinct was to raise a yell of triumph at the mighty achievement that confronted her.

(Homer 1946: 348–9)

The pattern is apparent even in Sendak's gentle tale, *Where the Wild Things Are*, in which the reader is not invited to disapprove of Max's wild behaviour but rather to feel the joy of his energy. Although it is not told in the first person the information which the anonymous narrator provides is all related to Max: we see what he does and what he sees. He is the initiator of the action. It is his wild behaviour at the beginning which causes him to be sent to bed without supper. He calls up the forest, the ocean, the boat and the wild things. He exerts his power over the wild things, orders the wild rumpus, and then commands its cessation. Even his mother's action in leaving his supper out for him is a response to his behaviour. Max is so central to the view of things provided by the text that his mother does not even appear in the pictures, though her relationship with him is crucial to the events. More telling, perhaps, is his father's absence from Max's consciousness. It is the wild things, Max's own imaginings, which fill the pictures and his awareness. This reflects his egocentric, oedipal stage of development, but it also suggests that the world exists to meet the needs of white, middle-class, male children, the future members of the patriarchy.

Thus hero tales insist upon the central importance of the hero in the scheme of things. Women matter only insofar as their actions affect him; in their own right they are of no interest or importance. Likewise his opponents are viewed simply as his opponents, not as people with complex lives and motivations of their own, and their fate is destruction or domination. Because the events are focalized through his consciousness and the reader's perceptions are focused upon him, his qualities are foregrounded and valued and others downplayed; the reader is required to admire courage, action, skill and determination, while qualities like creativity, sensitivity and self-questioning have no presence in the hero's world.

Rosemary Sutcliff's critically acclaimed historical novel for children, *The Eagle of the Ninth* [1954], provides a telling example of the way point of view in a hero story can function to naturalize the political values of the establishment. Although a more open and poetic text than many, this work is a classic example of the quest genre. It seeks both to chart the personal development of the protagonist, Marcus, and to explore the essential qualities of Roman and Celtic culture (or at least the versions of those cultures constructed in the text) while narrating a story of heroic endeavour and domination which turns upon the fundamental dualisms of civilization and wilderness, and reason and irrationality. Marcus, is a young ex-centurion who travels into the wild north of Britain to recover the lost standard of his father's former legion and so vindicate his honour. He also seeks a direction for his own future, having been permanently invalided out of the legions. His quest is successful on both counts: he eventually finds the golden Eagle hidden in the dark heart of a Celtic holy place and learns that his father died fighting bravely for Rome, and he also realizes that Roman Britain has become his home and decides to become a farmer there. In that he foreshadows the decision of many young Englishmen in the outposts of empire in the nineteenth and early twentieth centuries. The 'Roman' qualities which Marcus displays – courage, stoicism, conscientiousness, loyalty, a clear, logical mind – are also those that were prized in such English empire builders.

Although the story pivots upon the opposition between order and wilderness, and although Marcus is the focalizing character, it does not insist on the superiority of the qualities for which the Eagle stands in an absolute way. The countervailing system of values is presented sympathetically throughout, and the conclusion attempts, though with limited success, to suggest the possibility of an integration of the two cultures. Sutcliff provides Marcus with a companion on his quest, Esca, a Celtic warrior and tribal prince, who was enslaved by the Roman conquerors and forced to perform as a gladiator. After saving him from death in the arena, Marcus buys him as a personal slave and they gradually develop respect and affection for each other. Esca is used to make the qualities of Celtic culture explicit for the reader, and, through the richly metaphorical language, an impression is created of a way of seeing the world which is convincingly pre-literate and close to nature, with no sharp division between the understanding of the reasoning mind and unconscious intuitions. An example is the image Esca uses to indicate his willingness to remain with Marcus as his property: 'I am the Centurion's hound to lie at the Centurion's feet' (Sutcliff [1954] 1977: 77). A literate Roman (or Englishman) might express this complex attitude by the use of abstract terms such as 'submission', 'bitterness', 'admiration', 'loyalty' and 'irony' but the Celtic Esca conveys the whole constellation of feelings and ideas in a concrete image which would come readily to a hunter who lives close to animals and the natural world.

In a key passage Esca attempts to help Marcus understand the difference between Roman and Celtic culture by comparing a Roman dagger sheath and a Celtic shield boss. The dagger sheath is ornamented with tight little curves and stiff flowers, regularly repeated, while the shield-boss is covered with 'bulging curves that flow from each other as water flows from water and wind from wind, as the stars turn in the heavens and blown sand drifts into dunes . . . the curves of life' (p. 98). He generalizes from the comparison to sketch an inevitable and tragic clash of cultures, such as we see whenever a more technologically-advanced people impose their way of life upon a simpler, indigenous culture:

> You are the builders of coursed stone walls, the makers of straight roads and ordered justice and disciplined troops. We know that, we know it all too well. We know that your justice is more sure than ours, and when we rise against you, we see our hosts break against the discipline of your troops, as the sea breaks against a rock. And we do not understand, because all these things are of the ordered pattern, and only the free curves of the shield boss are real to us. We do not understand. And when the time comes that we begin to understand your world, too often we lose the understanding of our own.
>
> (Sutcliff [1954] 1977: 99)

This is a reflection of the situation of Aboriginal Australians whose way of life was subjected to the 'justice' and the ordered pattern of the invading British settlers, and, while such a conceptualization is perhaps not entirely convincing in the mouth of Esca, the passage comes close to a perception of human history as a process of inevitable change, with inevitable loss accompanying whatever might be defined as gain.

However, Esca exists only as part of Marcus's story, as does the Celtic girl, Cottia, whom he decides to marry in the concluding pages of the novel. Marcus is the hero, his concerns are primary and, although the novel is narrated in the third person, he is the focalizing character throughout. The reader sees Esca and Cottia only as he sees them and thus is required to accept the conclusion as a happy ending: Marcus has found his way in life, he has returned successfully from his journey into the wildness and 'darkness' of the tribal lands in the north, and from the darkness of his own despair at the pain caused by his injury and the destruction of his chosen career in the legions. The closure implies that in the future all will be well for Marcus and for Roman Britain. As the returning hero he will bestow a boon upon the land, living in harmony with the Celtic people, learning from them and adapting Roman ways to their needs. So he enters two symbolic unions: Cottia will be his bride and Esca, now freed, will work beside him on the farm.

The stories of Esca and Cottia are suppressed, but if they were told they would be tragedies, exemplars of the effects of imperialist expansion. Their land has been overrun by foreign invaders insensitive to the profound meanings it holds for them, invaders who build roads through their sacred sites. Esca's parents and most of his tribe have been killed. The tribal structure which gave his life meaning, and defined him as a warrior, is gone. The Celtic culture is being destroyed by Roman ways and Roman laws. They must live inside alien towns whose walls cut them off from the easy intercourse with nature which is vital to them; symbolically Cottia is forced to wear fashionable Roman clothes. Their only option for the future is to become assimilated, to relinquish their identity and live as ersatz Romans. For them the happy ending is a final defeat.

Despite Sutcliff's recognition of the imaginative and emotional limitations inherent in 'Roman' civilization *The Eagle of the Ninth* naturalizes imperialist domination of indigenous peoples. Marcus's essential decency and desire to understand enhance the impression that this process is an inevitable one, for insofar as Marcus stands for 'Rome', that is for Western civilization, there is no suggestion of cruel oppression involved. What is constructed for the reader is rather an image of natural selection, the unavoidable dominance of reason, order and efficiency over the unmoderated flux of life, no matter how poetic. This meaning, constructed by the story itself, is also imposed at the linguistic level by the light/dark imagery which pervades the text. The most powerful expression of this dualism occurs at the point in the story where Marcus and Esca find the Eagle in the underground holy place of a Celtic tribe. In the darkness Marcus is overcome by panic, and imagines that his candle flame is sinking:

> He felt not only the many-fingered dark, but the walls and roof themselves closing in on him, suffocating him as though a soft cold hand was pressed over his nose and mouth. He had a sudden hideous conviction that there was no longer a straight passage and a leather curtain between them and the outside world, only the earth-piled mountain high over them, and no way out. No way out! The darkness reached out to finger him softly. He braced himself upright against the cold stones, putting out his will to force the walls back, fighting the evil sense of suffocation. He was doing as he had told Esca to do, thinking Light with all the strength that was in him, so that in his inner eye, the place was full of it: strong clear light flowing into every cranny . . . He called it up now, like golden water, like a trumpet call, the Light of Mithras. He hurled it against the darkness, forcing it back – back – back.
>
> (Sutcliff [1954] 1977: 210–11)

Though there is no logical connection between Marcus' panic fear of the dark and the nature of Celtic culture, the light/dark opposition is attached to the Roman/Celtic opposition so that the reader is invited to feel that if the light of reason is to shine it must push back the world of the Celtic people.

Readers who belong to one of the groups marginalized by hero stories – primarily women and non-Europeans – are doubly affected by the narrative point of view of these tales. They see human beings like themselves depicted as unimportant and inferior, and sometimes as evil. But as they read they must participate in the hero's perspective and share the feelings of the narrator towards these characters. Thus they are taught to despise themselves, to collude in the construction of their own inferiority rather than to rebel against being so labelled. For generations girls, as well as boys, have read, and studied as class texts, classics like *Treasure Island*, *David Copperfield*, *Kim* and *The Eagle of the Ninth* – books whose implied reader is male, and in which females play circumscribed roles on the fringes of the action, but books which are vividly written, which stir the reader's emotions and compel the willing suspension of disbelief. For girls the cost of the pleasure these books provided was the internalization of their dismissive view of women. When these books, and others like them, were all that was available for 'young adults' the only possible stance of rebellion for girls was to wish to be a boy, for the idea of girls participating fully and freely in the action of life was barely conceivable. Girls who did not secretly wish to be boys adopted subservience as a virtue, defining themselves as existing only in relation to others, only in relation to the hero for whose coming they waited.

## THE LINEAR JOURNEY

In his study of conceptions of geological time, *Time's Arrow, Time's Cycle*, Stephen Jay Gould contrasts the two fundamental ways in which human beings have conceived of time: on the one hand as a continuous state, with no direction, in which 'apparent motions are parts of repeating cycles, and differences of the past will be realities of the future' (1988: 11); on the other, as a forward movement where 'each moment occupies its own distinct position in a temporal series, and all moments, considered in proper sequence, tell a story of linked events moving in a direction' (pp. 10–11). While ancient peoples believed that time was cyclic, as reflected in the recurrence of the seasons and the movements of the stars, a state in which all things are immanent, the Christian tradition, Gould points out, has conceived of time primarily as an arrow, a progress towards ultimate salvation:

> God creates the earth once, instructs Noah to ride out a unique flood in a singular ark, transmits the commandments to Moses at a distinctive moment, and sends His son to a particular place at a definite time to die for us on the cross and rise again on the third day.
>
> (Gould 1988: 11)

The idea of time as an irreversible sequence of moments has become the normal view of most educated Westerners and is, Gould argues (p. 80), an essential basis for the treatment of history as intelligible, although he qualifies this by pointing out that he is discussing 'a vision of the nature of things bound by both culture and time' (p. 12). The concept of the linearity of time is fundamental, not only for theories of evolution, but also for ideas of social progress and achievement. Ideas of purpose, goals, progress, success, are meaningful only if time is seen as linear.

Narratives encode the concept of time as linear. While a poem may express the essence of a moment, an apprehension of what Hopkins called inscape, a story moves from its beginning, through a series of incidents, to its end. In some narratives, however, the forward movement is less marked than in others. This is especially the case in postmodern, deliberately fragmentary and allusive works. Other more conventional stories achieve an effect of immanence and recurrence through imagistic and symbolic patterning and by modifying the linear structure of the narrative. Emily Brontë's *Wuthering Heights*, for instance, conveys a sense of permanent presence by associating the lovers Heathcliff and Catherine with the enduring landscape of the moors, the 'eternal rocks', and by embedding their story within two frame narratives – the story Nelly Dean tells to Lockwood and the story he narrates to the reader. Nor are the events presented in chronological order: the story begins at a time when Heathcliff is middle-aged and Catherine long dead, moves backward to tell of their childhood and young adulthood, and then returns to the time at which it began and moves forward. Other devices which enhance the impression of immanence include Lockwood's dream in which the child, Catherine, appears as a wandering ghost, a continuing presence, and the suggestion that she has survived in her daughter. Without sacrificing the intellectual notion of time as a continuous sequence of moments, such a work manages to suggest other ways of apprehending experience, other kinds of significance than the simply temporal.

In hero tales, however, the story takes the form of a journey and the sense of linear progression is strong. These stories are exciting and easy to read. They create pleasure by arousing excitement and desire, the desire to know 'what will happen next'. As each incident in the story concludes the desire is temporarily satisfied, only to be restimulated as the hero moves on to the next challenge. As Catherine Belsey puts it, the movement of the narrative is both towards concealment and towards disclosure, creating uncertainty and constantly promising the reader that all will be revealed (Belsey [1980] 1988: 106). The pleasure such stories arouse is very different from what Barthes in *Le Plaisir du texte* [1975] called *jouissance* or 'joy', a shock of revelation which involves a loss of the established sense of self. These stories rather reaffirm the reader's pre-existing sense of cultural identity, asserting the traditional patriarchal values, the fundamental dualisms which underlie Western culture, as each crisis in the story results in the hero's victory.

Because readers have experienced similar texts before they know that the hero will triumph and the story will assert the traditional dualisms, and so they have no difficulty in decoding it. For instance, as the reader learns how Jim Hawkins, hidden in the apple barrel on the *Hispaniola*, overhears Silver talking to a companion and realizes they are pirates, he or she experiences a shiver of excitement and wonders what will happen, but never doubts that Jim and his friends will somehow survive and gain the treasure, that the forces of 'good' will triumph over the wild irrationality of their adversaries. The same certainty sustains the reader through all the subsequent narrative crises. So far as significance goes they are exact repetitions of each other: Jim and his friends are good and they behave bravely, resourcefully and honourably, while the pirates are bad and behave selfishly, treacherously and less intelligently than the others. Therefore the good characters will win because it is in the nature of things for them to do so. *Treasure Island* provides pleasure in the arousal of curiosity, in anticipation, and in the satisfaction of anticipation, but no joy, no enlargement of understanding, no moments of insight.

It is rarely that a hero story constructed according to the traditional pattern of the journey into the wilderness and the final return manages to achieve more than the pleasure of repeated arousal and satisfaction of expectation. Ursula Le Guin's *A Wizard of Earthsea* [1968] does so because its successive incidents do not result in unequivocal victories for the hero, and because, as the story progresses, it undermines the very concept of 'victory' by subverting the dualisms which underlie conventional hero tales. When the hero, Ged, is a boy with his powers of wizardry just emerging he does achieve a simple victory, saving his village from invasion by viking-like marauders. Being only a boy he sees things simply – people are friends or enemies, actions are right or wrong – and the narrative voice invites the reader to share his perspective. We are told that the villagers realized he had 'saved their lives and their property' (Le Guin [1968] 1971: 23), and no other views of the incident are presented. But as the story continues and Ged grows older he is denied such certainties, and the reader is likewise required to question traditional beliefs and attitudes.

Pride in his powers causes Ged to overreach himself, and in trying to call up a spirit from the dead he inadvertently lets loose a shadow which attacks and severely wounds him. It disappears, but he is convinced that it is loose in the world and will eventually attack him again. He regards it as his enemy, flees from it, and then, changing his strategy, pursues it; but when at last he comes face to face with it he recognizes it as an aspect of himself which he must acknowledge if he is to be free and whole. Earlier incidents have led to similar reassessments. An unsuccessful attempt to use his magic powers to save the life of a dying child taught him to see death as part of nature, to feel the harmony of nature's cyclic processes, and strive to learn 'what can be learnt, in silence, from the eyes of animals, the flight of birds, the great slow gestures of trees' (p. 97). Thus the perception of existence as a process of opposition and mastery is replaced by a perception of complementarity and acceptance, and Ged's journey is essentially inward rather than forward. The poetic and philosophical insights and the multi-faceted symbolism of this fantasy for young adult readers combine with the excitement of the story to produce the kind of enhanced awareness which Barthes called joy, but it is rare amongst hero stories.

The linearity of most hero stories implies purposiveness as well as progress: the hero moves relentlessly forward through both space and time, travelling towards his goal. The shape of the story is an image of his ambition. It implies that failure to achieve the goal would render his life itself a failure, and perhaps bring disaster on his friends or his whole people. If Odysseus does not reach Ithaca and resume his kingship his honour will be destroyed and his fortune consumed by the rapacious suitors. Frodo's task, in *The Lord of the Rings*, like the task of many fantasy heroes who are depicted as struggling to save civilization, to preserve 'our' world from some threat of annihilation, is absolute and Christ-like – if he does not reach the crater of Mount Doom and throw the ring into its furnace depths the whole of Middle-earth will fall under the power of the Dark Lord. The point of such tales is that they advance towards their end; no matter how many exciting incidents and diversions occur along the way the final goal remains clear, and the achievement of the goal invests the narrative as a whole with meaning just as the Christian account of salvation implies a universe rendered orderly by God's purpose.

In this way the story of the hero's journey also encodes the metanarrative of progress, the vision of the Enlightenment which has been the guiding belief of modernism, the belief that the application of reason to nature and to human affairs must lead to solutions to the problems of society, to improvements in the material standard of living, and to steady advances in knowledge and understanding. The history of the twentieth century has made it difficult to sustain that belief, and postmodern thinkers tend to reject all such metanarratives, including Christian and Marxist accounts of reality as well as the myth of progress. If reality is fragmentary and plural then each moment in life is important in itself rather than as a stage on a journey to some distant goal, and the story of the hero's quest may be seen as illusory and distracting.

Hero stories imply the importance not only of a sense of rigorous purpose, but of successful achievement. The image of life they offer is of unremitting struggle in the pursuit of career goals. It is important to travel hopefully, but salvation is the prerogative of those who arrive. This is the message not only of fantasy adventures but also of the *bildungsroman* in which the hero's journey is primarily a progress through time as he moves from the uncertainties and powerlessness of childhood, through the difficulties of adolescence and the hostilities of the external world, to arrive finally at some form of successful adulthood. Although many of these works were originally written for adults they are routinely read by adolescents and often prescribed for study in schools. Dickens's *David Copperfield* [1850] is one of the best known. It is written in the first person and David's role as hero is announced in the opening sentence: 'Whether I shall turn out to be the hero of my own life, or whether that station will be held by anybody else, these pages must show' (Dickens n.d.: 7), and the reader is left in no doubt as to how to interpret his story when he explains that in his darkest days he sustained himself by reading books which had belonged to his father; they included *Humphrey Clinker*, *Tom Jones* and *Robinson Crusoe* – all traditional hero stories.

David is a middle-class child born into difficult circumstances; his father has died before his birth, and his mother's second husband is the cold and sadistic Mr Murdstone, a more fearsome ogre than most of those encountered by the heroes of fairy tales. David's life is full of challenges and reversals, but its general direction is forward and his progress is moral and spiritual as well as material. Although he arrives at a degree of material success it is his emergence as a writer, and his belated recognition of the virtues embodied in the self-sacrificing, beautiful and intelligent Agnes which constitute his real success.

Agnes is his reward, and David's marriage with her is in every way what Joseph Campbell in his analysis of early hero myths calls the 'mystical marriage . . . of the triumphant hero-soul with the Queen Goddess of the World . . . she is the incarnation of the promise of perfection; the soul's assurance that, at the conclusion of its exile in a world of organized inadequacies, the bliss that once was known will be known again . . .' (Campbell [1949] 1968: 109):

> And now as I close my task, subduing my desire to linger yet, these faces fade away. But one face, shining on me like a Heavenly light by which I see all other objects, is above them and beyond them all. And that remains.
>
> I turn my head, and see it, in its beautiful serenity, beside me. My lamp burns low, and I have written far into the night; but the dear presence, without which I were nothing, bears me company.
>
> O Agnes, O my soul, so may thy face be by me when I close my life indeed; so may I, when realities are melting from me like the shadows which I now dismiss, still find thee near me, pointing upward!
>
> (Dickens n.d.: 882)

Like Beatrice conducting Dante to Paradise she has led him to the brink of an ultimate goal, the attainment of enlightenment is linked to the attainment of worldly success, and the story parallels the archetypal Christian journey. *David Copperfield* inscribes the importance and possibility of spiritual as well as material success as effectively as the myths and fantasies in which the hero confronts dragons in a dark wood.

The narrative structure of the hero story is a paradigm of adolescent development, and specifically of male adolescent development. In Jungian terms it is an image of the outward journey of the ego, the concern of youth, as opposed to the later task of individuation, or inward journey in search of the Self, of wholeness and harmony. It could be argued, therefore, that hero tales are appropriate fare for younger readers simply because the story structure renders them both innately adolescent and easy to read, but this is to underestimate the capacity of children to respond to more complex narrative patterns. The enormous and enduring popularity of Frances Hodgson Burnett's *The Secret Garden* [1911] and, more recently, of Katherine Paterson's *Bridge to Terabithia* [1977], shows that children are able to construct satisfying meanings from stories which work symbolically, with a structure that focuses on a single place, and in which the essential movement of the plot is inward, rather than forward. These stories suggest that children, as well as adults, and boys as well as girls, seek a sense of wholeness, that they are not purely concerned with the assertion of the ego. In each of these works the successive events of the narrative involve further experiences of a single, central place which is a symbolic mandala, a closed space, complete in itself. It symbolizes the protagonist's self and is the site of inner growth. In Burnett's story it is the secret, walled garden, within a larger garden, to which the unhappy, resentful child, Mary, discovers the key:

> But she was *inside* the wonderful garden, and she could come through the door under the ivy any time, and she felt as if she had found a world all her own.
>
> The sun was shining inside the four walls and the high arch of blue sky over this particular piece of Misselthwaite seemed even more brilliant and soft than it was over the moor.
>
> (Burnett [1911] 1951: 70)

The garden is an overgrown wilderness because it has been kept locked for ten years, ever since the wife of the owner, Dr Craven, died in an accident there. However, the tangled rose bushes only appear to be dead, and as Mary works during successive visits to make them bloom again she slowly recovers her own joy in life. Later she introduces Dr Craven's depressed, hypochondriacal son to the garden and eventually he too achieves a renaissance of health and joy; this ultimately enables Dr Craven himself to emerge from his protracted grief. Most of the important scenes in the novel take place in the garden which accretes significance as the story unfolds.

In *Bridge to Terabithia* the symbolic place is a clearing in the woods where an imaginative child, Leslie Burke, helps an emotionally repressed friend, Jesse Aarons, create a magic kingdom which they call Terabithia. Before he met Leslie, Jesse's single ambition had been to win the fifth class running race, to move forward, hero-like, more swiftly than any of his peers, but once Terabithia has been summoned into existence, he feels the shallowness of this aim and becomes absorbed by the blossoming world of his imagination.

Jung regarded the mandala, a Sanskrit word, meaning 'magic circle', as an archetypal image of the Self (Fordham 1966: 64–8), and it is a common symbol in a number of religions, appearing for instance as the sun disc in ancient Egypt. It often has the form of a square within a circle, which is precisely the image of the secret garden with its four walls and the over-arching disc of the sky, and it clearly suggests wholeness and harmony. In *The Secret Garden* it can be read both as an image of Mary's self, which had been closed and neglected like the garden, and as a symbol of the vitality and harmony of nature. In *Bridge to Terabithia* the secret place has a similar dual significance. Terabithia is situated in the woods which Jesse at first feared as he feared all the darker aspects of nature, along with the depths of his own unconscious: 'There were parts of the woods that Jess did not like. Dark places where it was almost like being underwater, but he didn't say so' (Paterson 1980: 49). As their imaginative games allow him to explore his psyche he gradually loses his fear of nature and of himself, so that even after Leslie's death he retains the 'vision and strength' (p. 140) which he developed in Terabithia, and he is able to hand on to his sister, May Belle, the stimulus to imaginative growth which he received from Leslie.

Such stories enable young readers to construct a concept of time as both cyclical and linear. They suggest recurring patterns in human growth and the importance of a sense of immanence and harmony with nature to the achievement of psychic wholeness. Other widely-read children's books with a similar symbolic structure, which deal with the protagonist's inner growth include Philippa Pearce's *Tom's Midnight Garden* [1958], Betsy Byars' *The Cartoonist* [1978] and Ruth Park's *Callie's Castle* [1974]. The popularity of these works suggests that young readers are able to make meanings from narrative structures which go beyond the simple linearity of the hero tale and welcome texts that offer gender-neutral images of inner growth rather than the depiction of life as a succession of goal-oriented struggles in which success is dependent upon aggression and dominance.

## CLOSURE

Traditionally quest stories have a happy ending: the hero achieves his goal. Often this means that he attains a treasure which he brings back to his home, thus bestowing a boon upon it. So Jason returns from Colchis with the Golden Fleece, Jim Hawkins and his friends bring back the pirates' gold, Marcus recovers the golden eagle which was the standard of his father's legion, Jack escapes from the land at the top of the Beanstalk with bags of gold, a hen that lays golden eggs and a magic golden harp, Bilbo Baggins in *The Hobbit* helps the dwarves to recover the horde of gold and jewels guarded by the dragon, Smaug. The golden nature of these objects suggests a special significance, and generally quest objects symbolize the values of the cultures to which the stories belong. The Golden Fleece comes from a ram which was the offspring of the god Poseidon and is therefore an incarnation of the sacredness of the earth itself as well as a symbol of Hellenic pride. The Holy Grail which the pure hero, Galahad, achieves in Malory's *Le Morte d'Arthur* signifies the values of the Christian communion. The golden eagle in *The Eagle of the Ninth* is a symbol of the qualities admired by Roman and British imperialism, while the pile of money in *Treasure Island* is a fitting emblem of the values of nineteenth-century capitalism.

In some stories the hero's reward is not a golden object but a golden bride who is invariably beautiful and often a queen or princess. In the fairy tale 'The Sleeping Beauty' the prince, who makes his way through the forest of brambles surrounding the enchanted castle with truly heroic fortitude, comes at last:

> to a chamber which was all decked over with gold. There he encountered the most beautiful sight he had ever seen. Reclining upon a bed, the curtains of which on every side were drawn back, was a princess of seemingly some fifteen or sixteen summers, whose radiant beauty had an almost unearthly lustre.
>
> (Perrault [1697] 1969: 13)

Nineteenth-century *bildungsroman* often contained secular versions of this figure; David Copperfield's Agnes is an outstanding example. The significance of such brides is discussed in some detail in Chapter 4. Here it is necessary only to note that they function as symbols rather than characters. They are trophy brides who mark the hero's success, and as such, they are one of the ways in which the story inscribes the subordination of women: though both royal and beautiful they exist only in order to be bestowed upon the hero.

The sense of special significance with which the treasure or the bride is invested contributes to the effect of powerful closure which is a feature of these stories. Roger Webster defines closure as follows:

> The concept of *closure* refers to the ways in which a text persuades a reader to understand and accept a particular 'truth' or form of knowledge, to accept a certain view of the world as valid or natural.
>
> (Webster 1990: 53)

It is the point in a text where loose ends, doubts and uncertainties are removed, and the significance of the story appears clear and coherent, the point where the myth imposes its meanings upon the reader. The closure is ideological as well as narrative and aesthetic; it makes the values inherent in the structure and narrative point of view seem to 'go without saying', to be simply natural. Jason's attainment of the Golden Fleece in the face of such dangers seems to prove that it was meant to return to Hellas to mark the greatness of the Hellenes. When Odysseus proves his identity to the suitors in the great hall at Ithaca by stringing his mighty bow, preparatory to slaughtering them, the gods themselves indicate their approval: 'to mark the signal moment there came a thunderclap from Zeus, and Odysseus' long-suffering heart leapt up for joy at this sign of favour from the son of Cronos of the crooked ways' (Homer 1946: 337). So everything Odysseus has done, and the killing he is about to carry out, is endorsed by the highest authority. The text requires the reader to accept Odysseus' single-minded devotion to the cause of his own honour and authority as entirely admirable, and to accept also that any action undertaken in the furtherance of this cause is justified. When Marcus, in *The Eagle of the Ninth*, finds the Roman eagle hidden in a Celtic holy place and successfully recovers it the story imposes his perspective: his reason, courage and military training are seen to triumph over superstitious fear and over the Celtic tribesmen themselves thus demonstrating the 'natural' superiority of Roman culture.

The firm closure in these stories insists upon the particular values of the hero and his world, but the closure is meaningful in itself for it implies that unequivocal success is attainable, that all problems are soluble, that certainty is possible. Where the central binary opposition is defined as a conflict between good and evil the achievement of the hero's quest is a victory of the good and the closure asserts that evil can be clearly identified and defeated. This is the meaning of the conclusion of *The Lord of the Rings*. At the moment when the ring disappears into the crater of Mount Doom and Frodo's quest is achieved, the armies of the good, led by Gandalf and Aragorn, are engaged in a battle against the forces of Mordor. The effect of the ring's destruction reads very much like a description of a nuclear blast so that the forces of good are subliminally aligned with the Western powers which dropped the nuclear bombs on Hiroshima and Nagasaki:

> the earth rocked beneath their feet. Then rising swiftly up, far above the Towers of the Black Gate, high above the mountains, a vast soaring darkness sprang into the sky, flickering with fire. The earth groaned and quaked. The Towers of the Teeth swayed, tottered, and fell down; the mighty rampart crumbled; the Black Gate was hurled in ruin; and from far away, now dim, now growing, there came a drumming rumble, a roar, a long echoing roll of ruinous noise.
>
> 'The realm of Sauron is ended!' said Gandalf. 'The Ring-bearer has fulfilled his Quest.' And as the Captains gazed south to the Land of Mordor, it seemed to them that, black against the pall of cloud, there rose a huge shape of shadow, impenetrable, lightning-crowned, filling all the sky. Enormous it reared above the world, and stretched out towards them a vast threatening hand, terrible but impotent: for even as it leaned over them, a great wind took it, and it was all blown away, and passed; and then a hush fell.
>
> (Tolkien 1955: 227)

The consequences of this are represented as unequivocally good: evil is banished from the land, and the 'good' can return to their homes in peace. No suggestion of the ethical contradictions, impossible dilemmas and complex horrors of actual wars is present. The sufferings of the defeated Orcs have no reality within the text. Having been defined as evil they are treated as of no further account. All the focalizing characters in the narrative belong to the side of the good and are, by definition, concerned only to annihilate their opposites. For them Mordor is no Hiroshima, and the virtues of compassion and moral humility, which might have made them convincingly good, are beyond the range of Tolkien's heroes. The perspective of the narrative voice is no less limited: the fleeing and dying Orcs are compared to ants disoriented by the death of their queen, thus simultaneously distancing the reader from them and dehumanizing them. None of the characters in the trilogy has to struggle to understand what he should do. Those who do evil do it knowingly. They are not faced with situations where there seem to be no clearly good options available. The simplistic oppositions of the text deny the possibility of doubt or confusion about ethical issues. The moral difficulties, the indeterminacies and uncertainties, the 'bitter furies of complexity' (Yeats [1933] 1950: 281) which are intrinsic to the human condition, are absent in Tolkien, and denied absolutely by the closure.

Strong closures are especially characteristic of the endings of thrillers and detective stories, those modern, mundane versions of the hero tale. While much of the appeal of these stories for more sophisticated readers lies in the emergence of the aesthetic closure, the moment when the significance of previously puzzling incidents is made clear, hidden motivations are uncovered, confusions are clarified, and finally, like a completed jigsaw puzzle, the whole picture becomes apparent with every detail accounted for, the closure in such stories is also strongly ideological. They assert the efficacy and superiority of reason, and hence of the rational, scientific basis of Western civilization, and they insist upon the necessity of order: all must be analysed and categorized. There is no place in them for the 'negative capability' which Keats regarded as an essential condition for creativity: the capability of 'being in uncertainties, mysteries, doubts, without any irritable reaching after fact and reason' (Keats n.d.: Letter, 21 December 1817).

It seems likely that for many this constitutes much of their attraction. They construct a version of the modern world which is intelligible and unambiguous, where friends and enemies are clearly distinguishable and where there is no question that 'we' are right and will prevail. When, at the end of each case, Sherlock Holmes explains to Doctor Watson the processes of deduction by which he solved the mystery, his explanations simultaneously prove his superior rationality and reveal the wickedness of the criminal. Thus, for instance, in *The Hound of the Baskervilles* [1901–2] he explains how the incident of a stolen boot enabled him to deduce that the criminal intended to use a hound to track and perhaps attack Sir Henry Baskerville, recognizing his scent from the boot. This explanation shows the cold-bloodedness and premeditation of the criminal as well as Holmes' cleverness. Holmes remarks smugly that 'the more *outré* and grotesque an incident is the more carefully it deserves to be examined, and the very point which appears to complicate a case is, when duly considered and scientifically handled, the one which is most likely to elucidate it' (Doyle 1987: 348). Due consideration and scientific handling can make all clear because, in the world of Sherlock Holmes, the complexities are never ethical, political or emotional; the difficulties of real life do not exist. The completeness of the solution denies the possibility of doubt, and imposes the values which Holmes embodies, the values of the British establishment.

A conclusion does not necessarily entail such ideological closure, and many contemporary works feature deliberately open conclusions which allow the reader freedom to interpret them while implying uncertainty as a universal principle. The two alternative endings of John Fowles' metafictive work, *The French Lieutenant's Woman* [1969], is a famous example of a text which determinedly eschews closure and in so doing draws attention to the way the narrative point of view in Victorian social realist novels, and the 'justice' of their closures, imposed an ideological perspective on the reader. A.S. Byatt's *The Virgin in the Garden* [1978] ends suddenly at an arbitrary point in the lives of the major characters. What their futures might be is unclear not only to the reader but to themselves. While this leaves the way open for the sequels, *Still Life* and *Babel Tower*, the major effect of such abruptness is to emphasize the limited and uncertain control which people have over their lives and the inadequacy of any ideological explanations of human behaviour.

The reader response theorist, Wolfgang Iser, points out that all texts contain gaps or structured blanks – since no thought can be fully explained – which the reader must fill in, and it is these gaps which stimulate the processes of ideation and coordination between perspectives in the text that constitute interpretation (Iser 1980: 169). Formulaic texts, such as conventional hero stories, limit the reader's freedom to fill these gaps, since the reader knows and will apply the formula. On the other hand, texts which do not conform strictly to known patterns and which contain significant gaps and open endings encourage active, creative and critical interpretation. While open endings in adult literature are now common it is often argued, on the basis of Piagetian theories of child development, that young children need stories with clear cut distinctions between right and wrong and satisfying conclusions (e.g. Huck *et al.* 1987: 58–9). Some popular contemporary picture books, however, suggest that even quite young children are able to construct meanings from texts which contain significant gaps and avoid rigid ideological closure.

An Australian picture book of this kind is Jenny Wagner's *John Brown, Rose and the Midnight Cat* [1977], illustrated by Ron Books. Set in the Australian countryside this is the story of an elderly widow, Rose, who lives alone with her dog, John Brown. They share a self-sufficient contentment until a beautiful black cat appears in the garden one night, and stirs a desire in Rose to let it into the house. John Brown at first denies the cat's existence and then attempts to drive it away. When Rose takes to her bed declaring that she will never get up again, John Brown realizes he must let the midnight cat come in. Rose then leaves her bed to sit by the fire for a little while. The midnight cat sits on the arm of the chair and purrs, and John Brown sits beside her. The penultimate picture shows the three calmly sharing the domestic space. The narrative point of view moves between John Brown, Rose and the anonymous narrator so that no naive identification is possible.

To read this book children must do more than fill in gaps in a determinate but not fully disclosed design; they must engage in a task of genuine interpretation, selecting from a range of possible meanings at each point in the story and thus constructing personal readings valid for them at that moment. They must consider, for instance, the nature of the closeness between Rose and John Brown, the reasons for Rose's desire for the midnight cat and for John Brown's initial antipathy to it. The conclusion poses further questions, for the future of the three is uncertain. One easily accessible range of meaning focuses on the mother/child parallel in the relationship between Rose and John Brown and identifies John Brown's motivation as initial jealousy of a new family member followed by acceptance, but even at this level the closure remains indeterminate for there is no guarantee that John Brown's capitulation will ensure an equal and easy sharing of Rose's love. Another set of meanings connects Rose's grief for the death of her husband (whose photograph hangs on the wall) with her own movement towards death, and so John Brown's rejection of the black cat can be read as denial of death, followed again by acceptance. But the cat is equally suggestive of a wildness and glamour missing from the stuffy domesticity of Rose's house and, by implication, from her claustrophobic relationship with John Brown who can stand for husband as easily as child; in this reading, which raises issues of gender roles, the closure represents a defeat for John Brown whose future in the relationship is uncertain. At a more abstract level the cat, whose existence John Brown attempts to deny, signifies imaginative reality, the singing of the mermaids, the lure of the wild, while John Brown is the determined pragmatist his name suggests. Various modifications and combinations of these and other readings are possible, so that final meaning is indefinitely deferred.

The brief texts of picture books are perhaps inevitably more open than longer works but open endings which refuse ideological closure are now also no longer unusual in children's novels. The refusal is explicit in Katherine Paterson's *The Great Gilly Hopkins* [1978]. Gilly, an 11-year-old foster child, is the focalizing character in this text but the reader is required to criticize as well as share her point of view as she both misjudges well-meaning people because of her resentment against her fostered status, and romanticizes her irresponsible mother. By the end of the book she has developed real affection for her latest foster mother, a warm-hearted woman whom she calls Trotter, and wishes to stay with her, but her grandmother has decided that Gilly must live with her. No assurance is offered that she will be happy with her grandmother, and there is little suggestion that her mother's attitude to her will change. A range of issues about relationships, families and responsibility are raised in a sensitive way, but the text imposes no final answers. Trotter forces Gilly to recognize the compromises that all relationships entail and the uncertainty of the future: '". . . all that stuff about happy endings is lies. The only ending in this world is death. Now that might or might not be happy, but either way, you ain't ready to die, are you?"' (Paterson [1978] 1981: 138) The reader is left to ponder Gilly's future, to assess what she has learned, and to consider the motivations and problems of her mother and grandmother.

In summary, narrative and aesthetic closure does not necessarily entail ideological closure, and the strong ideological closure inherent in most hero tales is not an essential feature of literature for young readers, even very young readers. The structure of hero stories – the central binary oppositions, the use of the hero as the focalizing character, the linear plot and the strong sense of closure – inscribes the fundamental dualisms which underlie the values and world view of the Western patriarchal establishment and imposes those values on the reader, making them appear simply 'natural' and inevitable. Readers who believe in the absolute superiority of Western culture, who are suspicious of those who are different from themselves, who believe that women are innately subordinate, who believe that emotion is weakness and aggression strength, are confirmed in their views by the hero story. Further, the story discourages the questioning of received opinion, for the pattern of oppositions which it constructs implies that all is clear and unequivocal, that right and wrong are easy to determine, that what we see when we look at the world is not merely our perception, but reality as it is.

# 2

# THE HERO

The quest story is implicit in the nature of the hero. The sequence of events is the consequence of his will, his ambition, his activism, his rationality and his view of the world. He strives towards his goal never doubting the rightness or the primacy of his cause. He regards any opposition as evil, or at least as 'wild' and inferior, and he struggles to subdue it. His mode is domination – of the environment, of his enemies, of his friends, of women, and of his own emotions, his own 'weaknesses'. To many readers his certainty is enormously attractive because it reinforces established views of the way the world is. He embodies the privileged terms of the interconnected dualisms which have shaped Western thought and values.

## RACE

The hero is white, and his story inscribes the dominance of white power and white culture. In those versions of the myth which belong to the last four hundred years or so, the period of European expansion and colonialism, white superiority is frequently an explicit theme. In Daniel Defoe's *Robinson Crusoe* [1719], a major progenitor of later children's literature, Crusoe's superiority to the black natives who occasionally visit his island is strongly foregrounded. They are depicted as cannibals, 'brutish and inhuman' ([1719] 1981: 171). As the story is narrated in the first person the reader perceives them only from Crusoe's point of view, and he is so impressed by their inferiority he thanks God he is not like them. When at last he saves one of the cannibals' potential victims, a native of another tribe, he loses no time in establishing the proper relationship between them:

> first I made him know his Name should be *Friday*, which was the Day I sav'd his Life; I call'd him so for the Memory of the time; I likewise taught him to say *Master*, and then let him Know that was to be my Name.
>
> (Defoe [1719] 1981: 206)

Thus the identity of the master is made explicit.

The popularity of *Robinson Crusoe* with young readers (even though it was not written for them) gave rise to many imitations in which white lads are cast up on imaginary islands and proceed to demonstrate their cultural and moral superiority to the natives. R. M. Ballantyne's *The Coral Island* [1857] was one of the most widely read. Other adventure stories of the period dispensed with the island setting but used the Crusoe themes of struggle and survival to inscribe the white/non-white dualism in colonial contexts. Most of these are now deservedly forgotten, but they were very influential in their time. Ballantyne's *The Dog Crusoe and his Master* is typical. Set in America in the early days of westward expansion it focuses on a band of heroic white hunters who are depicted as innately superior to the native Indians:

> it had always been found in the experience of Indian life that a few resolute white men well armed were more than a match for ten times their number of Indians. And this arose not so much from the superior strength or agility of the Whites over their red foes, as from that bull-dog courage and utter recklessness of their lives in combat – qualities which the crafty savage can neither imitate nor understand.
>
> (Ballantyne n.d.: 169)

The whites are also morally superior: while the Indians are shown to be aggressive, cruel and deceitful, the stated aim of the white protagonists is to make peace with the tribes, and they treat them honestly and mercifully, permitting one group to go free even though they had captured two hunters with the intention of killing them. The actual history of white expansion is ignored and replaced with a flattering myth.

A similarly simplistic nineteenth-century tale which asserts the superiority of the white heroes to people of all other pigmentations is Gordon Stables' *Stanley Grahame: Boy and Man: A Tale of the Dark Continent* (n.d.). Although this work condemns the slave trade it is far from suggesting any notion of racial equality. Doubt is expressed about whether the African 'dwarfs' who live 'in tree-tops or in holes in the earth' (p. 291) are actually human and not 'wild beasts'. Stanley Grahame and his fellow white adventurers overcome treacherous Arab slavers and African 'savages' of several races on their quest to free a beautiful white girl from slavery. They invariably triumph with effortless mastery, while the narrator points out the inferior qualities of the coloured peoples. Stanley's approach is described succinctly: 'He rewarded honesty with a string or two of beads, he scorned cajolery, and when he met with a display of force he showed a bold front. He would not be turned aside' (Stables n.d.: 290).

Even in less crudely propagandist adventure stories the white supremacist message is pervasive. In Rider Haggard's *King Solomon's Mines* [1885] the culture of the imaginary African tribe, the Zulu-like Kukuanas, is depicted as impressive, though barbarous; the men are brave and disciplined warriors and, although the wicked king Twala is a cruel tyrant, the 'good' Kukuanas are loyal and just. The narrator, a British adventurer called Allan Quartermain, admires them. Nevertheless the three British heroes are able to precipitate the overthrow of Twala, and when a beautiful Kukuana maiden falls devotedly in love with one of them, Quartermain is perturbed because, in his view, 'the sun cannot mate with the darkness, nor the white with the black' (Haggard [1885] 1958: 227). This imagery suggests that white superiority is inherent in nature, something as unalterable and obvious as the brightness of the sun, that, as Aristotle said of dualities in general, 'it originates in the constitution of the universe' (Aristotle 1905: 33). The actual subjection of indigenous peoples, always predicated upon assumptions of white cultural superiority, proceeded with enthusiasm in America, Asia, Australia, New Zealand and South Africa during the period of these books' greatest popularity.

In *Kim*, Kipling shows the Indians as themselves recognizing and valuing the innate superiority of their white overlords which is exemplified in Kim himself. Because his childhood was spent in the streets and bazaars of Lahore Kim looks and outwardly behaves like an Indian: he is lithe and elegant, curious, observant, knowledgeable about human vices, cautious, capable of voluble abuse, but also affectionate, kind and courteous. However, these qualities are shown as merely supplementary to his essential whiteness which ensures that he is brave, intelligent and capable of rational, logical thought even before he begins his formal education. He is regularly reminded of his birthright by his Indian associates in the secret service, Mahbub Ali and Hurree Babu, who accept his superiority without question. Mahbub urges him to remember always that he is a sahib (p. 151) and Hurree, wishing to gain his assistance on a dangerous mission, praises his superior courage:

> 'Onlee – onlee – you see, Mister O'Hara, I am unfortunately Asiatic, which is serious detriment in some respects. And *also* I am Bengali – a fearful man. . . . It was process of Evolution, *I* think, from Primal Necessity, but the fact remains in all its *cui bono*. I am, oh, awfully fearful!
>
> (Kipling [1901] 1946: 236)

Thus *Kim* denies the reader a subject position critical of British dominance. In the world of this text, British superiority is self-evident and British rule is demonstrably efficient and benevolent. Commenting on Kipling's concept of the White Man and his role as overlord in the East Said says:

> What dignifies his mission is some sense of intellectual dedication; he is a White Man, but not for mere profit, since his 'chosen star' presumably sits far above earthly gain. . . . Yet, in the end, being a White Man, for Kipling, and for those whose perceptions and rhetoric he influenced, was a self-confirming business. One became a White Man because one *was* a White Man . . . Being a White Man was therefore an idea and a reality.
>
> (Said [1978] 1995: 226–7)

It was not only in fiction that the story of the white hero, dominating other races by his natural superiority, was told. It is the theme of much nineteenth-century historical writing. Prescott's widely admired *History of the Conquest of Peru* [1847] interprets the sixteenth-century conquest of the Incas by a band of Spanish adventurers as a function of the leader's heroic courage and determination: Pizarro is not deterred by hunger, heat, the terrifying wilderness or the enormous numerical odds stacked against him. When his men are fainting from exhaustion and want of food he:

> did not lose heart. He endeavoured to revive the spirits of his men, and besought them not to be discouraged by difficulties which a brave heart would be sure to overcome, reminding them of the golden prize which awaited those who persevered.
>
> (Prescott [1847] 1908: 129)

When he perseveres against the urgings of common sense and advice from his supporters in Spain, Prescott describes this as a deed of the most admirable courage:

> There is something striking to the imagination in the spectacle of these few brave spirits, thus consecrating themselves to a daring enterprise which seemed as far above their strength as any recorded in the fabulous annals of knight-errantry. A handful of men, without food, without clothing, almost without arms, without knowledge of the land to which they were bound, without vessel to transport them, were here left on a lonely rock in the ocean with the avowed purpose of carrying on a crusade against a powerful empire, staking their lives on its success. What is there in the legends of chivalry which surpasses it? This was the crisis of Pizarro's fate.
>
> (Prescott [1847] 1908: 160)

The signifiers 'knight-errantry', 'crusade' and 'chivalry' define the enterprise as heroic, and the ensuing events are represented as the outcome of Pizarro's unbreakable will. Although Prescott admires the civilization of the Incas, and calls Pizarro's execution of the Inca Atahualpa an 'atrocity' ([1847] 1908: 300), the text nevertheless naturalizes the domination of the New World by the Old. The energy, courage, adventurous spirit, dedication and determination attributed to Pizarro, and therefore defined, by implication, as the innate qualities of European conquistadors, are represented as an irresistible force against which no 'barbarian' (p. 300), no matter how subtle or cultured, could hope to stand. The text implies that the story could not have been otherwise.

In Western writing the hero has always been white, in 'fact' and fiction, even in fantasy tales, because the story is about the superiority of white culture. In C.S. Lewis' Narnia fantasies (1950–56) the human inhabitants of the good land of Narnia and the children who visit it, the heroes of the various adventures, are white-skinned and light-haired, while the major enemies of Narnia are 'dark, bearded men from Calormen, that great and cruel country that lies beyond Archenland, across the desert to the south' (Lewis [1956] 1964: 25). They smell of garlic and onions and their 'white eyes [flash] dreadfully in their brown faces' (p. 29). Ursula Le Guin has told how she attempted to subvert this symbolism in *A Wizard of Earthsea* by making her hero, Ged, dark-skinned, only to be defeated by the commercial imperatives of publishers who persisted in showing him as white in cover illustrations:

> I colored all the good guys brown or black. Only the villains were white. I saw myself as luring white readers to identify with the hero, to get inside his skin and only then to find it was a dark skin. I meant this as a strike against racial bigotry. I think now that my subversion went further than I knew, for by making my hero dark-skinned I was setting him outside the whole European heroic tradition, in which heroes are not only male but white. I was making him an outsider, an other, like a woman, like me.
>
> (You will not see that dark man on most of the covers of the Earthsea books, by the way; publishers insist that jackets showing black people 'kill sales', and forbid their artists to color a hero darker than tan . . . I think it has affected many readers' perception of Ged.)
>
> (Le Guin 1993a: 8)

We may be approaching the time when black heroes are possible in Western literature, but to date they have been almost a conceptual contradiction in terms. While black men could be noble, in the tradition of the 'noble savage', like Timothy in Theodore Taylor's perceptive children's book, *The Cay* [1969], they could not be heroes. Shakespeare's *Othello* is at one level the story of a black hero who destroyed himself because, ultimately, the white people in whose world he lived could not believe in him. The play shows how he was recreated by white perceptions, changed into what the wicked Iago wished him to be and most of the others feared he might be: not hero but monster, the 'thick lips', a dangerous Other, incapable of reason, ruled by passion, unable to love 'wisely', wild and violent.

## CLASS AND MASTERY

Plumwood suggests that 'it is the identity of the master . . . which lies at the heart of western culture' (Plumwood 1993: 42). One aspect of that identity, as we have seen, is a matter of race but the hero is also dominant over the lower orders of his own people. He is the symbol of an elite. In early legends he is typically a king or a prince, the leader and representative of his people, and his quest involves their aspirations. So Theseus destroys the Minotaur on behalf of the people of Athens, and Odysseus is a king whose adventurousness and assertiveness represent the Hellenes' emerging sense of cultural superiority.

Nevertheless it is the fate of the hero, not his followers, which is important in these stories.

It is sometimes assumed that this tradition has continued unmodified, that the hero is always upper-class. For example, Pearson and Pope in *The Female Hero in British and American Literature* say 'the hero is almost always assumed to be white and upper-class as well' (1981: 4), but this is something of an over-simplification. The hero is an emblem of the patriarchy, so, as political and economic structures evolved and power ceased to belong exclusively to kings and land-owning aristocrats, heroes from different backgrounds emerged. Thus a fifteenth-century 'true' hero story like 'Dick Whittington and his Cat', which appears in some of the chapbooks of the period, reflects both the growing power of the city merchants and the aspirations of the common people. Robinson Crusoe represents the established middle class; his father had 'got a good Estate by Merchandise' ([1719] 1981: 5) and Crusoe himself was educated for the law. Stevenson's Jim Hawkins is the son of an inn-keeper, and *Treasure Island* could be read as a fable about the financial opportunities which nineteenth-century capitalism offered to enterprising lads of the lower middle class.

But the Victorian hero, though not necessarily aristocratic, is almost always a 'gentleman', a member of the dominant social class. The notoriously unstable signifier 'gentleman' usually suggests education and polite manners, but often also implies an intellectual and moral superiority which justifies and naturalizes the class structure of society. This assumption underlies *David Copperfield* [1850] despite Dickens's biting awareness of the profound injustices of the unequal society of his day. *Copperfield* is typical of the *bildungsroman* in which the hero's journey is a progress through life, overcoming enemies and adversities along the way, and arriving finally at enlightened adulthood as a gentleman. This genre became popular in the nineteenth century as changing conditions provided more opportunities for advancement from relatively humble beginnings, and it owes much to the contemporary enthusiasm for self-help and the Protestant work ethic which conflated moral and material progress. It depends for one level of its meaning on the reader's acceptance of the ideology of the English class system, the assumption that the hierarchical class structure is a natural condition of social existence and that working-class life is inferior not only in material comforts but in opportunities for moral and intellectual growth. When sent by his step-father, Murdstone, to work in a wine-merchant's warehouse washing bottles David is profoundly distressed because he feels that the necessary conditions for personal development are being denied him in this lowly situation:

> No words can express the secret agony of my soul as I sunk into this companionship . . . and felt my hopes of growing up to be a learned and distinguished man crushed in my bosom. The deep remembrance of the sense I had of being utterly without hope now; of the shame I felt in my

> position; of the misery it was to my young heart to believe that day by day what I had learned, and thought, and delighted in, and raised my fancy and my emulation up by, would pass away from me little by little, never to be brought back any more; cannot be written.
>
> (Dickens n.d.: 159)

Thus one aspect of David's eventual success is the attainment of a moderately secure footing on one of the higher rungs of the class ladder and, despite its concern with social justice, *David Copperfield* accepts as 'natural' the existence of a hierarchy, dominated by 'gentlemen' who, because of their economic power and control of the professions, are the masters of society.

In the naive nineteenth-century boys' adventure stories which envisioned a world controlled and civilized by British (or at least European) rule support for a hierarchy of class is often quite overt. In Captain Marryat's *The Settlers in Canada* the father of a heroic British family which is building civilization in the wilderness, expresses profound misgivings about the recently established American republic and about democracy in general:

> where all men are declared equal (which man never will permit his fellow to be if he can prevent it), the only source of distinction is wealth, and thus the desire of wealth becomes the ruling passion of the whole body, and there is no passion so demoralizing . . . [and] where the people, or more properly speaking, the mob govern, they must be conciliated by flattery and servility on the part of those who would become their idols. Now flattery is lying, and a habit equally demoralizing to the party who gives it and the party who receives it. Depend upon it, there is no government so contemptible or so unpleasant for an honest man to live under as a democracy.
>
> (Marryat n.d.: 163)

Most contemporary realistic children's stories have moved beyond a preoccupation with social position but this is not the case with fantasy and science fiction where it is common to find pseudo-mediaeval societies and aristocratic heroes. Frank Herbert's widely admired and hugely influential, award-winning science fiction classic, *Dune* [1965], is set in a future so remote that interstellar travel is commonplace, yet the predominant social structure is an ersatz feudalism in which planets are fiefdoms ruled by lords whose attitudes and methods of government appear to be at least as autocratic and violent as those of their mediaeval originals. The text does not explain why society has reverted to a system of organization so inappropriate for a technologically sophisticated universe, nor is the system essential to the narrative. Its purpose appears to be to emphasize the mastery of the hero, Paul Atreides, whose superiority is further underlined when the reader is told that he is the product of many generations of selective breeding undertaken by the Bene Gesserit, an elite women's secret society, of which his mother is a member. The mother superior of this organization explains that the purpose of the programme is to separate 'human stock from animal stock' (Herbert [1966] 1984: 23). While in the final pages of the novel, in what is perhaps a gesture to post-Holocaust sensibilities, Paul is made to deride this distasteful 'master plan' (p. 549) the entire thrust of the work underwrites it for he is shown to be superior in intelligence, physical prowess, courage, extra-sensory perception, mystical insight, strength of character and moral purpose.

Tolkien's Middle-earth is also an essentially mediaeval world dominated by kings and small, aristocratic elites. Much is made of the responsibilities of the rulers to the ruled. Aragorn, the rightful king of Gondor, explains how he and the other men of his caste, the Dúnadain, have spent years patrolling the land, guarding the people from the depredations of the enemy: 'What roads would any dare to tread, what safety would there be in quiet lands, or in the homes of simple men at night, if the Dúnedain were asleep, or were all gone into the grave?' (Tolkien 1954: 261) While it avoids Herbert's crude invocation of the human (rational)/animal (irrational) dualisms the effect of this paternalism is to naturalize and justify the dominance of social elites, by suggesting that they alone possess the knowledge and understanding necessary for the protection of society. The ideology of these tales, and their innumerable imitators, is profoundly undemocratic for they imply that 'simple' people are inherently incapable of responsible participation in self-government.

Hierarchies are images of order, and this appears to constitute part of the appeal of these stories. To mediaeval and Elizabethan humanists the monarchical state in which each citizen had a precise place in the structure reflected the cosmic order of the universe, the Great Chain of Being. God had created an ordered cosmos with each sphere in its exact place, the sinful Earth at the centre and the moon, the planets, the sun and the fixed stars in ascending degrees of purity to the final Empyrean where God dwelt with the angels. So too every creature had its place in the hierarchy of the Great Chain ranging downwards from God, through the various ranks of angels, the classes of human beings, and the animals from the lion to the most insignificant insects. Beneath them came the plants from the oak tree to the tiniest mosses, and finally came inanimate things and the basic elements of air, earth, fire and water. They believed that the state must imitate God's creation with a prince as its supreme ruler and each individual member in his or her proper place in the hierarchy. Any attempt to disturb the social order was sinful, being contrary to God's intention, and in Tudor times this doctrine served as a powerful instrument of political control. The Tudor *Homily of Obedience*, one of the sermons which were regularly read in churches throughout the country, stresses the wickedness of rebellion and the importance of maintaining the hierarchy and obeying one's social superiors. Parts of it sound very like Aragorn's defence of the Dúnedain:

> Take away kings, princes, rulers, magistrates, judges, and such estates of God's order; no man shall ride or go by the highway unrobbed; no man

shall sleep in his own house or bed unkilled; no man shall keep his wife, children and possessions in quietness.

(*Homilies* [1574] 1850: 105)

It was feared that without hierarchy, without mastery, all would dissolve into chaos – physical, political and personal dissolution. This is the theme of Ulysses' famous speech in Shakespeare's *Troilus and Cressida*:

O, when degree is shaked,
Which is the ladder to all high designs,
The enterprise is sick. How could communities,
Degrees in schools and brotherhoods in cities,
Peaceful commerce from dividable shores,
The primogenitive and due of birth,
Prerogative of age, crowns, sceptres, laurels,
But by degree stand in authentic place?
Take but degree away, untune that string,
And hark what discord follows! Each thing meets
In mere oppugnancy: the bounded waters
Should lift their bosoms higher than the shores
And make a sop of all this solid globe;
Strength should be lord to imbecility,
And the rude son should strike the father dead . . .
This chaos, when degree is suffocate,
Follows the choking.

(I, III, 101–26)

The establishment of democratic regimes of one kind or another in most Western nations does not appear to have reduced the longing for an enduring social order. Perhaps insofar as democracies require their citizens to accept responsibilities and participate actively in making decisions they create discomfort which in turn increases the desire for certainty and simplicity. The hierarchical societies so common in modern fantasy adventures are images of an unattainable but longed for systemic security.

The American film and comic book super-heroes who emerged in the 1930s represent another response to the fear of democracy. The Lone Ranger, Superman, Batman, Zorro and the rest take upon themselves the responsibilities of moral judgement and the maintenance of order, that is of the capitalist establishment. Like traditional heroes their presence is a promise that order exists, that moral chaos and social uncertainty are not fundamental to the human condition. At the same time, however, these super-heroes are rabid individualists who operate outside the formal structures of social control and their appeal is partly to the suppressed anarchic longings of modern audiences, especially adolescent audiences, who dream of freedom from the innumerable constraints which modern society imposes. Superman and his kind owe no formal allegiance to anyone, nor does anyone have power over them. Therefore they are potentially wild and rebellious figures, but they voluntarily serve the interests of the establishment, appearing at moments of crisis to defeat evil doers and restore order. They are embodiments of an abstract ideal of social control, and they are profoundly conservative, opposing any agents of change who are always defined by the stories as criminals or dangerous malcontents. It is notable that each has two identities: they are simultaneously ordinary citizens (Clark Kent, Bruce Wayne, Don Diego) and incorruptible and invincible dispensers of justice, and when they assume their secret roles they adopt a special costume which marks their symbolic significance. [The Lone Ranger is a partial exception to this, but his mask gives him the appearance of an outlaw while concealing his 'real' identity as an enforcer of justice.] Thus the readers and audiences who envy their secret, powerful autonomy can identify with them in their everyday, vulnerable incarnations and are by this means aligned to their ideological position as conservative supporters of the establishment.

Ariel Dorfman, in his analysis of the Lone Ranger in *The Empire's Old Clothes: What the Lone Ranger, Babar and other Innocent Heroes do to our minds . . .* (1983), points out that these super-heroes appeared when capitalism was facing the crisis of the Great Depression. He suggests that they naturalized the increased state intervention which the economic crisis demanded while the commercial and technical development of the mass media ensured their enormous popularity (Dorfman 1983: 115–17). We could add that they also helped to divert discontent from capitalism itself and focus it upon the deeds of individual wrongdoers – criminals or profiteers – who are depicted as the causes of social problems, cancers in an otherwise benign system.

Dorfman also argues that changing social attitudes and growing doubts about the superiority of the American way of life since the Vietnam War have now made these superheroes anachronistic, so that recent Superman and Batman films are ironic and self-referential. He suggests that neither the films nor the audiences any longer take the heroes seriously. It is true that the recent films are full of high camp mockery, but since Dorfman's book was published the Rambo films and other 'realistic' works featuring super-violent and aggressive heroes have emerged to take the place of the earlier fantasies. Like Superman, Rambo and similar men of action played by actors such as Charles Bronson take the law into their own hands to enforce their own code of values. And, as life continues to imitate art, we have learned of the existence of private American armies of heavily armed vigilantes who are dedicated to the defence of their definition of 'the American way of life' against what they see as the hostile actions of their own government, and in the Oklahoma bombing we have seen some of their works. This is the ultimate expression of the ethic of the hero: he is the autonomous, uncontrolled and violent fighter for what he knows is 'right'.

## GENDER

As Ursula Le Guin points out (Le Guin 1993a: 8) heroes are traditionally male and the hero myth inscribes male dominance and the primacy of male enterprises. Stories about female warriors such as Boadicea and Joan of Arc may appear to be exceptions but in most retellings of their exploits they are little more than honorary men who undertake male enterprises in a male context and display 'male' qualities : courage, single-minded devotion to a goal, stoicism, self-confidence, certitude, extroversion, aggression. Heroism is gendered. This is readily apparent in C.S. Lewis' Narnia stories in which both girls and boys are transported into Narnia to play heroic roles, but the girls are required to behave exactly like the boys: they become proficient with bows and arrows and swords, take part in the fighting and never give in to weakness. Even in the dark moments of *The Last Battle*, Jill does not forget how a true warrior behaves: 'Even then Jill remembered to keep her face turned aside well away from her bow. "Even if I can't stop blubbing, I *won't* get my string wet," she said' (Lewis [1956] 1964: 115).

The one girl in the Narnia stories who does eventually develop an interest in conventionally female things suffers a heavy penalty. Towards the end of *The Last Battle* all the children who have visited Narnia over the years are transported there together, except for Susan. In fact, as Aslan presently explains, they have all been killed in a railway accident, and they are about to enter the 'real' Narnia, 'Aslan's own country'. Susan is absent because she is 'no longer a friend of Narnia' (Lewis [1956] 1964: 123). Jill dismisses her casually: '"Oh Susan! . . . she's interested in nothing now-a-days except nylons and lipstick and invitations. She always was a jolly sight too keen on being grown-up"' (p. 124). For playing a female role Susan has been denied entrance to heaven. Underlying this is a profound uneasiness about sexuality. Sex has never been a factor in the lives of the other children; even Polly and Digory who in their earthly lives have grown quite old by *The Last Battle* have remained in a state of uncomplicated celibacy, and Polly condemns Susan's interest in being a sexual creature as silly:

> She wasted all her school time wanting to be the age she is now, and she'll waste the rest of her life trying to stay that age. Her whole idea is to race on to the silliest time of one's life as quick as she can and then stop there as long as she can.
>
> (Lewis [1956] 1964: 124)

The hero typically avoids any significant sexual involvement for such a relationship would compromise his dedication to his mission, and one of the attributes of maleness, as defined by the story, is a contempt for such involvement, a preference for the sublimation provided by action and male bonding.

Hero stories inscribe the male/female dualism, asserting the male as the norm, as what it means to be human, and defining the female as other – deviant, different, dangerous. The essence of the hero's masculinity is his assertion of control over himself, his environment and his world. The world of these texts is a place of Manichean opposites: monsters exist and must be opposed. The hero's life, therefore, consists of a succession of struggles. No victory is sufficient, for the next challenge lies ahead. He must venture up the beanstalk once more to risk another close encounter with the giant. The final triumph comes only with the end of the story, and what follows the ending is a state as vague as heaven: 'happily ever after'. His struggle is with his own unconscious as much as with external opponents: he puts down the things which rise from the inner darkness, because to him they are enemies. Emotions and imagination threaten his control, and threaten to come between him and his goal; therefore they too must be suppressed. This is the definition of masculinity which the myth imposes.

Hero tales, especially nineteenth-century adventure stories written for young, potential empire builders, are often overtly concerned with the question of what it means to be a man – a state which is evidently not easily arrived at. Frequently the boy who would be a man must undergo a testing and toughening process, a version of ritual initiation. Gordon Stables' nineteenth-century tale *Stanley Grahame: Boy and Man* is centrally occupied with the nature of true manhood, as the title implies, and it constructs a definition of manhood which foregrounds action, courage and self-control and belittles intellectual and creative pursuits. The only son of a widowed mother, born in the highlands of Scotland, Stanley is marked out from childhood, like the miraculous heroes of myth, by his bold spirit, and at the age of 13 he is transported across the threshold to adventure by an extraordinary, if not exactly supernatural, helper, his uncle, Captain Mackinlay, who owns a beautiful plantation in the American south and who is resolved to 'make a man' of Stanley. (This estate has been given to Captain MacKinlay by a grateful benefactress whom he rescued from slavery, for Captain MacKinlay is himself a retired hero.) Having arrived at Beaumont Park, Stanley learns to use a gun and studies navigation, for he is destined to be a sailor. In hero tales of this period being a sailor is a common career choice and seems to be regarded as a particularly 'manly' vocation, doubtless because of the opportunities it provided to become involved in imperialistic enterprises. As part of his training Stanley goes on a sailing expedition in Captain Mackinlay's yacht and in the course of this adventure he is shot through the shoulder by hostile Indians. This is his first major test and ordeal. He proves his courage and skill and incidentally learns about the perfidy of the 'red men'.

When he recovers Stanley's uncle arranges for him to serve on a merchant ship, because the experience will be tougher than service in the fighting navy, and therefore will be more efficacious in transforming him into a man:

> 'Truth is Stanley I want to make a man of you, because the fact is there are the makings of a man about you. Well then, you want to be a sailor

> and I've got you a ship . . . Well, lad, I could have apprenticed you to one of the finest liners afloat, where you would have been treated like a young gentleman, and fed like a lady, and seldom required to soil your fine fingers. But would that make a man of you, think you? No, nor a sailor either. I want you to rough it a bit, just as I roughed it in my young days, and as every good man and true that now sails as master mariner has roughed it. Are you afraid to rough it, lad? Say so if you are, and I'll send you home again to your mammie.'
>
> (Stables n.d.: 100)

Stanley, of course, replies that he is 'not afraid of anything that's right', so he takes service on the *Trincomalee* where he is ill-treated and almost starved by a tyrannical captain for four years. While the narrative condemns this captain's behaviour the reader is left in no doubt that Stanley's sufferings contribute to his manhood. Thereafter he is ready to set forth on his quest to save a beautiful white girl from captivity in Africa, and throughout this undertaking he is unfailingly intrepid, strong, determined, self-controlled and dedicated to his goal, overcoming all adversaries, animal and human, who stand in his way. He has become a man.

The most cursory observation of the behaviour of men and boys in our society suggests that many still successfully internalize this absurd definition of masculinity. The following is a conversation between young businessmen overheard by a journalist on a plane flying from Sydney to Melbourne:

> First man: 'We've got to stop being f . . . ed over by these people. It's costing too much money.'
> Second man: 'F . . . ing right.'
> Third man: 'Yeh, f . . . it.'
> First man: 'So what I want you guys to do tomorrow is to go into that meeting and in a very unemotional way tell those f . . . ing jerks we're not going to be f . . . ed over anymore. Forget any emotion. Tell them we're f . . . ed off and this is just not on.'
> Second man: 'F . . . ing right.'
> Third man: 'Yeh, f . . . it.'
>
> (Leser 1995: 24)

It is all there: the refusal to be diverted from the goal of increased profit (the holy grail of our age), the simplistic division between them and us, the demonizing of 'them' as 'f . . . ing jerks', the determination to win, the suspicion and rejection of emotion, the imaginative deprivation suggested by the sad poverty of their language, the subliminal equation of sex and power.

Recently, however, there has been increasing concern about the psychic damage this conception of masculinity inflicts upon those who adhere to it. Rising rates of suicide amongst young men, the despair of many divorced fathers, the prevalence of male violence against women suggest that all is not well with men in the Western world. Shere Hite in *The Hite Report on the Family* [1994] reports ([1994] 1995: 245–51) the despair, loneliness and sense of powerlessness experienced by young men who have learnt to suppress their emotions and sensitivity in order to win admission to the male 'club'. The article from which the conversation quoted above is taken suggests that Western men today:

> operate almost always in the external world where occupation remains the cornerstone of their identity. They are compelled to know, to be right, to be pragmatic and in control, especially of their emotions. The result is a severing of their internal life from their external.
>
> (Leser 1995: 26)

The difficulty of being a hero, that is of being conventionally masculine, is one of the issues raised in Michael Ende's internationally popular metafictive children's story, *The Neverending Story* [1979]. This tale uses a number of devices to subvert the traditional image. The major strategy is to place the implied reader inside the book: Bastian is a decidedly unheroic child of 10 or 12 – fat, poor at sport and lessons, and a victim of school bullying, but with a passion for reading. He steals a wonderful book called *The Neverending Story* from a secondhand bookshop and becomes immersed in a tale about the land of Fantastica where a truly intrepid hero, Atreyu, embarks on a quest to save Fantastica from the mysterious Nothing (actually the withering of imagination) which is consuming it. An account of Bastian's reactions to the story is interwoven with the narrative of Atreyu's quest until, at a crucial point in the events, Bastian himself is transported into Fantastica and assumes the hero's role. This device positions the actual reader to share Bastian's point of view, rather than Atreyu's, and so to empathize with his longing to be like Atreyu – handsome, intrepid, physically strong and adept. Thus, when Bastian is magically endowed with these qualities in Fantastica and gradually becomes egocentric, arrogant, obstinate and irresponsible, it is easy for young readers to see the causes of his mistakes and perhaps to understand the lessons he learns.

Bastian had been traumatized by his mother's death and his father's subsequent emotional withdrawal; this had undermined his confidence in himself, making him timid and awkward, and feeding his secret desire to be a hero to compensate for the emptiness in his life. After his bad experiences in Fantastica he spends some time in the loving care of an Earth Mother figure and gradually regains the ability to offer affection to others. Having become a fat, unskilful little boy once more he leaves Fantastica, carrying with him an image of his father locked in a block of ice. With his new understanding he is able to melt this ice, saving both his father and himself from the loneliness of emotional repression. The story thus denies the value of heroic masculinity and asserts the supreme importance of relationships and the inner life of emotion and imagination.

Another technique used to undermine the conventional image is the introduction of a parodic version of the traditional hero in Hero Hynreck, a fair-haired knight in shining armour, straight from the world of mediaeval romance, who finds himself redundant in Fantastica because there is no call for his obsolete skills. Without proper employment he cannot impress the princess for whose love he conventionally languishes:

> After all he couldn't just go out and kill someone who had done him no harm. And as for wars, there hadn't been any for ages. He would gladly have fought monsters or demons, he would gladly have brought her a fresh dragon's tail for breakfast every morning, but far and wide there were no monsters, demons, or dragons to be found.
>
> (Ende [1979] 1984: 209)

The reader is thus offered a range of evidence in the case against the traditional hero with his masculinist qualities, but what meanings young readers are likely to make from this text, with its over-abundance of rather flat symbols and allegorical incidents, is uncertain. For many the colourfulness of the narrative is likely to distract attention from the somewhat portentous meanings.

In most popular twentieth-century hero tales, however, the hero displays nothing but the traditional gendered qualities. Superman and the other superheroes are parodies of masculinity, and the characters played by Stallone, Schwarzenegger and their like in contemporary Hollywood epics of mayhem redefine 'male' to exclude virtually all human qualities except strength, violence and aggression. Even in more benign works the conventions of stereotyped masculinity are endlessly reinscribed. In George Lucas' *Star Wars*, which is perhaps the paradigmatic late twentieth-century version of the story, Luke Skywalker is an idealistic hero and neither he nor his co-hero Han Solo are gratuitously aggressive, but they are certainly men of action with little time for creativity or contemplation. They pilot spacecraft, fight with laser swords and guns, climb precipitous structures and swing across crevasses. They are gallantly devoted to the cause of the Princess Leia, and their courage as they battle Darth Vader and the other agents of the evil empire never falters. They are never prey to self-doubt or uncertainty. Such figures are not helpful models for ordinary boys and men who are full of normal imperfections, who must live in a mundane world where there are no unequivocally evil enemies to fight against, and who must learn to develop their internal as well as their external lives.

## AGE

Heroes are young. In most versions of the myth there is no recognition of a future in which they will grow old. The closure is final and readers are not invited to consider further. Where images of old heroes do occur they are depicted as dissatisfied, dreaming of the past. In 'Ulysses' Tennyson imagines

Odysseus in old age still longing, with a kind of divine discontent, for the excitements of his youth, for the never-ending journey:

> I am become a name;
> For always roaming with a hungry heart.
> Much have I seen and known; cities of men
> And manners, climates, councils, governments,
> Myself not least, but honour'd of them all;
> And drunk delight of battle with my peers,
> Far on the ringing plains of windy Troy.
> I am a part of all that I have met;
> Yet all experience is an arch wherethro'
> Gleams that untravell'd world, whose margin fades
> For ever and for ever when I move.
> How dull it is to pause, to make an end,
> To rust unburnish'd, not to shine in use!
> As tho' to breathe were life.
>
> (Tennyson [1842] 1971: 89)

In Rosemary Sutcliff's *Warrior Scarlet* [1958] we are given a glimpse of an old hero who has become autocratic and embittered at the loss of his prowess: 'The Grandfather was sitting beside the fire as usual, on the folded skin of the bear that he had killed when the world was young; a man like a huge old brooding eagle that had once been golden' (Sutcliff [1958] 1976: 17). Still pre-occupied with the activist, goal-oriented striving of youth the old hero is unable to pursue the individuation process (Fordham 1966: 76–83), the pursuit of wholeness, or the self, which necessitates the creation of links between the conscious and unconscious aspects of the psyche, and which Jung regarded as the essential task of the second half of life.

Sutcliff's *Warrior Scarlet* is a work of great insight, revealing, perhaps more clearly than she realized, the limitations of the heroic. At the level of overt ideology it is concerned with what she called her one plot:

> a boy growing up and finding himself, and finding his own soul in the process, and achieving the aim he sets out to achieve; or not achieving it, and finding his own soul in the process of not achieving it. And becoming part of society.
>
> (Sutcliff 1974: 190)

Set in Bronze Age Britain it deals with a pre-literate, heroic society of red-haired Celts who form a warrior caste which dominates the smaller dark-haired indigenous people. For the young protagonist, Drem, there are only two life options: to be accepted as a warrior of his tribe or to be relegated to work as a shepherd with the small dark people. Drem is the focalizing character and he aspires intensely to the warrior status. The reader, therefore, is not required to be critical of the heroic way, but there are a number of motifs which nevertheless suggest its fundamental inadequacies, and one is the presence of the aged and discontented grandfather for whom the warrior society can offer no compensation for the loss of his youth. Another is the presence throughout of the indigenous people who have a profound empathy with nature which eludes their heroic rulers. Drem gains something of their understanding when he is forced to work with them, but abandons this path when he finally qualifies as a warrior. Although his ritual initiation forms the climactic closure of the story it seems somewhat forced and theatrical compared with an earlier, quieter scene where, with the aid of the ancient skills of an old shepherd, he helps save the life of a new-born lamb during a snow storm. The old shepherd feels none of the bitter discontent that afflicts Drem's grandfather for he has attained a sense of harmony with all things, something that the heroic life cannot provide.

The archetypal hero is not merely young, he is essentially adolescent. Sometimes, in children's literature, he is even younger. In some simplified versions of the story, such as *Where the Wild Things Are* and Beatrix Potter's *Peter Rabbit*, the protagonist is a small child (or his animal equivalent) and the story is concerned simply with the early assertion of will and dominance. But in the hero story proper the journey which shapes the plot signifies the protagonist's progress through adolescence, and the qualities of the hero are the qualities of the adolescent male invested with a self-serving gloss. The refusal to be diverted from his quest is a glamorized image of adolescent egocentricity. His courage and prowess are projections of adolescent fantasies of invincibility which are often expressed in real life in such anti-social activities as driving too fast and drinking too much. The dedication to his cause is an image of youthful idealism, always admirable but involving a simplistic view of the world. His struggle against the ogre or the dragon invests his aggressive instincts with dignity and purpose. He is Jack in 'Jack and the Beanstalk', full of energy and certainty and too egocentric to consider the effect of his actions on other people. Even when the protagonist is an adult, like Fleming's James Bond, his behaviour patterns are adolescent. Bond's dandyism, his liking for expensive brand-named consumer goods, his devotion to his fast and powerful car, his physical agility and resilience, and his brief and superficial relationships with women are all typical of someone much younger.

And the hero does not grow up because, for him, only the journey and the struggle are real. In real life those who are possessed by the myth try to repeat the excitement of that youthful struggle by means of various strategies: obsessive spectatorship of the sports they once played, the acquisition of fast cars and other symbols of potency, marriage to a succession of ever younger women. Likewise, for many fictional heroes there are successive incarnations: Sherlock Holmes, James Bond, Doctor Who, Batman, Indiana Jones and their like reappear in book after book and film after film hardly, if at all, older, to move again through the changeless pattern of the story. The actors who play them on the screen age and are replaced by others, but the hero himself is forever young.

The outstanding example of the hero's enduring immaturity is J.M. Barrie's Peter Pan who declares repeatedly that he wants to be a little boy forever. He has journeyed into the wilderness, the magical Never Land, but, unlike Sendak's Max, he refuses to return. When, at the conclusion of the play, Mrs Darling offers him a home and the opportunity to grow up he rejects it: 'I don't want to go to school and learn solemn things. No one is going to catch me, lady, and make me a man. I want always to be a little boy and have fun' (Barrie [1904] 1942: 574). Because there is no return for Peter there can be no closure; nor is there an open ending rich with possibilities for the future. The concluding tableau, which shows Peter and Wendy together again a year after the main events, suggests that Peter is trapped in a perpetual and meaningless present. He has forgotten the adventures of a year before, and has even forgotten the existence of his companions, the lost boys and the fairy Tinkerbell. Nothing is real to him except the moment, and so the events of the moment, related to nothing else, can have no significance, and he learns nothing – which is the necessary condition of remaining a child.

The Never Land which seemed so full of excitement and colourful figures is really an inane and unending emptiness. Peter's energy and zest are attractive, but he is also selfish, egotistical, boastful, manipulative, violent and cruel. He has no interest in, or even awareness of, other people's feelings. When he sees tears in Mrs Darling's eyes (p. 571) he does not know what they are. He does not recognize Wendy's or Tinkerbell's feelings for him. He regards people merely as sources of amusement, admiration or service; he wants Wendy to be his mother so that she will cosset and admire him. If this play is a celebration of childhood it is an ambivalent one, and Barrie's stage direction after Peter's assertion that he wants to be always a little boy, quoted above, suggests that the ambivalence is deliberate: 'So perhaps he thinks, but it is his greatest pretend' (p. 574). What can this mean except that a deliberate clinging to childhood in the belief that it is 'fun' is a desperate self-delusion?

Yet *Peter Pan* has been enormously successful ever since its first performance in 1904. Its appeal is partly due to its wonderful theatricality, and it must also have tapped into Edwardian sentimentality about childhood, for the prettiness of the motherless Peter, who will never turn into an awkward adolescent, is emphasized. But it is surely primarily the flying that entrances children. Flying is a common dream in childhood and, whether or not it has a sexual significance, it suggests a sense of absolute freedom and ecstasy. It is common in ancient myths, and in modern ones. The Olympian gods fly as does Perseus when Hermes gives him winged sandals. Angels fly. Superman flies, and so does the redoubtable Mary Poppins. These are free and powerful figures. They are not constrained by the mundane restrictions which tie the rest of us to the earth, and they fire our imaginations.

Childhood is a time of constraints which frustrate even the happiest children and the flying Peter is an emblem of freedom and autonomy. But more powerfully symbolic is the fact that he teaches the Darling children to fly, for they are surrounded by the kind of restrictions and impedimenta that children recognize – rules about bedtime, medicine, pyjamas, baths, night lights – so it seems that if they can fly then any child can break free. Their departure through the nursery window, 'like a flight of birds' (p. 522) is an exhilarating image of escape from the mundane. In liberating the children from the boring routine of school and office which Mr Darling represents, Peter, like Jack in 'Jack and the Beanstalk', overcomes the giant, the oppression of public authority. But this truly heroic achievement is followed by a plunge into the violence of Peter's imagined universe where, rather than the wit and absurdity of Alice's Wonderland, or the uninhibited joyousness of Max's wild rumpus, killing is the keynote. Peter Pan is an extreme manifestation of one aspect of the hero's nature: youthful energy and extroversion, but the energy is sterile, expressed only in self-glorification, rebellion and destruction. He is an all too appropriate idol for twentieth-century Western civilization which fetishises youth but provides few guides for the second half of life's journey which should be a progress towards wisdom and self-integration.

## RELATIONSHIPS

The hero's relationships are also typically adolescent. This is inherent in the linearity of the story, for as he journeys relentlessly onward he meets people, spends a little time with them, then leaves them behind, especially the women he encounters. Odysseus becomes the lover of both Circe and Calypso but refuses to remain with either of them, even when he is offered immortality as a bribe. Having rescued the Princess Sabra, Saint George rides on to deal with other dragons. The beautiful spies with whom James Bond dallies are left behind, or die, when each assignment is completed. The hero of the Hollywood Western moves on, riding tall into the sunset while the woman whose heart he has captured watches him go. The meaning implicit in this structure is that serial relationships of this kind are not only normal, but superior to the alternative of an established commitment because they allow the hero to remain dedicated to his goal.

His dealings with women and girls can hardly be described as relationships since the women exist merely as motifs in his story. His mother is more important to the hero than the women he encounters on his quest, but she is left behind when he goes off into the wilderness. The story inscribes the public/private dualism and asserts that the wilderness, the wide world, is a place for men. Women do not belong there: the domestic sphere of home is their place. Those who do turn up in the wilderness, being out of their place, are likely to be dangerous, aiming either to do away with the hero or to lure him from his quest. The women in the hero story are discussed in detail in Chapter 4. Here I want to consider the relationships which really matter to heroes.

Heroes are close to men, dogs, horses and, in some more recent stories, cars.

This pattern underlines the relegation of women and symbolizes the hero's domination of racial and social 'inferiors' and of nature, for his human companions are frequently subordinates removed from their own cultural or social group and his animals are often wild creatures who voluntarily leave the wilderness to serve him, recognizing him as their master.

If he does not travel alone the hero travels with a band of brothers, as Jason did with the Argonauts, or with a devoted male companion who is usually his inferior in some way. The hero and his companion are a very ancient couple. They appear as Gilgamesh and Enkidu in the oldest version of the story we have where the devotion of the wild man, Enkidu, to Gilgamesh is one of the ways in which *The Epic of Gilgamesh* symbolizes the triumph of emergent civilization. The relationship of Achilles and Patroclus which is of crucial importance in *The Iliad* is reflected in the later tradition of the knight and his squire which perhaps derives from the story of Roland and Oliver in the *Chanson de Roland* (*c.* 1100) and is important in Malory's *Le Morte d'Arthur*. This pattern which inscribes the hierarchical structures of heroic and feudal societies reappears metamorphosed into the American western hero and his sidekick, like the Lone Ranger and Tonto, where the primary symbolism is of the dominance of the white settlers over the indigenous people. Robinson Crusoe acquires a submissive companion in the savage Man Friday whose voluntary subservience illustrates the imperialist assumption of innate white superiority. Likewise Kipling's Kim travels India with the lama and although Kim describes himself as the lama's *chela* (disciple) his resourcefulness, rationality, and quick wits, his British heritage, make him the practical leader of the pair. The hero detective and his assistant – Holmes and Doctor Watson, Lord Peter Wimsey and Bunter – are a specialized version of the motif in which the superiority of the hero is primarily intellectual. In Rosemary Sutcliff's *The Eagle of the Ninth* Marcus is accompanied by his Celtic slave, Esca, their relationship symbolizing the inevitable triumph of rationality in the form of Roman civilization. These pairings are one of the ways the hero tale inscribes the basic dualisms of civilization/wilderness, master/slave (or subordinate), white/black and reason/emotion.

The hero is closer to his male travelling companion than to anyone else, and in earlier stories their relationship is sometimes clearly sexual. There is a sexual intensity to Achilles' love of Patroclus, and in Mary Renault's Alexander trilogy [1970–81] the sexuality of Alexander's relationship with Hephaistion, which Alexander liked to compare to that of Achilles and Patroclus, is foregrounded. The ancient accounts of Alexander's life – surely the most dazzling of all hero stories – bear this out, especially in their descriptions of the magnitude of Alexander's grief at his friend's death. Even the cautious chronicler Arrian, who dismisses some of the more extravagant accounts, agrees that he refused to eat for two days during which he lay prostrated by grief, that he had a funeral pyre prepared at a cost of 10,000 talents, and that he ordered sacrifices to be always offered to Hephaistion as a demi-god (Arrian 1958: 240).

He concludes that Alexander 'would rather have been the first to go than live to suffer that pain, like Achilles, who surely would rather have died before Patroclus than have lived to avenge his death' (p. 243).

In most later hero stories, however, the relationships are conspicuously asexual at the overt level, and this appears to be due less to prudery than to the privileging of reason over emotion. This is perhaps most strikingly the case in *Robinson Crusoe* which is in so many ways the 'onlie begetter' of later children's literature. Crusoe spends twenty-eight years on his island, alone for most of that time. Occasionally he longs for companionship, as when he observes a Spanish ship wrecked on the rocks with all aboard drowned, but what he desires is society, not intimacy:

> O that there had been but one or two; nay or but one Soul sav'd out of this Ship, to have escap'd to me, that I might but have had one Companion, one Fellow-Creature to have spoken to me, and to have convers'd with! In all the time of my solitary Life, I never felt so earnest, so strong a Desire after the Society of my Fellow-Creatures, or so deep a Regret at the want of it.
>
> (Defoe [1719] 1981: 188)

Most of the time he is content with the society of his domesticated animal companions: the parrot which he has taught to speak his name, his dog, his cats and some goats. He expresses no desire for female company, and he seems devoid of sexuality. As we have seen, when he at last acquires a companion in Friday, he reduces him to the level of servant and is certain that this is in accordance with God's design because Friday belongs to an inferior race.

The novel articulates the civilization/savagery dualism and superimposes the dualism of reason and passion upon it. Because passion, and especially sexual passion, would interfere with Crusoe's devotion to order and economic endeavour it has no place in his nature. His actions are always determined by reason; only the savages are depicted as driven by instinct and uncontrolled feeling. Despite his long years of solitary confinement, social categories and proprieties remain important to Crusoe because he regards them as part of a rational design, and from his respect for rationalism *per se* his devotion to economic rationalism arises. The ideology of Defoe's work is unequivocally capitalist for the acquisition of wealth is Crusoe's only vocation. It is true that when he is on the island he professes disdain for the money he finds on the Spanish wreck: ''Twas to me as the Dirt under my Feet', but this is only because, as he explains 'I had no manner of occasion for it' (Defoe [1719] 1981: 193). When he is rescued he does not fail to take it with him, and as soon as he is in touch with civilization again he begins to worry about setting himself up in the world, resolving to try to recover his plantation in the Brasils (p. 279). While most later heroes are less pure examples of economic man they are nevertheless always rational. They keep their passions under control and personal relationships are less important to them than their heroic purpose.

The class difference between the hero and his companion which is significant in earlier versions of the myth reflects the realities of the hierarchical societies of those times, but, as Ariel Dorfman points out, the companions of Hollywood superheroes make a voluntary submission to the hero. He argues that these companions represent a range of marginalized groups and that their alignment with the individualist heroes provides a subject position for the disempowered audiences which allows them simultaneous fantasies of rebellion against the society which oppresses them and of participation in its power.

> They are problematic and rebellious beings who come from submerged and seething zones of reality. They have agreed to subordinate their energies to the superhero in order to better serve their own pure, essential natures. The Lone Ranger has at his disposal an Indian; Batman, like Green Arrow, has an adolescent; Zorro, a mute; Mandrake, a black man; Buck Rodgers and Flash Gordon each have a woman. All who are mutilated or vexed, all who are excluded from power, either too young or too old, all who are resentful and sensitive, all the exploited, and all the potentially disobedient have their place alongside the Lone Ranger.
>
> (Dorfman 1983: 128)

But of course the stories, while acting as safety valves in this way, inscribe the assistants' continuing subordination and assimilation by the dominant group. Although he rides free across the ranges Tonto assists the Lone Ranger to regularize white, capitalist control of Wild Horse Valley, the land which has been taken from his people. The Ranger remains in control of the agenda, for the relationship is dedicated to the achievement of his goal. The Lone Ranger is also deeply attached to his faithful horse, Silver, who was once a wild horse. The Ranger rescued him when he was attacked by a buffalo and nursed him back to health, and although he then offered him freedom Silver chose to stay with the Ranger and serve him. Thus the Lone Ranger's relationships with his two subordinate companions symbolize the dominance of the white patriarchy over both the indigenous American people and the natural environment, and the story implies that this was inevitable and right, that the submission was voluntary. The reality of the bloody wars against the Indians to dispossess them of their land and the slaughter of the buffalo and other wild creatures is transformed into Tonto's and Silver's willing acceptance of their 'natural' master.

Close male friendships are common in children's adventure stories but do not necessarily involve a socially inferior companion and are sometimes quite emotionally complex and intense. The hero is usually very conscious of his dependence upon the support of his friend who often provides almost his only emotional warmth in a seemingly hostile or, at least, unwelcoming world. Thus the young wizard, Ged, orphaned and damaged by the consequences of his own pride, depends upon the support of his loyal friend, Vetch, as he pursues his quest to find and master the Shadow in *A Wizard of Earthsea*. In

Rosemary Sutcliff's works prior to *Song for a Dark Queen* the growth of a special male friendship is invariably a significant theme. After initial difficulties or misunderstandings are overcome this relationship provides the hero with a major source of fulfilment. So the friendship of Marcus and Esca in *The Eagle of the Ninth* deepens as Esca realizes that Marcus regards him as a fellow human being rather than a slave. Drem and the chief's son, Vortrix, in *Warrior Scarlet* are at first constrained by the difference of their status within the tribe and by the fact of Drem's withered arm, but eventually they become 'heart's brothers' and grieve when it appears they must be separated because of Drem's failure to achieve warrior status:

> 'My brother – oh, my brother – we have hunted the same trails and eaten from the same bowl and slept in the same bed when the hunting was over. How shall I go on or you turn back alone?'
>
> 'I do not know,' Drem said. 'It must be – it must be; but how I do not know.'
>
> They reached out their hands to each other, Vortrix's two hands, Drem's one, gropingly as though both of them were blind. Their arms were round each other in a close, hard embrace. They had always been equally matched, a team that had neither leader nor follower; but now in their parting it was Drem who was the stronger of the two, and Vortrix who cried like a woman, with his head bent into the hollow of Drem's shoulder, while beyond the wind-stirred branches of the oak and thorn the low sun set fire to the clouds, and the west was suddenly kindled to furnace gold.
>
> (Sutcliff [1958] 1976: 155–7)

Here the description of the sunset, building to the potent signifier 'gold', is used to invest this friendship with a numinous quality, suggesting that it partakes of the deep rhythms of nature and is of supreme worth, certainly more meaningful than any relationship with a female could be.

The centrality of the relationship of Drem and Vortrix is perhaps appropriate in a story dealing with early adolescent boys, but the same pattern appears in those Sutcliff works which feature adult heroes. In *Sword at Sunset* [1963], a version of the Arthurian story, the friendship between Artos and the Launcelot figure, Bedwyr, is more meaningful for both of them than Artos' relationship with his queen, Guenhumara, and it is the breach between them which marks the beginning of the end for the civilization they are struggling to maintain. In *Sun Horse, Moon Horse* [1977] the significant relationship for Lubrin Dhu, an artist and the leader of a defeated and enslaved Celtic tribe, is his friendship with Dara, his companion since boyhood. Lubrin trades his life for the freedom of his people, and so he must part from Dara who will lead them northwards. The account of their parting is reminiscent of the parting of Drem and Vortrix, and similarly suggests a spiritual dimension to the friendship:

For a breath of time Lubrin stood as rigid as the new timber of the gate pillar. Then he flung his arms round Dara, who had been heart-friend and more than brother to him since they were five years old. For one long moment they strained close, each driving his face down into the hard hollow of the other's neck.

'Heart-brother,' Dara said, 'wait for me in the Land of Apple Trees. Whether it be tomorrow, or when I am lord of many spears in the north, and too old to sit a horse or lift a sword, wait for me until I come. And do not be forgetting me, for I will not forget you.'

'I will not be forgetting,' Lubrin said.

(Sutcliff [1977] 1982: 106–7)

When asked in an interview about the homosexual feeling in the relationships between men in her books Rosemary Sutcliff said:

> I write mostly about men in a man's world, fighting men; and the homosexual relationship, or at any rate very deep friendship between men, tends very much to occur in this type of society. I imagine that the warrior 'blood brother' relationship was often far nearer to the homosexual than to any kind of brotherhood, though possibly the men themselves were not fully aware of this.
>
> (Sutcliff 1974: 184)

Such friendships, by their intensity and exclusiveness, deny the possibility of significant relationships with women, and so function as expressions of the male/female dualism, inferiorizing females by denying their participation in the special relatedness which, in these texts, is one of the things that give life meaning and worth. The vividness and poetic richness of Sutcliff's writing is compelling and her works convey the ideology of patriarchy with telling effect.

While the hero's relationships with human beings usually involve restraint there is a strong tradition of passionate friendship between boy, or man, and animal in children's hero stories. Frequently this is the most powerful emotional tie in the protagonist's life. Such a relationship is central to Jack London's *The Call of the Wild* [1903]. One of its explicit themes is the superiority of the noble dog, Buck, to women and to men who belong to inferior 'breeds' or who do not understand the hard, pure ways of the Canadian wilderness. The only woman in this story is depicted as pretty, shallow, silly and selfish; she disappears through a crack in the ice over White River, along with her useless husband and brother, without a hint of compassion in the words of the narrator. Compassion is reserved for Buck who was ill-treated by these people and has been rescued by John Thornton, a proper man, a hero, who knows the ways of the wild. Through much of this tale Buck is the focalizing character so the reader is privy to the movements of his canine heart, and witnesses the growth of his love for Thornton, 'love that was feverish and burning, that was adoration, that was madness' (London [1903] 1967: 96). Thornton reciprocates this passion: 'often, such was the communion in which they lived, the strength of Buck's gaze would draw Thornton's head around, and he would return the gaze, without speech, his heart shining out of his eyes, as Buck's heart shone out' (p. 98). The implication is that the strength and purity of this passion is beyond sex and that, while to love a woman would be foolish weakness, to love a dog is noble, an emotion befitting a real man.

The title of R.M. Ballantyne's *The Dog Crusoe and his Master* points to the primary relationship in the life of the protagonist, Dick Varley, who refuses to join an expedition to make peace with the Indians unless his dog accompanies him. The dog goes, saves his life and helps him kill a grizzly bear. Though this work lacks the mysticism and quasi-fascist ideology of London's tale the relationship between Dick and Crusoe is similar to that between Thornton and Buck. Like the Lone Ranger's horse both these noble dogs happily submit themselves to their masters because they instinctively recognize true superiority. In most of Rosemary Sutcliff's stories the hero has a close relationship with a dog as well as with his male friend. Just beyond this inner circle of three there is usually an older man who offers support and understanding, while on the periphery of his existence there is a girl, excluded from his heroic struggles, waiting for him to throw her a glance, though he is more likely to throw a bone to his dog. In *The Eagle of the Ninth*, Marcus' animal companion is an actual wolf cub which he acquired and trained when it was a whelp. When it is full grown he lets it go free but, like Silver again, it voluntarily returns to him.

Wonderful horses in hero stories, like the Lone Ranger's Silver and Shadowfax whom Gandalf rides in Tolkien's *The Lord of the Rings*, further emphasize the hero's superiority by refusing to let anyone else ride them. They seem to be imaginative descendants of Alexander's Bucephalus of whom Arrian says: 'he had shared with Alexander many a danger and many a weary march. No one ever rode him but his master, for he would never permit anyone else to mount him. He was a big horse, high-spirited – a noble creature . . .' (Arrian 1958: 181). In the best known Australian story of hero and horse, A.B. Paterson's 'The Man From Snowy River' [1895] the horse is 'a small and weedy beast' but possessed of great skill and courage: 'he bore the badge of gameness in his bright and fiery eye/And the proud and lofty carriage of his head' (Paterson [1895] 1972: 79). He proves his own and his master's superiority to all the other horses and riders who have gathered to try to recapture the valuable colt from old Regret, while the Man's amazing ride and conquest of the wild bush horses is an emblem of the white settlers' taming of nature.

Technology has made inroads into the hero story in the twentieth century and cars now frequently replace the horse as the hero's means of transport, but, like the horses, the cars are special, symbolizing the superiority of the man who has chosen them, and the relationship between man and car is close. Dorothy

L. Sayers' detective, Lord Peter Wimsey, owns a series of Daimlers, all archly called 'Mrs Merdle', and all both aristocratic and fast. In *Casino Royale* James Bond drove 'one of the last of the 4½-litre Bentleys with the supercharger by Amherst Villiers' (Fleming 1954: 36) and 'he drove it hard and well and with an almost sensual pleasure' (p. 37). Technology has become a new category over which the hero must assert his dominance, but it is at the same time one of the means by which he dominates the environment and his enemies. The increasingly bizarre, gadget-infested vehicles with which Bond is supplied in the later films make this point with heavy-handed humour.

As well as implying the benevolence of the hero's domination of the wilderness the faithful animals (and cars) in these stories provide a safe relationship for the hero because they cannot challenge his purpose or his rational self-control. There is no danger of his being diverted from his goal by the submissive and speechless devotion of a dog (or the sweetly purring engine of a car) whereas sexual passion is defined by the hero story as dangerous because it destroys the hero's control and can cause him to forget his purpose. The women who excite such passion, *les belles dames sans merci*, are to be feared and avoided.

In stories in which the hero travels with a band of comrades the bonds between the members of the group are stronger than any friendships with outsiders, especially with women, and are represented as somehow 'higher', more pure and more intense than any relationships involving sex. In this way they function as romantic images of the boys' gang, the sporting team, or the group of men who work and drink together and share a special camaraderie, which in Australia has been given almost mystical status in the concept of 'mateship' – something no mere woman can understand.

Probably the earliest extant story of such a band of adolescent wanderers is the legend of Jason and the Argonauts. While clearly well-known in very early times (it is mentioned by Homer) the fullest surviving version of this story is *The Argonautica* of the Hellenistic poet, Apollonius of Rhodes, who wrote in Alexandria in the third century BC. The first book of this epic establishes the glowing credentials of each of the heroes who volunteered to accompany Jason on his quest for the Golden Fleece. All are described as skilled and intrepid warriors, although some seem like desperadoes:

> After them came the two sons of Aiakos, though not together nor from the same place. After they had unwittingly killed their brother, Phokos, they fled to settle far from Aegina: Telamon settled on the Attic island, but Peleus made his home far away in Phthia.
>
> (Apollonius of Rhodes 1995: 5)

Nevertheless the narrator invites the reader's admiration for all members of the band who, we are told, were approved by the gods themselves: 'On that day all the gods looked from heaven upon the ship and the generation of demi-gods who sailed the sea, the best of all men' (p. 16).

They feel great comradeship and great loyalty to Jason. When the king of Colchis sets him a seemingly impossible task designed to end in his death, several Argonauts solicitously offer to take his place in the attempt to yoke the fire-breathing bulls, sow the dragon's teeth and deal with the armed men who will spring up from the soil. He is their leader and his welfare is important to them. On the other hand they feel little loyalty to Medea although Jason is finally able to gain possession of the coveted fleece only because she uses her sorcery to help him. They are ready to use and abandon her according to convenience. Medea assists Jason against her better judgement because she has fallen desperately in love with him; she flees with the Argonauts, leaving behind her home and her family, risking everything for her passion and their enterprise. Yet when her brother pursues them with an armed band the Argonauts are ready to hand her over (p. 107). Only her passionate reproaches make Jason change his mind. He decides instead to use her as a decoy to lure her brother to a lonely temple where he can murder him.

Apollonius' epic ends with the Argonauts' successful homecoming, but Euripides' tragedy, *Medea*, tells how Jason later deserts Medea for the princess of Corinth, a more prestigious bride than a runaway Colchian. From this act terrible consequences flow, for it drives the passionate and unhappy Medea to murderous despair. In both these works Jason seems self-centred and manipulative, unable to appreciate the depths of Medea's passion or the extent of the sacrifice she has made for him. He is clearly more at ease in the boys' gang. If it were stripped of the aura of its ancient origins and the glamour of the marvels the heroes encounter it would be difficult to see what inspiration this tale of adolescent expediency, treachery and self-promotion offers young readers.

The most popular English story of a hero and his band of companions is undoubtedly the legend of Robin Hood. The original sources of this tale are scanty (a few ballads, a late mediaeval long poem and two plays by the Elizabethan, Anthony Munday) but there are numerous later retellings for young readers which repeat the essential elements that must account for the enduring appeal of the legend. Although originally a yeoman, in later versions Robin became a nobleman, the Earl of Huntingdon, faithful vassal of the good King Richard I but outlawed by the wicked Prince John during Richard's absence at the Crusade. Robin flees to the wilderness (Sherwood Forest) where he is joined by others who resent the cruelty, injustices and extortionate practices of John and the time-serving lords and clergy who support him. There, while awaiting the return of the king, they rob from John's wealthy followers in order to give to the poor. Robin is joined in the forest by Marian, his betrothed. Their marriage has been prevented by John who does not want Robin to gain any title to the lands she will inherit. In some versions Robin lives to see Richard's return and proper justice is done him. In others, such as Roger Lancelyn Green's 1956 retelling for Puffin books, he dies still outlawed, having come at last, weakened and ill, to a nunnery where Marian has taken sanctuary from John's persecutions. Supported by his closest friend, Little John, he shoots a last arrow into the greenwood beyond the nunnery walls, and is buried at the spot where it falls.

Like the American superhero sagas the story of Robin Hood offers the reader the simultaneous subject positions of daring, anarchist rebel and loyal, devoted servant of the true establishment. It draws upon both the rhetoric of democracy and the mystiques of kingship, leadership and aristocracy. Likewise it glorifies the comradeship of the boys' band while simultaneously pointing towards the importance of marriage and true love. Thus readers can select from a range of ideological meanings according to their taste. Holt suggests that its original appeal was simply that it glorified violence at a time when law and order was uncertain, famines were frequent and people often resorted to violence to survive (Holt 1982: 10). Geoffrey Trease's children's version, *Bows Against the Barons* (1977), celebrates rebellion against the aristocratic system: the poverty and sufferings of the people are shown to be the results of structural inequality and class oppression. In Green's more ideologically conservative version Robin makes a speech to his followers insisting that they steal for 'the general good' and must seek out 'the poor, the needy, the widow, the orphan and all those who have suffered or are suffering wrong' (Green 1956: 45) but his programme to aid the poor is paternalistic, not democratic. He explains that he has been chosen as king of the outlaw band because 'one must rule and I come of a race of rulers' (p. 42). The opportunity to give faithful service to such a leader as Robin is shown to be the chief reward of his followers.

The delights of the boys' band in this story are described with plenty of appealing detail. There are countless opportunities for daring action of the kind which annoys the authorities, as when Robin and his followers attend an archery contest organized by Prince John at Ashby-de-la-Zouche, despite the danger of being taken by the Prince's followers. Of course Robin wins the prize because his skill with the bow is supreme, and he escapes to the greenwood unharmed but pursued by the Prince's men. The essentials of this exploit are endlessly re-enacted by groups of adolescents who taunt the authorities by committing acts of vandalism and minor lawlessness for the sake of the thrill and the chase. There is also a lot of merry-making and eating and drinking in the forest – that is, in the wilderness which is the domain of men, not the domestic sphere which is controlled by women. This is the spirit which ensures the success of late night take-away pizza parlours today!

The emotional bonds that link the outlaws to each other are of prime importance in the legend of Robin Hood. We see this when Will Scarlet is killed in a fight against the Sheriff of Nottingham's men and the retainers of the wicked Guy of Gisborne. Robin is so distressed by his friend's death that he turns on a group of the Sheriff's men, saying:

> 'I exact vengeance from you alone, for you have this day slain my friend Will Scarlet. Run now to Nottingham – the gate is but a mile away! He who passes the gate may live: but so long as you are on the road, I shoot, and Robin Hood's arrows do not miss!'
>
> (Green 1956: 205)

Robin shoots and kills all fifteen of them, never missing, 'so great was his grief and his rage at the death of Will Scarlet' (p. 206). Their devotion to each other is expressed in action, and develops in the context of shared action. It does not evolve beyond this simple, primary commitment, but it is presented as overriding any limitations prescribed by laws or customary morality. It is unspoken and unexamined, and the implication is that it is somehow too pure and precious for verbal expression. This is the ethos of the sporting team, of the gang, and, at its worst, of quasi-military fascist brotherhoods.

Tolkien's band of adventurers, the 'fellowship of the Ring' who accompany Frodo on his quest to save their world from the power of the evil lord Sauron, contains representatives of the various human-like creatures who inhabit Middle-earth – hobbits, dwarves, elves and men, but women are completely excluded. Relationships between members of the band are both high-minded and full of good fellowship. They share dangers, excitements and transcendent experiences such as their visit to Lothlórien, the domain of the elf queen, Galadriel. By the omission of women from the company (as they were omitted from Tolkien's own world of Oxford colleges) the text implies their irrelevance to life's significant and rewarding experiences.

In twentieth-century children's literature many of the stories which feature bands of companions are Viking tales, perhaps because the popular conception of Viking culture is of something inherently adolescent – adventurous, violent, outward-thrusting, focused upon action rather than contemplation. Henry Treece's trilogy *Viking's Dawn* [1955], *The Road to Miklagard* [1957] and *Viking's Sunset* [1960] are probably the best known and most respected of these stories. The focalizing character in each is Harald Sigurdson who is only a boy in *Viking's Dawn* where the real interest centres on the other members of the band, especially the leader, Thorkell Fairhair, who is the epitome of the hero: beautiful, bejewelled, charismatic and supernormally brave, for he is a Berserk. His glamour is enhanced because we see him through the eyes of the young and impressionable Harald:

> It was at this stage of the fight that many men heard a curious and monotonous chanting from above. They looked up to see Thorkell, his golden mail-shirt discarded, his wild hair flying about his shoulders, his pale blue eyes full of an empty ecstasy. In his hand the sword whirled so rapidly that the sun seemed to create a new globe of light about him. Harald understood the man's secret then; he was a Berserk. That was why the others followed him.
>
> (Treece [1955] 1967a: 80–1)

With such a captain the team would seem destined for victory, but this is not so, for the entire band, except Harald, are killed or drowned, supporting each other to the end and dying bravely but pointlessly. The attitude of the text to the ethos of the brotherhood is ambivalent. Their relationships, which Treece renders with considerable insight, are complex but finally unfulfilling, and it is a Christian monk, the Vikings' prisoner, who comes nearest to providing Harald with a genuinely enriching closeness. He also stirs a sense of discontent in Thorkell, temporarily and symbolically blinded by the effects of the salt wind, who gropes for a greater understanding than the illiterate, action-centred Viking culture can provide. The text intimates the limitations of the endless adolescence which constitutes the Vikings' way of life, but at the same time the closeness and courage of the band are depicted as deeply admirable, and this is the note which is emphasized by the closure: '"You have sailed with men, viking. The world will never see their like again"' (p. 174). The emptiness which awaits those who fail to outgrow the gang and the brotherhood is ignored by most such tales, which end either with a reaffirmation of its values or with a suggestion that the hero is moving on to marriage, while relegating that step to a vague and unconvincing future beyond the text.

The American Beat writers of the 1950s exalted the male bonding of the gang, and to a degree exemplified it in their own lives. In a recent review of Allen Ginsberg's *Journals, Mid-fifties 1954–1958*, James Campbell quotes the view of a member of the Beat group: '"The social organization which is most true of itself is the boy gang (not society's perfumed marriage)"' (Campbell 1995: 22). The quintessential Beat novel, Kerouac's *On the Road* [1957], celebrates the anarchic wanderings of a group of young male misfits who closely resemble Kerouac and his friends. Dean Moriarty, the hero, is based on Neal Cassady whose friendship was the pre-eminent relationship in Kerouac's life and Sal Paradise, the first person narrator, is a thinly disguised projection of Kerouac himself. Dean arouses a nostalgic longing for the pleasures of adolescence in Paradise:

> And in his excited way of speaking I heard again the voices of old companions and brothers under the bridge, among the motorcycles, along the wash-lined neighbourhood and drowsy doorsteps of afternoon where boys played guitars while their older brothers worked in the mills.
>
> (Kerouac [1957] 1972: 13)

The members of the group talk a lot about heterosexual sex, but throughout the story women are abandoned, rejected and marginalized. (It is perhaps relevant that the 1950s was the decade during which sex roles in Western culture were widely redefined by the media along traditional lines, largely obliterating the progress towards autonomy and financial independence which women had achieved during the war years.) But the romanticism of the boys' gang is not enough to sustain its adherents in adulthood. At the end of the novel Dean Moriarty is still travelling pointlessly from one side of the continent to the other, and Campbell notes Kerouac's sad inability, in real life, to make a transition from the boys' band to an adult mode of existence. His final years were spent as a registered disabled, living with his mother and appearing as a drunken heckler at gatherings of 1960s youth. 'Emptiness – Siberian emptiness – consumed his last years' (p. 23). This is the emptiness in which Peter Pan is trapped in the Never Land when the Lost Boys have gone.

These stories of brotherly adventurers inscribe the divisions between males and females and feed the contempt for women which is still prevalent in Western society. By exalting wordless and unexamined male bonds that find their only expression in shared physical action they offer young male readers no insights into adult communion beyond the content-free companionship of the football team, the boozy camaraderie of the pub and the mutual dependence imposed by war.

## RATIONALITY

Historically the hero opposes the darkness. He stands for the power of reason, the transforming strength of human intellectual energy. But while reason and its products, science and technology, have produced innumerable benefits, the exaltation of reason, which has been the primary characteristic of Western culture since the Enlightenment, has encouraged a corresponding devaluing of emotion and imagination and a profound fear of the unconscious. The relentless pursuit of reason in human affairs has led to such conclusions as widespread environmental degradation, the horrors of the 'final solution', Hiroshima and the logic of the nuclear balance of terror. The reason/nature and reason/emotion dualisms which the hero story inscribes and the determined privileging of reason in these stories encourages the perception of social complexities and the ambivalences of human motivation and behaviour as a set of simplistic oppositions which militates against a better understanding of our condition.

In early legends the hero's task is to defeat the forces of chaos, fear and ignorance and so ensure the survival of the state, the realm of civic order and rational behaviour. When Athens is threatened by the demands of remote and mysterious Crete which exacts an annual tribute of youths and maidens to be fed to the Minotaur, the young prince Theseus ventures into the labyrinth beneath the palace of Knossos, at the heart of which the Minotaur lurks. Both the labyrinth and the Minotaur are images of chaos, the antithesis of reason and order. The labyrinth is dark and deep, baffling, confusing, mind-numbing. To be lost there is to be trapped in primitive fear. Thus when Theseus kills the Minotaur and uses the logical device of the ball of thread to mark the way out of the labyrinth, Athens, the city of light and reason, is saved from the threat of ancient darkness.

Perseus, a son of Zeus and a favourite of Athena, had a similar mission. He was despatched by the wicked king Polydectes to bring back the head of the Gorgon Medusa who turned all who looked upon her to stone. Her hair of hissing serpents, which were sacred to the earth, suggests that she is an incarnation of the ancient power of earth and night, of the mental and spiritual darkness which can petrify the consciousness. Perseus is her opposite. He is aided by the bright gods of Olympus – his father, Zeus, Hermes who gives him winged sandals, and especially Athena who lends him her golden shield so that he may see Medusa's reflection and avoid looking upon her directly as he cuts off her head. This is a compelling image of the way the terrors Medusa represents can be rendered harmless when refracted by reason and logic. Like Theseus, Perseus is successful and Medusa is destroyed.

It is not necessary to have a detailed knowledge of Greek mythology to be able to make meaning from these stories. Nor is it especially helpful to subject them to specifically Freudian or Jungian analyses which tend to focus on the conflicts of the individual psyche rather than the sense of an emerging intellectual and cultural energy. The images of light and strength on the one hand and stifling darkness on the other, make their impact with minimum context, so the tales are still vivid for young readers today.

The Old English epic *Beowulf*, which probably dates from the eighth century AD but depicts an even simpler heroic society than that of early Greek legend, recounts a similar struggle to preserve society from the inroads of darkness. The monsters, Grendel and his mother, who threaten King Hrothgar's people rise from the depths of the sea and attack in darkness. They devour the flesh of the unfortunates they kill. Like the Minotaur and Medusa they represent fear of the violence of nature and also fear of fear. The lives of Hrothgar's people are made wretched by their own terror as much as by the depredations of Grendel. In this story the hero Beowulf relies purely on his enormous strength and courage to kill the monsters. It is not reason which defeats them, but it is the basis for the development of reason – social order – which he protects.

In many hero tales the senses and the imagination are as much enemies of reason as primitive darkness. The enchantresses Circe and Calypso use their beauty and sexuality to entice Odysseus, the sirens lure men by the beauty of their singing, while the lotus eaters offer the delights of drug-induced forgetfulness. Odysseus has difficulty getting his men away from them:

> All they now wished for was to stay where they were with the Lotus-eaters, to browse on the lotus and to forget that they had a home to return to. I had to use force to bring them back to the ships, and they wept on the way, but once on board I dragged them under the benches and left them in irons. I then commanded the rest of my loyal band to embark with all speed on their fast ships, for fear that others of them might eat the lotus and think no more of home.
>
> (Homer 1946: 143–4)

Odysseus's unwavering aim is to escape from the realms of seductive magic and return to 'the clear skies of Ithaca' (Homer 1946: 141), to the light and order of the rational mind. He has encountered wonders and gathered a vast amount of information on his journey, but he is unchanged by his experiences, and in this he is the ancestor of later heroes such as Crusoe for whom bourgeois rationalism is more a limiting prison than a state of enlightenment.

Crusoe is concerned to re-create on his island, as far as possible, the achievements and order of eighteenth-century British materialism. He is a creation of the Enlightenment and, whether consciously or not, a disciple of Descartes:

> So I went to work; and here I must needs observe, that as Reason is the substance and Original of the Mathematicks, so by stating and squaring every thing by Reason, and by making the most rational Judgement of things, every Man may be in time Master of every mechanick Art.
>
> (Defoe [1719] 1981: 68)

He becomes, successively, a hunter, a herder, an agriculturalist (using the seed corn conveniently available from the wreck) and a manufacturer, paralleling even the beginnings of industrialism when he manages to fire the earthenware pots he has made (Defoe [1719] 1981: 120–1). He builds dwellings and furniture which imitate those of his homeland. He devises a calendar so he will always know the Christian sabbath, and he is pleased that he has rescued mathematical books, compasses and bibles from the wreck. His concept of order is entirely Western and external to the reality of the island which is by definition savage because it is not European. Crusoe reasons, measures and plans, and he uses the language of the accountant as well as that of the philosopher:

> as my Reason began now to master my Despondency, I began to comfort myself as well as I could, and to set the good against the Evil, that I might have something to distinguish my Case from the worse, and I stated it very impartially, like Debtor and Creditor, the Comforts I enjoy'd, against the Miseries I suffer'd . . . Upon the whole here was an undoubted Testimony, that there was scarce any Condition in the world so miserable, but there was something *Negative* or something *Positive* to be thankful for in it; and let this stand as a Direction from the Experience of the most miserable of all Conditions in this World, that we may always find in it something to comfort our selves from, and to set in the Description of Good and Evil, on the Credit Side of the Accompt.
>
> (Defoe [1719] 1981: 65–7)

His perceptions are those of emergent capitalism, of economic, as well as philosophical, rationalism. But in the first-person account of the twenty-eight years he spent on his island there is not one comment on the aesthetics of the environment, and the only emotions he expresses are those related to his immediate practical situation – dejection at being cast up alone, satisfaction when his enterprises go right, discouragement when they do not, a conventional religious conversion brought on by sickness and loneliness. His general demeanour is one of equanimity as he goes about his business guided by reason.

He is finally able to establish a colony on the island based on a group of shipwrecked Spaniards whom he rescues, and supplemented later with settlers whom he ships from 'the Brasils', along with appropriate supplies. So the wilderness is tamed: that is, a European form of economic and social order is imposed upon it. His experiences on the island do not challenge Crusoe's values or conceptions. Unlike the protagonists of Conrad's *Heart of Darkness* and Golding's *Lord of the Flies*, and the Brando character in Francis Ford Coppola's film, *Apocalypse Now*, he is not threatened by the encroachments of inner darkness or the disintegration of civilized moral and intellectual belief systems. His grip on the rationalist values and materialist conception of reality which he brought with him is never weakened; the superiority of European civilization and the efficacy of rationalism as a means of making sense of reality remain unquestioned.

In the many nineteenth-century derivatives of *Robinson Crusoe* such as R.M. Ballantyne's *Coral Island* [1857] civilization continues to be equated with Western culture which is based upon reason, while the natural condition of those uninfluenced by the West and ungoverned by reason is defined as 'savagery'. This simplistic dualism is still present at the end of the nineteenth century in Conan Doyle's hugely popular Sherlock Holmes stories which exalt rationalism to new heights, combining imperialist values with enthusiasm for scientific knowledge and method to create a new form of the myth. Three of Doyle's four novel-length Holmes stories, *A Study in Scarlet*, *The Sign of Four* and *The Valley of Fear*, embody the European/non-European dualism in their narrative structure. In each case the story begins in England where a crime is committed and Holmes is called upon to investigate it. Subsequent chapters are set in an exotic location – respectively Utah, India, and Vermissa, 'the most desolate corner of the United States of America' (Doyle 1987: 424) – and the crimes are revealed as the outcomes of earlier dark deeds in those exotic wildernesses. The final chapters again take place in England where Holmes's deductive powers enable him to unravel the mysteries, uncover the criminals and restore the order of civilization which had been temporarily fractured by incursions of evil from without. The structure of the narratives in itself 'proves' the superiority of English civilization and justifies imperial domination as a safeguard against chaos.

The emergence of the detective story as a form of popular literature in the nineteenth century is a dramatic index of the faith in reason as the mechanism for material and moral improvement. The task of the detective hero is to venture into the moral wilderness, to find and defeat the modern version of the wicked ogre of fairy tales – the criminal who threatens the good order of society from within. In this mutation of the hero story, reality is reduced to the material – footprints, bullets, corpses, stolen objects, bloodstains – and the hero dominates by his superior ability to interpret these material clues and deduce the truth from them. Criminals, though not necessarily unintelligent, are depicted as driven by passions which erupt from the dark unconscious levels of the psyche, while the detective is the embodiment of the reasoning intellect. Catherine Belsey, in her analysis of the Holmes stories, says: 'The project of the Sherlock Holmes stories is to dispel magic and mystery, to make everything explicit, accountable, subject to scientific analysis' (1988: 111). Agatha Christie's Poirot is less concerned than Holmes with the scientific interpretation of fingerprints and bloodstains, but he also emphasizes the crucial importance of logic: 'It is an exercise, this, of the brain' (Christie 1959: 141). The detective heroes of later writers are sometimes more multi-faceted and more subject to moments of uncertainty, but all ultimately triumph by the exercise of reason. These stories thus set up an opposition between rationality and emotion, associating emotion with lack of control, violence and evil, while reason is portrayed as the essence and salvation of civilized society.

Detective stories are a product of the increasing urbanization and democratization of Western life. As the old hierarchical structure of power was modified by the evolving realities of capitalism and imperialism it became necessary to redefine the superiority of the patriarchal elite so that its dominance would continue to appear natural and inevitable. In social Darwinian terms the establishment needed to be defined as the 'fittest' to rule. In the detective story courage and physical prowess by themselves are manifestly insufficient to deal with the complexities of the modern urban wilderness. The implication is that where evil-doers can operate in the vast anonymity of the metropolis, plotting secretly to disrupt civilized order by perpetrating crimes against decent people, knowledge and the intellectual power to outwit them are essential weapons. Early detective stories define these qualities as the preserve of a male elite and show the heroic detective as a supporter and protector of the establishment, the only one able to defeat the criminals who threaten the moral and social order.

Edgar Allan Poe's aristocratic detective, the Chevalier Auguste Dupin, the first of his kind, possesses a power of analytical penetration which far exceeds that of the plodding police officers who consistently fail to solve crimes which are transparent to Dupin. As Jon Thompson points out, in *Fiction, Crime and Empire*:

> Dupin not only represents values antagonistic to democracy, but his rationalism is repeatedly valorized over the narrow empirical values of the police, which, Dupin makes clear, are also held by the inferior democratic masses. For Poe, rationalism and empiricism represent ways of understanding the world that are linked to different social formations – rationalism to the superior capabilities and values of the aristocracy, empiricism to the creation of a democratic, industrializing society built on philistine values.
>
> (Thompson 1993: 45)

In the famous story of 'The Purloined Letter' [1844] Dupin uses his powers of ratiocination to protect the reputation of a female member of the French royal family. He is able to deduce the whereabouts of an embarrassing letter which the police have failed to discover because he does not rely, as they do, upon searching with mere system and thoroughness. Rather he uses his knowledge of the character of the thief, a clever minister of the crown, to duplicate his reasoning processes. He deduces that the thief would anticipate a thorough search of his home and his person, and would therefore resort to simplicity, leaving the letter in such an obvious place that it would be bound to be overlooked. Dupin is correct and retrieves it from the minister's letter rack. The story thus simultaneously implies the value of a royalist, aristocratic social structure and asserts the importance of the intellectual elite in protecting it.

The superiority of the detective's intellectual rationalism to the limited understanding of the ordinary police is a recurring motif in the work of Conan Doyle, Agatha Christie, Dorothy L. Sayers and P.D. James, the most popular and influential writers in the classical whodunnit tradition, and the detectives in each case are either aristocrats or 'gentlemen' standing for elite values in the egalitarian hurly-burly of modern life. The aristocratic detective has reappeared in the 1990s in the novels of Elizabeth George, whose hero, although employed as a policeman, is Thomas Lynley, Lord Asherton, a wealthy member of the nobility, whose powers of deduction, like those of his predecessors, outshine all about him. In all these stories the effective exercise of analytical reason is shown as being beyond the range of ordinary people. The detective is superior and special, a hero upon whose strengths others must be prepared to depend, and the linking of masculinity and intellectual and social superiority makes these stories myths of patriarchal domination.

Despite the popularity of his various descendants Sherlock Holmes remains the paradigmatic detective. Unlike Poe's Dupin stories Conan Doyle's tales have retained the enormous popularity which began with the publication of *A Study in Scarlet* in 1888. This is partly attributable to their atmospheric evocation of the London of fogs, gas lamps and hansom cabs – but the essence of their appeal lies in the effectiveness with which they construct the myth of the detective hero. Holmes, although idiosyncratic, is both brave and infallible and he is a symbol of the London he inhabits, the solid hierarchical society of the Victorian metropolis and the wealth which underpinned it. What he defends by the exercise of his intellect is the British way of life and the British empire itself, and his successes reassuringly suggest their durability. Current enthusiasm for the Holmes stories is no doubt largely due to nostalgia for such certainties.

Holmes' intellectual brilliance is consistently foregrounded by contrasting him with the pedestrian first-person narrator of the stories, Dr. Watson, who conscientiously 'records' both his observations of Holmes' methods and Holmes' own explanations of them. In *A Study in Scarlet* Holmes explains the superiority of the rational mind:

'In solving a problem of this sort the grand thing is to be able to reason backwards. That is a very useful accomplishment, and a very easy one, but people do not practise it much. In the everyday affairs of life it is more useful to reason forwards, and so the other comes to be neglected. There are fifty who can reason synthetically for one who can reason analytically.'

'I confess,' said I, 'that I do not quite follow you.'

'I hardly expected that you would. Let me see if I can make it clearer. Most people, if you describe a train of events to them, will tell you what the result would be. They can put those events together in their minds, and argue from them that something will come to pass. There are few people, however, who, if you told them a result, would be able to evolve from their own inner consciousness what the steps were which led up to that result. This power is what I mean when I talk of reasoning backwards, or analytically.'

'I understand,' said I

(Doyle 1987: 104)

Watson's respectful humility indicates the response of the implied reader to Holmes' displays of rationalism.

The structure of these stories with their carefully arranged and causally connected pieces of information which are finally fitted together to achieve a clear and comprehensive closure imposes a single, unarguable meaning upon the reader: the criminal is discovered, the puzzle is solved and the analytical brilliance of a patriarchal elite is established as essential for the solution of problems and the maintenance of order. But the image of reality these stories construct denies the actual complexities of society, and the closure insists that ultimately everything is understandable and all problems are soluble. Criminals are presented as simply aberrant individuals; questions of poverty, inequality, unemployment, inadequate systems of education and social welfare are not recognized as relevant to the issue of crime. Likewise the stories deny the paradoxes and ambiguities of human character and motivation. Because the reader is primarily engaged with the puzzle, which focuses attention on the brilliance of the detective, interest in the victim and the criminal must remain limited and so they are flattened into stereotypes.

The detectives themselves are almost as two-dimensional as the stories they inhabit, for intellect is their only significant quality. Their other characteristics are merely decorative. Details such as Holmes's cocaine habit and violin playing or Poirot's vanity, while adding texture to the surface of the texts, are little more than the colouring in of cardboard shapes because these additional traits have no structural function in the narratives. The events of the stories, the processes of detection, are not generated by the heroes' non-professional attributes but purely by their analytical powers. The result is an implicit denial of the importance of most of the qualities which make us human – emotion, imagination, the capacity for personal relationships, creativity, aesthetic sensibility, spirituality, and fallibility.

Recent stories featuring women detectives are in some sense a challenge to the myth, but insofar as these women exhibit the same behaviour patterns as their male counterparts the challenge is doomed to fail. The meaning to be constructed from the story of the smart, street-wise, gun-toting female detective, like the meaning to be derived from most retellings of the history of Joan of Arc, is not that women can be heroes too, but rather that, if they want any part of the important action, they must become as much like men as possible. In the web of interrelated dualisms which underlie Western thought and culture reason, action and maleness are linked.

In hero stories written specifically for children the dominance of reason is often depicted symbolically rather than in the pyrotechnical displays of ratiocination typical of the detective story, but is nevertheless firmly insisted upon. In Tolkien's *The Hobbit* [1937], in an incident that has several parallels to the story of Theseus's encounter with the Minotaur, the hero, Bilbo Baggins, comes face to face with Gollum who lives in the caves and passages beneath the Misty Mountains. These passages recall the Cretan labyrinth in their darkness and confusion. Gollum is slimy, secretive, repulsive, and he intends evil. Like the Minotaur he is an image of atavistic forces lurking deep in the unconscious which threaten the mind's equilibrium and which it is the task of reason to subdue. Bilbo succeeds in outwitting him in a riddle contest. He then reasons that Gollum must know his way through the maze of dark passages and so follows him secretly to the higher levels from where it is possible to escape. His plan succeeds because it is logical, just as the ball of thread by means of which Theseus marks his way through the labyrinth is a logical device.

Fairy tales also inscribe the power of reason over both the dark forces of the unconscious and the external dangers of existence. The English folk tale, 'The Three Little Pigs', is a simple hero story which tells how the third little pig repeatedly uses his wits to defeat evil and aggression in the form of a wolf. Having left home to make his way in the dangerous world he is wise enough to build his house of bricks so that the wolf cannot blow it down and eat him up as he ate his siblings who foolishly built their houses of straw and sticks. The wolf repeatedly tries to lure him out but on each occasion the pig is too clever for him, and when the frustrated wolf attempts to climb down the chimney the pig outwits him once more by putting a cauldron of water on the fire so that the wolf falls into it, ending up as wolf stew. At every stage the wolf's reasoning skills prove deficient compared with those of the pig, and although in this tale the wolf has become a stock symbol of evil with a quality of burlesque about him, rather like the Vice in mediaeval morality plays, the essential meaning remains similar to that of the legends of Perseus and Theseus: the determined application of reason can dispel the dark horrors which threaten us.

This is also one of the interrelated meanings of Sendak's *Where the Wild Things Are*. The wild things who roar their terrible roars, gnash their terrible teeth, roll their terrible eyes and show their terrible claws, are an image of Max's temper tantrum and the 'wild rumpus' in which they engage, a prelinguistic flux of movement, gesture, sound and rhythm, stretches over six full pages of illustration devoid of text. Max dances, leaps and howls with them, abandoning himself to wildness, but finally he controls them with a grammatical imperative: 'Now stop!' And he sends them to bed without their supper. The victory here is specifically that of language, the essential basis of reason.

The wordless wild rumpus is a depiction of what the French psychoanalytic critic, Julia Kristeva, calls the semiotic chora. She believes that the acquisition of language goes hand in hand with the stabilization of the concept of self in relation to the maternal other, but argues (1986: 130–31) that, while the establishment of autonomy is necessary, and language is the means by which we transcend our earlier archaic state, poetry, and creativity in general, depend upon the possibility of keeping open access to this state of anarchic pleasure. She believes that it is language itself which provides this possibility: 'the semiotic chora in language produces poetry. It can be considered as the source of all stylistic effort, the modifying of banal, logical order by linguistic distortions such as metaphor, metonymy, musicality' (p. 131).

It is just this access to the unconscious and nourishment of imagination which is implicitly denied by the traditional hero's role as the instrument of reason, but *Where the Wild Things Are* modifies the pattern of the story in this crucial respect. Although Max enters the domain of language and logic and his reward will be participation in the patriarchy (He is one of those for whom hot suppers are provided!) his time with the wild things is joyous, and they do not suffer the fate of the dragons, wolves and ogres of traditional stories. While he establishes control over them he does not kill them, so presumably he has the power to revisit them when he wishes. Max perhaps retains access to his emotions and his imagination. The story articulates the reason/emotion dualism but, for all its conformity to the ancient structure, Sendak's reworking of the myth contains a significant ambiguity.

## ACTION AND VIOLENCE

The hero is a man of action and it is in action that he expresses his nature – skill, courage, dominance and determination. He is neither contemplative nor creative. He marches onward, and when he encounters a dragon or a difficulty he deals with it. In some versions of the story it is action itself, as much as the final goal, which is the point of the quest. Action involving an extreme level of skill or great danger is depicted as providing extraordinary fulfilment akin to that of a mystical experience.

Australian hero myths are very much concerned with this kind of action as a supreme value. The best known Australian fictional version of the myth is undoubtedly Andrew Barton (Banjo) Paterson's narrative poem 'The Man from Snowy River' which celebrates the Man's outstanding riding skill. Originally published in 1895, during the first period of fervent Australian nationalism, it has been taught in schools across the country ever since and has been filmed twice, in 1982 and again in 1988. It is not only firmly imprinted in the national psyche, it is printed on the currency – the first lines of the poem and a drawing of the Man appear on the ten-dollar notes released in 1993. The story follows the pattern of the hero myth in a somewhat simplified form: A band of crack horsemen have gathered at a station to try to recapture a valuable colt which has 'got away/ And joined the wild bush horses'. Amongst them is 'a stripling on a small and weedy beast' who comes from the Snowy Mountains and is therefore skilled at riding in difficult mountain country. The riders chase the mob in a spirited fashion, but the horses manage to reach the hills and only the man from Snowy River has the courage to pursue them down the treacherous hillsides:

> The wild hop scrub grew thickly, and the hidden ground was full
> Of wombat holes, and any slip was death.
> But the man from Snowy River let the pony have his head,
> And he swung his stockwhip round and gave a cheer,
> And he raced him down the mountains like a torrent down its bed,
> While the others stood and watched in very fear.

He runs the mob until they can go no further and 'alone and unassisted' brings them back. Thus he overcomes the dangers of the wilderness to achieve his goal.

The values of the poem are secular. It establishes the wilderness, the bush (which to most Australians, even in 1895, was a virtually mythical place, far from the cities in which they lived), as the site of self-realization and fulfilment, and it establishes it as a male domain. In this version of the myth women are not only marginalized; they are obliterated. And because it is only in this world of masculine adventure and challenge that transcendent physical achievement is possible women are defined, by implication, as impediments to the attainment of this experience which alone invests existence with significance. The reward of the Man is the attainment of iconic status:

> And where around the Overflow the reedbeds sweep and sway
> To the breezes, and the rolling plains are wide,
> The man from Snowy River is a household word to-day,
> And the stockmen tell the story of his ride.

Just as bards in ancient times sang the stories of Jason, Odysseus, Beowulf and the rest! But what matters most is the experience itself, the exercise of his supreme physical skill, which generates, briefly, an intensity of being that raises him beyond the mundane, but which, nevertheless, is achievable only in the physical world. Because this experience is ineffable it is not described directly; the reader is required to infer it as the Man is observed through the eyes of the other riders who see him, for a moment, as a god-like figure:

> Then they lost him for a moment, where two mountain gullies met
> In the ranges, but a final glimpse reveals
> On a dim and distant hillside the wild horses racing yet,
> With the man from Snowy River at their heels.

'The Man from Snowy River' does not merely privilege physical action over the life of the mind, and over creativity and imagination, it constructs a world in which these aspects of human life, like women, are not conceptually present at all, and yet the narrative voice presents it as a world whose inhabitants find it utterly sufficient. There is no Thorkell from *Viking's Dawn* here groping hesitantly towards an awareness beyond the edges of the mental universe constructed by his culture. The poem is a much more simplistic piece of writing than *Viking's Dawn*, even though the latter is a children's book, and it exemplifies the profoundly sexist and anti-intellectual strains in traditional white Australian culture.

Actual Australians who have achieved iconic status in the national culture are all men noted for their physical achievement – except for Phar Lap who was a male racehorse. They include the boxer, Les Darcy, the bush-ranger, Ned Kelly, and the cricketer, Sir Donald Bradman. The predominance of sportsmen is significant: in modern Western life sport has been elevated to an activity of national significance and commercial importance. It provides arenas for the endless re-enactment of the hero story and affirmation of national superiority, and likewise ensures the constant restatement of the related dualisms, especially, perhaps, the male/female dualism. In her analysis of the contribution of sport and sports reporting to hegemonic masculinity Gay Mason says of this worship of the physical:

> At times this attitude finds expression in description of sport in quasi-orgasmic terms, overlaid with suggestions of divine communication. As one author writes: Watching a football team that has suddenly lifted itself and found its feet is to observe a collection of individual, fast-running men become one organism and in a state of collective ecstasy achieve a superhuman level of control in which the speeding ball moves as if in total obedience to some hidden law with which they too are now utterly in tune. It is as if some unseen hand is guiding things. (John Carroll, 'Sport: Virtue and Grace', *Theory Culture and Society*, Vol. 3, No. 1, 1986 p. 97)
>
> (Mason 1995: 2–3)

The darker side of the hero's commitment to action is the naturalization of violence. In ancient versions of the story it is his status as a great warrior, able to destroy the enemies of his people, which marks the hero out. The heroes of

Troy are, above all things, formidable in battle. In *The Iliad* their deeds are described in great detail and always with the utmost adulation:

> And now the pair, when each had pulled his long spear out, fell on each other like flesh-eating lions, or like wild boars, whose strength is not to be despised. Hector struck Aias with a spear on the centre of his shield. But the bronze did not break through: the stout shield turned its point. Then Aias leaping in caught Hector on the shield. Hector was brought up short and the spear passed clean through his shield with force enough to reach his neck and bring the dark blood gushing out. Yet even so, Hector of the flashing helmet did not give up the fight.
>
> (Homer 1950: 138)

In mediaeval romances a knight's ability to slay his opponent is likewise proof of his eminence. Malory is full of accounts of knights engaging in single combat for no better reason than to prove their honour, as in the following extract where Launcelot fights and kills Sir Turquine:

> Then they hurtled together as two wild bulls rashing and lashing with their shields and swords, that sometimes they fell both over their noses. Thus they fought still two hours and more, and never would have rest, and Sir Turquine gave Sir Launcelot many wounds that all the ground thereas they fought was all bespeckled with blood . . . Then at last Sir Turquine waxed faint, and gave somewhat aback, and bare his shield low for weariness. That espied Sir Launcelot, and leapt upon him fiercely and gat him by the beaver of his helmet, and plucked him down on his knees, and anon he rased off his helm, and smote his neck in sunder.
>
> (Malory [1485] 1906 Vol. 1: 163)

The reader's response to this is guided by Gaheris' words to Launcelot a few lines later: 'ye are the best knight in the world, for ye have slain this day in my sight the mightiest man and the best knight except you that ever I saw' (p. 164).

Sir Walter Scott draws on this tradition in *Ivanhoe* [1820], and the nineteenth-century adventure story, born of Defoe and Scott, is always constructed so as to elicit the reader's admiration for the violent exploits of the hero. Hundreds of adventure stories, usually conforming more or less to the structure of the hero tale, were turned out in the nineteenth century by writers such as W.H.G. Kingston, R.M. Ballantyne, Gordon Stables, Stevenson and G.A. Henty who, according to John Rowe Townsend, 'had a horror of any lad who displayed any weak emotion and shrank from shedding blood, or winced at any encounter' (Townsend [1965] 1976: 63). They invariably contained a generous measure of violent action by means of which the hero established his credentials. In Stables' *Stanley Grahame* (n.d.), for instance, the hero and his followers are attacked in quick succession by a lion (p. 277), crocodiles (p. 280) and gorillas (p. 287) as well as being constantly beset by hostile natives. They deal death to all opponents.

A quality peculiar to nineteenth- and early twentieth-century children's adventure stories is the depiction of this violence as fun. The lads in these tales generally greet the prospect of a fight with enthusiasm. Kingston's sailor hero in *True Blue* 'was in his glory' (Kingston, n.d.: 186) when he was permitted to fire at a French ship. The crew of HMS *Tonitru* in *Stanley Grahame* cry 'Hurrah!' (Stables, n.d.: 142) when they are informed that a fight with an Arab dhow is about to commence. The swashbuckling Alan Breck Stewart feels nothing but delight after the sword fight in the round-house in Stevenson's *Kidnapped* [1886], and his eyes are 'as bright as a five-year-old child's with a new toy' (Stevenson [1886] 1925: 237). He asks 'in a kind of ecstasy, "am I no a bonny fighter?"' (p. 236).

The construction of violence as a jolly romp is perhaps at its most pronounced amidst the whimsy of the pernicious *Peter Pan* [1904]. Peter's declared intention is to spend his life having 'fun', and his idea of fun is fighting and killing pirates. He crows with delight as he kills the pirates with his sword. Of course, the murderous action on the pirate ship is presented as a kind of children's game, but the nastiness of Hook's sadism, Peter's lust for killing and the bloody effects of the fighting are emphasized in both the dialogue and Barrie's coy and knowing stage directions ('There is no boy whose weapon is not reeking' (Barrie [1904] 1942: 566)). The play seeks the audience's complicity in the enjoyment of bloodshed by rejecting Wendy's distress which is made to appear as weakness:

> Michael (*reeling*). Wendy, I've killed a pirate!
> Wendy. It's awful, awful.
> Michael. No it isn't, I like it, I like it.
>
> (Barrie [1904] 1942: 566)

Humphrey Carpenter notes that in childhood Barrie was 'an adventure story addict' (Carpenter 1985: 178) who 'soaked himself' in Ballantyne, Stevenson and the rest. He suggests that insofar as Peter's adventures in the Never Land are derived from *Coral Island* the play is a joyful celebration of children's literature itself. But, while it all too obviously owes a debt to Barrie's favourite reading, *Peter Pan* is different in several ways from the tales of the previous generation. For one thing it is aimed primarily at young children whereas the works of Marryat, Ballantyne, Kingston, Stevenson and the rest were directed at adolescents. Furthermore the protagonists in these stories are, as we have seen, engaged in the process of becoming 'men' while Peter specifically refuses to leave childhood behind. Barrie's play presents violence as *fun for children*, as excitement without consequences, but Peter's games are the kind of games William Golding exposed in *Lord of the Flies* (another work derived from *Coral Island*) where the build up of aggression and excitement to an orgasmic crescendo releases the boys from their civilized inhibitions and results in the murder of one of their fellows. *Peter Pan* implies that heroes, that is dominant European males, have the right, and the duty, to kill those who are 'evil' and it encourages demonizing and stereotyping, but it goes further, suggesting that violence is natural for boys, the only truly enjoyable activity, the essence of maleness.

The boys who absorbed these glorifications of action and violence were ready for the real action when it came. Four years after 'The Man from Snowy River' was published 'Australian horsemen went off to fight for the Empire against the Boers, reciting "The Man from Snowy River" on their troop ships at night. Paterson went with them as correspondent for the *Sydney Morning Herald* and *The Age*' (White 1995: 15). And in 1914 young men from all the countries of the Empire went to war, possessed by the myth, like 'children ardent for some desperate glory' (Owen 1933: 66). One of those who did not return from the killing fields of Flanders was George Llewelyn Davies, the eldest of the family of five boys for whom Barrie wrote *Peter Pan*. Llewelyn Davies went to war carrying a copy of *The Little White Bird*, Barrie's 1902 story in which Peter Pan makes his first appearance, and he is reputed to have once said to Barrie: 'To die will be an awfully big adventure' (Carpenter 1985: 185). Barrie gave this line to Peter at the end of Act III where he is marooned on a rock with the tide rising. But Peter is a hero, the play is a game, and therefore he cannot die; he escapes almost immediately in the Never Bird's nest. But there was no escape for the boys who went off to adventure in 1914. *Peter Pan* is an irresponsible denial of the realities of violence. The poet Wilfred Owen who witnessed the realities of the 1914–18 war described the departure and return of one of the myth-dazzled youths in 'Disabled':

> Smiling they wrote his lie; aged nineteen years.
> Germans he scarcely thought of; all their guilt,
> And Austria's, did not move him. And no fears
> Of Fear came yet. He thought of jewelled hilts
> For daggers in plaid socks; of smart salutes;
> And care of arms; and leave; and pay arrears;
> *Esprit de corps*; and hints for young recruits.
> And soon he was drafted out with drums and cheers.
>
> . . .
>
> Some cheered him home, but not as crowds cheer Goal.
> Only a solemn man who brought him fruits
> *Thanked* him; and then inquired about his soul.
>
> . . .
>
> Now he will spend a few sick years in Institutes,
> And do what things the rules consider wise,
> And take whatever pity they may dole.
>
> (Owen 1933: 76)

Despite the experiences of 1914–18 the spirit of Peter Pan survived in stories such as W.E. Johns' Biggles books which featured a hero of whom Henty and the others would have approved, the determinedly adolescent

Captain James Bigglesworth, dedicated enemy of the Hun, who found war frightful fun. In more recent children's adventure stories violence is perhaps less glamorized, but often still abundant. Some of these works are set in the past or in a fantasy world so that the bloodshed is somewhat removed from the reader's own reality, but they still naturalize the use of violence in the pursuit of mastery. Fighting is a major ingredient of Viking adventure stories such as Treece's trilogy. Ronald Welch's historical adventures contain colourful accounts of battles and his young protagonists routinely find them exhilarating. Philip d'Aubigny in *Knight Crusader* [1954] feels a sense of destiny as he faces an infidel army and kills several of his opponents with alacrity:

> he was worked up to a high pitch of exhilaration by the raucous voices of the trumpets and the infectious feeling of wild excitement that sweeps over anyone taking part in a great concerted manoeuvre such as a cavalry charge. This was the moment for which he had been trained all his life: to be a part, however small, in a mass attack upon the hereditary enemy of the knights of Outremer.
>
> Then the two armies met in a shattering crash, a blending of many sounds, the splintering of lances, the screams of horses, the clatter of sword on sword, and the gasping shouts of men hacking furiously at each other with all the concentrated bitterness of religious hatred, fear, blood lust, and exultant rage and fury.
>
> Philip saw his lance go home. He felt the familiar jar, and saw a swarthy face under a white turban grimacing in the sudden agony of death.
>
> (Welch [1954] 1970: 110)

This does not exactly glamorize war, but it certainly implies that a real man can handle violence as a matter of course. The deliberately structured sentences and the authoritative narrative voice suggest that reason and self-control are entirely compatible with the dealing of death.

But Welch's relatively straightforward treatment of violence which demands that it be accepted as normal is ultimately less disturbing than its metamorphosis into a children's game as in *Peter Pan* and, notably, in C.S. Lewis' Narnia fantasies. The protagonists of the various Narnia books are simultaneously game-playing children in their own world and adult kings and queens in Narnia where they engage in ongoing conflicts with Narnia's enemies. They bring the attitudes of children with them to these war games and this has the effect of presenting violence as both ordinary and enjoyable. In *The Horse and His Boy*, for instance, when told that there will be a battle that day, the boy Corin is delighted and determined to take part in it:

> 'I know,' said Corin, 'Isn't it splendid!'
>
> 'Splendid or not,' said Thornbut, 'I have the strictest orders from King Edmund to see to it that your Highness is not in the fight. You will

be allowed to see it, and that's treat enough for your highness's little years.'

'Oh what nonsense!' Corin burst out. 'Of course I'm going to fight. Why, the Queen Lucy's going to be with the archers.'

(Lewis [1954] 1965: 152)

The language here – 'splendid', 'treat' – is that which might be used about a sporting event or some spectacular children's entertainment.

Violence is also presented as inescapable, for Narnia is a fiercely dualistic, Manichean world where all creatures are either good or wicked, and the good are constantly under threat. In *The Last Battle*, the final book of the sequence, this dualism is explicitly affirmed and modern notions of pluralism rejected as iniquitous. A wicked Ape who is in league with the Calormenes, the enemies of Narnia and of Aslan, says that Tash, the god of the Calormenes, and Aslan are but two names of the same reality, and he attempts to reject the labelling of people as either right or wrong: 'All that old idea of us being right and the Calormenes wrong is silly. We know better now. The Calormenes use different words but we all mean the same thing. Tash and Aslan are only two different names for you know Who' (Lewis [1956] 1964: 34). This is bitterly denied by Tirian, the good young king of Narnia, who cries out passionately: 'You lie damnably' (p. 36). And, of course, the text as a whole supports Tirian's assertion, for the entire Narnian sequence is constructed on the premise of the absolute opposition of good and evil and their incarnation in individuals and groups: the Narnians *are* good, the Calormenes *are* wicked (although one of them – like one of the thieves – is saved (Lewis [1956] 1964: 146–50)). At the conclusion of *The Last Battle* this is made explicit when, in a version of the last judgement all the creatures come before Aslan at the entrance into heaven, and some feel fear and hatred and vanish into a vast black shadow, but others feel love and pass through the door. The implication is that violence is necessary and justified against enemies who are inherently evil.

One of the pre-texts of Lewis' Narnia stories is Blake's poem 'The Tyger' which confronts the problem of the existence of violence and destructiveness in a universe supposedly created by a benign deity. The key questions in this poem, which consists entirely of unanswered questions, occur in the penultimate stanza:

When the stars threw down their spears,
And water'd heaven with their tears,
Did he smile his work to see?
Did he who made the Lamb make thee?

Having evoked the beauty and the terror of the tiger's 'fearful symmetry', the poem leaves the reader to contemplate the significance of its existence. No answers are offered to the appalled questions it raises. Lewis' stories do not so much attempt to suggest an answer as to deny the questions. Aslan the great golden lion, who is both god the creator and Christ who suffers the little children to come unto him, is related to Blake's tiger in his beauty and strength, but he is unquestionably benign to those who are good; only the evil feel his wrath. In *The Lion, the Witch and the Wardrobe*, Aslan is loving and gentle to the children and the good talking beasts but in the battle which concludes the story he flings himself upon the White Witch and kills her, simultaneously unleashing an avalanche of violence against her supporters:

> and at the same moment all war-like creatures whom Aslan had led from the Witch's house rushed madly on the enemy lines, dwarfs with their battle-axes, dogs with teeth, the Giant with his club (and his feet also crushed dozens of the foe), unicorns with their horns, centaurs with swords and hoofs. And Peter's tired army cheered, and the newcomers roared, and the enemy squealed and gibbered till the wood re-echoed with the din of that onset.
>
> (Lewis [1950] 1959: 161)

This violence, initiated and endorsed by Aslan, is not seen as problematic in any way because it is directed at 'the enemy'. Aslan's supporters remain unscathed and thus the whole issue raised by the suffering of the innocent is obliterated, and violence is made compatible with virtue by demonizing the victims.

In an unmistakable allusion to Blake's poem the stars and their spears are introduced towards the end of *The Last Battle* where the death of the Narnian universe is described. Early in this process the stars fall from the sky:

> Stars began falling all round them. But stars in that world are not the great flaming globes they are in ours. They are people (Edmund and Lucy had once met one). So now they found showers of glittering people, all with long hair like burning silver and spears like white-hot metal, rushing down to them out of the black air, swifter than falling stones. They made a hissing noise as they landed and burnt the grass. And all these stars glided past them and stood somewhere behind, a little to the right.
>
> (Lewis [1956] 1964: 137)

In the poem the stars throw down their spears and weep when they see the implications of the tiger's creation, the 'deadly terrors', but Lewis' stars do neither. They retain their spears and presumably march into heaven along with the other creatures who pass through the door. Lewis makes no attempt to describe his final vision of heaven, but it seems not to exclude the potential for violence.

In his 1973 landmark essay on the Narnia stories David Holbrook quotes from a radio talk by Lewis in which he expressed his approval of fighting:

> What I cannot understand is this sort of half-pacifism you get nowadays which gives people the idea that though you have got to fight, you

> ought to do it with a long face as if you were ashamed of it. It is that feeling which robs lots of magnificent young Christians in the Services of something they have a right to, something which is the natural accompaniment of war – a kind of gaiety and whole-heartedness.
>
> (Holbrook 1973: 5)

The right not to be perturbed by the thought that your enemy is human and capable of suffering seems an odd right to claim in the name of Christianity.

Fighting is featured in each of the Narnia books except *The Magician's Nephew* and in *The Last Battle* it makes up the major part of the action. The children, Eustace and Jill, are fully involved in the killing of the Calormenes, and as they bring down their enemies they encourage each other, crying out 'Oh well done. *Well* done!' (p. 114) like polite parents at a rugby match. Holbrook comments:

> In C.S. Lewis there is a particular emphasis on a *continual* aggressive stance: indeed, in a sense nothing happens in the Narnia books except the build-up and confrontation with paranoically conceived menaces, from an aggressive posture of hate, leading towards conflict. And in this there is so often an intense self-righteousness which must surely communicate itself to children?
>
> (Holbrook 1973: 5)

Children are also likely to infer from these stories that violence is an appropriate solution to all problems. When the heroes of these tales feel threatened their first response is to draw their weapons. For instance, in *The Voyage of the Dawn Treader* when Lucy reports to Prince Caspian that she has overheard suspicious voices his response is: '"We must go and face them. Shake hands all round – arrow on the string, Lucy – swords out, everyone else – and now for it. Perhaps they'll parley."' The thought of parleying is very much an afterthought.

Of course the fighting in these tales is partly allegorical, a representation of the Christian struggle, but many of the children who enjoy these books do not recognize the Christian parallels, and in any case the stories make their major impact at the literal level. Children have found these works enchanting ever since their first appearance in the 1950s and this can hardly be because of the religious symbolism for similar symbolism is a component of other far less popular works. As with Tolkien the rich inventiveness is compelling, encouraging the suspension of disbelief, a surrendering to the world of the text, which is further facilitated by the roles given to the child protagonists who are independent of adult control and fill positions of importance and dignity. The endorsement of violence is unfortunately made more effective by the power and persuasiveness of Lewis' writing.

The existence of nuclear weapons has forced us to realize that, at the political level, the automatic resort to violence and intimidation as a response to perceived threats is no longer an available option. Human survival depends upon the development of alternative modes of dealing with disagreements. Nevertheless our culture continues to celebrate the hero and his violence. In contemporary thrillers for adolescents and adults whose taste in entertainment remains adolescent, the story often seems a somewhat perfunctory vehicle for scenes of mayhem, especially in movies where technology enhances effects of speed, explosion, horror and pain. The torture scene in *Casino Royale* (Fleming 1954: 111–20) where the bound and naked James Bond is beaten about the genitals with a cane carpet sweeper, which made such an impact when the novel first appeared, seems like elegant understatement compared with what has followed. The pre-eminent figure of contemporary mass entertainment is a super-violent hero destroying his enemies with maximum bloodshed and dramatic effect. The dialogue is usually minimal but the camera lingers on the details of shattered bodies and spilled innards. The slightness of the plot in many of these films suggests that the enjoyment of vicarious violence has become an end in itself. Perhaps because Western domination of the globe and the environment is now virtually complete the image of the brute assertion of superior power for its own sake, the most atavistic gesture of mastery, the stance of the playground bully, has become the West's pre-eminent cultural product.

# 3

# THE WILD THINGS

'"Monsters," said Hykrion, winking at Bastian and stroking his huge moustache, "monsters are indispensable if a hero is to be a hero."'
(Michael Ende, *The Neverending Story* [1979] (1984): 231)

The hero's triumph over the wild things dramatizes the mastery of the patriarchy. Their confrontation forms the climax of the story and encodes the major dualisms which shape it and which underlie Western attitudes and values: the opposition of the civilized and the wild, of order and chaos, of 'good' and 'evil', of reason and basic instinct. The story defines reality in terms of these binary oppositions, insisting upon their inherent antagonism. It does not envisage the possibility of *rapprochement* between the hero and his opponents for the aim of the wild things, as the story tells it, is always to destroy him.

This perception, repeatedly restated in the tale which has been basic to Western culture for at least three thousand years, has justified the hunting of wild animals to near extinction and the genocidal killing of indigenous peoples in countries colonized by the West. By casting people of other nations, religions or political persuasions as the wild things it justifies wars, pogroms and oppression. At the level of professional and personal relationships it offers a model of confrontation and dominance. In our culture it is admirable for men to be 'strong', to make the acquisition of power and wealth their primary goal, to defeat opponents, regardless of who they are, to win – in everyday life as in war and on the football field, and many men still regard the exercise of power over women as a natural aspect of human relationships.

The wild things symbolize both the external 'others' and the hero's inner fears and passions, and it is probably because the story has both ideological and psychological significance that we have told it for so long and continued to believe it, for each level of meaning seems to guarantee the truth of the other. We must all make the journey from childhood to adulthood and overcome the disabling doubts and terrors that beset us on the way and so the struggle against the monster resonates with personal meaning. In most hero stories this level of personal symbolism is conflated with other levels of significance:

readers are invited to see their inner demons embodied in animals or in people with different coloured skins, to deal with self-doubt by hating or opposing someone else who can be blamed for their insecurities, and to project their longing for inner harmony onto the social environment or the landscape itself, the creative disorder of nature.

However, in our postmodern era, when the old certainties have been undermined by the Darwinian and Freudian revolutions, by the end of empire, by the brute facts of the Holocaust and Hiroshima, and by our awareness of environmental degradation, or, in deconstructive terms, when discourse has become decentred, the meanings of a particular version of the story can become unstable. Images which once seemed to embody the traditional dualisms and assert the superiority of the European patriarchy may now seem to reveal an opposite reality. The wild things which the hero dominates or destroys may now seem to possess qualities the hero himself sadly lacks, so that he appears their self-deluded inferior, and at the level of psychological symbolism the passions and dark denizens of the unconscious which the hero struggles to master may seem to be precisely those aspects of the self with which we need to establish contact.

The Minotaur whom Theseus tracked to the centre of the dark labyrinth and slew with his bright sword is an example of an archetypal, polysemic wild thing which has acquired a shifting significance. This struggle of the hero against the bull monster is regularly re-enacted in the bull-ring to this day. The matador's richly ornamented costume emphasizes his role as the representative of culture and civilization in contrast to the unmodified brute strength and savagery of the bull which is finally despatched with Theseus's weapon – a sword. It is a popular spectacle which stirs ancient instincts, but it is now passionately opposed by many who regard it as a display of gratuitous cruelty. They see the bull as a beautiful and noble creature which the matador is able to kill only because the structure of the arena and the assistance of the picadors make the contest unequal. These contrasting attitudes to the bullfight are reflected in the varying ways in which the image of the Minotaur has been used in Western culture.

The tale of Theseus occurs early in the cycle of Greek legend and at the political level the Minotaur symbolized the power of the ancient Minoan kingdom which the younger city of Athens perceived as frightening and oppressive. It was the offspring of Pasiphae, the queen of Crete, and a magnificent white bull which came out of the sea. Bulls were important in the culture of the earthquake-prone island of Crete and appear to have been sacred to the Minoans; they suggest both sexual potency and the strength and violence of nature. This bull had been sent to King Minos by the dark god Poseidon, the earth-shaker. The Minotaur therefore symbolized these natural forces, and, in addition, because of its parentage, it suggested the danger of passion uncontrolled by reason, for reason would have forbidden the queen's congress with the bull. In particular it attested to the dangerous results of unbridled female sexuality. Hidden in the darkness at the heart of the labyrinth it also functions, at least for modern readers, as an image of the terrors that dwell in the depths of the unconscious.

In killing the Minotaur, Theseus is therefore simultaneously asserting the autonomy of Athens, the dominance of humanity over nature and the power of reason to control irrational passions and fears. He is destroying the dangerous myths that such passions breed! His bright sword is wielded by the keen power of mind, and the ball of thread with which he marks his way through the labyrinth is logic in action. Significantly, he is also asserting the primacy of the patriarchy over the older, female-influenced culture of Crete where the mother goddess was still worshipped and where, Pasiphae's exploit suggests, female sexuality was allowed expression. It is this ancient religion in which female power is enshrined that is the real object of his aggression. The incident of Pasiphae and her passion constitutes what Derrida called an *aporia*, or fracture, in the story where the otherness which the myth conceals becomes apparent and where its meaning can become reversed. It is possible to perceive Theseus not as a hero but as an oppressor intent upon destroying the indigenous, female-centred culture of the Minoans. His cruel treatment of Ariadne, whose name meant 'holy' and 'pure' (Kerenyi 1958: 237), and whom he abandoned on the island of Dia, can be read as further evidence of this.

The Minotaur has continued to resonate with contradictory meanings and to accrete additional significance as it is reinterpreted in different cultural contexts. In the 1930s Picasso produced a series of drawings of a grotesquely powerful and muscular Minotaur, an obvious emblem of male potency, shown in a variety of relationships with women, including rape, but in two of the later pictures he is blind and helpless, and a small girl leads him by the hand. These later images seem to look forward to 'Guernica' (1937), Picasso's comment on the destruction inflicted on the Basque town of Guernica by German bombers acting on behalf of Franco's army, where a bull-Minotaur stands at one side, contemplating the carnage created by human beings, the incarnations of reason. In all these works the Minotaur's animal energy is immense and terrible but also vulnerable. One critic suggests that Picasso's Minotaur is a metaphor for the troubled self and the powerful passions of the creative life (McCaughey 1984: 212). While any interpretation must be reductive the drawings clearly suggest that the passions which rise from the unconscious, while dangerous, are nevertheless the source of vigour and creativity, and that the simple project of the hero – to destroy the Minotaur – is ultimately life-denying. They also seem to imply that our animal passions are perhaps finally less dangerous than our reason. Thus they reinterpret the myth, requiring us to make new meanings from it.

Ian Fleming also made use of the Minotaur myth in the first James Bond novel, *Casino Royale*. The story reasserts the fundamental oppositions of the hero story in the context of the Cold War, with communists and communist spies as the evil opponents of civilization, virtue and reason. Bond's assignment is to destroy Le Chiffre, a Russian agent and boss of a communist-controlled French trade union. Le Chiffre is in financial difficulties having secretly used union funds in an unsuccessful business venture, and is planning to make good his losses at the baccarat tables of the Casino Royale. Bond's task is to outgamble and ruin him, thus bringing the communist union into disrepute. The reader sees Le Chiffre through Bond's eyes as he observes him across the gaming table:

> Bond had coldly held the banker's gaze, taking in the wide expanse of white face surmounted by the short abrupt cliff of reddish brown hair, the unsmiling wet red mouth, and the impressive width of the shoulders, loosely draped in a massively cut dinner-jacket. But for the high-lights on the satin of the shawl-cut lapels, he might have been faced by the thick bust of a black-fleeced Minotaur rising out of a green grass field.
>
> (Fleming 1954: 74)

The point of the allusion is to define Le Chiffre as brutish and evil, a wild thing, in contrast to the suavity, intelligent self-control and implied superior morality of the hero, Bond, who represents 'our' way of life. To make meaning from the text, the reader must accept this interpretation of reality as the narrative provides no perspective other than Bond's. However, at a later point in the story, Fleming draws attention to the way meaning is dependent upon perspective and can slip into reverse if the point of view is altered. Lying in hospital recovering from the effects of torture Bond reflects upon the purpose of his activities:

> 'when one's young it seems very easy to distinguish between right and wrong; but as one gets older it becomes more difficult. At school it's easy to pick out one's own villains and heroes, and one grows up wanting to be a hero and kill the villains.'
>
> (Fleming 1954: 131)

He continues:

> 'Now . . . that's all very fine – the hero kills two villains; but when the hero Le Chiffre starts to kill the villain Bond and the villain Bond knows he isn't a villain at all, you see the other side of the medal. The villains and heroes get all mixed up.
>
> 'Of course . . . patriotism comes along and makes it seem fairly all right, but this country-right-or-wrong business is getting a little out of date. Today we are fighting communism. Okay. If I'd been alive fifty years ago, the brand of conservatism we have today would have been damn near called communism, and we should have been told to go and fight that. History is moving pretty quickly these days, and the heroes and villains keep on changing parts.'
>
> (Fleming 1954: 133)

This meets with horrified rejection from Mathis, the French agent, who asserts that the actions of communist agents prove them to be evil, and the remainder of the story, focalized through Bond and narrated entirely from 'our' perspective, reinforces Mathis's view. However, the passage quoted above invites the reader to interpret the events of international espionage, as constructed in the text, as merely part of a cynical power struggle in which both sides are motivated entirely by self-interest. If Le Chiffre is a monster, as the Minotaur allusion suggests, Bond is perhaps no less so. Since the collapse of communism in eastern Europe the conceptual centres which existed during the Cold War have disintegrated and it is impossible to read *Casino Royale* today without experiencing this slippage of meaning.

Further parallels to the Theseus story in this novel add the male/female dualism to its pattern of binary oppositions. Bond is assisted by Vesper Lynd as Theseus was assisted by Ariadne, and after he has recovered from the torture which Le Chiffre inflicted upon him, they go to a secluded pensione on the French coast just as Theseus and Ariadne went to the island of Dia. 'Dia' means 'godly' or 'heavenly' and this is how Bond sees their seaside retreat with its golden beach and good provincial food: '"This is heaven," he said' (p. 151). But the heavens to which their heroes lead them are fatal for both Ariadne and Vesper. Theseus abandoned Ariadne and, although in one version of the story she is rescued by Dionysus and becomes his wife, Homer says that Artemis 'killed her in sea-girt Dia' (Homer 1946: 184). In Fleming's story Vesper kills herself because she is a double agent but has fallen in love with Bond. Just as Ariadne belonged to the Cretans but turned against them because of her love for Theseus, Vesper turns against her Russian employers because of her love for Bond. Both women are thus shown as ultimately ruled by passion rather than reason and, from the hero's point of view, they are therefore untrustworthy and treacherous. This invites a misogynist reading, but from a different perspective the women appear morally superior, putting love ahead of politics and pragmatism. Fleming's text comes very close to deconstructing itself.

To modern readers many hero stories now reveal their structure in this way and the wild things often seem more appealing than the heroes, but traditionally the stories served to define the wild things as dangerous others which had to be destroyed.

## DRAGONS

The image of the mounted knight in armour slaying the dragon is genuinely iconic, a picture which symbolizes a whole system of values and beliefs. Both the knight and the dragon are armoured and armed, but whereas the dragon's scales, claws and fiery breath are natural attributes the knight's mail coat, heraldic shield and sword are the products of technology and culture. He represents a complex, aristocratic social system and military organization, whereas the dragon is an emblem of the fiercer aspects of nature, its huge size and destructive flames and smoke suggesting volcanic forces. Thus both the culture/nature and the human/nature dualisms are invoked.

These dualisms are fundamental to human self-definition and symbolic dragons appear very early in Western mythology. One of the tales which tell how the Olympian gods overthrew the Titans is the story of Zeus and the dragon, Typhon (Kerenyi 1958: 22–4), the son of Gaia, who was so huge that he was taller than the highest mountain and his arms reached the stars. He was extremely ferocious, flinging stones at the heavens and bellowing, for he wished to rule both gods and humankind. Zeus's battle with him represents the struggle of humanity to control the power of nature; in Greek art (for example a shield relief of *c.* 580 BC (Schefold 1966: 53)) Zeus is shown as a naked, classically proportioned human figure while Typhon is a writhing, alien form. Zeus strikes him with lightning but also with an iron sickle – like the knight's sword a creation of culture – and finally manages to subdue him.

One of the tasks of Herakles, the strongest of all Greek heroes, was to steal the golden apples of the Hesperides which grew in a divine garden, guarded by a dragon called Ladon (Kerenyi 1958: 46–8). Ladon is also a son of Gaia or, in some versions, of Typhon but, unlike Typhon, he can speak. The garden and the golden apples belong either to Hera or to Aphrodite, while the beautiful nymphs, the Hesperides, renowned for their singing, were the daughters of night. Their name connects them to the evening star, the star of Aphrodite. Clearly the golden apples, the nymphs and the dragon are all sacred to the great goddess who presides over music and language, and Herakles' assault on the sacred garden dramatizes the challenge to the ancient religion by emergent, patriarchal power. It is difficult to feel any enthusiasm for the victory of the muscle-bound hero over these symbols of nature, beauty, love, language and art, and the meanings of this myth are shifting and contradictory.

Dragons, however, are usually more terrifying than Ladon, suggesting the profound fear evoked in earlier times by the might of nature. The dragon which guarded the Golden Fleece in Colchis stirred terror in all who heard it roar:

> Directly in front of them the dragon stretched out its vast neck when its sharp eyes which never sleep spotted their approach, and its awful hissing resounded around the long reaches of the river-bank and the broad grove. It was heard by those who dwelled in that part of the Colchian land which lies very far from Titan Aia, beside the streams of the Lykos; this river breaks off from the crashing Araxes and unites its sacred stream with that of the Phasis to flow as one into the Caucasian sea. Women who had just given birth woke in terror, and in panic threw their arms around the infant children who slept in their arms and shivered at the hissing. As when vast, murky whirls of smoke roll above a forest which is burning, and a never-ending stream spirals upwards from the ground,

> one quickly taking the place of another, so then did that monster uncurl its vast coils which were covered with hard, dry scales.
>
> (Apollonius of Rhodes 1995: 102)

Some dragons, like the one from which Perseus rescued Andromeda, came from the sea and thus suggest the power of oceanic forces, but most are associated with the earth and fire, and the dragons which appear in fantasies for children and young adults almost invariably belong to the fiery tradition. The fearsome Smaug who guards a vast hoard of gold and jewels in Tolkien's *The Hobbit* is typical. He is specifically compared to a volcano (Tolkien [1937] 1966: 199) and he erupts into rage when Bilbo manages to enter his lair with the intention of stealing something from his treasure:

> His rage passes description – the sort of rage that is only seen when rich folk that have more than they can enjoy suddenly lose something that they have long had but have never before used or wanted. His fire belched forth, the hall smoked, he shook the mountain-roots. He thrust his head in vain at the little hole, and then coiling his length together, roaring like thunder underground, he sped from his deep lair through its great door, out into the huge passages of the mountain-palace and up towards the Front Gate.
>
> To hunt the whole mountain till he had caught the thief and had torn and trampled him was his one thought. He issued from the Gate, the waters rose in fierce whistling steam, and up he roared blazing into the air and settled on the mountain-top in a spout of green and scarlet flame.
>
> (Tolkien [1937] 1966: 199–200)

Both these descriptions illustrate another fundamental dualism symbolized by the encounter of the dragon and the hero: the opposition of reason and irrationality. In each case the hero is motivated by a considered purpose: Jason's aim was to fulfil the task imposed upon him – regaining the Golden Fleece; Bilbo has agreed to help the dwarves regain their treasure and their ancient home. And in each case the hero is guided by reason as he proceeds. The dragons, on the other hand, are shown to be moved only by passions – greed, anger and aggression. When they feel their treasures threatened they respond with rage and seek to destroy the source of the threat.

While the totemic beliefs of tribal peoples stress their sense of human contiguity with animals, in the Western tradition, at least since Plato, human beings have consistently defined themselves in contradistinction to nature. That which is conceived as the essence of the human is precisely that which is absent from animals. For Plato this essential quality is reason which inheres in the human soul but is impeded by the body and its demands. He divides reality into two spheres: the physical or 'natural' to which the body belongs, and the divine, of which the soul partakes. This position is emphatic in the *Phaedo* in which Socrates looks forward to death as an escape from the distractions of the body:

> 'Surely the soul can best reflect when it is free of all distractions such as hearing or sight or pain or pleasure of any kind – that is, when it ignores the body and becomes as far as possible independent, avoiding all physical contacts and associations as much as it can, in its search for reality.'
>
> (Plato 1954: 109–10)

In the *Republic* he describes the soul itself as having three parts: the rational part, irrational appetite, and passionate feelings, the 'spirited' part. This spirited part he says is shared by children and animals who are not rational (Plato 1941: 133–5). Thus the capacity for reason is seen as unique to human beings (although not all human beings develop it) and as that which raises them above the level of animals and above the animal instincts of their own bodies.

In Christian philosophy, which drew heavily on Plato, animals were regarded as devoid of souls and so of reason. In the mediaeval metaphor of the chain of being, the divine order of creation, human beings ranked below god and the angels, while animals ranked below humans and were regarded as a resource for humans to exploit. The position of human beings in the chain was crucial to the concept for they were seen as linked to the angels by virtue of their immortal souls and capacity for reason but sharing also in the nature of animals because of their physical bodies, appetites and passions. This is the belief which informs Hamlet's description of them:

> What a piece of work is man, how noble in reason, how infinite in faculties, in form and moving how express and admirable, in action how like an angel, in apprehension how like a god: the beauty of the world, the paragon of animals!
>
> (*Hamlet* II, ii, 303–7)

Because of their animal bodies, the concept implied, human beings could lose sight of their divine nature and succumb to the body's temptations, thus reducing themselves to the level of animals, as Hamlet believed his mother had done in rushing to remarry so soon after his father's death: 'O God, a beast that wants discourse of reason/ Would have mourned longer'. (I, ii, 150–1) In the *Republic* Plato had spoken of the cruel despot as 'becoming' a wolf (p. 285) and of the wild beast within us:

> then the wild beast in us, full-fed with meat or drink, becomes rampant and shakes off sleep to go in quest of what will gratify its own instincts. As you know, it will cast away all shame and prudence at such moments and stick at nothing. In phantasy it will not shrink from intercourse with a mother or anyone else, man, god, or brute, or from forbidden food or any deed of blood. In a word it will go to any length of shamelessness and folly.
>
> (Plato 1941: 290)

Our everyday language is full of expressions which demonstrate the continuing power of the idea of the beast within. Most of our less pleasant behavioural characteristics are described in animal terms: 'the man is a brute', 'that was a beastly thing to do', 'he has rat cunning', 'she is a snake in the grass', 'she's a bitch', 'he's just an animal' and so on. In her very useful study *Beast and Man: the Roots of Human Nature*, Mary Midgley quotes as typical a *Guardian* report headed 'ANIMAL' MOTHER GAOLED: 'An unmarried mother who brutally beat up her three young children was told by a judge when he sent her to prison for two years on assault and wounding charges, "You behaved like a wild animal"' (Midgley 1995: 34). Midgley points out that, if wild animals did in fact normally attack their young, they would soon become extinct. She further points out (Midgley 1995: 37) that actual animals do not lack inhibitions in their behaviour – most do not, for instance, mate indiscriminately – and that Plato's abstract wild beast is a fantasy. A dragon, of course, is just such a fantasy, and any behaviour, no matter how vile, may be attributed to it.

This habit of thought facilitates the interpretation of the hero's conflict with the wild things as a symbolic struggle to control his own violent and irrational impulses. Psychoanalytic interpretations of the significance of the dragon in hero tales vary but usually see the hero's victory as an act of repression. For Campbell the dragon is both 'the tenacious aspect of the father' which must be overcome in order to release 'the vital energies that will free the universe' ([1949] 1968: 352) and 'repressed id' (ibid.: 130). Bettelheim likewise regards dragons and other 'dangerous' animals as 'the untamed id, not yet subjected to ego and superego control, in all its dangerous energy' (Bettelheim 1976: 76), but he also sees them as an image of the father as perceived by the (male) child at the oedipal stage:

> the story implies: it's not Father whose jealousy prevents you from having Mother all to yourself, it's an evil dragon – what you really have in mind is to slay an evil dragon. Further the story gives veracity to the boy's feeling that the most desirable female is kept in captivity by an evil figure, while implying that it is not Mother the child wants for himself, but a marvellous and wonderful woman he hasn't met yet, but certainly will.
>
> (Bettelheim 1976: 111–2)

For the Jungian Joseph Henderson the battle with the dragon represents the ego's conflict with the 'shadow', 'the dark or negative side of the personality' (Henderson 1964: 112), although he also interprets a dragon in a patient's dream as the 'devouring' aspect of his attachment to his mother (Henderson 1964: 117).

While readers may derive some of these meanings from some stories in which dragons appear a dragon is clearly *always* a wild creature and a powerful force of nature, and traditionally the hero's task has been to subdue it, if not to kill it. (The work of Ursula Le Guin in which the hero relates somewhat differently to dragons is discussed in the final chapter of this book.) The image of the hero and the defeated dragon suggests the Western drive to dam rivers, clear forests, bridge torrents, mine the earth, sail tiny ships across huge oceans. It implies the linear progression of the story with its affirmative closure, the ultimately triumphant struggle to tame wild nature and establish human civilization, a state of order based on reason. Because we live in a world which has been largely shaped by these visionary endeavours it is difficult for us to imagine what it might be like to be part of a culture in which people are content to admire and respect the great forces of nature – and leave them alone. The philosophies of modern green movements have developed within the context of Western culture and they can only be reformist. We have, however, learned to read the story deconstructively, to see the triumph as entailing terrible costs. Our consciousness of the need to preserve surviving wilderness areas and threatened species is contingent upon our awareness of the extent of the destruction which has already occurred.

The general revision of Western views about nature has seen significant changes in attitudes to the killing of wild animals. While hunters still vigorously defend their 'right' to engage in their 'sport', and will often argue that 'culling' is beneficial for a particular species, and some seem able to affirm their own existence only by destroying other living creatures, many people in the West now regard the slaughter of animals for sport with abhorrence. Along with this moral position there is a growing awareness of the need to maintain biodiversity, and if dragons actually existed there would undoubtedly be a strong movement to preserve such a rare and threatened species! Certainly the once widespread belief in the innate wickedness of some wild animals is in retreat, but the still routine designation of dragons, the mythical quintessence of wildness, as 'evil' testifies to the earlier strength of the idea. The passage quoted above from Bettelheim twice applies the qualifier 'evil' to 'dragon' as a matter of course.

In Geraldine McCaughrean's *Saint George and the Dragon* [1989], an illustrated retelling of the tale for children, discussed in Chapter 1, the dragon's name is Wickedness:

> Its red mouth gaped as it panted in the hot sun. Its ragged teeth bulged through rolled green lips. And awake or asleep, its lidless eyes stared and its claws stretched and withdrew, stretched and withdrew in the waterside mud. Its foul breath hung in a green haze. Its father was Evil, its mother Darkness, and its name was Wickedness.
>
> (McCaughrean [1989] 1994)

Ted Hughes has argued that the story of Saint George and the dragon is detrimental for children because: 'It sets up as an ideal pattern for dealing with unpleasant or irrational experience the complete suppression of the terror . . . It is the symbolic story of creating a neurosis' (Rees 1980: 81). This seems a restrained criticism, for the postulated existence of the dragon is more disturbing than Saint George's need to suppress it. This dragon is not, like pre-Christian dragons such as Typhon, simply symbolic of the destructive forces of nature which are indifferent to the creatures in their path. This dragon's evil is deliberate, it is directed against the people of the town and it means to devour them all. It signifies the existence of evil as a powerful, active and autonomous force in the universe, intent upon the destruction of human beings. It implies a paranoid vision of reality.

The major source of Saint George's dragon is the Book of Revelation. In Chapter 12 of Revelation a woman who is about to give birth appears in heaven 'clothed with the sun' and is menaced by a dragon:

> And there appeared another wonder in heaven; and behold a great red dragon having seven heads, and ten horns, and seven crowns upon his heads.
> And his tail drew the third part of the stars of heaven, and did cast them to the earth; and the dragon stood before the woman which was ready to be delivered, for to devour her child as soon as it was born.
> And she brought forth a man child, who was to rule all nations with a rod of iron: and her child was caught up unto God, and to his throne.
> And the woman fled into the wilderness, where she hath a place prepared of God, that they should feed her there, a thousand two hundred and three score days.
> And there was war in heaven: Michael and his angels fought against the dragon; and the dragon fought and his angels.
> And prevailed not; neither was their place found anymore in heaven.
> And the great dragon was cast out, that old serpent, called the Devil, and Satan, which deceiveth the whole world.
>
> (Revelation 12: 3–9)

In Chapter 19 the dragon reappears (now referred to as 'the beast') and it is opposed by Christ seated, hero-like, on a white horse. The beast and his sinful followers are defeated and cast into a lake of fire burning with brimstone.

Here the materials of the early Greek hero myths which expressed the dualisms of human/nature, culture/nature and reason/irrationality are used to encode the Christian dualism of good and evil, the dragon is defined as the incarnation of Satan, and this additional layer of significance is attached to the symbol as it coils its way through the forests of Western imagination. A precisely similar seven-headed dragon, spitting fire, appears in the Grimm brothers fairy story 'The Two Brothers' (Grimm 1994: 296–316) where a young hunter is the hero who kills it and rescues the princess it was about to devour. And here it is, still single-mindedly intent on destroying the hero, in *The Warlock of Firetop Mountain* (1982), a 'Fighting Fantasy Gamebook' in which the reader is cast as the hero and left in no doubt about what must be done to the dragon:

> As you shine your lantern around the cavern, you hear a rumble. A dull glow flickers in the blackness. Suddenly, a jet of fire shoots from the depths of the cavern, narrowly missing you and singeing the mossy growths on the wall! You throw yourself onto the ground and look up to see a large DRAGON stalking out of the darkness towards you. Smoke curls from its nostrils. Its scaly red skin glistens with an oily covering. The beast is some fifteen metres long! How will you attack the creature?
>
> (Jackson and Livingstone 1982: 107)

The text does not permit the option of not attacking the dragon. The good/evil opposition is assumed and aggression is defined as the only response possible.

But *why* was evil conceived as inherent in animals (wolves and serpents, for example, as well as the symbolic dragon), and not in something else? Mary Midgley argues (Midgley 1995: 40–9) that it is essentially the consequence of the Platonic concept of the beast within. Being social animals human beings have inhibitions about killing others within their group, but the inhibitions are weak enough to be often overborne. Primitive human beings must, Midgley argues, frequently have been appalled and puzzled by the things they did, and just this puzzle must have contributed to the development of intelligence and morality. She suggests that the preoccupation of early literature with bloodshed, guilt and vengeance is evidence of a very early concern with these problems. Using the *Iliad* as evidence she argues that human beings sought to explain their violent actions, which troubled their consciences, by attributing them to some agency outside themselves, and originally they attributed them to the gods. Agamemnon, for example, explains his quarrel with Achilles by saying that Zeus filled him with madness. However, this useful and satisfying position became untenable as the gods came to be defined as good. Plato, who consistently defined the gods as good, was also the first consistent exponent of the theory of the beast within. He viewed evil as alien to the soul and so concluded that human beings' evil deeds must be caused by their bodily instincts, by that part of them which they share with non-human animals. From there it is a short, although logically invalid, step to the view that (some) animals themselves are evil. Ultimately Midgley's theory must remain a matter of speculation, but it is unarguable that belief in the inherent evil of wild beasts has had a profound influence on Western habits of thought.

## WOLVES AND OTHER BEASTS

In many stories the hero's opponents are actual wild beasts rather than symbolic dragons or other fabulous monsters. The human/nature dualism is inscribed in these tales and the animals, as the representatives of nature, are defined as objects for human beings to dominate or destroy. As a result of this perception many animals over the centuries have suffered appalling persecutions while others have been enthusiastically hunted to the point of actual or near extinction, and routine cruelty to animals such as battery hens is still unthinkingly condoned by most Westerners.

While Plato's concept of the beast within established the basis for the perception of wild animals as the natural and symbolic enemies of rational human beings it was in the Middle Ages that particular animals, especially wolves, came to be regarded as guilty of human sins such as greed and sexual predatoriness and, in some cases, as incarnations of Satan himself. When Dante entered the dark forest of error and began his allegorical journey through hell and purgatory to paradise in *The Divine Comedy* [1307–21], the first creatures he encountered were three beasts: a leopard, a 'bright beast so speckled and so gay', a lion 'swift and savage' and finally a wolf, the worst of the three, who filled him with terror. His guide, the poet Virgil, explained the wolf's nature to him:

> The savage beast that makes thee cry for dread
> Lets no man pass this road of hers, but still
> Trammels him, till at last she lays him dead.
>
> Vicious her nature is, and framed for ill;
> When crammed she craves more fiercely than before;
> Her raging greed can never gorge its fill.
>
> With many a beast she mates and shall with more . . .
> (Dante, *Inferno*, Canto 1, [1307–21] 1949: 72–4)

In the allegorical structure of the work these beasts are the images of different types of sin: the leopard of thoughtless, self-indulgent sin, the lion of rage and violence, and the wolf of malicious and wilful sins. These sins must, of course, be mastered by reason, the hero within.

Murderous aggression, greed and lust are routinely attributed to wolves during the Middle Ages and beyond, and these qualities, with the addition of cunning, are seen in the wolves of fairy tales. In 'Little Red-Cap', the Grimm version of 'Little Red Riding Hood', the narrator tells us that the wolf is 'a malicious beast' (Grimm 1994: 108). A few lines further on we learn the wolf's thoughts: '"She is a nice tender little thing, and will taste better than the old woman: I must act craftily, that I may snap them both up"' (p. 108). When the huntsman appears on the scene he calls the wolf 'you old sinner' (p. 109) and shoots it dead. In the Perrault version of the story the wolf, who eats both the grandmother and Red Riding Hood, is referred to as 'wicked' (Perrault [1697] 1969: 28) and his sexual predatoriness is strongly implied in the concluding verse moral and in the reference to his large arms which are 'all the better to embrace' Red Riding Hood.

More fundamentally there is a sexual dimension to the notion of 'devouring' in fairy stories, clearly indicated in Perrault when Red Riding Hood takes off her clothes and climbs into bed with what she takes to be her grandmother (Perrault [1697] 1969: 28). This meaning is underlined in Gustave Doré's 1867 illustrations, which show a lusciously rounded Red Riding Hood under the covers beside an alert wolf. Bettelheim's Freudian reading of the story (Bettelheim 1976: 166–83) takes the wolf's role as seducer for granted, but ignores the darker suggestions in the fact that the child cannot distinguish the wolf from her grandmother. This confusion, which is essential to the impact of the story, suggests a link with the werewolf hysteria of the fifteenth and sixteenth centuries (see below), but also suggests that the tale is perhaps as much about sexual abuse within the family as about the dangers of wolves, the wilderness and male predation. It is the complex interplay of latent meanings which accounts for this story's continuing appeal.

The more light-hearted tale 'The Three Little Pigs', discussed in Chapter 2, stresses the wolf's greed, murderousness and cunning. Two other fairy tales which illustrate the evils commonly attributed to wolves are 'The Wolf and the Fox' (Grimm 1994: 341–3) in which a wolf is destroyed by his own greed and 'The Wolf and the Seven Little Goats' (Grimm 1994: 25–8) in which several components of 'Little Red Riding Hood' are reworked. In this tale a wolf, which is referred to as a 'villain' and a 'monster', tricks the seven children of a goat into believing he is their mother by softening his rough voice and rubbing his black feet with flour to make them white. When the goat children let him in he devours them all except for the youngest who is so small he is able to hide in the clock case. When the mother returns home and learns what has happened she is able to save her children by cutting the wolf open while he is asleep. The six young goats spring out and the mother puts stones in the wolf's stomach and sews him up again. The stones are so heavy that when he goes to drink he falls into the brook and drowns. He is thus punished for his murderousness, greed and deception.

Twentieth-century observations of actual wolves in their natural habitats have shown them to be very different from these mythical monsters. They are extremely social animals who rarely kill human beings and whose behaviour is similar to that of humans in significant ways. Hall and Sharp argue that because both wolves and human beings evolved as hunters and gatherers who were too small to overpower or outrun large prey they both developed intelligence to outwit their prey and learned to practise co-operation and division of labour within the group. Not all members of a wolf pack engage in hunting. The non-hunting members include the young who are carefully protected by their elders. Food procured by the hunters is shared with the rest of the pack which normally consists of about seven animals – roughly the size of a human family group (Hall and Sharp 1978: 1–5). Because their diet of meat is high in protein wolves do not need to spend all their time searching for food and so are able to play and socialize, and because, as hunters, they need to communicate over distances as well as at close quarters they have developed a vocabulary of howling. The affinity between humans and dogs which gives pleasure to so many is the result of our ancient evolutionary parallels with wolves. There were, of course, stories which recognized wolves' intelligent and nurturing behaviour, such as the tale of Romulus and Remus, the legendary founders of Rome, who, as babies, were reared by a she-wolf. However, such stories were overshadowed during the Middle Ages by the myth of the wolf as the embodiment of evil.

The charge of cunning and deceitfulness levelled against wolves no doubt arose from human frustration at being frequently outwitted by these intelligent animals. Even in recent times government hunters in North America, armed with high-powered rifles, have been unable to destroy certain legendary wolves (Fox 1978: 25). But this does not explain why they were persistently condemned as murderous, greedy and lustful. Clearly they were the victims of humans' desire to externalize their own shortcomings, but this fate could have befallen any other wild animal. It is possible that linguistic confusion helped to link wolves to the Devil because the Greek for 'wolf', *lukos* is very close to *leukos* (light) and 'Lucifer' means light (Lopez 1978: 209). But the more important answer seems to be that the Church took advantage of their availability. In Europe in the Middle Ages there were more wolves than any other large predators living in close proximity to human beings. They did attack sheep and possibly, on occasions, did kill lone travellers. Lopez suggests that, to distract attention from actual grievances and smother social and political unrest, 'the Roman Church, which dominated mediaeval life in Europe, exploited the sinister image of wolves in order to create a sense of real devils prowling in a real world' (Lopez 1978: 208).

This propaganda campaign was very effective. People became obsessed with wolves. They believed that wolves could strike a person dumb with their gaze. They believed that highway robbers were reincarnated as wolves. The poisonous plant aconite became known as 'wolfsbane'. Peasants referred to both famines and avaricious landlords as wolves (Lopez 1978: 206). As early as the tenth century King Edgar of England had imposed an annual tribute of 3,000 wolves on the king of Wales, and in the twelfth and thirteenth centuries the English Kings Richard I, John and Henry III made land grants to individuals who undertook to keep the number of wolves in check (Fiennes 1976: 168).

The hysteria intensified in the fourteenth, fifteenth and sixteenth centuries. Wolves were persecuted, poisoned and burnt in Church sponsored programmes, and the Inquisition condemned hundreds of human beings to be burnt at the stake as werewolves. The *Malleus Maleficarum*, published in 1486 and reprinted fourteen times by 1520, encouraged the hunt for werewolves as well as for witches. The theological position of its authors was that the apparent transformations of humans into wolves were merely illusions caused by the Devil, but a 'werewolf', by dealing with the Devil, was guilty anyway (*Malleus Maleficarum* in Otten 1986: 112–3). While the werewolf legend goes back to antiquity (there is a werewolf story in Petronius's *Satyricon*) it was in this period that they became a European obsession. Lopez suggests (p. 228) that the pressures of famines and plagues and the stifling ignorance of the Middle Ages encouraged mass neuroses and that the belief in werewolves was such a neurosis. There was an orgy of accusation and condemnation, and also of confession. These confessions, recorded by the Inquisition, include those of Jean Peyral who, in 1518, said that he had committed murder while in the shape of a werewolf and Gilles Garnier who confessed to devouring young children as a wolf in 1573. Both of these, along with numerous others who confessed to similar crimes, were burnt at the stake (Copper 1977: 44–7).

Perhaps the best known confession was that of Stubbe Peeter who, in 1590 in Germany, confessed to numerous murders including that of his own son, and to rape, incest and sodomy while in the form of a werewolf. He was tried and condemned to torture and beheading and his body was burnt. A pamphlet describing his trial and his crimes was circulated throughout Europe and England shortly after his conviction. According to this pamphlet the Devil had promised to give him whatever his heart desired whereupon he asked to be allowed to prey on human beings in the form of a beast. The Devil gave him a girdle which transformed him into a werewolf whenever he put it on:

> he was transformed into the likeness of a greedy, devouring wolf, strong and mighty, with eyes great and large, which in the night sparkled like brands of fire, a mouth great and wide, with most sharp and cruel teeth, a huge body and mighty paws.
>
> (*A True Discourse Declaring the Damnable Life and Death of One Stubbe Peeter*, in Otten 1986: 69)

One of his habits when in wolf form, according to the pamphlet, was to roam the fields seeking any women or girls he could get alone. When successful he would rape and then murder them and devour their hearts. He claimed to have killed thirteen children and two women in this way. This sounds very like a possible origin of 'Little Red Riding Hood', and in a version of the story which, according to Douglas (1992: 175), seems to date back to seventeenth-century France, although not recorded until 1885, the wolf is actually a werewolf. He kills the grandmother, tricks the girl into eating her grandmother's flesh and drinking her blood, and then, pretending to be the grandmother, entices her into bed. If this version does belong to the early seventeenth century it predates Perrault and must have been influenced by the notorious Stubbe Peeter pamphlet.

The psychology of the self-proclaimed werewolf is explored in Webster's tragedy, *The Duchess of Malfi*, probably first performed in 1616, where the werewolf is Ferdinand, Duke of Calabria, who was obsessed by an incestuous passion for his sister, the widowed Duchess. When she secretly remarries he arranges to have her murdered, but is then racked by grief and guilt, and falls victim to lycanthropy. This 'very pestilent disease' is described in a speech by the Doctor who attends him in his madness:

In those that are possessed with't there o'erflows
Such melancholy humour they imagine
Themselves to be transformed into wolves;
Steal forth to churchyards in the dead of night,
And dig dead bodies up: as two nights since
One met the duke, 'bout midnight in a lane
Behind Saint Mark's church, with the leg of a man
Upon his shoulder; and he howled fearfully;
Said he was a wolf, only the difference
Was, a wolf's skin was hairy on the outside,
His on the inside; bade them take their swords,
Rip up his flesh, and try: (V, II)
(Webster [1623] 1956: 199)

Ferdinand's incestuous desires are typical of the kind of physical appetite that werewolves symbolized while his self-loathing suggests the sorts of mental disturbance which may have prompted confessions by mediaeval 'werewolves'.

The werewolf remained popular in sensationalist literature and is still a staple of horror films. Copper (1977) includes a bibliography of several dozen books and films which feature them. In all cases the werewolf symbolizes the violence of the 'beast within'. Typical of the novels are George W.M. Reynolds' *Wagner, the Wherwolf* [1857] and *The Werewolf of Paris* by 'Guy Endore' [1934]. Reynolds' tale was a penny dreadful which first appeared in monthly episodes published by John Dicks of the Strand in London. It tells of an old man, Wagner, to whom the Devil offered renewed youth, good looks and riches on the condition that he became a werewolf at certain times and preyed upon human beings. Wagner accepted this Faustian bargain and pursued a long career of violence but was eventually captured and brought to trial. During his trial he changed into his wolf shape, broke out of his prison cell and rushed through the crowd '"with savage howls, glaring eyes and foaming mouth"' (Copper 1977: 126)

Guy Endore (Harry Relis) was an American who wrote film scripts as well as novels, so *The Werewolf of Paris* may have been produced with the movies in mind. It is a complex story set in nineteenth-century Paris. The central character, Bertrand Aymar Chaillet, is born as the result of an innocent girl's seduction by a priest, one of whose noble ancestors had been imprisoned for fifty years and had developed wolfish behavioural characteristics while incarcerated in his tiny cell. Bertrand is born with hair on the palms of his hands! Of course he becomes a werewolf who robs graves, rapes his own mother by mistake and kills his best friend. The hero and narrator, his stepfather Aymar Galliez, feels both pity and disgust for him, but eventually decides he must be stopped and pursues him through Paris during the siege of the Franco-Prussian War. The famine precipitated by this siege was said to be marked by a wolf stalking the suburbs! Bertrand is finally captured and incarcerated in an asylum.

Famous werewolf films include *The Wolf Man* (1940) in which Lon Chaney delivers a bravura performance, *The Werewolf of London* (1935), *The Werewolf* (1956), *I Was a Teenage Werewolf* (1957) which overtly attributes the violence and lack of control in adolescent males to 'the beast within', *The Curse of the Werewolf* (1961) which stars Oliver Reed, *Werewolf of Washington* (1973) and *The Howling* (1981). In all these stories and films the werewolf is eventually destroyed by the representatives of social order, hero figures whose purpose is to control the wildness of nature and of human nature which is, by implication, an ever-present threat to civilization. The skill of the make-up artist is essential to the success of the films and it is significant that the werewolves, while impressively horrific, never look like wolves. They are recognizably human, walking upright and wearing clothes. Their wolfishness is signified by fangs, copious facial hair and hairy hands with claws, and it is this melding of the human and the beastly that constitutes their appeal: they are a visual image of 'the beast within', of the human capacity for violence, cruelty and slaughter. Thus they imply that human beings must control their passionate natures, their savage instincts, for reason alone raises us above the beasts.

Welch Everman in *Cult Horror Films* remarks on the fundamental conservatism of most horror films which define anyone who is different as dangerous and deserving of death (Everman 1993: 3), but in werewolf films the conservatism goes further than this. By demonizing the 'wild' aspects of human nature these works encourage sexual and emotional repression, and by attributing violent crimes and social disorder to individual aberrance they discourage investigation of urgent social problems.

Wolves and werewolves turn up in conventional, terrifying form in nineteenth- and twentieth-century children's hero stories conveying the same constellation of meanings as in the fairy tales and the werewolf films. In Marryat's *The Settlers in Canada*, two girls are menaced by a wolf which kills their dog and then confronts them 'bristling his hair and showing his powerful teeth' (Marryat, n.d.: 115). In Ballantyne's *The Dog Crusoe* the hero hunters encounter a variety of wild beasts including white wolves whose size, cunning and ferocity are stressed. The story condemns the cruelty of catching them in traps, but generally presents them as deserving of what they get: their killing of horses is described as 'cold-blooded murder' (Ballantyne: 194). Tolkien casts wolves and Wargs, an especially large and evil variety of wolf, as the allies of the wicked goblins in *The Hobbit*: 'the goblins gathered again in the valley. There a host of Wargs came ravening' (Tolkien [1937] 1966: 260).

In C.S. Lewis' *The Lion, the Witch and the Wardrobe* the White Witch has a grey wolf called Maugrim as Chief of her Secret Police (Lewis [1950] 1959: 91). He is despatched to kill her enemies in secret raids, perhaps recalling the Nazis' Operation Werewolf, an organization established by Goebbels in the last months of World War II to harass Allied lines of communication (Douglas 1992: 26). In a semiologically crucial incident in the story Peter, the eldest of the children, who eventually becomes king of Narnia, proves his heroic status by fighting and killing a wolf, perhaps Maugrim himself, and saving the life of his sister who was fleeing from the beast. The wolf confronts him, howling with anger and with its eyes 'flaming' (p. 120), but Peter manages to plunge his sword into its heart. When he has cleaned the wolf's hair and blood from the 'bright blade' (p. 121) Aslan uses the sword to knight him as Sir Peter Wolf's-Bane. Thus the wolf functions as an emblem of both natural savagery and evil, and the civilization/nature and good/evil dualisms are casually conflated. Peter's action and the reward which Aslan bestows upon him define destruction as the necessary response to natural savagery.

Werewolves are also common in the more banal fantasy adventure tales and fantasy games. Ian Livingstone's werewolf in *The Forest of Doom* (1983) is typical. Livingstone is less subtle and less effective than Lewis, but the message is the same:

> There is a full moon in the sky and the light casts eerie shadows all around. You hear soft footsteps and sniffing, followed by another low growl. Then a shape which looks like a man steps out of the shadows to your right; as he gets closer you see that his chest, arms and face are covered with thick brown hair and long teeth protrude from his mouth. He is a WEREWOLF and you must fight him.
>
> (Livingstone 1983: 285)

Rosemary Sutcliff's *Warrior Scarlet*, set in Bronze Age Britain, dramatizes humanity's struggle to maintain a small ordered space of emergent civilization against the always encroaching wilderness. Wolves symbolize the terrors of nature and are aligned with darkness in this text's pervasive light/dark imagery. The central conflict is between the hero, Drem, and the wolf he must kill in a ritual fight to establish his status as a warrior of the tribe. The wolf's savagery is stressed in a series of descriptive touches: there is 'menace in every raised hackle', it has 'savage amber eyes', a 'snarling head', 'yellow fangs and a wet black throat' (Sutcliff [1958] 1976: 143). Drem fails in his attempt and is badly wounded, physically and psychologically, but later he meets the wolf again when, driven by winter famine, wolf packs attack the sheep folds and the shepherds of the village. He recognizes its 'wicked grin' and 'savage yellow eyes' (p. 199) and is glad of a second opportunity to kill it. He expects to die but, in a desperate struggle, manages to drive his spear into the wolf's body. His friends arrive just in time to save him from death in the jaws of its companions. His feat wins Drem admission to the warrior ranks and symbolizes humanity's difficult but determined subjugation of the wild.

An earlier incident in this story links wolves to the destructive effect of panic fear on human reason. Drem is lost in the forest as night falls and gradually loses all grasp on reality, feeling himself menaced by the 'furry darkness' (p. 27) as if it were some monstrous wolf:

> he heard that soft, stealthy panting as though the Thing prowled at his heels. But it was not only at his heels now, it was all around him, in front as well as behind. . . . This was what the hunters spoke of under their breaths around the fire. This was the Fear that walked the forest, the Terror of the Soul. He had never felt it before, but the hunter within him knew it; the Fear that prowled soft-footed beyond the cave mouth and the firelight.
>
> (Sutcliff [1958] 1976: 28)

This evokes the human/nature, reason/emotion and culture/nature dualisms in a compelling way and superimposes the evocative light/dark opposition upon them so that it is difficult to read this book, especially because of its setting in the primitive past, without accepting the wolf as the incarnation of all that Drem fears and without believing that its deliberate aggression is directed at him. Nevertheless the description of the wolf's aggression is entirely traditional, and its 'savage amber eyes', huge mouth and 'yellow fangs' seem, like so many of the descriptions of wolves and werewolves in our literature, to derive ultimately from the Stubbe Peeter pamphlet of 1590.

As Lopez points out 'we create wolves' (Lopez 1978: 203). Every perception of reality is a cultural construct and Western culture constructed in the 'wolf' a monster so powerful that we could not see beyond it. The image survives despite current scientific interest in monitoring the lives and habits of actual wolves. The terms 'wolf' and 'werewolf' still turn up in the media to signify extreme violence. For instance, Douglas cites a report in *The Independent* of 3 July 1990 of a sex-attacker guilty of a series of rapes across south-east England who was known as the werewolf rapist. Of course, as deconstructive theory insists, even a scientific perception is just that – a perception; but a perception of wolves based on careful observation of actual animals is likely to be less wildly unjust to them than the tradition based on fear and opportunistic theological subtleties, and it can be used in the process of deconstructing that tradition. That task is urgent, for the effect of the folkloric and literary tradition on living wolves has been catastrophic. Wolves became extinct in England between 1485 and 1509. They survived longer in Scotland but were eventually eliminated and according to the records the last one died in 1848 (Fiennes 1976: 169–71). They are now extremely rare in Western Europe. In the United States only Minnesota has a wolf population large enough to maintain itself. In Canada and Alaska their numbers have diminished and there is concern for their survival: Henry S. Sharp comments that 'many' have been shot and an 'inestimable number' have been poisoned (Sharp 1978: 64). In 1993 the Alaskan government allowed the killing of 150 wild wolves, and in 1994 approximately a hundred were slaughtered under the government's management plan. It is heartening to note that in 1995 the wolf kill was cancelled (Antonio 1995: 224), perhaps giving the wolf a chance of survival.

Literature is at last beginning to come to the aid of the wolf, and the field of children's literature has produced at least one outstanding novel which presents an informed and sympathetic picture of north American wolves: Jean Craighead George's *Julie of the Wolves* [1972]. This work is discussed in the final chapter of this book.

European penetration into India, the Americas and Africa during the era of imperialism provided opportunities for confrontation with other large beasts, and the popular adventure literature of the period made use of this chance to demonstrate the superiority of the Western patriarchy in a new context. In these tales intrepid white heroes, armed with rifles and other products of Western technology, kill tigers, grizzly bears, lions, gorillas, rhinoceroses – almost every large mammal now threatened with extinction – thus demonstrating the dominance of civilization over the wilderness, the superiority of 'nurture' to 'nature'! These animals are not normally depicted as evil in the theological sense but a degree of deliberate malevolence is usually attributed to them so that insofar as they symbolize nature it is presented as powerful, dangerous and hostile. Ballantyne in *The Dog Crusoe* (n.d.) repeatedly refers to the beasts which his hero, Dick Varley, encounters as monsters: 'It is scarcely possible to conceive a wilder or more ferocious and terrible monster than a buffalo bull' (p. 57). And of a grizzly bear: 'Yes there he was at last, the monster to meet which the young hunter had so often longed – the terrible size and fierceness of which he had heard so often spoken about by the old hunters' (p. 151). Dick has little trouble in killing the bear and he makes himself a collar from its claws which he wears with great pride, thus signifying his mastery over wild nature just as the representatives of the British raj turned the skins of the tigers they shot into rugs and stood upon them before the fireplaces in their drawing rooms.

Even in a pedestrian story like G.A. Henty's 'The Man-Eater of the Terai' [1894] tigers are powerful symbols of India, as well as of nature itself. Completely lacking in character interest, local colour or narrative suspense, this tale seems to exist purely as an excuse for its climactic closure in which a 16-year-old English lad shoots a tiger that had killed his father. The story foregrounds his courage and dedication to his task: he spends months obsessively practising his marksmanship and then tracks the tiger relentlessly for three weeks. The moment when he shoots it between the eyes as it is about to spring upon him (Henty [1894] 1995: 106) is an image of British self-discipline and superiority to the undisciplined power of nature, but modern readers are likely to perceive the mirror reverse of the image: British control of India was not a 'natural' consequence of innate superiority, but rather was achieved and maintained only by the rigorous, ruthless and ultimately self-destructive application of force.

Likewise imperialist adventure stories set in Africa, which offered an even greater variety of large animals for heroes to kill, appear today like evidence of the ignorance and ineptitude of the white masters rather than testaments to the inevitability and beneficence of their dominance. The animals emerge as symbols of the beauty and strength of nature and the powerful vitality of Africa, which the Europeans spectacularly failed to understand. In Gordon Stables' *Stanley Grahame* (n.d.), Stanley and his band of adventurers in the 'dark continent' face, within the space of ten pages, a 'monster lion' (p. 277), a swamp full of crocodiles, 'monsters' which attack the men with 'roaring and champing and splashing' (p. 284) and a 'monster gorilla' (p. 287). Even a black rhinoceros (now one of the most endangered species on Earth) and her calf are killed because they happen to rush along the path being taken by the smallest member of the expedition (p. 276). In 'A Tale of Three Lions' [1889] Rider Haggard's hunter-hero, Allan Quartermain, the first person narrator of the story, emphasizes the nobility of the wild beasts but shoots them nevertheless. As well as disposing of the lions which form the chief interest of this tale, he and his son shoot a 'noble koodoo bull' (Haggard [1889] 1995: 69–70). Having killed it they cut off a few slices of 'the best meat' and leave its corpse in the wilderness. In *King Solomon's Mines*, Quartermain and his two white companions dispose of a variety of animals including elephants which Quartermain hunts professionally. Even the giraffes are not safe: one of Quartermain's associates, kills one simply because he had a loaded gun in his hand and 'could not resist' (Haggard [1885] 1958: 47).

Mary Midgley says of this opposition between white hero and wild beast:

> That nervous white man with his heart in his mouth and his finger on his trigger, was amongst the most dangerous things in the jungle. His weapon was at least as powerful as those of the biggest animals, and while they attacked only what they could eat or what was really annoying them, he would shoot at anything big enough to aim at. Why did he think they were more savage than he? Why has civilized Western man always thought so?
>
> (Midgley 1995: 30)

She answers her question by suggesting that '*man has always been unwilling to admit his own ferocity*, and has tried to deflect attention from it by making animals out to be more ferocious than they are' (p. 31). This may be true, but it is equally true that the attribution of extreme ferociousness to large beasts, like the attribution of savagery to indigenous peoples, justified the white man's programme of domination.

Midgley's point about the comparative dangerousness of hunter and hunted highlights the reversibility of the iconic image of the hero confronting the wild things. It is only because of the structure and narrative point of view of hero tales that the reader is able to interpret the hero's actions as heroic. If the point of view is changed he appears as a violent and dangerous predator killing innocent wildlife, attacking indigenous people, occupying their land and destroying their culture, or as an arrogant oppressor denying the autonomy of women and imposing laws and customs upon the common people which enrich and advantage him at their expense.

We have learnt, too late, to regret the victory of the hero over the great beasts as we contemplate the likelihood that many will soon be gone from the planet, but whether this represents a real change of attitude in the majority of human beings is uncertain. Are we horrified at tales of rhinoceros poaching only because they are scarce, or because we have really come to value and respect all other living creatures? Most Westerners now seem to be vigorously opposed to the hunting of mammals but attitudes to non-mammalian predators that are not in short supply do not seem to have changed very much. Sharks, which occasionally attack and kill human beings, are still hunted without much compunction, and the 1975 film *Jaws* which exploited fear and hatred of sharks made record-breaking profits. In her 1994 *Report on the Family* Shere Hite records the testimony of young men who had taken part in hunting expeditions. While some expressed revulsion at the killing others enjoyed it and felt empowered:

> 'I went hunting a few times with other men, with a .22 rifle, when I was eighteen to twenty-two. It was, admittedly, a fun game, feeling the surge of power.'
>
> 'I grew up hunting and fishing. Most hunters pretend to hunt for something called 'sport'. But I know that what makes hunting game attractive is the killing of the animal. I like to kill things. The very real sense of power over life and death projected through space.'
>
> (Hite [1994] 1995: 239)

One of the things that hero stories do is to define animals as legitimate and appropriate targets for human violence. By articulating the human/animal opposition, and asserting a separation between the two categories in the very way the narrative is structured, they deny our interconnectedness with other living things, and by defining the destruction of wild beasts as one of the proofs of patriarchal superiority they encourage those who need to prove their masculinity to continue with the killing.

## SAVAGES: 'HUMAN BEASTS'

Edward Said remarks that people often define themselves negatively, as different from 'them', the others who live 'out there', beyond one's own territory, but often have a quite unrigorous idea of what the others are like (Said [1978] 1995: 54). The European elite have had a lively sense of their own difference and superiority to others from early times, and one function of the hero tale has been to express this in dramatic form. We have noted Odysseus's contemptuous account of the Cyclopes as 'fierce and uncivilized' (Homer 1946: 144), a people who had no laws and did not know how to govern themselves. But it was the discovery of the New World and the advent of imperialism that provided Europeans with the most striking examples of 'uncivilized' peoples, the most vivid contrasts to themselves, the most dazzling demonstrations of their superiority. As the conquest and appropriation of the New World (and of Africa and Australasia) proceeded, stories in which morally upright European heroes out-fought and outwitted 'savages' proliferated.

Most Europeans had no familiarity with the 'savages' who inhabited these distant parts of the world but, as Said suggests, this proved no bar to the conceptualization of savages as utterly different from Europeans and inferior in manners, morals, intellect, sensibility and appearance. This is the process which Plumwood, in her account of the operation of dualism, calls 'radical exclusion' (Plumwood 1993: 49–51): the differences between the two groups are maximized to the point where continuity between them is virtually denied. They appear to be two different orders of beings so that the domination of the one over the other seems simply in the nature of things. Odysseus said of the Cyclops that no one could have taken him for 'a man who ate bread like ourselves' (Homer 1946: 146). Likewise, when Crusoe first set eyes on the savages that visited his island he:

> look'd up with the utmost affection of my Soul, and with a Flood of tears in my Eyes, gave God Thanks that had cast my first Lot in a Part of the World, where I was distinguish'd from such dreadful Creatures as these.
>
> (Defoe [1719] 1981: 165)

Another feature of the construction of dualism, as Plumwood describes it (p. 53–5), is stereotyping or homogenization. From the perspective of the superior and dominant race differences between the inferior 'others' are of no significance. What matters, what marks them out, are their differences from the masters. To recognize individual differences could begin to call into question the comfortable sense of self-evident superiority so, in a process which is still too familiar, they are all labelled with the same terms, dismissed as interchangeable members of a group and so branded as inherently inferior. They are all 'wogs' or 'blacks' or 'abos' or 'gooks'. This facilitates the treatment which such creatures 'deserve'. Thus Europeans and their descendants in America, Australia and Africa, people who would have regarded themselves as moral and honourable human beings, have enslaved, beaten, raped, shot and massacred other human beings whom they had assigned in their minds to the category of the inferior, to the class of 'human beasts'. This was the term applied to the natives of the New World in the Council of Virginia's *True Declaration of the state of the Colonie in Virginia, with a confutation of such scandalous reports as have tended to the disgrace of so worthy an enterprise* (1610): 'there is no trust in the fidelitie of human beasts' (Kermode 1964: xxxi).

More than two hundred years later the young British heroes in Ballantyne's very influential tale *The Coral Island* [1857] still shared the Council's view. Before they have even seen a native at close quarters Jack, the eldest of them, says, when he recognizes canoes on the horizon: '"They are canoes Ralph! whether war canoes or not I cannot tell; but this I know, that *all* the natives of the South Sea Islands are fierce cannibals, and they have little respect for strangers"' (Ballantyne [1857] 1953: 170; my italics). As they watch the natives land on the shore of their island paradise the narrator, Ralph, tells us that they yelled like 'incarnate fiends' and 'looked more like demons than human beings' (p. 172). Thus they are stereotyped as 'all the same' and the good/evil opposition is constructed before any behaviour of the natives is described as evidence to support it.

The evidence is not long in coming, however. Not only do the two canoe-loads of natives fight and kill each other, they are cannibals. The victorious group begin their feasting without delay:

> Next moment one of the savages raised his club, and fractured the wretched creature's skull. He must have died instantly; and strange though it may seem, I confess to a feeling of relief when the deed was done, because I now knew that the poor savage could not be burned alive. Scarcely had his limbs ceased to quiver when the monsters cut slices of flesh from his body, and, after roasting them slightly over the fire, devoured them.
>
> (Ballantyne [1857] 1953: 174)

They are 'monsters' because of their cannibalism, and the moral and cultural superiority of the British lads is demonstrated by their revulsion at the practice. There is no more suggestion here of a cultural context in which cannibalism has ritual significance than there is in *Crusoe* which was written almost one hundred and forty years earlier: the savages are cannibals simply because they are less fully human than the British observers. They are innately inferior.

As the heroes of *The Coral Island* gain more experience of the various cannibal tribes the evidence of their monstrousness increases: these natives eat not only their enemies but also their friends and they do it for pleasure (p. 214). They feed their babies to enormous eels which they worship (p. 223). They launch a new war canoe by running it over the bound bodies of living victims so that their eyeballs burst from their sockets and their blood gushes out of their mouths (p. 237). When a chief's house is being built they bury a man alive beside the main supporting post (p. 289). The heroes' horror increases proportionately and so the process of radical exclusion proceeds. The suggestion that the savages are less than human, that they are indeed 'human beasts', is underlined by the imagery. One of them has 'wolfish eyes' (p. 183), they look like 'demons' (p. 172), they are 'incarnate fiends' (p. 210), there is nothing too 'fiendish or diabolical' for them to do (p. 223), they are capable of 'diabolical enormities' (p. 237).

Crusoe had likewise labelled his cannibals as 'inhumane', that is 'not human':

nor is it possible for me to express the Horror of my Mind, at seeing the Shore spread with Skulls, Hands, Feet and other Bones of humane Bodies; and particularly I observ'd a Place where there had been a Fire made, and a Circle dug in the Earth, like a Cockpit, where it is suppos'd the Savage Wretches had sat down to their inhumane Feastings upon the Bodies of their Fellow-Creatures.

I was so astonish'd with the Sight of these Things, that I entertain'd no Notions of any Danger to myself from it for a long while; All my Apprehensions were bury'd in the Thoughts of such a Pitch of inhuman, hellish Brutality, and the horror of the Degeneracy of Humane Nature; which though I had heard of often, yet I never had so near a View of before; in short I turn'd away my Face from the horrid Spectacle.

(Defoe [1719] 1981: 164–5)

The contrary idea of the noble savage had, of course, long been propounded, most famously by Montaigne in his essay 'Of the Caniballes' which is recognized as a source of *The Tempest*. (John Florio's English translation of Montaigne's *Essays* was published in 1603.) Montaigne regarded the natives of the New World as uncorrupted humanity, 'wilde' only in the sense that plants which have not been modified by sophisticated gardeners are wild, an example of nature in 'her puritie' (Montaigne [1603] 1965: 219). He praised them because they *lacked* the characteristics of civilized society:

It is a nation . . . that hath no kind of trafficke, no knowledge of Letters, no intelligence of numbers, no name of magistrate, nor of politike superioritie; no use of service, of riches or of povertie; no contracts, no successions, no partitions, no occupation but idle; no respect of kindred but common, no apparrell but naturall, no manuring of lands, no use of wine, corne or mettle. The very words that import lying, falshood, treason, dissimulations, covetousness, envie, detraction and pardon, were never heard amongst them.

(Montaigne [1603] 1965: 220)

He regrets their cannibalism, but suggests that eating people when they are dead is less horrific than some of the practices of civilized Europeans such as systematic torture of the living: 'I am not sorie we note the Barbarous horror of such an action, but grieved, that prying so narrowly into their faults we are blinded in ours' (p. 223). Montaigne's work fed dreams of rustic idylls and Rousseau gave fresh impetus to the concept of the noble savage with the publication of *Emile* in 1762 but the idea proved less popular than its opposite: the savage who is violent, cruel and irrational, whose very existence proves the superiority of civilized Europeans.

In *The Tempest*, Shakespeare explores the concepts of nature and nurture, civilization and savagery, but accepts neither of the extreme views of the savage. The kindly old courtier, Gonzalo, expresses Montaigne's ideal but the play does not allow the audience to accept this view. Caliban, the native of the island on which the civilized and learned Prospero and his daughter, Miranda, were cast ashore, is driven by basic instincts and resists attempts to teach him civilized ways, although he acquires language and clearly has a fully human aptitude for learning. Prospero becomes convinced of his innate wickedness when he attempts to rape Miranda, and dismisses him as:

> A devil, a born devil, on whose nature
> Nurture can never stick.
>
> (IV, I, 188–9)

But Prospero's judgement is also brought into question for Caliban is shown to have sounder instincts and more sense than the debased products of civilization, represented by the shallow drunkards Stephano and Trinculo, and to be no more cruel or treacherous than the ambitious lords, Sebastian and Antonio, who plot to murder the king. He is also shown to be moved primarily by a profound attachment to the land of which he has been dispossessed, an empathy that Prospero does not understand. He cries out against his loss:

> This island's mine, by Sycorax my mother,
> Which thou tak'st from me.
>
> (I, II, 333–4)

And it is this which makes him surly and resentful, ready to strike at Prospero when he believes he has the chance. This is the crux or aporetic fracture where the logic of the text may be seen to reverse itself: Prospero's arrival on the island 'to be the lord on't' (V, I, 162) was an act of usurpation no less unjustified than his brother Antonio's usurpation of his own dukedom, but all the wisdom which he gains does not enable him to see this. From Caliban's point of view Prospero is an oppressor who robs him of both his land and his freedom, and Prospero's values and morality are irrelevant to him.

The play explores the effects of European colonization on indigenous peoples, and suggests the tragic inadequacy of assumptions of white cultural superiority and policies of assimilation. In a prophetic vision of the fate of the Australian Aborigines, Caliban, having been dispossessed of his land, is derided as 'filth' (I, II, 348), reduced to the status of a slave, physically ill-treated and, finally, corrupted by alcohol, which had been previously unknown to him. Yet Prospero was guided by reason and good intentions. No 'solution' is offered to this impasse; there can be no 'true' view of the situation, for truth is shown to be irreducibly relative. What is seen depends absolutely upon the point of view of the observer. The audience is invited to share a number of points of view, although that of Prospero is privileged, but the audience's perspective is itself yet another point of view and what meanings any member of an audience derives from the play will depend upon the prior experiences he or she brings to the act of observation. *The Tempest* is, in Barthes's term, a profoundly *scriptible* work, requiring the active participation of the audience (or reader) in the construction of meanings, not only because it is a mimetic, rather than a diegetic, text, but because its complex, multi-layered symbolism precludes unequivocal interpretation, and this complexity in itself suggests the limitations of rationalism.

Nevertheless, within this complex pattern of significance, it is the flowers of civilization, the young lovers Ferdinand and Miranda, in whom natural goodness has been refined by all the benefits of nurture, who represent the highest potential of human kind and the bright hope for the future. Caliban is a lesser creature. In the Names of the Actors he is listed as 'a salvage and deformed slave'. While 'Caliban' appears to be an anagram of 'cannibal' and so associates him with the inhabitants of the New World, Kermode suggests (Kermode 1964: xxxviii–xxxix) that he is also derived from 'the wild or salvage man of Europe', a familiar figure in contemporary paintings and masques. Possibly based on unfortunates who had been abandoned in the woods as children and survived to lead a feral life, 'salvage' men, always depicted as unchaste, were regarded as falling below human beings but above beasts in the chain of being.

Prospero regards Caliban's physical 'deformities' as emblematic of his moral imperfections:

> And as with age his body uglier grows,
> So his mind cankers.
>
> (IV, I, 191–2)

However, the term 'deformed' implies a norm from which the deformed deviates, and in Caliban's case this norm is obviously the physical appearance of the Europeans who have usurped his isle. This process by which a difference is defined as inferiority, which Plumwood terms 'relational definition' (Plumwood 1993: 52), is intrinsic to the logic of dualism and condemns the unequal 'other' to an inescapable position of 'natural' inferiority. If Europeans are the norm then savages are inherently inferior, and it is natural for Europeans to be their masters. Thus colonization is seen to be both justified and inevitable.

This is the perspective of the eighteenth- and nineteenth-century adventure stories which take no account of *The Tempest*'s depiction of the effects of colonization. Because these stories are always related from the hero's point of view the savages, measured against the hero, are seen as hideous or deformed, immoral and irrational, and their inferiority is as self-evident as their need of redemption. Thus Ralph, the young British first person narrator of *The Coral Island*, describes one of the natives who land on the island:

> His hair was frizzed out to an enormous extent, so that it resembled a large turban. It was of a light-yellow hue, which surprised me much, for the man's body was as black as coal, and I felt convinced that the hair

> must have been dyed. He was tattooed from head to foot, and his face, beside being tattooed, was besmeared with red paint and streaked with white. Altogether with his yellow turban-like hair, his Herculean black frame, his glittering eyes, he seemed the most terrible monster I ever beheld.
>
> (Ballantyne [1857] 1953: 172)

Of course this man seems a monster to Ralph because he does not have short hair in the British style, white skin and an absence of tattoos and face-paint. Today, when Afro hair-styles are deliberately created at considerable expense, the beautiful bodies of black athletes are envied, tattoos are in fashion, and face-painting is a holiday entertainment for children, he might not appear so monstrous!

Savages are similarly defined as monstrous at the end of the century in Conan Doyle's *The Sign of Four* [1890] in which the origins of the crime Holmes is called upon to investigate lie in an intrigue concerning treasure in India at the time of the Mutiny. India is defined as a place of precarious order dependent upon British rule: 'One month India lay as still and peaceful, to all appearance, as Surrey or Kent: the next there were two hundred thousand black devils let loose, and the country was a perfect hell' ([1890] 1987: 182). Even more savage than the Indians are the natives of the Andaman Islands in the Bay of Bengal. Their description in a supposed gazetteer recalls Crusoe's horrified account of the cannibals who visited his island:

> The average height is rather below four feet, although many full-grown adults may be found who are very much smaller than this. They are a fierce, morose and intractable people, though capable of forming most devoted friendships when their confidence has once been gained. . . . They are naturally hideous, having large, misshapen heads, small, fierce eyes, and distorted features. Their feet and hands, however, are remarkably small. So intractable and fierce are they, that all the efforts of the British officials have failed to win them over in any degree. They have always been a terror to ship-wrecked crews, braining the survivors with their stone-headed clubs, or shooting them with their poisoned arrows. These massacres are invariably concluded by a cannibal feast.
>
> (Doyle [1890] 1987: 159)

In this passage the savagery and 'otherness' of these people are defined entirely in terms of their relationship to, and differences from, the English or European norm: their size is abnormal because they are notably smaller than the English. They are 'hideous' and 'distorted' in comparison to a European standard. They are 'intractable' because the British have been unable to control them. Their evil is demonstrated by their behaviour towards shipwrecked Europeans. Their very existence functions as a justification for imperialist domination of the 'wilderness' and the efforts of the heroes who guarantee 'our' safety from such savagery.

However, while Doyle defines the Andaman islanders as intractable, most imperialist adventure stories suggest that savages are capable of learning orderliness and decency and are greatly benefited by doing so. Imperialism is thus presented as an altruistic enterprise: the natives are in need of salvation from the chaos and moral darkness in which they are lost. This salvation is to be achieved partly by the imposition of orderly government and European social practices, but above and beyond that it is to be achieved by the introduction of Christianity, and the opportunity to spread the true faith is an additional justification for colonialism. Crusoe first teaches Friday to refrain from eating human flesh and to perform useful work, but then sets about his religious education. Friday proves an apt pupil and after some time Crusoe is able to declare that: 'The savage was now a good Christian, a much better than I' (Defoe [1719] 1981: 220). So the dual programme for the reclamation of benighted souls and the extension of European power is established in what is essentially the archetypal text of children's literature.

In many popular nineteenth-century children's adventure tales the conversion of cannibals to Christianity is easily achieved. The superiority of white culture and white religion is presented as so absolute that no savages could fail to see it and to welcome the light when it shines upon them. In Gordon Stables' *Stanley Graham*, the white heroes confront African savages such as:

> the terrible Makalala – sometimes called Makula-men, whose motto is 'war', constant war with every race they come in contact with, and who, horrible to say, capture victims but to kill them, and rear slaves only to minister to human sacrifices.
>
> (Stables, n.d.: 297)

But even people like these are easily converted by the beautiful white girl Ida who lives imprisoned, with her elderly father, on an island in a lake where she is served by a small household of native retainers. In the four or five years of her captivity she has taught these fortunate few simple English, provided them with English names, converted them to Christianity, and inspired them with such loyal devotion that they fight to the death for her, against their own people, when the inevitable climax comes:

> Ida ran rapidly over the names of the eight men who lived in the island garden with them. English names every one of them, though they were black men, savages. Nay, not now, for Ida had not left them in their darkness all these years. She had taught them to pray, and though books were things unknown in these regions, Captain Ross and Ida every morning and evening gathered them together and told them tales, and one tale that they all delighted most to listen to was the Gospel tale – the story of the cross. There were in addition to these men, or boys, as

Captain Ross called them, three female servants, one a grey-haired negress who took quite an interest in her 'dear chile Idee', as she called our heroine.

'Trust them, father! Yes, they would die for us.'

(Stables, n.d.: 304)

The link between the signifiers 'black' and 'darkness' in this passage illustrates the inextricable overlapping of the related dualisms which structure the values at the heart of our culture. 'Black' refers to both the actual colour of the Africans' skin and to intellectual and moral 'darkness'. It further implies that such ignorance and moral benightedness are consequences of blackness, conditions which can be rectified only by the intervention of educated and enlightened whites. So the ambiguities of the language itself are used to signify the benevolence of the imperialist enterprise. There is, of course, no suggestion that the denial of these people's very identities along with an absolute devaluation of their culture could be anything but beneficial to them.

Ida's activities suggest idealized accounts of the work of missionaries, and in *The Coral Island* the wondrous effects of missionaries on the savage and lawless natives is a major theme. Ralph, the narrator, several times reports the testimony of a 'good' pirate on this point: 'I know that when any o' the islands chance to get it [the Gospel], trade goes all smooth and easy; but where they ha'n't got it, Beelzebub himself could hardly desire better company' (Ballantyne [1857] 1953: 209). 'I never cared for Christianity myself . . . but a man with half an eye can see what it does for these black critters' (p. 215). 'It's a curious fact, that whenever the missionaries get a footin' all these things [cannibalism and savage practices] come to an end at once, an' the savages take to doing each other good, and singin' psalms, just like the Methodists' (p. 224). Ralph prompts the reader's response saying: 'God bless the missionaries!' He gains first-hand evidence of these reports when they visit a tribe who were converted to Christianity a year earlier. Within that space of time a wonderful transformation has occurred: the natives who had previously practised 'the most cruel system of idolatry' (p. 274) have built a Christian church large enough to accommodate 2,000 people, adopted an approximation of European dress, learned to labour diligently at taro growing and cloth manufacture, and created an English-like village, 'perfectly straight', with a wide road down the middle and little cottages with gardens and pebbled walks in front. The natives themselves are still black externally but their cottages, which have been plastered with lime made from coral, are white. In essence the savages have become whiter as they have adopted European manners and morals and the beginnings of European economic behaviour. *The Coral Island* and stories like it suggest that it is not necessary to destroy the savages or to subdue them by military might: their wildness can be modified. They can be assimilated into the order of the Western world.

Ariel Dorfman's analysis of Jean De Brunhoff's Babar books (Dorfman

1983: 17–64) shows how these charming picture books for very small children, first published in France in the 1930s but now amongst the best-known works of children's literature, convey similar meanings in what appear to be guileless stories about a small elephant/child's gaining admission to the world of adult culture. *The Story of Babar the Little Elephant* [1934], the first book in the series, is, on the surface, a very juvenile form of the *bildungsroman* – the hero story as the tale of growing up and making one's way in the world. Babar is a small elephant who lives in an unspecified (but obviously African) jungle where he plays on all fours in animal, or childlike, innocence. When his mother is shot by a cruel hunter he flees to an unnamed (but obviously Parisian) city. There he encounters a rich and kindly Old Lady, a substitute mother, who gives him money and everything he wants. The first thing he does is to buy some smart European clothes. When he puts them on he stands upright and begins to behave like a European, or an adult. He dines with the Old Lady at a formal dinner table, drinking red wine from a glass which he holds carefully with his trunk, sleeps in a bed and bathes in a bath with a sponge. The Old Lady buys him a motor car, and a learned professor gives him lessons. Soon he is able to take his place at evening parties, in elegant evening dress, and converse politely with the Old Lady's friends.

When Babar's two little elephant cousins, Arthur and Celeste, come to the city to seek him out he buys them some 'lovely clothes' ([1934] 1955: 26) and takes them to a tea shop for 'some delicious cakes' (p. 27), thus passing on the civilization he has acquired. He decides to return to the jungle with them and they depart, fully clothed, in his car. When they arrive in the land of the elephants they are greeted with enthusiasm. The elephants, all walking on four feet, cry: 'What lovely clothes! What a beautiful car!' (p. 36). They have arrived at an opportune moment for the king of the elephants has just died, and the oldest elephant, Cornelius, advises the others to make Babar their new king because: 'He has come back from the town, where he has lived among men and learnt much' (p. 38). They agree and Babar accepts the offer on condition that Celeste, whom he has decided to marry, is made queen. Babar sends to the city for grand wedding and coronation clothes. The story ends with a joyous celebration with the royally clothed Babar and Celeste dancing among the other elephants who are naked but who are shown as now standing on two feet instead of four.

Babar, originally an inhabitant of the wilderness, has learned the ways of civilization and become its emissary, the hero who, like the missionaries in *The Coral Island*, brings enlightenment to the elephants/savages of Africa, who recognize its benefits immediately and voluntarily begin to adopt the ways of the 'city'. In subsequent books Babar establishes a European-like city, Celesteville, in the land of the elephants and the civilization of the wilderness proceeds apace. When these books were being written the French colonies in Africa had not achieved independence, and the Babar stories represent a dream of painless domination and transmutation. The actual horrors of the early history of the 'jungle' – the French Congo, the Ivory Coast, Dahomey – have vanished, and the happy elephants look towards their enlightened future with joy. Edward Said writes that, while the French acquisition of empire was motivated no less than the British by the desire for profit, plantations and slaves, it was also energized by 'prestige' (Said [1993] 1994: 204). The French believed that theirs was a *vocation superieure*, a *mission civilisatrice*. Said quotes from the opening address to the second international congress of geographical sciences, attended by the President of the Republic, in 1875: '"Gentlemen, providence has dictated to us the obligation of knowing the earth and making the conquest of it. This supreme command is one of the imperious duties inscribed on our intelligences and on our activities"' (p. 205).

The Babar books represent the vision achieved. As Dorfman says: 'the reader is being handed an easy-to-grasp, easy-to-swallow historical version of the incorporation of Africa (and, by analogy, that of other out-of-the-mainstream continents, namely Latin America and Asia) into the contemporary world' (Dorfman 1983: 23). The story is compelling for children because of the parallels it draws between childhood and primitivism, adulthood and civilization. By showing the colonization and 'civilizing' of the elephants/natives as the process of learning adult ways it naturalizes imperialism; it seems self-evident that countries, like people, must go through different stages of development and that primitive countries, like young children, need to be educated by those which are already civilized:

> This superimposition of the individual on the social, of the biological on the historical, is at the heart of the way that books like Babar educate children . . . The stages of colonial penetration, the stages in which the native assumes Western norms as his models, are felt by the reader to be the stages of his own socialization.
>
> (Dorfman 1983: 43–4)

In the second of De Brunhoff's books, *Babar's Travels* [1935], a distinction is drawn between 'good' savages, who are capable of learning civilized ways and happy to do so, and 'bad' savages who are irredeemably wild and inferior. In this story Babar and Celeste set off for their honeymoon in a hot air balloon but are blown off course and land on an island where, Crusoe-like, they try to establish as much civilized order as possible. While Babar is exploring the island Celeste has a nap after lunch and is captured by cannibals. These cannibals are drawn as black, African-like human beings, naked except for red skirts made from leaves. They are armed with spears and bows and arrows, they carry shields decorated with 'African' designs, and they are clearly more ferocious and less civilized than the elephants. Babar returns just in time to save Celeste from death. He attacks the cannibals heroically and triumphs over them.

The distinction is repeated in the second part of the story where the role of the unreformed savages is taken by the rhinoceroses who make war on the elephants for no good reason. They ravage the land, destroying the trees of the Great Forest. (Thus the degradation of the environment is blamed not on the colonizers but on the indigenous inhabitants.) While this is happening Babar and Celeste have fallen into the hands of a circus manager who makes them perform for the public, but when the circus visits the city they escape and go to the Old Lady for help. They all return to the land of the elephants and the Old Lady acts as nurse to the elephants who have been wounded by the rhinoceroses. A final battle ensues in which the elephants are victorious because Babar devises a stratagem which deceives the rhinoceroses: he camouflages the elephants' rear ends by painting enormous round eyes on them and topping them with red and green hair. When the rhinoceroses attack they are confronted by the elephants' rumps and think they are 'faced by monsters' (De Brunhoff [1935] 1953: 45). Panic-stricken, they flee in confusion and their leaders are captured. Thus reason is victorious over savagery, over brutishness, and over childishness. Babar, in a smart blue suit and white waistcoat, an elegant Parisian, is carried shoulder high in triumph. Clearly there is no place in the emerging world order for recalcitrant savages.

Dorfman points out the symbolic importance of the Old Lady in these stories. At the end of *Babar's Travels* she is formally rewarded for her work tending the wounded and she accepts her honour clothed in a white nun's habit. This suggests the missionary spirit, but she also acts as a teacher and surrogate mother figure among the elephants. She spreads the light of the metropolis, fount and source of all that is good, to all her 'children' and 'foundlings' (Dorfman 1983: 37–8).

Just as the concepts of childhood and primitivism are superimposed on Babar and the elephants, so the Old Lady simultaneously represents motherhood, selfless virtue and French civilization. It is thus impossible for the reader not to conclude that what she bestows upon the elephants/savages is of inestimable worth. And in the later books in the series, such as *Babar at Home* [1938] we see her gift in its full flowering. Celesteville has become an orderly and elegant city in the French style. There is a royal palace with gilded wrought iron railings, a well-laid-out park and a fort manned by the King's Artillery who wear red military jackets with gold epaulettes. The elephant citizens who throng its prosperous spaces wear smart French clothes – well-cut overcoats, top hats, homburgs and berets, fur collars and dashing floral chapeaux. All walk upright on two legs. The savages have been assimilated, the *mission civilisatrice* accomplished.

The story of the white hero's subjugation and salvation of the savages, which justified European imperialism, remained popular for over three hundred years, from Shakespeare to Ballantyne, De Brunhoff and beyond, but since World War II, British and European imperialism has been everywhere in retreat. Though it has been succeeded in many ways by the American hegemony and by economic colonization, many formerly-subject peoples are beginning to recover a sense of identity by telling their own stories, and by retelling some of the European stories which inscribed their subjection. Edward Said instances modern Caribbean versions of *The Tempest* as attempts to reclaim authority over their own region. ('Cannibal', of which 'Caliban' is usually considered a variation, is derived from the Spanish *Caribe*):

> The core of Aimé Césaire's Caribbean *Une Tempête* is not *ressentiment*, but an affectionate contention with Shakespeare for the right to represent the Caribbean. That impulse to contend is part of a grander effort to discover the bases of an integral identity different from the formerly dependent, derivative one . . . Caliban must be shown to have a history which can be perceived on its own, as the result of Caliban's own effort.
>
> (Said [1993] 1994: 256–7)

I recall being startled into awareness when, in 1980, I first heard an Aboriginal story-teller describe the arrival of the First Fleet in Sydney Harbour from the perspective of the local Eora tribe. Like all white Australians I had grown up with the story of how those first British settlers, from Captain Arthur Phillip and his officers to the unfortunate convicts, their understandings shaped by life in the towns and settled countryside of Georgian England, had perceived the Australian land and its people as disturbingly 'other', the bush full of alien trees, monotonously grey-green, the soil sandy and infertile, the light harsh, the people primitive, naked and dirty. As I listened I learned to see the white-skinned British in their complex clothes, so unsuited to the climate, with their guns and paraphernalia and their huge ships which appeared to be monstrous sea birds, as terrifying visitants, inexplicable invaders whose origins could not be imagined. If meaning depends upon *différance*, as both Saussure and the deconstructionists have shown, then the concepts of 'savage' and 'civilized' can have meaning only in relation to each other, but those meanings are shifting and unstable, dependent upon the viewpoints of the narrator, the protagonist and antagonists, and the reader or audience.

So have the savages disappeared from Western hero stories in this post-colonial and postmodern period? Has the myth which inscribed the innate superiority of Europeans been abandoned or has it merely acquired some post-colonial clothes? Science fiction and fantasy stories are amongst the most popular contemporary entertainments for adults and children and in their imagined fields mutations of the cannibals roam. There intrepid representatives of the European patriarchy confront an endless variety of beings who share many of the characteristics of the early savages, especially uncompromising aggression and an insatiable desire to destroy their opponents. *Doctor Who*, the longest running television serial (transmuted in 1996 into a slick American tele-movie), and arguably the best-known and most influential of all science fiction hero tales, endlessly repeats the confrontation between the Doctor, the rational, humane and rather dandyish embodiment of all the best qualities of Western culture, and one or another tribe of evil opponents. Just as the heroes of stories like *The Coral Island* ventured into the wild regions of our planet and did their best to impose some civilized decency while struggling to survive against a variety of dangers, so Doctor Who roams the wilds of our galaxy on a similar mission.

The cybermen, mechanical creatures who inhabit a distant planet called Telos, are typical of his antagonists. Originally human they perfected the art of cybernetics, gradually replacing every part of their human bodies with plastic and steel, and finally replacing brains with computers. They are thus immortal but devoid of feelings:

> They lived by the inexorable laws of pure logic. Love, hate, anger, even fear, were eliminated from their lives when the last flesh was replaced by plastic.
>
> They achieved their immortality at a terrible price. They became dehumanised monsters. And, like human monsters down through all the ages of Earth, they became aware of the lack of love and feeling in their lives and substituted another goal – power!
>
> (Davis 1974: 7)

The overt meaning here is that reason is not enough and emotion is essential for both humanity and real understanding, but the cybermen's ruthless drive for power is a basic instinct entirely comparable to the ruthless aggression attributed to the cannibals of earlier texts. And, of course, there is nothing inherently logical about desiring power; it is a lust like any other. The cybermen resemble the cannibals in several ways: they kill without a qualm, their behaviour is militaristic and, although their bodies are silver, being made of metal, their leader wears a black helmet. As they prepare to attack the Doctor and his friends in their small base on the moon the text itself invokes the comparison with nineteenth-century conflicts between black and white. Watching their slow advance Doctor Who says: 'this march towards the base is probably a show of strength, to scare us the way the Zulus used to intimidate their enemies with their famous slow march' (p. 117).

The Doctor and the other representatives of Earth (all of whom have European names: Hobson, Benoit, Jamie, Nils, Sam) are, of course, victorious. They employ an instrument called the Gravitron in their defence, and the cybermen, robbed of gravity, float off into space. The closure, which is repeated with minor variations in every adventure in the series, demonstrates that the Doctor and his friends are rationally as well as morally superior to the cybermen, despite the latter's computerized brains. If eighteenth- and nineteenth-century hero tales inscribed the superiority of Europeans to all other races on the planet, *Doctor Who* reassures its readers and viewers that they are the moral and rational lords of the universe.

Tolkien's hugely influential fantasy *The Lord of the Rings* likewise establishes a confrontation between the European-like heroes and a race of dark, savage and evil opponents, the Orcs, servants of the dark lord, Sauron. The conflict between good and evil is the explicit theme of this work, but the pattern of subordinate binary oppositions reveals its inherent racist and classist ideology. Mapped onto the primary good/evil dualism are the oppositions of white/black, aristocratic/common, European/foreign. The heroes and their supporters, essentially European in appearance and manners, use formal and at times slightly archaic language, their sentences given an aura of dignity by occasional grammatical inversions: '"To that the Elves know not the answer," said Legolas' (Tolkien 1955: 149). The Orcs' speech is more colourful and more loosely structured, suggesting creatures who are less educated, less intelligent and less courteous: '"Curse you, Snaga, you little maggot! If you think I'm so damaged that it's safe to flout me, you're mistaken. Come here, and I'll squeeze your eyes out, like I did to Radbug just now. And when some new lads come, I'll deal with you: I'll send you to Shelob"' (pp. 181–2).

The suggestion of racial difference is given weight by Tolkien's invented languages, phrases of which are used throughout the text. The 'good' peoples' languages are based on various European tongues. The Riders of Rohan speak in something very close to Old English; Elvish has a Celtic quality; the hobbits use the Common Speech which is rendered in modern English. But the language of the Orcs, the 'Black Speech', looks very different from English (and from romance languages) because of its un-English morphemes, especially the frequent 'uk' and 'zg'. Tolkien says of this language:

> It is said they had no language of their own, but took what they could of other tongues and perverted it to their own liking; yet they made only brutal jargons, scarcely sufficient even for their own needs, unless it were for curses or abuse. And these creatures being filled with malice, hating even their own kind, quickly developed as many Barbarous dialects as there were groups or settlements of their race, so that their Orkish speech was of little use to them in intercourse between different tribes. So it was that in the Third Age Orcs used for communication between breed and breed the Westron tongue . . .
>
> (Tolkien: 1955: 409)

With its references to 'race', 'tribes', 'breed' and 'jargon' this sounds very like a dismissive colonialist view of the inferior languages of 'lesser breeds without the law' who can communicate with each other only by using English, the superior language of their conquerors.

The success of Tolkien's work has prompted numerous other fantasy sagas turning upon similar oppositions, and the fantasies have in turn provided the inspiration for many contemporary computer games in which both the violence and the starkness of the oppositions are heightened. One of the currently most popular games, 'Doom' is described on its package as follows:

> This time the entire forces of the netherworld have overrun Earth. To save her you must descend into the stygian depths of Hell itself. Battle mightier, nastier, deadlier demons and monsters. Use more powerful

weapons. Survive more mind-blowing explosions and more of the bloodiest, fiercest, most awesome blastfest ever!

(ID Software inc, GT Interactive Software)

'Flashback' (1992–1994, Delphine Software), a mild example of its kind, features a 'cool dude' white American hero called Conrad Hart who carries a gun with which the player must make him destroy a variety of opponents. These include aliens and primitive-looking, near-naked forest dwellers. The aim of the aliens is to invade Earth and Conrad's quest is to prevent them by destroying them.

So the savages and their heroic opponents are loose in cyberspace, and the dualisms which define the superiority and naturalize the dominance of the European patriarchy continue to find popular expression. In these games the player enters the action and so actually 'becomes' the hero; there is not even the minor distancing provided by the narrative voice of a written or spoken story, or the possibility of detachment which exists for the audience of a play or film. In these stories and games it is not merely the behaviour of the savages, the cybermen, the Orcs and their like which is condemned, it is their very natures. And 'we', the heroes with whose perspective the readers, viewers and game-players are required to identify, are defined as correspondingly superior simply because we are who we are. The relative nature of terms such as 'superior' and 'inferior', 'civilized' and 'savage,' the dependence of meaning upon point of view, is denied by the rigid perspective of the story which, in whatever form it is experienced, implies the existence of *innately* superior and inferior people. This is the false logic that makes possible the gas chambers, the My Lai massacre, the routine brutalities which black and indigenous peoples have suffered at the hands of their white masters everywhere.

## PIRATES, CRIMINALS AND SPIES: 'WHITE SAVAGES'

The ambiguous significance of the hero and his wild opponents is most apparent in stories in which the hero or his adversaries, or both, are lawbreakers, or at least hostile to the social establishment. When read deconstructively these stories suggest the arbitrariness of many laws and the relativism of concepts of right and wrong, for the behaviour of the hero, when examined objectively, is frequently little different from that of his opponents. Often the definition of right and wrong seems to be merely a matter of the point of view from which the story is told. Just as the hero in old Hollywood westerns wore a white hat to distinguish him from his black-hatted enemy whom, in every other way, he closely resembled, so it is often simply his role as the protagonist in these stories which labels the hero as good. The circumstances which have made the criminals what they are, or the values which label and reward the hero, are not examined.

The development of relatively effective law enforcement agencies in the nineteenth and twentieth centuries saw the emergence of the detective and the intelligence agent as mutations of the hero and the corollary of this was the definition of criminals of various kinds as the hero's opponents – wild things threatening the good order of society, vermin needing to be eradicated. The essential purpose of social regulation was to protect the power and property of the patriarchal elite and facilitate those activities, such as trade and imperialistic expansion, which supported their wealth and dominance. Both individuals and groups whose background or poverty denied them the opportunity to participate in the activities of the patriarchy and who tried to function outside the system of legal regulation were therefore defined as criminal. Smugglers, pirates, gypsies, prostitutes and others whose attempts to make a living were not sanctioned by the system, as well as thieves, pickpockets, highwaymen and other predators were so defined, and the poor whose economic position was marginal could easily find themselves on the wrong side of the law. While some of these people were undoubtedly cruel and irresponsible and some psychopathic, many were no more than the helpless victims of an unjust society as contemporary works of social criticism such as Dickens' *Great Expectations* attempted to show.

In hero stories, however, criminals who are perceived as threatening the establishment are not analysed but condemned. While Dickens, in *Great Expectations*, shows how the homelessness and poverty into which Magwitch was born made it inevitable that he would break society's laws and then become a scapegoat for the injustices which made him a criminal, the behaviour of Conan Doyle's criminals is not explained in any social or psychological context. They are presented as innately wicked, agents controlling their own destiny who have voluntarily chosen to perpetrate their crimes for personal gain. Stapleton in *The Hound of the Baskervilles* [1901–2], for instance, is described as a 'clever criminal [who] may be too confident in his own cleverness' (Doyle 1987: 322). The stories construct the concept of criminals who belong to a different category from the rest of us, creatures who are naturally 'wild', whose existence is a threat to the good order of society and who must, therefore, be put down. The ultimate example of this type in the Holmes stories is, of course, Professor Moriarty, whose intellectual brilliance supposedly makes him a worthy opponent for the great detective who, in *The Valley of Fear* [1914–15], describes him as: 'The greatest schemer of all time, the organizer of every devilry, the controlling brain of the underworld – a brain which might have made or marred the destiny of nations' (Doyle 1987: 355).

By setting up the binary opposition of hero and criminal and stressing the separation between them these stories are simultaneously reassuring and disturbing. By splitting off the dark side of the psyche and reconstituting it as a separate being they reassure their readers that they belong comfortably to the class of the non-criminal, that they do not have the capacity to commit a crime. (In contrast to these stories a work like Camus' *The Outsider* is disturbing because of the very ordinariness of the protagonist and killer.) On the other hand, by postulating the existence of a category of criminals who do not share society's ordinary moral assumptions, the Holmes stories imply that we are constantly at risk from the predatory actions of these malevolent and irrational creatures. This dualism underlies much popular present-day journalism which simultaneously excites and frightens its readers by reporting the deeds of serial killers, mass murderers, child abductors and their like as though they are a different species who lurk all around us in the interstices of respectable society, likely to strike anyone at any time.

Criminals in adventure stories which condemn them as wild things are often guilty of no worse deeds, by conventional standards, than the heroes but they are seen from the hero's point of view and the inferior terms of the basic dualities are attributed to them. They are depicted as uncivilized, irrational, governed by uncontrollable drives and passions, animal-like. In Ballantyne's *Coral Island* the narrator, Ralph, refers to the pirates whom he falls among as 'white savages' (Ballantyne [1857] 1953: 191), equating them to the bloodthirsty cannibals whose behaviour has already been described. The pirates in Stevenson's *Treasure Island* are similarly defined but with much more colour and bravura. The contrast between the 'gentlemen' heroes and the pirates is presented to the reader in the opening chapter when Jim Hawkins, the young narrator, contemplates the visual differences between Doctor Livesey and Billy Bones, the pirate whose treasure map is the catalyst of the adventure:

> I remember observing the contrast the neat, bright doctor, with his powder as white as snow, and his bright, black eyes and pleasant manners, made with . . . that filthy, heavy bleared scarecrow of a pirate of ours, sitting far gone in rum, with his arms on the table.
>
> (Stevenson [1883] 1946: 5–6)

Some of the constituent elements of the central binary opposition are established here: gentlemen are neat, sober and well-mannered; pirates are filthy, drunken and ignorant of nice manners. Other elements of the opposition emerge as the story progresses. With the exception of Silver, the pirates are depicted as lacking in emotional control and unable to act on the basis of reason. In the speech which Jim overhears from the apple barrel Silver laments the fact that the pirates would not have enough self-control to wait until the others had collected the treasure and steered them well on their way home before attacking them. This would clearly be the most intelligent plan, 'but', he says, 'I know the sort you are' (p. 69). Their irrationality and lack of self control is demonstrated on the island where their chances of defeating the 'gentlemen' and gaining the treasure for themselves depend absolutely on remaining sober and alert. They are unable to appreciate this, and give themselves up to rum and carousing (p. 119).

The term 'gentlemen' recurs at crucial points in the narrative to underline the distinction: when Jim realizes that what he has in his possession is a pirate's treasure map he determines to show it to Doctor Livesey because he is 'a gentleman and a magistrate' (p. 34); after the apple barrel incident where Jim learns that Silver and many other members of the crew are indeed pirates, the squire, Doctor Livesey and Captain Smollett are differentiated from them by being described as 'the three gentlemen' (p. 76); Silver himself says that he knows Captain Smollett will not break their bargain (although the pirates might) because Smollett is a 'gentleman' (p. 122), and when he is demanding his word of honour from Jim he describes him as 'a young gentleman . . . though poor born' (p. 193). These gentlemen are representatives of the British establishment in particular and of the patriarchy in general. The story permits no questioning of their moral authority, but when their motives and deeds are examined it is difficult to see them as noticeably more virtuous than the pirates.

The object of their quest is the pirate gold, and they seek it for their personal enrichment. Trelawney, already a wealthy man, says: 'We'll have favourable winds, a quick passage, and not the least difficulty in finding the spot, and money to eat – to roll in – to play duck and drake with ever after' (p. 40). Both pirates and gentlemen lust after the gold and both are prepared to engage in killing in order to acquire it. Even such an admirer of the book as John Rowe Townsend concedes, in *Written For Children*, that 'Our side, Squire Trelawney, Dr. Livesey and the rest – is not particularly in the right' (Townsend [1965] 1976: 66). He contends, however, that Stevenson engages in a refreshing blurring of 'the usual black-and-white of right and wrong', (p. 66), but in fact a whole range of black and white signifiers is attached to the respective groups, and Jim's first person narrative is vigorously employed to underline the virtue of the gentlemen and the wickedness of the pirates. The pirates are referred to by such terms as 'treacherous demons' (Stevenson [1883] 1946: 191), 'rogues' (p. 192), 'wicked' (p. 189), 'like monkeys' (p. 130), while their opponents are described again and again as 'honest' (e.g. pp. 65, 68, 83), 'brave' (p. 88) and 'faithful' (p. 133). A striking instance of the use of the animal/human duality to condemn the pirates is Doctor Livesey's description of the killing of the pirate, Pew, as 'an act of virtue, sir, like stamping on a cockroach' (p. 36).

Because the story is narrated in the first person (by Jim and Doctor Livesey) the pirates are seen only through the eyes of their opponents. A comparison of Jim's account of the first murder committed by the pirates' leader, Silver, with Doctor Livesey's account of Squire Trelawney's first shooting of a pirate makes clear the effect of this perspective. Silver's killing of the honest hand, Tom, is given in extreme close-up, so much so that Jim 'could hear him pant aloud as he struck the blows' (p. 88) and see him twice bury his knife in Tom's body. The reader is made to experience a sense of the physical actuality of the deed. The death of the pirate whom Trelawney shoots, however, is observed from a desensitizing distance; Livesey simply notes that the shot misses Hands and another man falls instead. Silver's killing of Tom is described in highly emotive language which stresses the 'monstrousness' of the action: Tom is a 'brave fellow', 'poor Tom', 'defenceless'; he is struck with 'stunning violence' and

Silver is 'agile as a monkey' and a 'monster' who cleanses his 'blood-stained knife' upon the grass (pp. 88–9). Trelawney's action, on the other hand, is recounted in bland, objective terms except for the observation that he was 'as cool as steel' (p. 106).

Finally, the responses of Jim and Livesey to the respective murders are used to define the one as a deed of horror and the other as a straightforward and dutiful action, though each is committed for the same reason – to reduce the numbers in the opposing camp. Jim is so appalled by Silver's deed that his sense of reality is turned upside down; he faints for the first time in his life: 'the whole world swam away from before me in a whirling mist; Silver and the birds, and the tall Spy-glass hill-top, going round and round and topsy-turvy before my eyes' (p. 89). On the other hand, Livesey is so unaffected by Trelawney's action that he continues to keep a sharp look-out and draws brisk attention to the other pirates who are climbing into the gigs (p. 106). The reader has no access to the perspective of the pirates who exist only as the opponents of the gentlemen.

The structure of the story further reinforces the distinction between the 'goodness' of the gentlemen and the 'evil' of the pirates, and makes clear what these signifiers mean in this text. Though the pirates' desire for the gold is the original motivating force of the story, at each critical juncture thereafter it is the desire of the gentlemen which determines the direction of the action: Jim's taking of the packet of papers from Bones' chest, Trelawney's decision to hire a ship and go in quest of the treasure, Smollett's decision about where to store the guns and ammunition, their decision to fortify the stockade, their decision to give Silver the map once they know that Ben Gunn has moved the treasure, and so on. It is only in very minor ways that the pirates influence the movement of events. The gentlemen are in control because, in the world of *Treasure Island*, that is in the nature of things. The point of closure, the moment when the pirates behold the great excavation from which the treasure has been taken, underlines the relationship between the haves and the have-nots. The gentlemen actually have no more legal or moral right to the treasure than the pirates do; they have taken possession of it simply as a prerogative of their class. And, although the gold is worth 700,000 pounds, they give Ben Gunn only 1,000 pounds even though they could not have acquired it without his help. Because he is an ex-pirate, not a gentleman, he is not considered worthy of a fair share. (The careful notations in Billy Bones's note-book of the portions he has been allocated from other treasures suggest that the pirates would have made a more equitable division.)

Throughout the story the gentlemen identify strongly with law and sovereignty, even when they are behaving most lawlessly: when they fortify the stockade and use it as a base from which to shoot the pirates, they run up the British flag (p. 111) and behave as though they are fighting in the service of their sovereign. Nor do they ever consider that they might be punishable at law for the killings they have perpetrated, though the pirates live in constant fear of hanging; even Silver says 'I've the shakes upon me for the gallows' (p. 194). The gentlemen have no fear of the law because they embody and administer it. So Livesey, who is magistrate as well as doctor, tends the pirates' ills and announces cheerfully that he makes it a point of honour 'not to lose a man for King George (God bless him!) and the gallows' (p. 191). The order of the world from which the gentlemen come, and to which they return, is not a moral or intellectual order at all but simply one of institutionalized privilege and power – the class structure of English society; and the primary signification of 'good' in this book is: belonging to the social class of gentlemen and exhibiting certain behavioural characteristics pertaining to that class, such as dressing neatly and keeping one's word. Conversely the significance of 'evil' relates not so much to the deeds of the pirates which are little different from those of the gentlemen, but to their position outside respectable society.

Despite the increasing effectiveness of the forces of law and order, social inequality and the oppressive nature of many aspects of the legal system in the eighteenth and nineteenth centuries meant that colourful opponents of the law often came to be seen as heroes of the people, fighters against injustice. Famous highwaymen were cheered by huge crowds on their way to be hanged at Tyburn, and in Australia bushrangers such as Ned Kelly were extensively mythologized. Stories written from the point of view of such figures reverse the hero/criminal opposition, casting the law enforcers as brutal oppressors and setting up a hierarchy of moral values which transcends the legal rules of the period and establishes the hero as superior to his adversaries, even though he might be officially a criminal. Popular versions of the legend of Robin Hood, the earliest criminal-hero of the people, set up generosity and a concern for the poor as defining virtues and attribute these behaviours to Robin while depicting Prince John, Guy of Gisborne and the Sheriff of Nottingham as ruthlessly extortionate. Likewise Alfred Noyes' poem 'The Highwayman' [1913], for many years a staple of high-school English curricula, sets up romantic love and loyalty as the overriding virtues, so that the highwayman, who dies for love of the woman who has died for him, is seen as morally superior to the heartless troopers even though he is an active robber who is 'after a prize.' [All quotations are from the 1983 Oxford Softcover edition of the poem, illustrated by Charles Keeping.]

No attempt is made to justify the highwayman's career of crime which is relegated to the background of the tale. His heroic status is implicit in the passionate sacrifices which the story foregrounds and the suggestion of his superiority is enhanced by the description of his dandified clothing which marks him, like the matador, as a symbol of civilized elegance:

> He'd a French cocked-hat on his forehead, a bunch of lace at his chin,
> A coat of the claret velvet, and breeches of brown doe-skin.

When he is shot down 'like a dog on the highway' the bunch of lace at his throat is again mentioned, implying that, though the troopers' bullets have found their mark, they have failed to reduce him to the level of a mere animal and, even in death, he remains their superior, the essence of elegant humanity. His ghostly survival further underlines this meaning. In this the poem is similar to A.B. Paterson's 'Waltzing Matilda', Australia's unofficial national song, which celebrates an outback swagman and sheep thief who defied the state troopers by drowning himself in a billabong rather than surrendering. The swagman also survives as a ghost and a symbol of the individual's stand against unjust authority.

These stories are popular expressions of Romanticism, of the valuing of individualism above the limiting structures of society, and of passion, energy and courage above the sterile rationalism of law enforcement agencies which represent the interests of the establishment, and they demonstrate the relative nature of the terms 'good' and 'evil'. The instability of these signifiers was, of course, not a discovery of the deconstructionists. Shakespeare focuses attention on the issue in *King Lear* where one of the causes of Lear's despair on Dover Beach is his recognition, after a long lifetime of moral certainty, that such terms, as they are commonly used, are frequently meaningless:

> see how yond justice rails upon yond simple thief. Hark in thine
> ear: change places, and, handy-dandy, which is the justice, which
> is the thief? Thou hast seen a farmer's dog bark at a beggar?
>
> . . .
>
> And the creature run from the cur? There thou might'st behold
> The great image of Authority:
> A dog's obey'd in office.
> Thou rascal beadle, hold thy bloody hand!
> Why dost thou lash that whore? Strip thine own back;
> Thou hotly lusts to use her in that kind
> For which thou whipp'st her.
>
> (IV, vi, 149–61)

*King Lear* is a painful and unflinching investigation of human behaviour and of the possible meanings of 'good' and 'evil'. It attacks the audience's comfortable preconceptions relentlessly as Lear's own arrogant certainties are destroyed. But *Treasure Island*, one of the most widely read and influential of all children's books, is content with a casual employment of the conventional assumptions about law and order. For all its liveliness and colour the world of Stevenson's classic is chilling and repellent, a place of violence, materialism and rampant self-interest, which admits no challenge of any kind to the social and psychological dominance of the patriarchal elite, and no pity for the underclass of an inequitable society. Nor does it acknowledge the possibility of any other system of moral values in the light of which the reader might question the behaviour of the leading figures. The concepts of good and evil are subordinated to the overarching significance of social power and position, and in this it is typical of many children's adventure stories.

## OGRES, DARKNESS AND SHADOWS

Stevenson's pirates carry a degree of imaginative conviction because, at one level, they are creatures of the unconscious. This is vividly suggested in the opening chapters when they enter the daylight world of the well-kept Admiral Benbow Inn, one by one, like maggots emerging from some hidden putrescence. They are strange, deformed, dark and terrifying in their various ways: Bones is 'tall, strong . . . his hands ragged and scarred, with black, broken nails; and the sabre cut across one cheek, a dirty, livid white' (Stevenson 1946: 1); Black Dog is 'a pale, tallowy creature, wanting two fingers of the left hand (p. 8); Blind Pew is 'hunched, as if with age or weakness, and wore a huge old tattered sea-cloak with a hood, that made him appear positively deformed' (p. 19) and is a 'horrible, soft-spoken, eyeless creature' (p. 19). Their names are suggestive of nightmare and Jim says that Bones's description of the seafaring man with one leg 'haunted my dreams' and was 'the worst of nightmares' (p. 3). The journey to the island which has 'a kind of poisonous brightness' (p. 81) that Doctor Livesey associates with fever, is a journey into that nightmare, the human potential for violence and horror. One of the meanings this story imposes on the reader is the need to suppress the emanations of the unconscious, to deny the human capacity for the irrational, and to live according to the clear light of rational certainty, the vision of neat, bright Doctor Livesey.

The ogres in folk tales and children's stories have a similar psychological significance. Freudian critics see the ogre figures in hero tales as always in part embodiments of the (male) child's fear and resentment of the father. For Joseph Campbell the punitive aspect of God the Father is itself a projection of this fear and is likewise present in the threatening figures of the tales:

> the ogre aspect of the father is a reflex of the victim's own ego – derived from the sensational nursery scene that has been left behind, but projected before; and the fixating idolatry of that pedagogical nonthing is itself the fault that keeps one steeped in a sense of sin, sealing the potentially adult spirit from a better balanced, more realistic view of the father, and therewith of the world. Atonement (at-one-ment) consists in no more than the abandonment of that self-generated double monster – the dragon thought to be God (superego) and the dragon thought to be Sin (repressed id).
>
> (Campbell 1968: 129–30)

It is not necessary to share Campbell's view of the myth as ultimately beneficent to agree with much of his interpretation of figures like the ogre in 'Jack and the Beanstalk'. The ogre is large, powerful, frightening, and has taken over both Jack's father's wealth and his significance in Jack's life. Bettelheim describes this ogre as 'the oedipal father' (Bettelheim 1976: 190) and argues that, in cutting down the Beanstalk and killing him, Jack frees himself from a view of the father as destructive and devouring. Like Campbell he sees the story as concerned with the child's need to develop a 'correct', that is an accepting, view of the father, and of patriarchal power. A firm faith in Freud is necessary to read Jack's final act in this way. For most readers the felling of the ogre evokes a richer and less comfortable complex of personal, social and political meanings than Bettelheim allows. It certainly celebrates the assertion of youthful male energy against the entrenched power of an older generation, and at the political level it is an image of rebellion against feudal oppression, or, more generally, against unjust authority. But the story also endorses both the highly questionable means by which Jack acquires the ogre's wealth and his exploitation of the ogre's wife. The ogre does, in part, represent fears which must be confronted, but the overarching significance of this tale is the celebration of Jack's entry into the patriarchy, his joyous achievement of dominance.

Sometimes the psychological or metaphysical significance of an ogre figure is indicated by his name or by the symbolic structure of the narrative. Bunyan's Giant Despair locks Christian and Hopeful in his dungeon, where Christian toys with the idea of suicide (Bunyan [1678] 1954: 114–15). The significance of the Dark Lord, Sauron, the ultimate enemy against whom the small hero, Frodo, must struggle in Tolkien's *The Lord of the Rings*, is made unequivocal by the pattern of the story's Christian iconography. The vague powers against which Will Stanton struggles in *The Dark is Rising* are routinely called 'the Dark'. These works seek to invoke the good/evil opposition in a purely symbolic way, and generally lack the power of stories which particularize the significance of terms such as 'light' and 'dark' as Rosemary Sutcliff does in her historical novels for young readers.

In Sutcliff's stories the imagery of light and dark is employed to colour their dramatization of British history from the Bronze Age to the period after the withdrawal of the Roman legions. Her texts depict this sweep of time as a continuing conflict between the transforming forces of order and rationality, and the 'darkness' of superstition and submission to the imperatives of natural rhythms. That is, they are shaped by the civilization/wilderness dualism. In each work the protagonist is a member of a relatively complex and self-consciously ordered culture who becomes involved in a struggle against the representatives of a simpler and more primitive one. In *Warrior Scarlet*, the Bronze Age Celtic tribe to which the hero, Drem, belongs dominates the indigenous inhabitants but it is the darkness of fear and ignorance which are Drem's chief opponents. In *The Eagle of the Ninth* the Romans have established dominance over the Celtic people and built straight roads across their tribal lands, imposing order and logic upon their ancient customs. In *The Lantern Bearers* the Romans have withdrawn and the civilized ways of the Romanized Britons are threatened by the invading Jutes. In *Sword at Sunset* Artos (Arthur), a Romanized British war leader, struggles to hold back the Saxons and preserve something of the intellectual legacy of Rome. *Dawn Wind* deals with the last defeat of the Romanized

British at Aquae Sulis, three generations after the death of Artos; the despair which the hero, Owain, feels after this disaster is eventually lightened a little when he is able to envisage a future far ahead when British and Saxon together will have built a new civilization.

The symbolism of light and dark is realized not only in the events of the narratives but in scenes of actual light and dark such as the contrast between the dark interior of the Celtic holy place and the small bright flame of Marcus' glim in *The Eagle of the Ninth* (Sutcliff [1954] 1977: 211). Perhaps the most powerful and moving of these symbolic scenes is the last igniting of the beacon at Rutupiae on the night the Roman legions leave Britain forever in *The Lantern Bearers* [1959]. Aquila, a young auxiliary officer stationed at Rutupiae, decides to stay behind when the others leave, and as the galleys set sail for Rome leaving Britain in darkness, he is moved to fire the Light for the last time:

> He flung water from the tank in the corner onto the blackened bull's-hide fireshield, and crouched holding it before him by the brazier, feeding the blaze to its greatest strength. The heart of it was glowing now, a blasting, blinding core of heat and brightness under the flames; even from the shores of Gaul they would see the blaze, and say, 'Ah, there is Rutupiae's light.' It was his farewell to so many things; to the whole world that he had been bred to. But it was something more: a defiance against the dark.
>
> (Sutcliff [1959] 1972: 21)

A sense of loss and desolation pervades the novel and convinces the reader of the worth of what was lost, the rational order and certainty of 'Rome'.

Despite the poetic power of this opposition as it is constructed in these texts the dominant meanings which emerge evoke the constellation of traditional dualisms and naturalize the project of imperialism – the conquest of a more primitive people, the occupation of their land and the destruction of their culture – in the name of civilization, of spreading the light. This causes tensions in the works because the culture of the Celtic peoples is depicted sympathetically, their empathy with nature contrasted favourably with the coldness of Roman logic. Finally in a late work, *Song for a Dark Queen* [1978] Sutcliff abandons the Roman perspective and narrates the Icenian revolt of AD 61 from the point of view of the conquered people, the Celtic Iceni, led by their queen, Boudicca. The first person narrator is a Celtic bard, but his sympathetic, poetic account of Boudicca's ill-treatment by the Romans and the subsequent revolt is interspersed with imagined letters from Gneus Julius Agricola who was on the staff of the Roman governor and whose letters home reveal the Roman perspective, a dogged struggle to maintain order in the face of chaotic violence. Thus this text demonstrates the inadequacy of a simple dualistic interpretation of history. It is the story of a clash of cultures which can have no satisfactory resolution. Unlike the earlier works it is not a hero tale but a tragedy which foregrounds the inevitable loss involved in conquest.

Ursula Le Guin uses the imagery of darkness and light to symbolize psychological experiences in her powerful and compelling fantasy, *A Wizard of Earthsea* [1968]. The shadow which the young wizard, Ged, unleashes by an act of rash over-confidence invites a Jungian interpretation, 'shadow' being the term Jung uses to denote the repressed aspects of the psyche:

> Such tendencies [repressions] form an ever-present and potentially destructive 'shadow' to our conscious mind. Even tendencies that might in some circumstances be able to exert a beneficial influence are transformed into demons when they are repressed . . .
>
> Our times have demonstrated what it means for the gates of the underworld to be opened. Things whose enormity nobody could have imagined in the idyllic harmlessness of the first decade of our century have happened and have turned our world upside down. Ever since, the world has remained in a state of schizophrenia.
>
> (Jung [1964] 1968: 83–4)

Ged is pursued and tormented by the shadow until he at last confronts it and recognizes it as an aspect of himself:

> As they came right together it became utterly black in the white mage-radiance that burned about it, and it heaved itself upright. In silence, man and shadow met face to face, and stopped.
>
> Aloud and clearly, breaking that old silence, Ged spoke the shadow's name, and in the same moment the shadow spoke without lips or tongue, saying the same word: 'Ged.' And the two voices were one.
>
> Ged reached out his hands, dropping his staff, and took hold of his shadow, of the black self that stretched out to him. Light and darkness met, and joined, and were one.
>
> (Le Guin [1968] 1971: 197–8)

After this Ged is healed and goes on, in the third volume of the series, to become the Archmage, the spiritual and intellectual leader of his world. We are reminded of Prospero, another great wizard, and wielder of a magic staff, who finally said of Caliban: 'this thing of darkness I/Acknowledge mine' (*The Tempest* V, i, 275–6). The story suggests a range of possible meanings in addition to the primary struggle for psychic wholeness. It raises issues about the dangers and responsibilities of intellectual and creative gifts, and it could be read as a fable about the artist/intellectual and the perils of experimentation with mind-altering drugs. *A Wizard of Earthsea* is a text which demands active participation by the reader in the construction of meaning, and, despite its obvious debt to Jung, the richness of the imagery and the clarity with which the character of Ged is realized, provide more than a merely cerebral significance.

It is when the hero's wild adversaries carry this kind of multiple significance that the story achieves its maximum power to shape our perceptions of reality, when it seems, in Barthes' term, an image of what is 'natural and *goes without saying*' (Barthes [1957] 1973: 143), for each layer of meaning seems to guarantee the truth of the others. The seamless complexities of significance which attach to the wild things in Sendak's *Where the Wild Things Are* make it one of the most brilliant, though one of the briefest, examples of the genre. The wild things are the creatures of Max's dream, incarnations of his own wildness and loss of control, denizens of the unconscious, like the Minotaur, who threaten to overwhelm the mind if they are not controlled. And Max controls them; he is made king of 'all wild things' (Sendak [1963] 1967) by the creatures themselves when he orders them to 'be still!' and 'tames' them by staring into their eyes until they submit to him. In the illustration he is shown wearing a crown and a smug expression and holding a sceptre, thus suggesting actual political control, but his power over them is clearly psychological and intellectual. He dominates them by the grammatical imperative, by the instrument of reason, and the assertion of his will, and their submission is voluntary. They recognize their master. He is naturally their master because he is civilized and they are wild. He is the representative of home, of Western order; he is the white colonizer, while they are the inhabitants of the wilderness, the island – savages like Man Friday and Caliban, alien others. Max's wolf suit is only a disguise (like Kim O'Hara's Hindu dress); beneath it is a neat white boy, but they are shaggy, scaly and bare-footed, with horns and claws – monstrous. So his mastery of the wild things is mastery of himself, the triumph of reason over emotion and instinct, but it is also an image of European patriarchal power. Max's crown evokes the range of dualisms which have shaped Western culture.

# 4

# THE WOMEN

Women make up over 50 per cent of the world's population, they have always performed much of the world's work, often toiling alongside men, and they have played crucial roles in the social and cultural life of all communities, but this is not reflected in the hero myth as it recurs throughout the centuries. In these stories women are few, and most of those few function only in the domestic sphere. Many of these are mothers – gentle creatures with expressions of beatific sweetness, or plump warm bodies who dispense food unfailingly. Others are golden-haired brides in the first flower of youth. On the other hand the few females encountered in the wilderness possess amazing powers and perform extraordinary functions: they are goddesses, fairy godmothers, evil witches, sirens. Their appearance tends to indicate their nature. Those who are beautiful and blonde, like Tolkien's Galadriel, are certain to be benevolent. But some dark beauties are evil, deceptive and dangerous; they are La Belle Dame Sans Merci in one of her guises. Those who are ugly are, without exception, evil embodiments of cruelty and malice or of smothering destructiveness. All these women are, of course, stereotypes, but that is not sufficient to explain their functions in the story and their influence on the way we conceptualize reality.

## MARGINALITY AND INFERIORIZATION

Firstly it is necessary to realize that the women are, essentially, not 'characters' at all but symbols of events in the hero's psyche. Because the story is always narrated from the hero's point of view women appear only insofar as they are involved in his adventures, and the effect of this is to suggest that women are of no significance except when they make an impact upon men. Women haunt the margins of these stories like the girl, Blai, in Rosemary Sutcliff's *Warrior Scarlet*, who is dependent on the kindness of the hero's family where she lives as something between adopted daughter and servant, patiently performing household tasks. She adores Drem who is only intermittently aware of her existence, and the best she can hope for is to go on serving him humbly as his wife. She plays no part in his heroic struggle to become a warrior of the tribe, nor does her life have any purpose of its own. Drem's mother, similarly marginalized, patient but unfulfilled, says: '"Sometimes I wish that I had been born to the Men's side; sometimes I grow weary of the spinning and the weaving and the grinding corn."' (Sutcliff [1958] 1976: 18) Despite Sutcliff's obvious sympathy for these characters they remain shadowy presences on the periphery of the action. Interest centres on 'the Men's side', the male world of action and achievement.

In some stories with young heroes in the age range when the peer group is of paramount importance there are virtually no women at all. Children's literature contains many such tales, designed to appeal to boy readers who are believed to be intolerant of girls. *Treasure Island* is typical. In a letter to his friend, W.E. Henley, Stevenson said that he omitted all women from the book on the orders of his 13-year-old stepson, Lloyd Osbourne, for whose amusement the story was written (Stevenson [1883] 1946: viii). Whether this explanation provides the whole truth or not, the reader of *Treasure Island* certainly enters a world inhabited entirely by males except for the presence of Jim's mother in the early chapters.

It is easy to exclude women from the enclosed world of shipboard life as Stevenson does, and stories of sailors and pirates have been popular from the earliest years of children's literature. Robinson Crusoe excluded women from his life by going to sea. The hero of W.H.G. Kingston's *True Blue* (n.d.), typical of early nineteenth-century sea-going adventure tales, is actually born on a British naval vessel and becomes an intrepid fighter against the French. In Edward Ardizzone's Little Tim picture books which first appeared in the 1930s and are still being reprinted, Tim, a child of no more than 8, becomes involved in adventures with benevolent sailors and spends weeks at sea without, apparently, causing any particular alarm to his parents. John Ryan's best-selling Captain Pugwash picture books, first produced in the 1970s, are aimed at early readers and reproduce many of the features of the Little Tim stories. The milieu is the seagoing life of a 'good' pirate, Captain Pugwash, whose crew includes a small boy who invariably plays a heroic part in their adventures. Both Ardizzone and Ryan use the comic strip technique of pictures with speech balloons to supplement their simple texts. Dialogue thus predominates and the language of the short narrative sections is seemingly neutral and transparent, but the very lack of emotion and comment naturalizes the oppositional, single-sex world of the texts, as though life consisted of an on-going boys' team game.

In earlier years stories of this kind were often specifically addressed to boys alone. Kingston dedicated *True Blue* to 'the brave defenders of England's shores – the seamen of Great Britain, – and to all boys who speak the English language in all parts of the world' (Kingston, n.d.: vi). But later works, like the Pugwash stories, by their silence on the subject of their intended readership, imply that girls will happily accept stories about a world from which they are totally excluded because that world is where interest lies. One of the subliminal meanings young readers are likely to derive from such tales is that women and girls are neither interesting nor significant, and just as stories in which the hero rescues a beleaguered maiden and makes her his sexual partner naturalize adolescent male fantasies, so these fictions naturalize the pre-adolescent male disdain and fear of females, and inflate this attitude so that it appears as a quintessential quality of masculinity.

Insofar as their narrative structure implies that the actions of real consequence are those undertaken by men, hero stories resemble the historical record from which women are also largely obliterated. We know they were there, but what they did, what they thought, how they felt, even what their names were, we can mostly only conjecture. Their omission seems to prove their unimportance. Rosalind Miles in *The Women's History of the World* (1989) provides a literal example of this process of obliteration: the names of all the Pilgrim Fathers who sailed in the historic *Mayflower* expedition to settle America in 1620 are inscribed in stone on the Plymouth quayside, but of the eighteen women who went with them there is no mention. Their names are not carved in stone, for their existence was regarded as merely contingent (Miles 1989: 197). The process still continues. Most people are familiar with the name of Lech Walesa, the heroic leader of Solidarity; but how many have heard of Anna Walentynowicz? Marilyn French tells her story in *The War Against Women* (1992). She was active during the 1970s in agitating for free democratic trade unions and it was she, together with another woman, Alina Pienkowska, both workers in the Lenin shipyard where Walesa was also employed, who persuaded the workers not to give up the historic 1980 strike but to remain out in solidarity with the other shipyards. From this Solidarity was born. When the Polish government invoked martial law in December 1980, Walentynowicz continued to organize at the yard. As a consequence she was imprisoned. Men took over Solidarity, and when, after her release, she tried to return to the yard she was sent to a prison hospital for psychiatric observation. Walentynowicz lost her job, her pension and her possessions when her flat was looted during her imprisonment. Lech Walesa became president of Poland.

As French points out (p. 450), the men of Solidarity did not just appropriate a union Walentynowicz started, they pushed her out of it and then impugned her sanity. Like so many other women whose actions were of crucial significance she has been obliterated from history. If it were not for *MS* magazine, we would not know she existed. On the other hand almost everyone has heard of an earlier revolutionary woman, Charlotte Corday, for she murdered Marat, one of the leaders of the French Revolution, in his bath, thus making a very direct impact on the affairs of men. Her action is recorded in the history books and is commemorated in a striking painting by the French nationalist painter, David. Significantly, however, it is the only action of her life which is well known.

Why does this process occur? One reason is that in the past men have controlled, and largely still control, the academic institutions, the discipline of history, and the publishing industry, so that at every level, decisions about what should be recorded have traditionally been made by men. But it is simplistic to see this as a conscious campaign to marginalize women. The chroniclers and historians believed they were recording the important events, those which determined the course of human development. As they saw it the details of a war in which many people were killed were more significant, and more worthy of record, than information about such things as changes in diet or child care, even though those changes often saved and improved innumerable lives. They simply believed that women and their actions *were* marginal and inferior. This belief is reflected in the structure of the hero story.

Recently anthropologists have reconsidered the perceived significance of male and female activities. Nancy Chodorow's influential paper 'Family structure and feminine personality' presents a persuasive psychological-anthropological explanation of the universal secondary status of women which can also help to account for the fictional existence of idealized and idolized figures such as goddesses and good fairies along with their opposites, the witches and other evil female predators. Chodorow rejects biological determinist explanations for the development of masculine and feminine personality traits, and regards the concentration of Freudian theory on isolated behaviours such as weaning and toilet training as limited. Her focus is on the ongoing interpersonal relationships which give behaviours meaning. She argues that the nature and quality of the relationships a child experiences are internalized and come to constitute her/his personality (Chodorow 1974: 45).

The crucial feature of infantile existence is dependence upon, and primary identification with, the mother which is first experienced as an extension of the prenatal state of being physically part of her body. In most societies a close dependent relationship continues because of the mother's lactation, and even if the biological mother does not undertake the primary care of the infant, a child's earliest experiences are still involved with attachment to women. Chodorow suggests that even at the pre-oedipal stage the experiences of boys and girls are different. She argues (p. 47) that a woman identifies with her own mother and in her relationship with her child she re-experiences herself as a cared-for child, but, because she was a female child, her identification with her daughter is likely to be stronger than with her son; mothers therefore tend to treat infants of different sexes differently, pushing their sons to assume a sexually toned male role.

At the oedipal stage the differences between male and female experiences become explicit. From about the age of 3, the father, and men generally, begin to become important in a child's primary object world and children of this age have a concept of gender. A boy's masculine gender identification must come to replace his former identification with his mother and Chodorow argues (p. 49) that, because most male activities take place outside the domestic sphere in which the small boy spends his time, the boy's gender identification becomes a 'positional' one, not easily apprehensible in the world of his daily life. His identification also often becomes negative: he defines masculinity primarily in terms of that which is not female and does not have to do with women. This means that for a boy masculinity becomes a matter of denial of relationship as he differentiates himself from his mother, and a devaluation of the female on both the psychological and cultural levels. For a girl, however, gender identity does not involve a rejection of her early identification with her mother and, because her involvement with her mother and other females continues, her gender role identification is mediated by real affective relationships. It is not merely positional and it is not apprehended negatively. Chodorow suggests that women's lives generally are characterized by a quality of embeddedness in social interactions and personal relationships whereas men's lives are more likely to be concerned with wider social organizations within which they function in individualistic and objective ways. She notes (pp. 58–9) that for Western women this can result in a sense of a loss of self in inescapable responsibility for others and a sense of guilt even for situations which are not in any way the result of their actions: women apologize for others' difficulties in dealing with the world, and apologize if it rains on a family picnic. That is, women have internalized a sense of their inferiority, while men have learnt to disdain the doings of women because that is how they define their masculinity.

Sherry B. Ortner, in her paper 'Is female to male as nature is to culture?' builds on Chodorow's analysis of universal female subordination. She argues that while women are not identified with nature they are seen as *closer* to nature than men because of their procreative functions and their traditional domestic and child care role which produces the kind of psychic structure described by Chodorow. Women's association with the domestic sphere evokes the domestic/public opposition which she argues, following Lévi-Strauss, is present in every social system. Domestic, biological units are related to one another by a system of rules (for example the incest prohibition and insistence on marriage outside the group) which are logically at a higher level than the units themselves and which structure society. Because they lack a natural basis for a familial or domestic orientation (i.e. parturition and lactation) men tend to be associated with this 'higher' level of organization, with society and its activities, that is with 'culture', whereas women are associated with the domestic sphere, that is with 'nature'.

This is the basis of the assumption that it is only the doings of men that are worthy of record, for history has been conceived as an account of human interaction at the public, not the private, level, as an account of the construction of culture. Where a woman's doings have been included in the record it is because she has functioned in the world of public affairs. So queens rate a mention, and so does Joan of Arc; often, however, the achievements of women who have so acted are minimized or obliterated (as in the case of Anna Walentynowicz) so strong is the feeling that they *ought* to stay at home. Thus the public/private dualism is constructed and attached to the male/female dualism.

Women, then, are widely perceived as subordinate to men because they are regarded as closer to nature, but this perception of the female as intermediate between culture and nature produces symbolic ambiguities. Depending upon the viewer's perspective this liminal position may be seen as either ignoring and subverting cultural values, or else as transcending them, as standing for purer and nobler qualities of love and caring as opposed to the pragmatism of public life. Julia Kristeva's view, as summarized by Toril Moi, is similar:

> if patriarchy sees women as occupying a marginal position within the symbolic order, then it can construe them as the *limit* or borderline of that order . . . Women seen as the limit of the symbolic order will in other words share in the disconcerting properties of *all* frontiers: they will be neither inside nor outside, neither known nor unknown. It is this position that has enabled male culture sometimes to vilify women as representing darkness and chaos, to view them as Lilith or the Whore of Babylon, and sometimes to elevate them as the representatives of a higher and purer nature, to venerate them as Virgins and Mothers of God. In the first instance the borderline is seen as part of the chaotic wilderness outside, and in the second it is seen as an inherent part of the inside: the part that protects and shields the symbolic order from the imaginary chaos.
>
> (Moi 1985: 167)

Both Ortner and Moi make the point that, of course, neither position corresponds to any reality about women who are, in actuality, no closer to 'nature' than men. These analyses provide a context in which to consider the meanings of the female figures who appear in hero stories and who continue to influence popular perceptions of the nature and roles of women.

## MOTHERS

Mothers often appear at the beginnings of hero tales. They preside over the home which the hero leaves when he sets out on his quest, remaining there when he has gone. Sometimes they reappear at the end of the story to welcome him home. These mothers are invariably good, nurturing, sometimes almost saintly. They are the presiding spirits of the domestic sphere. A typical example from a Victorian adventure story is the mother of Dick Varley the young hunter-hero in R.M. Ballantyne's *The Dog Crusoe*:

> Dick's mother was thin, and old, and wrinkled, but her face was stamped with a species of beauty which *never* fades – the beauty of a loving look. Ah! the brow of snow and the peach-bloom cheek may snare the heart of man for a time, but the *loving look* alone can forge that adamantine chain that time, age, eternity shall never break.
>
> (Ballantyne, n.d.: 21–2)

Mrs Varley is saddened when her son asks leave to go on an expedition into the wilderness to make peace with the Indian tribes, but she gives her permission because she approves of the purpose: 'Blessed are the peace-makers.' When eventually Dick returns, having become a great hunter during the course of the expedition, his reunion with his mother is so moving that the narrator shrouds it from the reader's eyes: 'Before another word could be uttered, Dick Varley was in the room. Marston immediately stepped out and softly shut the door. Reader – we shall not open it!' (Ballantyne, n.d.: 243). She is clearly an idealized embodiment of home, the private sphere where the gentle virtues flourish. In the story she never appears outside her house; the men who inhabit the public world – the meeting place in the town square, the trails, the woods – visit her there and pay homage.

As the hero story is, at one level, the story of a boy's journey to maturity, Mrs Varley and her like also signify the all-giving mothers of the child's preoedipal stage. The hero must go forward without her, survive without her constant nurturance, since that is his essential developmental task. Bettelheim argues that this is made almost explicit in 'Jack and the Beanstalk' when Jack is sent forth by his mother to sell the cow which had provided them with an unfailing supply of milk:

> Every child can easily grasp the unconscious meaning of the tragedy when the good cow Milky White, who provided all that was needed, suddenly stops giving milk. It arouses dim memories of that tragic time when the flow of milk ceased for the child, when he was weaned. That is the time when the mother demands that the child must learn to make do with what the outside world can offer. This is symbolized by Jack's mother sending him out into the world to arrange for something (the money he is expected to get for the cow) that will provide sustenance.
>
> (Bettelheim 1976: 188)

Other mothers who make typically brief appearances include Robinson Crusoe's mother who begs him passionately not to go to sea, Jim Hawkins' mother in *Treasure Island*, Stanley Grahame's mother in *Stanley Grahame: Boy and Man* (she weeps when her son goes to his uncle to be 'made a man' but knows it is necessary), Mrs Rabbit in *Peter Rabbit* who goes off to buy brown bread and currant buns for her children, Drem's mother in *Warrior Scarlet* and Max's invisible mother in *Where the Wild Things Are* who provides her son with his famous hot supper on his return from his adventures. In all these tales the hero makes significant progress towards maturity before he returns at the end of the story. Will Stanton's mother in Susan Cooper's *The Dark is Rising* sequence has nine children and is unsurprisingly preoccupied with domestic things, often 'bent broad-beamed and red-faced over an oven' (Cooper 1976: 12). Will's fantasy adventures in which he is an Old One caught up in the struggle of good against evil often read like the hallucinations of someone on the brink of adolescence glimpsing the terrors of the world that lies beyond his mother's warm domestic sphere. In Ann Holm's best-selling children's novel, *I am David* [1963], the hero has been separated from his mother for most of his twelve or thirteen years, having grown up in a concentration camp from which she has previously been released, and she appears only in the final sentence to welcome him home. His journey in search of her parallels his psychological development which had been arrested during the years in the camp, and when they are finally reunited he is ready for the next stage of personal growth which must involve renewing his relationship with her. Only after that will he be able to move onwards to adulthood. There are few fathers in these tales. Either the mothers are widows or, as in *Where the Wild Things Are*, the father is simply not mentioned, so that the first part of the story concentrates on the psychic drama of the child's separation from the mother. It is later, during the course of his adventure, that the hero confronts and overcomes intimidating male figures – giants, savages, pirates, Mr McGregor!

Sometimes the good and loving mother is dead, or dies at an early point in the story, so that the hero is doubly severed from her when he sets out on his adventure. In these cases he must somehow make good this central psychic lack; otherwise he risks remaining trapped by his memory of her in a state of emotional childhood. David Copperfield's widowed mother, Clara, is gentle, sweet and loving but she mishandles the process of David's separation from her. When he is a small boy she marries the cold and punitive Murdstone, as terrifying a figure, from a child's perspective, as any fairy-tale giant or ogre. His name with its suggestions of hardness and murderer implies his nature as David perceives it. Murdstone destroys the closeness between mother and son, forbidding his wife to express affection for her child and subjecting David to a harsh and repressive regime. Eventually he sends him away to school.

While he is at school David's mother has another child and David is able to spend one happy day with her and his new brother during a school vacation while his step-father is absent. However, both his mother and his baby brother die shortly after and he is left with nothing but a memory of her. Significantly what he remembers is their earliest closeness:

> From the moment of my knowing of the death of my mother, the idea of her as she had been of late had vanished from me. I remembered her, from that instant, only as the young mother of my earliest impressions, who had been used to wind her bright curls round and round her finger, and to dance with me at twilight in the parlour. What Peggotty had told me now, was so far from bringing me back to the later period, that it rooted the earlier image in my mind. It may be curious, but it is true. In her death she winged her way back to her calm, untroubled youth, and cancelled all the rest.

> The mother who lay in the grave, was the mother of my infancy; the little creature in her arms, was myself, as I had been once, hushed for ever on her bosom.
>
> (Dickens [1850], n.d.: 137)

David here perceives his pre-oedipal self as dead, but he has not yet negotiated a voluntary separation from a mother who supports his progress towards adulthood and no real advance is possible for him. He overcomes this problem when he runs away from Murdstone's persecutions to find sanctuary with his great-aunt, Betsey Trotwood, who functions as a second mother to him and sets him upon the road to maturity.

In *The Neverending Story* a major concern of Bastian's quest is finding the means to heal the psychic wound inflicted by the death of his mother when he was a small boy. Because he lost her before he was ready to grow towards independence Bastian is lonely, withdrawn and timid. He is unhappy at school and poor at school work. One day his psychological withdrawal is actualized when he hides himself in the school attic to read a book he has stolen from a magic bookshop. He immerses himself in a fantasy version of the hero tale, *The Neverending Story*, the story within the story, and the vicarious experiences this tale provides enable him to overcome some of his psychological problems. One of the meanings to be derived from Michael Ende's metafictive work is concerned with the therapeutic power of fiction and the psychological function of story in general.

Towards the end of his adventures in Fantastica Bastian encounters Dame Eyola, an earth mother figure, who feeds him delicious and spiritually nourishing fruits and lets him slip into a suppressed memory of babyhood:

> He had slipped into a sweet half-sleep in which he heard her words as a kind of chant. He heard her stand up and cross the room and bend over him. She stroked his hair and kissed him on the forehead. Then he felt her pick him up and carry him out in her arms. He buried his head in her bosom like a baby. Deeper and deeper he sank into the warm sleepy darkness.
>
> (Ende [1979] 1984: 349)

After a long summer in her care he gradually comes to crave her fruits and her tenderness less until he realizes he is ready to leave behind the self-absorption of the small child and learn to relate to others. He parts from her voluntarily to continue his quest and is able to return to the real world with enhanced self-confidence, and to offer love to his still grieving father.

C.S. Lewis' *The Magician's Nephew* [1955], the second Narnia book to be written, but the first in the Narnian chronology, is also concerned with the relationship between a son and his terminally-ill mother, but concludes with a denial of the necessary separation. It is an allegory of the Biblical creation story and therefore the hero, Digory Kirke, is accompanied on his quest by a girl, Polly, and together they travel to a paradisal place in the centre of which a wonderful tree grows. Aslan, the creator of Narnia, has asked Digory to bring him one of the fruits from the tree, but when he has plucked it Digory is tempted by the evil witch, Jadis, who urges him to take the fruit instead to his dying mother whom it will certainly cure. The novel inverts the Genesis story in a number of ways: It is Adam, not Eve, who is tempted; the tempter is female, not a subtle male serpent, and Digory/Adam resists the temptation. His sense of decent behaviour prevails! He obediently takes the fruit to Aslan and it is planted in Narnia where it grows into a tree which will guard the land and ensure that it remains a place of innocent joy for hundreds of years. As a reward for his virtue Digory is given a fruit from this new tree to take home to his mother. When she has eaten it she grows well again, and life for Digory returns to what it was before she became ill, a time of innocent delight blessed by her presence:

> windows were opened, frowsy curtains were drawn back to brighten up the rooms, there were new flowers everywhere, and nicer things to eat, and the old piano was tuned and Mother took up her singing again, and had such games with Digory and Polly that Aunt Letty would say 'I declare, Mabel, you're the biggest baby of the three.'
>
> (Lewis [1955] 1963: 169)

Thus Digory remains in an emotionally static, dependent relationship with his mother, and in Narnia the fall and expulsion from Paradise is avoided.

If, symbolically, the expulsion from paradise, the 'fortunate fall', is the beginning of humanity's development into adulthood which is dependent upon the experience of suffering, the essential basis of compassion and altruism, then Narnia is a land of perpetual childhood and Digory, unlike Bastian Bax, makes no progress on the journey towards full humanity. David Holbrook suggests that the Narnia stories owe their existence to the fact that Lewis' mother died when he was a baby, leaving him with a psychic hunger for nurturance. He sees the stories as an attempt to find a way into the other world to which the mother had gone, the world of death, so that Narnia is a place which denies real life and growth (Holbrook 1973: 6). Whether or not one wishes to go along with Holbrook's essentially Freudian reading, these stories certainly depict childhood as a state more desirable than adulthood, a time when access to paradise is still possible.

Barrie's *Peter Pan* is, as we have seen, another story in which the protagonist refuses the opportunity to move forward from childhood. Except for the Darling children all the males in this play – the pirates as well as the Lost Boys and Peter – are motherless and yearn to fill that emptiness. When Wendy arrives in the Never Land she plays mother to the Lost Boys, mending socks, dispensing medicine and supervizing bath time, but Peter, who remembers or imagines rejection by his real mother, is bitter about motherhood:

> Wendy, you are wrong about mothers. I thought like you about the window, so I stayed away for moons and moons, and then I flew back, but the window was barred, for my mother had forgotten all about me and there was another little boy sleeping in my bed.
>
> (Barrie [1904] 1942: 552)

This unresolved resentment at displacement by a younger sibling appears to be the reason Peter is unable to negotiate the transition to maturity, remaining stranded in an endless and meaningless childhood. But despite Peter's resentment the play itself is a sentimental celebration of idealized motherhood, with Wendy as the representative in the Never Land of Mrs Darling who presides in the domestic world of home. She embodies gentleness and affection and eventually adopts the Lost Boys, welcoming them into a seemingly limitless maternal embrace. The impact of this work on twentieth-century perceptions of gender roles was considerable and a Wendy House was an almost universal feature of pre-school and infants' classrooms in Australia until well into the 1970s. This miniaturized domestic setting provided little girls with the chance to grow familiar with what was considered their destined future.

The mother figures in these tales, then, symbolize the pre-oedipal closeness of mother and child, but they are also significant at the ideological level of the story, inscribing the perception that 'a woman's place is in the home' (especially if she has children) naturalizing the restriction of women to the domestic sphere, and thus authorizing the strategies which have been used over the years to keep them there, strategies ranging from unequal educational opportunities for girls and the simple refusal to admit women to many occupations, to practices such as unequal pay, denial of tenure and promotional opportunities, and lack of child care facilities. The stereotype of the gentle mother content with her role in the home is, of course, not restricted to hero tales. It is widespread in advertising and it abounds in children's literature of all kinds, functioning as a powerful tool of social conditioning. In 1992 a random selection of 282 children's picture books published since 1970 revealed that 62 per cent of the mothers in these books were depicted in a purely home-making role, with another 29 per cent in an indeterminate role. Only 9 per cent were shown in professional or professional/home-making roles, despite the fact that 1986 Bureau of Statistics figures showed that almost half the married mothers in Australia were employed. Interestingly, 36 per cent of the home-making women in these books were depicted wearing aprons. Earlier studies had shown this badge of domestic servitude to be rampant in children's picture books and while this study revealed some lessening of the phenomenon it was still quietly flourishing (Tunstall 1992). Despite decades of equal opportunity legislation, and despite the reality of Western women's involvement in a range of professional and community activities, the perception that women belong in the home, in the private, not the public sphere, persists, and hero stories consistently reinforce that perception.

## GODDESSES, FAIRY GODMOTHERS AND OTHERS

Meek domestic creatures like Mrs Varley and Mrs Darling accord well with the ideology of female subordination and male dominance but in some hero tales more powerful maternal and quasi-maternal figures – strong, autonomous beings – appear at the hero's times of great need to assist him in his quest. These women do not lend themselves nearly so well to the ideology of female domesticity. Consequently they have been relatively ignored by popular image-makers.

In early myths mothers of heroes are sometimes powerful figures themselves, often goddesses who are responsible for the extraordinary powers of their sons. Ninsun, the mother of Gilgamesh, in the ancient Assyrian epic, is a goddess and a priestess 'gifted with great wisdom' (Sandars 1960: 64) who is consulted by her son about the meanings of his dreams, and who intercedes for him with the god Shamash. Thetis, the mother of Achilles, is a sea goddess who visits Olympus to persuade Hephaestus to forge new armour and a new shield for her son so that, properly equipped, he may avenge the death of his friend, Patroclus. A number of other goddesses play equally significant roles in the *Iliad*, including Athene who is also a major player in the *Odyssey* where she consistently aids Odysseus, to the point of actually intervening in the battle with the suitors, causing their spears to miss their marks (Homer 1946: 345). In the story of Perseus his mother, Danae, is a princess who is seduced by Zeus as a consequence of which she gives birth to the semi-divine Perseus. And Perseus, like Odysseus, is aided by Athene when he sets out on his quest to behead Medusa. Both Theseus and Jason are assisted in their tasks by strong women – Ariadne who defies her father to help Theseus defeat the Minotaur, and Medea who likewise defies her father to help Jason steal the Golden Fleece, using her magic powers to enable him to defeat the dragon which guarded it.

These powerful female figures are not restricted to the private domestic world, or to the beginning and end of the hero's story; they can appear in any place and influence events at any point. They might seem, therefore, to constitute a challenge to Chodorow's theory that women are universally seen as subordinate to men, but these goddesses and goddess-like women are survivals from an earlier pattern of thought: they are descendants of the great mother goddess, universally worshipped, under many names, in early human history (Lethbridge 1962: 23–7). Before the connection between intercourse and birth was understood animal and human life seemed to be the exclusive gift of the female, and the earth itself, from whose body crops are brought forth, was perceived as female. The great goddess was honoured as the source of life and, as the giver of milk and the bearer of crops, she was also worshipped as the sustainer of the life she created. In her earliest incarnations she was always a mother, and early depictions of her, such as the famous Venus of Willendorf, emphasize her breasts and sexual organs. Gradually, however, various aspects of female existence were split off and she was worshipped as both maiden and mother (for example as Persephone and Demeter), and as the incarnation of eroticism in, for instance, the great goddess Aphrodite. She was all-powerful, and in early mythologies male figures are merely her temporary consorts.

Human societies of this early period appear not to have been matriarchies in the sense of organizations in which female power was structurally entrenched, but rather woman-centred and relatively egalitarian. The power bestowed by the goddess was believed to pass from mother to daughter, so that a man could become king only by marrying the queen who was also the priestess, or incarnation, of the goddess. This custom survived in the dynasties of ancient Egypt, where the son of a pharaoh commonly entered into a formal marriage with his sister so that he could assume the throne when she became queen. Where this did not occur the daughter became pharaoh in her own right, as in the case of Hapshetsut to whom Thutmose I had to yield the throne on the death of his wife, even though he had two sons (Miles 1989: 46–7). In very early societies the practice of ritually sacrificing the king each year, as an offering to the goddess to ensure the annual rebirth of the crops, appears to have been widespread, and is reflected in innumerable myths such as the stories of Venus and Adonis and Isis and Osiris. In these myths the mother goddess is the bestower of death as well as the giver of life.

In effect the great goddess was 'Mother Nature' and women were honoured *because* of their perceived closeness to nature. But, as human understanding of cause and effect developed, the role of men in fertilization and pregnancy became clear and phallus worship and male gods appeared. As new mythologies developed mother goddess figures were gradually sanitized and incorporated as consorts or subordinates of male god kings. So in the Hellenic world the ancient goddess Hera became the wife of Zeus who was king of the gods, and other ancient female goddesses were redefined as members of the Olympian pantheon over which he ruled. Simultaneously, as organized agriculture developed from earlier horticulture and societies acquired stored surpluses of wealth, social structures became more complex and organized war between different groups emerged as a feature of human existence. The culture of war facilitated the dominance of men who possessed superior physical strength and lacked the encumbrance of physically dependent children. So war leaders became entrenched as kings, defeated groups became slaves, hierarchies developed and women were relegated to subordinate roles. The public and private spheres of life became increasingly separated. Patriarchies evolved and their project was domination – domination of the land by agriculture, domination of enemy groups, and domination of women whose traditional, rival powers had to be suppressed.

The struggle between the ancient power of women and the emergent power of the patriarchy is dramatized in *The Epic of Gilgamesh*, in which the hero, Gilgamesh, the ruler of Uruk, opposes the will of the great goddess Ishtar. After Gilgamesh and his friend, the wild man Enkidu, have successfully conquered the forest and its guardian, the giant Humbaba, Ishtar wishes to take Gilgamesh as her bridegroom. She woos him in grand style:

> I will harness for you a chariot of lapis lazuli and of gold, with wheels of gold and horns of copper; and you shall have mighty demons of the storm for draft mules. When you enter our house in the fragrance of cedar-wood, threshold and throne will kiss your feet.
>
> (Sandars 1960: 83)

But Gilgamesh knows that her consorts are regularly sacrificed after enjoying her favours for a short time, and he refuses her: 'And if you and I should be lovers, should not I be served in the same fashion as all these others whom you loved once?' (p. 85). Enraged, Ishtar appeals to her father Anu to create the Bull of Heaven for her so that it can kill Gilgamesh for his impertinence. Anu obliges her but Gilgamesh and Enkidu manage to slay the bull. Ishtar is then further enraged and cries out: 'Woe to Gilgamesh, for he has scorned me in killing the Bull of Heaven' (p. 86). But the people of Uruk celebrate Gilgamesh's victory, acclaiming him as the greatest of heroes: 'Gilgamesh is the most glorious of heroes, Gilgamesh is most eminent among men' (p. 87). In the event Enkidu falls ill and dies as punishment for the sacrilege, but Gilgamesh remains unscathed although he grieves deeply for his friend. Thus the patriarchy is triumphant and the goddess is forced to submit.

Later hero myths inscribe the project of patriarchal dominance as the hero goes forth, subduing the land and all those who oppose his power – and in these stories he is *assisted* by female power, by the descendants of the great goddess, who are shown as accepting his dominance and working to further it. For the worship of the goddess and all she stood for did not disappear. Something so fundamental in human symbolic thought could not be easily eradicated. In the face of this the stratagem of the stories is to co-opt her later manifestations into the service of the patriarchy. So the Olympian goddesses in Greek hero tales are consistently shown as aiding and supporting the heroes because they approve of their character and their enterprises. When Odysseus at last reaches the shores of Ithaca on his homeward journey he is confronted by Athene who sums up the assistance she has rendered him and the reasons for her support:

> [I am] Pallas Athene, Daughter of Zeus, who always stand by your side and guard you through all your adventures. Why, it was I who made all the Phaecians take to you so kindly. And here I am once more to plan your future course with you; to hide the treasures that the Phaecian nobles, prompted by me, gave to you when you left for home, and to warn you of all the trials you will have to undergo within the walls of your palace . . . I cannot desert you in your misfortunes; you are so civilized, so intelligent, so self-possessed.
>
> (Homer 1946: 216–7)

Likewise, as Apollonius of Rhodes relates, Jason was aided in his quest for the Golden Fleece by Athene who built the Argo for him, and by the goddesses Hera and Aphrodite (Kypris) who persuaded Eros to cause Medea to fall in love with him and assist him to steal the fleece from her father. Hera explains that Jason had always been dear to her because of his graciousness in assisting her across a river when she was disguised as an old woman (Apollonius of Rhodes 1995: 67) and she extricates him and his followers from many difficulties on their long voyage.

Even after the triumph of Christian monotheism, with its jealous male god, reverence for the goddess persisted, transmuted at an official level into worship of the Virgin, but also surviving underground in a debased form in village beliefs in witches and fairies and in practices such as May Day celebrations. In mainstream mediaeval Christian stories such as the Arthurian tales it is the Virgin who assists the hero, but in the more subversive fairy tales good fairies and fairy godmothers abound, attesting to the persistence of belief in a powerful female principle. Thus, in the magic land at the top of the Beanstalk, Jack is accosted by an infirm-looking old woman with wrinkled skin and tattered garments (Opie and Opie 1974: 165) who reveals that she is a fairy. She tells him how an evil giant had stripped his father of all his possessions, and insists that Jack must recover them and punish the giant. Jack feels her presence as powerful and menacing, but she has clearly enlisted on his side even though he has behaved like a lazy ne'er-do-well. The great mother goddess was still not completely vanquished, but she was reduced to shabby disguises and collaboration with the enemy.

In hero tales of the post-Enlightenment era, which has seen rationalism in the ascendant, avatars of the great goddess are relatively rare. Sweet mothers who sanctify the home by their presence and leave the great world to their sons are far more in accord with the agenda of the times, but the goddess reveals her presence occasionally in the feisty, usually eccentric old women who cross the hero's path and offer him aid, although they are very much circumscribed by the cultures they inhabit. David Copperfield's great-aunt, Betsey Trotwood, is such a one – an independent, strong-minded, autocratic, fanatically neat, fierce but benevolent old woman with a rather poor opinion of men in general, except for those who need her support. She is not dismayed when David turns up on her doorstep, grubby and exhausted, having run away from his stepfather's ill-treatment. She sees through the odious Murdstone at their first encounter and vanquishes him in fine style. She then takes the runaway David in and launches him into a new life. Like the goddesses in ancient myths and the fairy godmothers of folk tales she is powerful and autonomous and, to that extent, potentially disruptive of the establishment, but, like the goddesses and godmothers, she uses her power in the service of the hero because she approves of his project. Her animosity is not directed at the status quo of unequal male/female power relationships in Victorian England, but only at those men who abuse their power thus threatening the social equilibrium:

> 'Mr Murdstone,' she said, shaking her finger at him, 'you were a tyrant to that simple baby, and you broke her heart. She was a loving baby – I know that; I knew it years before *you* ever saw her – and through the best part of her weakness you gave her the wounds she died of. There is the truth for your comfort, however you like it.'
>
> (Dickens [1850], n.d.: 217)

For all its reformist spirit the ideology of *David Copperfield* is essentially conservative because it directs its criticism at the unjust behaviour of individuals rather than at the structural injustices of a society based upon a system of profoundly unequal rights.

In Kipling's *Kim* another strong and idiosyncratic old woman is shown as accepting and supporting a complex of inequalities: the dominance of men over women, of high caste over low caste, and of the British over India. The old woman of Saharunpore is a wealthy widow who encounters Kim and his lama when they have first set out upon the road together. She befriends them, at first because she finds Kim's engaging impudence charming and because she believes the lama may be able to give her a spell to ensure her daughter-in-law will bear a second son, but later because she comes to appreciate the lama's true goodness and to recognize Kim's heroic qualities. In the final chapters, when Kim and the lama are exhausted and ill from the rigours of their adventures in the mountains, she provides them with unstinting hospitality and facilitates their physical and spiritual recovery. It is at her home that each achieves the epiphany which is, in effect, the object of his quest.

She is of aristocratic descent and mistress of a large household which she runs with great efficiency and energy, but the structure of the narrative, in which she appears only when she is addressing some need of Kim's, implies that she is of less importance than he is although he is a vagabond child only provisionally adopted by the British establishment. Further, she is shown as accepting without question the social and political conditions which circumscribe her freedoms. She remains behind curtains in her litter when she converses with men, never revealing more than a jewelled forefinger which she shakes at her interlocutors. And she is shown to approve of British rule, believing that it is the only guarantor of justice in India. When an English District Superintendent of Police, 'faultlessly uniformed', trots past her litter and greets her with some friendly banter she says:

> 'These be the sort to over-see justice. They know the land and the customs of the land. The others, all new from Europe, suckled by white women and learning our tongues from books, are worse than the pestilence. They do harm to Kings.'
>
> (Kipling [1901] 1946: 80)

Her criticism of the raw recruits is far less important to the ideology of the novel than her acceptance of the old hands for the comment implies the inevitability and rightness of rule by one kind of Englishman or another. With her colourful personality, her energy, her humour and her inexhaustible kindness the old woman of Saharunpore functions as something akin to an embodiment of India. Her endorsement of British and patriarchal dominance is crucial to the way in which the novel naturalizes these structures of inequality.

In twentieth-century high fantasies for children and young adults the symbolism often has a quasi-Christian significance, and female figures compounded of aspects of the Virgin and the great goddess appear, to inspire and consecrate the young hero, but their role is marginal. They may be present at moments of great crisis, either bodily or as a numinous image in the hero's mind, but they take almost no part in the action. Their semiotic function is to invest the hero and his quest with significance, to underline his transcendence. *The Lord of the Rings* contains several passive but inspirational female figures, but it is the elf-queen, Galadriel, who is most clearly descended from the Virgin. She is tall, golden-haired, grave and beautiful, she wears white, she lives in Lothlórien, the golden wood, and she is referred to as the Lady. When the heroes prepare to leave her presence she bestows a gift on each. To Frodo she gives a phial of light resonant with Christian significance: 'It will shine brighter when night is about you. May it be a light to you in the dark places, when all other lights go out. Remember Galadriel and her mirror!' (Tolkien 1954: 393). While there is a suggestion of the society hostess about Galadriel, the description of the autumnal beauty of the golden wood evokes both the biblical lost paradise and the sense of a vanished Arcadia, achieving a fusion of the ancient and the Christian traditions.

Susan Cooper's *The Dark is Rising* sequence which has many echoes of Tolkien also contains a numinous figure known as the Lady who greets the hero, Will Stanton, in the second book of the sequence, when he steps through a pair of mysterious carved doors which lead from one time to another, to begin the first stage of his quest. In this book her association with nature and ancient Celtic mythology is emphasized: she is accompanied by Merriman/Merlin and she is described as small, immensely aged and 'fragile as a bird' (Cooper [1973] 1976: 43). Later in the story the bird imagery is repeated with more force: in another incursion into past time Will observes a pagan ceremony known as the Hunting of the Wren in which a group of boys carry the body of a wren on an ivy-covered bier; as he looks the bird is transformed into the Lady, 'a small, fine-boned woman, very old, delicate as a bird, robed in blue' (p. 174). But in the final book of the sequence, *Silver on the Tree*, her identity as the Virgin is unmistakable. She appears to one of the children in a vision, floating on the air, delivers a cryptic prophecy to aid them in their final struggle against 'the Dark', and at a climactic moment in this struggle she again appears, looking now neither old nor young, and wearing a robe 'blue as an early morning sky' (Cooper [1977] 1979: 258).

Both these fantasies implicitly recognize the submerged tradition of the great goddess and the power of the female principle, but the images of Galadriel and Cooper's Lady are images of co-opted power. Their function is only to bless and encourage the heroes. They are reduced to decorative presences, bright figures on the periphery of the structural pattern; action and accomplishment is seen to be the prerogative of males.

A much more vigorous figure is Princess Leia in George Lucas' 1977 film *Star Wars*. She enlists the hero, Luke Skywalker, in her cause, and takes an active part in the struggle against the evil Empire and the dark lord, Darth Vader. She resembles the goddess Athene of the *Odyssey* in several ways: her white gown and coiled hair have a somewhat Greek quality, she is dignified rather than alluring, and her role is Olympian – she is concerned with the struggle for control of the universe. Nevertheless most of the action, and the audience's interest, belongs to Skywalker and his friends. Leia's semiotic function in the narrative is to invest their actions with ultimate approval and to mark them as true heroes. She performs this function formally at the end of the film when she bestows gold medals upon them at a victory ceremony which perhaps intentionally recalls a medal presentation at the Olympic games: in the simplistic opposition of good rebels and evil empire and the aerobatics of the final contest the film resembles the televised coverage of a sporting contest.

Women in science fiction hero stories are usually entirely marginal, but another interesting exception is the hero's mother in Frank Herbert's *Dune* [1966]. She is Jessica, the concubine of a duke, and has been rigorously trained by the Bene Gesserit, an elite women's secret society. This organization is a priestly caste which works within the male power structure to influence events, as cults of the great goddess must have done in earlier times as the patriarchy entrenched its ascendancy. As a result of her training Jessica has acquired exceptional mental insight, skill in martial arts, and supreme self-control. She is also beautiful, devoted to her husband and son, and accepting of women's subordinate position in the male supremacist society of the novel. Initially it seems that the character of Jessica is the outcome of an attempt to depict a strong woman while simultaneously feeding male readers' fantasies of gender superiority, but, as the story develops, what initially appeared as a conflict of intention is realized as a dramatization of the inner conflict of an intelligent and independent woman who has internalized her society's view of women's subordination, who accepts but resents her husband's political reasons for denying her the status of wife, and who is unable to use her strength and talents for any purpose other than furthering her son's ambitions.

Whether by design or not she emerges as by far the most interesting character in the novel, the only one apart from her son, Paul, who evolves as the events of the story unfold. And, while his development into a prophetic messiah taxes the reader's ability to suspend disbelief, she becomes increasingly convincing despite the improbabilities of the plot. When she and Paul are forced to flee from their enemies she learns new depths of patience in the desert. Although she finds a new role for herself as a holy woman with the desert people she still struggles to aid her son, continuing to teach him the skills and insights she has acquired from her life and training, while coming to feel, as most mothers do, that she knows him less as he grows older and so has less power to aid him. Finally, after a series of trials and losses, she comes to see personal relationships as more important than power and feels that her worldly plans for Paul were misguided – just as he becomes engulfed by the hubris of imperial ambition. Her role in the story is unusual because, although she is the hero's mother, she is present throughout, playing a significant part in all the main events, and because her relationship with her son is a developing one which remains important to him. She functions in the novel as a fully realized character, not merely as a symbol of pre-oedipal security or as a *dea ex machina* who appears at moments of crisis to render the assistance necessary to extricate the hero from his difficulty. Sadly she is a rarity in hero tales.

Older women, substitute mothers who turn up to help the hero achieve his goal, appear from time to time in contemporary children's hero stories. Sophie Bang in *I am David* (Holm [1963] 1980) emerges at an amazingly convenient moment to help David locate his mother. In Allan Baillie's *Little Brother* (1985) an Australian doctor, Betty Harris, large in body and heart, becomes fond of the orphan Cambodian refugee Vithy and decides to take him to Australia with her. They and their like are important in the plot but unconvincing and undeveloped as characters and, like the goddess Athene who comes down from Olympus to help Odysseus, they naturalize the concept of women's inherently ancillary role.

## WITCHES AND BITCHES

While strong, beneficent female figures have a somewhat ambiguous function in the hero tale, and do not fit comfortably into the pattern of interrelated dualisms at the centre of Western culture which assert the supremacy of the European patriarchy, their dark counterparts, the witches, sirens, fatal enchantresses and other evil female creatures, serve the ideological purposes of the myth perfectly. They are 'wild' and irrational, governed by emotions and physical hungers, whereas the hero, as Athene said of Odysseus, is 'so civilized, so intelligent, so self-possessed'. These dark and dangerous women are the hero's opponents and, unlike other females, they often play a major part in the story for they have broken out of the domestic sphere and are loose in the wilderness. They naturalize and justify male dominance because they show what iniquity uncontrolled femaleness is capable of! They threaten the hero's rationality, self-control and purpose. They try to divert him from his goal, tempting him to linger in sexual dalliance with them. Often, like the wicked witches in fairy tales and the beautiful spies who serve the enemy in the James Bond stories, they threaten his very life. Or, like the spirit who appears as Helen of Troy in Marlowe's *Faustus*, they would suck forth his soul (Marlowe [*c.* 1604] 1909: 154) leaving him doomed to perpetual torment. The stories assert the need to destroy them or, at the very least, to rob them of their power.

In pre-Christian stories fatal women are manifestations of the dark side of the great goddess whose consorts were once annually sacrificed to ensure the fertility of the land. To the emergent patriarchy she seemed an emanation of darkness and chaos, a threat to order and to life itself. Medusa is one of her best known incarnations in early European legend and has remained a potent symbol in the work of many later writers and artists. She was one of three sisters, the Gorgons, who lived at the farthest northern end of the earth, and the hero, Perseus, was able to find them only with the help of three other sisters, the Graiae, who were immeasurably aged and who alone knew where the Gorgons dwelt. The isolation of her dwelling place suggests dangerousness and extremity, perhaps the furthest reaches of the unconscious. According to the myth she had once been beautiful but had offended the goddess Athene who punished her by changing her beauty into an appalling hideousness and replaced her hair with hissing serpents. The serpents are present in all depictions of Medusa, but in some accounts she is described as still beautiful apart from the snaky hair, and it is this combination of beauty and horror which captured the imagination of later writers and artists.

If Perseus embodies the young, patriarchal spirit of the Hellenes, Medusa suggests the ancient female power of the goddess in its most terrifying form. She is sometimes regarded as the dark side of the beautiful Persephone since, like Persephone, she was ravished by a dark god, Poseidon, and spent some of her time in the Underworld (Kerenyi 1958: 43). That she represents a very ancient power is implied by the extreme old age of the Graiae who seem to stand for time itself, and who point the way to her. The snakes that hiss about her head were associated with the goddess of Minoan Crete, and the Greeks regarded them as sacred to the earth. So she stands for ancient chaos, for the darkness of fear and ignorance which possessed human minds before the emergence of reason. Her power to turn all who look upon her to stone suggests the way primitive terror can overcome the mind, even the mind of a hero, destroying reason, 'petrifying' consciousness.

Greek legends contain many other fatal women, all of them aspects or servants of the great goddess. The great mother goddess herself is Gaia, the earth, who emerged from Chaos. She bore a son, Ouranos, who later became her consort, and who hated and stole the children she bore him. Gaia then brought forth iron and made a sickle with sharp teeth. She persuaded a surviving son, Kronos, to use this sickle to castrate his father as punishment for his wicked deeds. Aphrodite, the beautiful goddess of love, was born from the foam created by the semen and genitalia of Ouranos which Kronos flung into the sea. Thus this legend associates the very principle of female sexuality with castration, with the destruction of masculine potency, and this theme is repeated in other myths such as the story of Aphrodite's love for the beautiful boy, Adonis, who was killed by a boar while hunting. Although in some versions Aphrodite warned him not to go on the hunt the essence of the legend is that his association with her caused his death. Red roses sprang from the earth where his blood fell, and red flowers were part of the rites of Adonis which were widely celebrated in Greece from the fifth century BC (Rose 1964: 125). Lesser deities fatal to men include the Sirens, goddesses of love and death, who were said to be companions of the Queen of the Underworld and daughters of Chthon, the depths of the earth. They are famous, of course, for their singing which lured wandering heroes to their death.

The story of Medea provides a somewhat more subtle example of the supposed violence and dangerousness of uncontrolled female power. Both the dramatist Euripides and the Hellenistic poet, Apollonius of Rhodes, depict her as unintentionally evil, a passionate woman used and abused by the hero Jason whom she loved, a woman who was able to do terrible deeds in his service and then wreak murderous vengeance upon him because of the magic powers she possessed. Without her powers, the stories imply, she would have remained just another meek and obedient, if ill-used woman, another tragic victim who could have been pitied for her suffering – obviously a preferable state of affairs. Apollonius relates the first part of her story in *The Argonautica* where he tells how, as a young girl, a daughter of the king of Colchis, she fell passionately in love with Jason who had come to retrieve the Golden Fleece and take it back to Hellas. Because she was a priestess of Hecate and 'mistress of drugs' she was able to provide Jason with magical assistance in carrying out the tasks her father had imposed upon him with the intention of bringing about his death. Medea was reluctant to provide this aid but did so because she was overcome by passion:

> Often her heart fluttered wildly in her breast. As when a sunbeam which is reflected out of water that has just been poured into a bowl or a bucket, dances inside a house and darts this way and that as it is shaken in the rapid swirl, so did the young girl's heart quiver in her breast. From her eyes flowed tears of pity, and within her the pain wore her away, smouldering through her flesh, around her fine nerves and deep into the very base of the neck where the ache and hurt drive deepest, whenever the tireless Loves shoot their pains into the heart. At one moment she thought that she would give him the drugs as charms against the bulls; then she would not, but would herself face death; then she would not die and would not give the drugs, but with calmness would endure her misery just as she was.
>
> (Apollonius of Rhodes 1995: 84)

She flees with the Argonauts because she fears the consequences of her father's rage, and, when they are pursued and trapped by a party of Colchians led by her brother Apsyrtos, she helps Jason deceive him into meeting with her alone, thus providing the chance to murder him. As Jason leaps upon him with his sword she turns her face away and covers her eyes with her veil, but she is fully complicit in the murder nevertheless.

Apollonius does not deal with the development of Jason and Medea's ill-fated relationship after the Argonauts reach home, but this is the subject of the earlier work, Euripides' *Medea*. In this tragedy Jason, now the father of two sons by Medea, has seized the opportunity to enhance his power by marrying a princess, the daughter of Creon, king of Corinth. Medea and her children are to be banished, but Jason insists that he will provide for them richly in their exile, and clearly has no doubts about the morality of his behaviour. The play is constructed so as to avoid making Jason's actions the issue, for the focus is on Medea's revenge and it is she with whom the Chorus pleads. Medea is unable to return to her homeland and, having lost Jason, believes that she has lost everything. Determined at least to avoid being scorned by her enemies she uses her arts to murder the new bride; pretending to accept the situation she sends her a poisoned robe and golden crown. She then kills her own sons, partly to complete the destruction of Jason's house and partly to save them from suffering vengeance for her own deeds. The play foregrounds her agony, but she is nevertheless seen to be guilty because of the excesses of her passion and the irresponsible use of her arts. Jason is given a speech summarizing the troublesomeness of women. As he sees it their very existence is an affliction:

> Some other way to beget sons should mortals
> Have found, and the race of women ne'er have been.
> No woes then had there been to afflict mankind.
> (Euripides 1949: 158)

From these and similar myths the figure of the fatal woman in European culture took initial shape, but it was Christianity which provided the context for the full flowering of the stereotype. The Biblical stories of Eve, of Delilah, who betrayed the hero Samson, and of Salome, who persuaded her stepfather, Herod, to behead John the Baptist, provided vivid paradigms of female malevolence towards men. In all these instances it is the active sexuality of the women which makes them dangerous and establishes them as archetypes of evil. In Christian teachings women are both a source of temptation for virtuous men by reason of their sexuality and also the cause of humanity's fallen state. In the Genesis story, Eve's moral weakness in allowing herself to be persuaded by the serpent is the origin of all humanity's woes, and in tempting Adam to share the forbidden fruit she involved him in her sin. Thus, in this tradition, women are naturally inferior, being created second to Adam and made from a part of his body, and they are also guilty. They are dangerous, corrupting, and they have dealings with the powers of evil. Centuries of persecution of women and denial of their most basic human rights have been justified by these beliefs.

Many stories of witches and evil enchantresses emerged during the Middle

Ages and there are several such figures in the Arthurian material that Malory gathered together and shaped into *Le Morte d'Arthur* which has been the basis of many fantasies for young readers. Malory eliminated much of the supernatural material which he found in his sources, but the enchantress Morgan le Fay remains an important and enigmatic presence. She was Arthur's half-sister and 'a passing fair lady' (Malory [1485] 1906 vol. 1: 35) who seduced the young Arthur without his realizing who she was when she was already the wife of King Lot of Orkney and the mother of four sons. As a result of her incestuous and adulterous liaison with Arthur she bore another son, Mordred, who eventually brought about Arthur's death. She is thus a figure of potent sexuality, and, at the level of the tale's Christian significance, an embodiment of evil. It was shortly after his encounter with Morgan that Arthur was given the magical sword, Excalibur, by another mysterious woman, the beautiful Lady of the Lake. The possession of Excalibur marked him as the supreme hero and destined leader, but he was already fatally damaged, having produced the instrument of his own destruction. His death at the hands of Mordred was a matter of prophecy, and the entire romance becomes a tragic progress towards this inevitable end.

Despite an overlay of Christian symbolism the Lady of the Lake and Morgan le Fay suggest the two opposite aspects of the great goddess. The Lady is a beneficent force but her powers are ancient, pagan and magical rather than Christian. In Malory she serves the cause of heroism and the tradition of chivalry. It was she who taught Lancelot, the greatest of all knights, and she intervenes to further Arthur's heroic progress, giving him Excalibur whose scabbard ensures that, so long as he has it, he can receive no mortal injury. On the other hand Morgan uses her wiles to make him her lover, and consistently seeks his death. In a later section we learn how she uses enchantment to steal Excalibur and give it to her paramour, Sir Accolon, so that he may fight with Arthur and kill him. Arthur is sorely wounded in the fight but eventually the Lady of the Lake, who is aware of Morgan le Fay's evil plans, intervenes once more, causing Excalibur to fall from Accolon's hand so that Arthur is able to recover it and deal his enemy a mortal blow. Thus the light and dark aspects of the goddess, struggle for the life of the hero.

When Arthur is fatally wounded by Mordred in the final battle of Camlann, as was foretold, he orders Sir Bedivere, one of his few surviving knights, to throw Excalibur into the lake. When Sir Bedivere reluctantly obeys a hand appears from the water to grasp the sword and pluck it back into the depths. So Arthur's career as a hero reaches its end and a barge with three queens, veiled in black, appears to bear him off to Avalon. Significantly one of these queens is Morgan le Fay. Malory writes:

> Thus of Arthur I find never more written in books that be authorised, nor more of the very certainty of his death heard I never read, but thus was he led away in a ship wherein were three queens; that one was King

> Arthur's sister, Queen Morgan le Fay; the other was the queen of Northgalis; the third was the Queen of the Waste Lands.
>
> (Malory [1485] 1906 vol. 2: 390–1)

When he is lifted onto the barge Arthur lays his head in Morgan's lap and she says: '"Ah, dear brother, why have you tarried so long from me?"' (p. 389) Malory makes no attempt to explain the seeming contradiction between this scene and Morgan le Fay's previous behaviour. It is likely that he simply recorded incidents from his source material without attempting to reconcile them completely, but there is no contradiction if we assume that in earlier versions of these tales Morgan le Fay was an incarnation of the dark goddess who took Arthur as her lover, lost him for a time to the world of heroic action, but appeared at last to claim him back. Like the Lady of the Lake she is a pagan figure, a force of nature rather than an embodiment of evil in the Christian sense, the details of her various intrigues being added later and her real significance forgotten, as the stories moved further from their origins. In Malory she is a memorable and influential version of the fatal woman. It is she, rather than Mordred, who is the binary opposite of Arthur in the pattern of the romance, the symbol of the forces of nature, of passion, fertility and death, against which the hero opposes his will and his reason to establish a structure of order, the perfect circle of the Round Table, by means of which nature may be mastered.

The witches that haunt fairy tales and fly on their broomsticks through modern children's literature derive chiefly from images created during the witchcraft hysteria of the late Middle Ages, overlaid by Shakespeare's Weird Sisters in *Macbeth* with their choppy fingers, beards and skinny lips. The Church's persecution of witches, the overwhelming majority of whom were women, may have been partly a political stratagem to deflect popular discontent away from the Church itself as Lopez suggests (Lopez 1978: 208). It may also have been a move to counter new currents of thought, both the worldly cult of courtly love, celebrated in the songs of the troubadours, which glorified sexual passion and elevated women, and the questioning of Church doctrines which culminated in 1517 in Luther's Ninety-five Theses that precipitated the Reformation. But belief in witches was certainly widespread amongst all classes in the fifteenth and sixteenth centuries. Just why the hysteria took such hold during this period, and how far any of these women were practitioners of a surviving form of the religion of the great goddess it is impossible to say, but they were accused of consorting with Satan and claiming to consort with heathen goddesses.

The text book of the witch hunters, the *Malleus Maleficarum* ('Hammer of the Witches'), the work of two German divines, Heinrich Kramer and Jakob Sprenger, was first published in 1486. Although there had been witch hunts in the earlier years of the fifteenth century it was this work, endorsed by Pope Innocent VIII, which fuelled the craze and established the definitive concept of the 'witch'. It proclaimed magisterially that:

> It must not be omitted that certain wicked women perverted by Satan and seduced by the illusions and phantasms of devils, believe and profess that they ride in the night hours on certain beasts with Diana, the heathen goddess, or with Herodias, and with a countless number of women, and that in the untimely silence of the night they travel over great distances of land.
>
> (*Malleus Maleficarum*, in Otten 1986: 108)

Although the authors insist that the witches' claims to fly and consort with Diana are 'altogether false' (p. 108), illusions perpetrated by Satan, the image persisted in the popular imagination, along with claims that witches had sexual intercourse with devils. One William West of the Inner Temple in a work called *Symbolaeographie* [1594] said of witches that they:

> shake the air with lightning and thunder, to cause Hail and tempests, to remove green corn and trees to an other place, to be carried of her familiar which hath taken upon him the deceitful shape of a goat, swine, or calf etc. into some mountain. . . . And sometimes to fly upon a staff or fork, or some other instrument.
>
> (Quoted in Bradbrook [1951] 1977: 19)

Here is the witch of children's literature, flying on her broomstick, casting spells, and accompanied by her black cat. It is her sexuality, her irrationality, her links with nature and with the powers of evil that make her the binary opposite of the hero in a range of traditional and modern stories. The power of stories and stereotypes is evident in the fact that during the two hundred years from the late fifteenth to the late seventeenth century in Europe and Britain thousands of women were tortured, burned or hanged as witches, and many thousands more were persecuted and brought to trial though they escaped execution.

The literary home of the wicked witch is the fairy tale of which the simple hero story 'Hansel and Gretel' is typical. As in most hero tales the opposition between home and the wilderness, or the forest, is central but in this story home is not safe for the young hero and his sister because it is dominated by their wicked stepmother whose *alter ego* is the witch who lives in the forest. The children are abandoned in the forest because their stepmother insists there is not enough food to feed them, and after wandering for three days, facing death by starvation, they are led by a white bird to the house of the witch. This house is made of bread, cake and clear sugar, so they are able to satisfy their hunger. The witch takes them in, pretending to be loving and benevolent, a representative of the safe domestic world. She provides them with a delicious meal and comfortable beds but then reveals her true aim which is to eat them both. They eventually escape when Gretel is able to push the witch into the oven, and they fill their pockets with the jewels they find in the house. On their homeward journey they are assisted by a white duck who bears them across a river on her back, and they are finally welcomed by their father who had never been a willing participant in their abandonment. The stepmother has died, so father and children are able to live happily and prosperously on the proceeds of the jewels.

Anthony Browne's illustrations for this Grimm Brothers' story in the 1981 Julia MacCrae picture book edition employ a number of devices to suggest a symbolic identity between the witch and the ruthless, rejecting stepmother. The shape of a tall, pointed witch's hat, formed by the window curtains, is added to the shadow of the stepmother in an early illustration. The same shape formed by the division of the curtains appears in a later picture of the witch's house, framing the head and torso of the witch herself. The face of the stepmother in a close-up illustration of her is the same as the face of the witch in this later illustration, except that the witch is depicted as old while the stepmother is young and beautiful except for her narrow, down-turned red lips. The story itself invites this conflation insofar as the deaths of the witch and the stepmother coincide and both try to bring about the children's deaths. Like most fairy tales 'Hansel and Gretel' has several layers of significance, but the witch and her malevolence is crucial to all of them.

Jack Zipes reads it as a tale about pre-capitalist social conditions in eighteenth century Germany, where evil members of the aristocracy had houses 'made' of food and hoards of hidden treasure, while the peasantry were reduced to such penury that they could not afford to feed their children. The actions of Hansel and Gretel offered hope that the common people might be able to use their initiative and take action to survive in an unjust society (Zipes 1979: 32–4). It seems unarguable that the version which the Grimm Brothers collected does relate to the extreme poverty of a period when the abandonment of children was far from unknown. In the Grimms' retelling the story gains a more spiritual quality: the white birds flicker with suggestions of Christian symbolism and hint at the continued presence of the dead mother's spirit watching over her children and saving them from the witch. (Marina Warner points out (Warner 1994: 211) that in the original tale it was the real mother who abandoned the children, but the Grimms, with Victorian sensibility, softened its harshness by turning her into a stepmother.) For modern readers, however, the main significance of the story is likely to inhere in the children's relationship with their father and stepmother and the struggle against the witch, rather than in Christian symbols.

Bettelheim sees this struggle as essentially concerned with the need to move beyond oral gratification, to overcome the sense of rejection we experience when weaned from the mother's breast. In his analysis the children's perception that the stepmother wishes to leave them to starve is an expression of this sense of rejection. Likewise, he says, the witch at first appears to be a good mother figure but then she too turns out to be rejecting, because, far from continuing to feed them, she wishes to eat them (Bettelheim 1976: 163). He argues that the children's experiences in the witch's house purge them of their oral fixations and their return home across the river, assisted by the white duck, represents a transition to a more mature stage of development, one where they are able to contribute to the family's support (by means of the jewels) rather than being merely dependent. This analysis, while interesting, does not account for either the extreme malevolence of the witch who does not merely reject the children, but wishes to devour them, or the closure where happiness is attained only after the destruction of the stepmother/witch.

A sense of female power as dangerous and perverse is central to this story. If Hansel and Gretel are to survive childhood, survive their journey through the forest and reach adulthood, they must overcome it. The stepmother's power is shown to be out of control in the private world of home, while the witch is loose in the forest and her intentions are murderous. The task, as always in the hero story, is to defeat the wild things, and here the wild things are aberrant women who do not conform to their proper role.

The witches in stories written specifically for children similarly suggest dangerous, and implicitly sexual, female power. The story of Salome eventually inspired Oscar Wilde's play of that name [1894] in which the link between female sexuality and evil is made vivid when Salome kisses the lips of the severed head of Jokanaan who had dared to repulse her advances. Wilde's play, in turn, inspired a notable series of black and white drawings by Aubrey Beardsley which seem to have established twentieth-century conceptions of the appearance of the fatal woman. In these works Salome is slender and sinuous, with dark, elaborately coiled hair, high cheek bones and upward slanting eyes; like all Beardsley's women she exudes a decadent sexuality. Beardsley's influence is apparent in many Hollywood productions and in children's book illustrations by artists such as Kay Nielsen and Edmund du Lac. Walt Disney's cartoon images of the evil stepmother in the film of *Snow White* and of Cruella De Vil in his 1960 adaptation of Dodie Smith's *One Hundred and One Dalmatians*, which is currently enjoying a revival, also conform to the pattern. The implication that female sexuality equates with evil has become a commonplace of popular entertainment for children.

This is particularly clear in the case of the White Witch, Jadis, the personification of evil in C.S Lewis' Narnia stories. Her physical attractiveness has a hint of Hollywood glamour:

> She also was covered in white fur up to her throat and held a long straight golden wand in her right hand and wore a golden crown on her head. Her face was white – not merely pale, but white like snow or paper or icing-sugar, except for her very red mouth. It was a beautiful face in other respects, but proud and cold and stern.
>
> (Lewis [1950] 1959: 33)

When she encounters Edmund, morally the weakest of the four children who make their way into Narnia in *The Lion, the Witch and the Wardrobe* [1950], she gains power over him by giving him some magic Turkish Delight which creates an insatiable craving for more, a craving she alone can satisfy. While this clearly symbolic sweetmeat suggests the effect of an addictive drug Edmund's response to the Turkish Delight is also strongly suggestive of sexual arousal: 'His face had become very red and his mouth and fingers were sticky' (p. 39). When the Witch describes her house which she wishes him to visit she asks him to look at 'two little hills' and says 'my house is between those two hills' (p. 40). The words evoke a sense of the female body, and of the possibility of entering it. While children are extremely unlikely to pick up these suggestions at a conscious level the whole scene with the Witch evokes the excitement of forbidden, secret things.

At the theological level of the story the Witch is cast as Satan, suggesting that Lewis shared the view of female sexuality held by many mediaeval theologians – that it was intrinsically evil, a snare to entrap righteous men. The White Witch is also clearly related to several specific incarnations of the dark aspect of the great goddess. Like Medusa she can turn living creatures into stone; the courtyard of her home is full of her victims. Like La Belle Dame she creates an unending winter in which nothing blooms, no new life emerges, no birds sing. Narnia is perpetually covered with snow until the arrival of Aslan brings spring and the beginning of the defeat of her power. Her dead white skin and red mouth recall Coleridge's Life-in-Death in 'The Ancient Mariner':

> Her lips were red, her looks were free,
> Her locks were yellow as gold:
> Her skin was white as leprosy,
> The Night-mare Life-in-Death was she,
> Who thicks man's blood with cold.
> (Coleridge [1798] 1906: 128)

Death is the fate of those who succumb to the White Witch's seductions. When the battle with Aslan and the forces of good is in progress she determines to kill Edmund and it is clear that his death would be part of a long tradition. She says: '"I would like to have done it on the Stone Table itself... That is the proper place. That is where it has always been done before"' (Lewis [1950] 1959: 123). When she is defeated in the battle she claims the right to the traitor Edmund's life according to the rules of the 'Deep Magic': '"His blood is my property"' (p. 129). But the Christian allegory is pursued and Edmund is saved when Aslan offers to die in his place. The Witch's links to the ancient goddess and to unholy sacrificial rites are suggested as she whets her knife in preparation for killing Aslan: we are told that it was 'made of stone, not of steel, and it was of a strange and evil shape' (p. 140). She symbolizes 'evil' female power and sexuality as defined in both the Christian and pre-Christian traditions, power capable of diverting male energy away from the cause of 'virtue' and patriarchal dominance.

There are many similar witches in other children's hero stories, such as the Wicked Witch of the West in L. Frank Baum's *The Wonderful Wizard of Oz*

[1900] and the evil and deceitful Zayide in Michael Ende's *The Neverending Story* [1978] who manipulates the hero, Bastian, by feeding his egotism and his delusions of power. They are realized with varying degrees of effectiveness but all are produced from the traditional template. The witch Serret in Ursula Le Guin's *A Wizard of Earthsea* [1968] conforms to the type in that she is dark-haired and deceitful, but she is a more subtle creation than most of her kind. The text hints that, although she has given herself to the service of evil as a means to power, she has done so only because she can see no other way for a woman to achieve self-realization. All the wizards in Earthsea are men. Le Guin's imaginary world is similar to mediaeval Europe in many ways including the exclusion of women from access to higher learning and Serret's situation mirrors that of many actual women in former times who turned to witchcraft as the only source of knowledge accessible to them. Although women are marginalized in this tale, as in most hero stories, simplistic stereotyping is avoided, and the reader is invited to share the pity which the hero, Ged, the focalizing character, feels for Serret's lonely exile in her enchanted castle.

In *King Solomon's Mines* [1885], H. Rider Haggard created a variant in the African witch, Gagool, who does her best to thwart the heroes, Allan Quartermain and his companions, in their quest to discover a hidden diamond mine. All the fundamental dualities which have structured Western thinking are evoked by the opposition of Gagool and the British heroes. Not only is she 'wild' in contrast to the civilized gentlemen adventurers, she is black, alien, female, immensely aged and a hysteric who utters prophecies in a thin, wailing voice before falling to the ground 'foaming in an epileptic fit' (Haggard [1885] 1958: 123). The Zulu-like African tribe which she controls through her influence over their tyrannical king is itself constructed as a contrast to Quartermain and his friends, but the men of this tribe are in many ways noble savages, and the implication is that they would progress further towards true civilization if it were not for the grip Gagool has on their minds. As opposed to both the cultivated intellects of the British adventurers and the calm, sensible thinking of the good native leader, Ignosi, she is depicted as the embodiment of irrationality and destructive passion, conducting vindictive witch hunts and handing out random sentences of death. Her animosity towards the white adventurers is represented as further evidence of evil, and her death as a victory for reason and British civilization. *King Solomon's Mines* was followed in 1887 by *She*, another popular story of an evil female, in this case a *femme fatale* who lures men to their destruction.

The fatal woman who uses her sexuality to bewitch the hero and then destroy him is a common variant of the witch in adult literature from the Romantic period to the present. Deriving from figures such as Salome and Morgan Le Fay, in poetry, fantasy, horror stories and horror films she is frequently a supernatural being who deceives the hero into believing she is human, but she appears also, without supernatural qualities, in 'realistic' adult fiction. Keats' 'La Belle Dame Sans Merci' is perhaps her best known literary incarnation. In this poem a knight-at-arms tells how he met a beautiful woman, long-haired and wild-eyed, who lured him to her 'elfin grot' where she made love to him and then cast him into an enchanted sleep. While asleep he dreamed of all the others she had treated in the same way:

> 'I saw pale kings and princes too,
> Pale warriors, death-pale were they all;
> Who cried – "La belle Dame sans Merci
> Hath thee in thrall!"
>
> 'I saw their starved lips in the gloam
> With horrid warning gapèd wide,
> And I awoke and found me here
> On the cold hill's side.
>
> 'And this is why I sojourn here
> Alone and palely loitering,
> Though the sedge is wither'd from the lake,
> And no birds sing.'
>
> (Keats [1819] 1995: 208)

La Belle Dame is the exemplar of her type. Her *raison d'être* is the destruction of the wandering heroes she encounters, and what she inflicts upon them is a spiritual death. The knight's will to act has been destroyed by his sexual encounter with her, and his very will to live is withering like the sedge on the lake, for his life has lost all possibility of joy. For him there is nothing but the cold hill's side where no birds sing. The heavy spondees in the last line sound with the finality of a death knell; there will be no reprieve.

Fatal women appear frequently in the work of French *fin de siècle* writers such as Baudelaire, Barbey d'Aurevilly and Huysmans, and they are omnipresent in Swinburne. In his sado-masochistic fantasies their cruelty is celebrated, but although the men in his works are victims for whom pleasure is pain and love delicious martyrdom they are victims nevertheless. A few stanzas from the diffuse and repetitive 'Dolores' are sufficient to indicate the essence of the whole:

> Cold eyelids that hide like a jewel
> Hard eyes that grow soft for an hour;
> The heavy white limbs, and the cruel
> Red mouth like a venomous flower;
> When these are gone by with their glories,
> What shall rest of thee then, what remain
> O mystic and sombre Dolores,
> Our Lady of Pain?
>
> . . .

Fruits fall and love dies and time ranges;
Thou art fed with perpetual breath,
And alive after infinite changes,
And fresh from the kisses of death;
Of langours rekindled and rallied,
Of barren delights and unclean,
Things monstrous and fruitless, a pallid
And poisonous queen.

. . .

There are sins it may be to discover,
There are deeds it may be to delight.
What new work wilt thou find for thy lover
What new passions for daytime or night?
What spells that they know not a word of
Whose lives are as leaves overblown?
What tortures undreamt of, unheard of,
Unwritten, unknown?
(Swinburne [1887] 1919: 126–8)

Swinburne's work can seem both pathological and an affectation possible only within the milieu of pre-Raphaelite fascination with the sadness and cruelty of an imagined mediaevalism, but the fatal woman has a vigorous life in works from all periods, including contemporary literature. She appears in banal form in numerous paperback romances, and she dominates Josephine Hart's modishly successful novel, *Damage* [1991], the tale of a hero who leaves the fashionable respectability of home to adventure in a psychological-sexual wilderness with a woman who shares Dolores' ability to devise new passions for daytime and night, and who consumes and destroys him. He cannot find his way back from the wilderness, so the novel ends in tragedy rather than triumphant return.

The unnamed hero/narrator of this work is a middle-aged Conservative member of the British parliament with a promising career ahead of him. He is wealthy, attractive, well-dressed, conventional, with a beautiful, gentle, blonde wife and two pleasant grown-up children. Anna Barton is the fiancée of his son, Martyn. Until his meeting with her the protagonist's life has been comfortable but superficial: nothing has aroused his commitment and he has experienced no profound emotion. He has always behaved honourably but with rational self-interest, furthering his career in the world of politics. He is a modern, diminished King Arthur, supported by a pure, fair Lady of the Lake, and destroyed by an incarnation of Morgan Le Fay. When he meets Anna at a party he is deeply stirred and, although he knows she is his son's fiancée, they embark almost immediately on a passionate, increasingly sado-masochistic affair. He experiences this as a journey into a previously unimagined wilderness: 'And at last the age-old ritual possessed us, and I bit and tore and held her, round and round, as we rose and fell, rose and fell into the wilderness' (Hart [1991] 1992: 38).

Anna, dark-haired (of course) and self-contained, has had previous passionate relationships and her younger brother killed himself because of his desire for her. Thus she functions as an embodiment of 'wild', devouring female sexuality. She is content to divide herself between father and son, but the protagonist grows jealous of his son. When, inevitably, Martyn discovers them together, both men are destroyed. Disoriented by shock Martyn falls to his death from the landing of the stairs. Anna withdraws immediately into her own life, leaving the protagonist distraught and disgraced, unable to continue with his career, his marriage or even the ordinary routines of his existence. He retires to an anonymous apartment painted entirely in white with no decoration except for two blown up photographs – of Anna and Martyn. In this white space he lives the life of a solitary automaton – alone and palely loitering, waiting, like the knight-at-arms, for the kindness of death to overtake him.

These works suggest that female sexuality will destroy the hero should he succumb to it because it will submerge reason. This idea is explicable in the context of Ortner's and Kristeva's theories of the perceived liminality of women, their imagined position at the boundary between nature and culture, or between civilization and wilderness, and probably derives ultimately from ancient belief in the destructive power of the goddess. The hero's fear is that to submit to a woman, to turn away from rationality and self-control in a moment of sexual surrender, is to risk being permanently overwhelmed by 'nature', by chaotic, messy physicality and illogical emotion. This is precisely what happens to the hero of *Damage* as his passion for Anna overwhelms and destroys his hitherto successful career in politics. The actual spilling of semen thus becomes a metaphor for the loss of 'manhood', the loss of rational control and secure membership of the public world of affairs and heroic enterprises. A sexually active woman is 'fatal', a witch, a vampire, a belle dame sans merci, because she threatens such a loss. The lovers of the great goddess were always symbolically sacrificed after a short period as her consort so that to submit to her is to ensure that death will soon follow. It is a form of suicide, a choice of death over life. Thus to look upon the face of the Medusa was to be turned into stone.

The obverse of the fatal woman's deadliness is her attraction, which is perversely enhanced by the danger inherent in her beauty. In the *Odyssey*, Calypso and Circe, the enchantresses who try to deter Odysseus from his homeward path, are consistently described as 'lovely' (e.g. Homer 1946: 92, 167) and in Greek art Medusa is sometimes shown as beautiful despite the serpents which sprout from her head. It was this oxymoronic quality which made her a popular subject for the Romantic poets of the nineteenth century. A poem of Shelley's, inspired by a Renaissance painting of Medusa which he saw in Florence, illustrates this attraction:

It lieth, gazing on the midnight sky,
Upon the cloudy mountain-peak supine;
Below, far lands are seen tremblingly;
Its horror and its beauty are divine.
Upon its lips and eyelids seem to lie
Loveliness like a shadow, from which shine,
Fiery and lurid, struggling underneath,
The agonies of anguish and of death.

Yet it is less the horror than the grace
Which turns the gazer's spirit into stone,
Whereon the lineaments of that dead face
Are graven till the characters be grown
Into itself, and thought no more can trace;
'Tis the melodious hue of beauty thrown
Athwart the darkness and the glare of pain,
Which humanize and harmonize the strain.
(Shelley [1819] 1970: 582)

It is beauty and pain, together, which '*humanize* and harmonize' the strain. For the Romantics the beauty of the Medusa was an alternative to the proportion and perfection of Praxiteles, the classic ideal which was a visual representation of the harmonies of mathematics and logic, inhuman because of its perfection. Their celebration of Medusa is a recognition that life is as full of pain and horror as of beauty, and that awareness of the pain and horror makes the beauty more precious. This is not Swinburne's sado-masochistic delight in cruel beauty, but a recognition that it is necessary to embrace the whole of life, that insistence upon balance and perfection is a form of denial. Romanticism represents the most significant rebellion in Western culture against the programme of the hero, against the exaltation of rationalism in the service of patriarchal dominance. The Romantics celebrated the energy of uncontrolled nature, of cataracts and storms, as well as of 'wild things', the tiger burning bright.

For the classical hero and his descendants, however, the dark goddess in all her incarnations is unequivocally an enemy. To escape actual or spiritual death at her hands he must kill her, or ensure that her death occurs. So Perseus beheads Medusa with a sickle presented to him by the bright male god Hermes, and those who fail to do what Perseus did are doomed, like the protagonist of *Damage*. James Bond, an omnipresent modern hero, frequently encounters beautiful and dangerous women, but manages to destroy them or neutralize their power and emerge triumphant and unchanged. As well as constructing a political version of the wilderness/civilization dualism the Bond stories inscribe the opposition of rational, male virtue and unprincipled female deviousness. In the first Bond novel, *Casino Royale*, Vesper Lynd is dangerous because she has been ordered to betray Bond to the enemy, but there is an underlying suggestion that she is more subtly dangerous in a way that is intrinsic to her beauty and sexuality. Bond's commitment to the cause of espionage is weakened by his growing passion for Vesper. Eventually, lulled by the natural beauty of the French seaside and the physical and emotional delights of their love-making, he decides that he will ask her to marry him. Such a step would displace his dedication to the Secret Service. It would amount to a renunciation of the public, political world ruled by Cold War logic in favour of the private world of emotion and personal relationships. It would represent the triumph of Nature, of the power of the ancient goddess, over Reason and the power of the patriarchy. But Bond is saved for politics and patriarchy because Vesper, a double agent, kills herself rather than risk SMERSH destroying both of them. When Bond reads her farewell letter in which she proclaims her love and explains her treachery all his doubts about his role vanish:

> He saw her now only as a spy. Their love and his grief were relegated to the boxroom of his mind. Later, perhaps they would be dragged out, dispassionately examined, and then bitterly thrust back with other sentimental baggage he would rather forget. Now he could only think of her treachery to the Service and to her country, and of the damage it had done.
>
> (Fleming 1954: 174)

He dedicates himself anew to the cause, deciding that SMERSH will be his particular target. When he contacts his superiors in London to report Vesper's betrayal his concluding words define her role in the hero's story: '"The bitch is dead now"' (p. 176).

Although *Casino Royale* creates considerable sympathy for Vesper Lynd who is trapped by the ruthlessness of male politics, and points to some of the ways in which the hero tale constructs meanings that serve the interests of the patriarchal establishment, it does not pursue these issues. Instead it settles for a conventional appeal to adolescent male fantasies of superiority and dominance over adoring but nevertheless treacherous women who deserve what they get. The closure reinforces the conventional meanings, restates the fundamental dualisms, and re-imposes all the limitations of the genre. The sequels and the Bond movies which followed have continued to assert the values of Western patriarchy, and in particular the subordination of women, in a context of consumerist glamour and technological gimmickry. Their popularity shows that this is a formula with wide appeal, and the money they generate serves the cause they proclaim.

Another form of popular entertainment which draws on the tradition of the fatal woman and has established the stereotype in the public imagination is the horror movie. The vampires and wolf women who roam the sets of these productions are sexually active females who are out of control. Their consistently reiterated meaning is that female sexuality is likely to be murderous unless it is dominated by a strong man, and it is the duty of strong men to destroy such women, or force their submission, for the common good. For example Rino di Silvestro's *Legend of the Wolf Woman* (1977) contains a protagonist who realizes she is the reincarnation of a werewolf ancestress. In response to this knowledge she tears out the throat of her sister's husband and then goes on a rampage, killing any man who responds to her sexual overtures, until she is finally trapped by a heroic police inspector. She is incarcerated to prevent her doing further harm. Mel Welles' *Lady Frankenstein* (1971) perverts Mary Shelley's tale and shifts most of the guilt to a woman, Frankenstein's daughter, who sets out to avenge her father's death by creating another monster to destroy the one which has killed him. But this second creature is both good-looking and intelligent, and she has sex with him. This is sufficient evidence of her infamy – the creature kills her, thus conveying the message that a woman who is both clever and sexually active is too dangerous to live. Ted Mikels' *Blood Orgy of the She Devils* (1973) contains a coven of attractive witches and a hero who is a theology professor. As a result of his exorcising intervention the minor witches kill each other and the leader who turns herself into a bat is captured and burned – as witches should be. Harvey Kumel's *Daughters of Darkness* (1971) adds lesbianism to vampirism. In this film the beautiful evil-doer seduces women and exercises hypnotic power over them. With the assistance of her latest conquest she kills the male protagonist (her lover's husband) and together they drink his blood. As a lesbian vampire she is doubly an affront to the notion of proper, submissive femininity, a threat to women as well as men. The taste for such tales, like the vampiresses' taste for blood, appears to be insatiable. In our culture the message about the dangerousness of female sexuality does not pall.

It is appropriate to conclude this section with the most striking instance of a devouring female in twentieth-century young adult or children's literature. The name of Shelob, the giant spider in Tolkien's *The Lord of the Rings*, suggests that she is meant to signify the essence of the female, and the fact that she is a spider implies that that essence is animal – appetite and sex devoid of reason. The virtuous women in the trilogy are two-dimensional asexual figures who provide decorative touches in the semiotic patterns of the story but make little emotional impact. Shelob, however, appears to have been conceived out of a real sense of horrified revulsion. She guards one of the entrances to Mordor, the kingdom of the Dark Lord, Sauron. Her lair is in a deep cave approached by dark, narrow passages through the rock. This recalls the Minotaur at the heart of the labyrinth, and Gollum in his cave beneath the Misty Mountain in Tolkien's earlier work, *The Hobbit*. Like both these symbolic figures Shelob suggests the fear which lurks deep in the unconscious, but because of the emphasis on her femaleness, her lair also suggests the passages of the female body, and the small heroes, Frodo and Sam, become engulfed in these dark, repulsive passages.

Their first awareness of her is a foul and all pervasive smell which afflicts them as they approach her lair. This is an overture to the description of her body from which the stench emanates:

> Great horns she had, and behind her short, stalk-like neck was her huge swollen body, a vast bloated bag, swaying and sagging between her legs; its great bulk was black, blotched with livid marks, but the belly beneath was pale and luminous and gave forth a stench.
>
> (Tolkien 1981: 420)

This image of grotesque pregnancy is followed by a metaphorical account of coition which outdoes it in the sense of revulsion it conveys. Shelob has overwhelmed Frodo. He lies helpless beneath her swaying bulk when Sam comes to his aid with a sword in his hand. He manages to get beneath her and strikes upwards:

> She yielded to the stroke, and then heaved up the great bag of her belly high above Sam's head. Poison frothed and bubbled from the wound. Now splaying her legs she drove her huge bulk down on him again. Too soon. For Sam still stood upon his feet, and dropping his own sword, he held the elven-blade point upwards, fending off that ghastly roof; and so Shelob, with the driving force of her own cruel will, with greater strength than any warrior's hand, thrust herself upon a bitter spike. Deep, deep it pricked, as Sam was crushed slowly to the ground.
>
> (Tolkien [1954] 1981: 424)

Shelob's function as an image of female sexuality – hideous, repulsive, overwhelming, devouring – is underlined by contrast with the Elf Queen, Galadriel who stands for spirituality and virginity. As they are fleeing from Shelob a bright image of Galadriel, white and golden against a green meadow, comes into Sam's mind, and Frodo holds aloft the phial she gave him which emits a star-like radiance. In case the iconography should not be enough by itself to ensure that Galadriel is associated with the Virgin she is referred to as 'the Lady' (p. 413) while Shelob is several times called simply 'She' (p. 414). A link to the ancient cult of the goddess is implied when we are told she is immeasurably old, predating even the Dark Lord, and that she lusts to kill 'Elves and Men' (p. 418). So female virginity and sexuality are opposed, and equated, respectively, with good and evil.

There is a reprise of Shelob and her death on the point of Sam's small phallic sword in the *Alien* trilogy of horror films (1979–92) in which a huge female ant-like creature from outer space reproduces endlessly and oozes deadly sticky fluids which destroy her victims. She has a cavernous, blood-dripping mouth ringed with cruel teeth, an image of the 'voracious vagina' (Miles 1989: 107) the fear of which lies behind so many myths. The hero who eventually destroys her and so saves humanity is a woman, Ripley, and this might seem to contradict the horror of the female implicit in the alien image. But Ripley shoots her down with the most phallic of weapons, a large machine gun, and the orgasmic explosion of bullets signifies the salutary power of male potency.

The description of Shelob is extreme in the intensity of revulsion implicit in it, but in all these texts the fatal female is viewed through the eyes of her victim, or a narrator who shares the victim's perspective and values, and what the reader sees is not the similitude of a human being but a symbol of the hero's fear and fascination. The qualities attributed to these female figures suggest the kinds of unconscious fears which haunt many men in Western civilization, just as the demonic powers attributed to women burnt at the stake for witchcraft in earlier centuries exemplified the pathological contents of their accusers' imaginations. Belief in the actual existence of evil, 'castrating', fatal women has always been widespread. In 1933 the distinguished literary critic Mario Praz wrote in *The Romantic Agony*:

> The type of the fatal *allumeuse* was very widespread, and though it may be too arbitrary to try to trace it always to literary models such as Matilda, Carmen or even Cécily – for, after all, *it is a type of which examples are not so very rare even in actual life* – it is, on the other hand, quite easy to discover elements of these characters in such figures as Rosalba 'la Pudica' (Barby d'Aurevilly, *A un dîner d'athées*) in Conchita (who is Carmen and Cécily rolled into one) and in the innumerable other creations of the lower grades of Romanticism.
>
> (Praz [1933] 1960: 225; my italics.)

The film industry has produced a steady stream of supposedly realistic movies which depict independent women as dangerous and destructive. *Working Girl*, *Fatal Attraction* and *Presumed Innocent* are recent examples. The popular media seize upon supposed examples of the fatal woman at work in real life. A recent example is a story reported in the Australian press of a sexually promiscuous HIV-infected woman allegedly travelling across the continent with the explicit intention of spreading death amongst the males of the eastern states. (*Sydney Morning Herald* 22 March 1996: 17). According to the reports she had been convicted in Western Australia of having unprotected sex and, when released from prison, announced that she planned to move to Victoria. This provoked outrage and alarm as though she could force her deadly attentions on innocent men who would be helpless in the face of her sexuality.

These clearly pathological fears continue to exert an influence on the way men perceive women and women perceive each other and themselves. The terms 'witch' and 'bitch' are regularly used as pejoratives to condemn women of whom the speaker disapproves and fear of being so labelled constrains the way many women dress, speak and act. The enduring stereotype encourages and justifies acts of violence against women who become labelled in the minds of their attackers as witches and bitches, deadly predators whose sex itself is proof of their guilt.

## BRIDES

If the witch and the fatal woman have functioned over the centuries as warnings to women who might be tempted to act autonomously or enjoy their own sexuality, the beautiful brides of hero tales have compounded women's psychological oppression by providing a model of what they 'ought' to be like – in appearance, attitude and behaviour. This model has profoundly influenced women's perceptions of themselves and has contributed to their pervasive self-consciousness about their looks and body shape. It has also helped create a lingering belief that it is natural for women to be submissive and self-denying, sacrificing their interests to the needs of the men in their lives.

It is hardly necessary to describe the physical attributes of the hero's bride as her late twentieth-century incarnations smile at us every day from advertisements, fashion magazines, film and television screens, but a consideration of the significance of her appearance is instructive. She is, of course, beautiful; in one of the most popular fairy tales 'Beauty' is her only name. But her beauty is of a particular kind, and advances in the technology of printing and the reproduction of works of art, together with the advent of film and television, have made the visual definitions of Western female beauty as familiar as the motifs of the hero story itself. From the nineteenth century, if not before, women have known not only that they must strive to be beautiful, but precisely what the essential attributes of 'beauty' are.

To begin with the bride is white, and usually blonde. In fairy tales golden-haired beauties abound; the only memorable dark-haired heroine is Snow White whose hair is in stark contrast to the pallor of her skin. Rapunzel is more typical: she had 'long and beautiful hair, as fine as spun gold' (Grimm 1994: 81), which she let down from her tower window to allow the witch and the prince to climb up. In 'The Goose Girl' the true princess each day 'unloosened her hair, which was of pure gold' (Grimm 1994: 410) and combed it out so that it dazzled both the goose boy and the king. The story of 'Goldilocks and the Three Bears' did not become popular until the late nineteenth century when it was modified to emphasize the golden hair. Originally the intruder who enters the bears' house was an old woman, a later version made her into a little girl who was at first called 'Silver-Hair', then 'Golden Hair' and finally she became 'Goldilocks' (Bettelheim 1976: 216–7). In Geraldine McCaughrean's recent retelling of 'Saint George and the Dragon' the Princess Sabra whom George rescues is described as 'a golden-haired maiden dressed in a lightly blowing smock' (McCaughrean 1994). Where the colour of her hair is not specified in the words of the story illustrators more often than not give the heroine of a hero tale golden tresses. George Cruikshank gave Cinderella golden curls in his drawings for an 1854 translation of Perrault (Opie and Opie 1974: 125) and Gustave Doré, Arthur Rackham and Walt Disney, amongst others, have ensured that she has remained glamorously blonde ever since.

Like the white skin of the hero which signifies the superiority and dominance of the European patriarchy the bride's blondeness carries racial connotations but it also draws on a more complex tangle of symbolism. Fairness has implied beauty in European literature at least since Homer described Helen as golden-haired (*xanthe*), and in English the word 'fair' means both blonde and beautiful. There are many famous visual representations of beauty which emphasize golden hair. The most well known is probably Botticelli's *Birth of Venus* in which the goddess stands on her shell enswathed in golden knee-length tresses which are her only covering and adornment. The golden hair of Titian's more voluptuous Venus of Urbino gleams from the wall of the Uffizi, and other blonde goddesses abound in all the galleries of Europe. The colour gold has connotations of value because of the preciousness of the metal, and the golden-haired maidens are, by implication, of great worth. Sometimes, as in the case of the miller's daughter who spun straw into gold in 'Rumplestiltskin', they are associated with actual golden treasure, but more often it is moral worth that is signified by their beauty and blonde locks. The suggestions of high moral value derive from the ancient symbolism of gold which is the colour of the sun and so of light itself. Because it is very unreactive and therefore resistant to tarnish, as well as because of its colour, the alchemists believed gold possessed a mystical purity, and it had a similarly special significance in most ancient cultures. The worship of the sun was central to the religion of ancient Egypt, and the golden sun disc is ubiquitous in Egyptian art. In the Old Testament the first words that God utters are 'Let there be light'. Because light is essential for all life, and because our circadian rhythms ensure that we wake and feel alive when day dawns and begin to feel tired as it darkens, it is natural for human beings to celebrate light and brightness, and so, perhaps, it was natural to regard it as an attribute of whatever heaven and god they believed in. In Christian iconography gold was used to colour the haloes of angels and saints and, from the Renaissance onwards, the hair of the Virgin is almost always depicted as golden.

These associations have been consistently exploited in literature, painting and film. Donne uses them brilliantly in 'The Relic' when he imagines his grave reopened to reveal the evidence of his love: 'A bracelet of bright hair about the bone' (Donne 1973: 76). More conventionally Rossetti's 'Blessed Damozel' leaned out from heaven and 'Her hair that lay along her back/Was yellow like ripe corn'. The girl on the beach in Joyce's *A Portrait of the Artist as a Young Man* [1916] who appears to Stephen Daedalus as an 'angel of mortal youth and beauty' has long fair hair (Joyce [1916] 1952: 195–6). Much of the work of the French Impressionists is a celebration of the beauty of light, and blonde hair glows in many of their canvases. The Hollywood fashion for blonde beauties, from Lillian Gish to Marilyn Monroe and Nicole Kidman, draws upon all this and spices it with sexual suggestiveness. And the naturally dark-haired Madonna dyes her hair blonde to exploit the whole tradition with postmodern irony.

However, the celebration of golden hair casts a shadow. It can be employed in the demonization of people with dark skin and dark hair, as the Nazis demonstrated. Marina Warner, in an interesting and detailed chapter on the symbolism of hair in *From the Beast to the Blonde*, says:

> For fairness was a guarantee of quality. It was the imaginary opposite of 'foul', it connoted all that was pure, good, clean. Blondeness is less a descriptive term about hair pigmentation than a blazon in code, a piece of a value system that it is urgent to confront and analyse because its implications, in moral and social terms, are so dire and are still so unthinkingly embedded in the most ordinary, popular materials of the imagination. The Nazis' Aryan fantasies were partly rooted in this ancient, enduring colour code.
>
> (Warner 1994: 364)

The golden-haired bride who is the hero's reward is usually also slender, delicate and very young. In earlier times female slenderness was regarded as indicative of aristocratic status since physical work builds strength and a more muscular conformation. To be a fitting reward for the hero his bride needed to be a lady of high degree and so she was described as small and delicate. In 'The Goose Girl' the king is impressed by the true princess's appearance even when she seems to be a mere servant, because she is so 'delicate and beautiful' (Grimm 1994: 409). Cinderella's tiny foot is the outstanding symbol of desirable smallness and delicacy. Although this detail appears to have originated in China when foot-binding was in fashion (Opie and Opie 1974: 120–1) and foot binding has always been regarded with horror in the West, innumerable Western women, until very recently, have attempted to fit their feet into the smallest possible shoes, with dire consequences for both their feet and their general health. Likewise the emphasis on slenderness has fuelled the diet industry and the epidemic of anorexia in modern times, despite the alternative fashion for fitness.

The extreme youth of fairy tale heroines, of which their slenderness is an indication, is in part a reflection of the actual age at which many women were married. Beauty, in Perrault's version of 'Sleeping Beauty' is 15 or 16 when she pricks her finger and falls asleep to await the coming of her prince. In the Grimm version she is just 15. Rapunzel was locked up at the age of 12 and it was 'a couple of years' later (Grimm 1994: 81) that the king's son heard her singing and tricked his way into her tower. In Victorian hero stories heroines are likewise usually very young and this is also partly related to the custom of early marriages for females, but many are still children when they first appear: Stanley Grahame's Ida is 'little Ida', an orphan child under his uncle's protection. David Copperfield's Agnes Wickfield is of school age when he first meets her. Even in twentieth-century stories heroines are sometimes mere children. Marcus's Cottia in *The Eagle of the Ninth* is 'a girl of perhaps 12 or 13, with a sharply pointed face that seemed all golden eyes in the shadow of her dark hood' (Sutcliff 1977: 68). It is a commonplace that twentieth-century Western culture, especially American culture, fetishises youth in a way that devalues the experience and wisdom of older people and contributes to their neglect while ensuring the commercial success of the fitness, hair-dye and beauty industries. But the taste that perceives barely pubescent girls as pinnacles of beauty and erotic attraction is something more than this, and it is fed by the same fantasies of domination that are inscribed in the hero stories. This taste means that contemporary fashion and photographic models are often very young, and always unnaturally thin, so that even when they are in fact adults their bodies appear to be those of young teenagers. Most women's clothes are designed with this image in mind, and many women of normal adult shape complain that fashionable clothes are not available in their sizes. (In recent years this trend has become so marked that specialist designers and niche marketers have profited from the situation by producing clothes especially for 'big' women.) The fetish for extremely young beauties encourages domination fantasies and at its worst it supports the child pornography industry which enables some men to nourish their fantasies by the degradation of actual children.

The effect of the heroine's slenderness and youth in the semiotic patterns of the hero story is to emphasize her virginity and her subordination to the hero. Unlike the dark seductresses she does not threaten his manhood. Even if she is lively and has a mind of her own, like Cottia, the hero's greater age, experience and strength means that he is inevitably dominant in their relationship. In most cases, however, she is passive and submissive, and it is this attitude of voluntary submission which is naturalized by the story. Fairy tale heroines are always sweet and gentle. In the Grimm version of 'Sleeping Beauty' the princess is 'so beautiful, gentle, virtuous and clever, that every one who saw her fell in love with her' (Grimm 1994: 239). Cinderella, in the Grimm version, is 'good and pious' (p. 115); in Perrault she 'endured everything patiently' (Perrault [1697] 1969: 67). The true princess in 'The Goose Girl' is too gentle to resist the bullying of her wicked maidservant, and Rapunzel submits without a struggle to the domination of the witch and, when he appears, the demands of the prince.

The relationship between the hero and his bride is always profoundly unequal as he alone possesses power; the women are either completely without volition or so restricted by circumstances that their capacity for making choices about what will happen to them is virtually nil. The traditional stories are indices of women's actual powerlessness in earlier centuries in Western society, of the way their lives were entirely at men's disposal, yet the hero's encounter with these women is always presented in a very favourable, even glamorous, light. Often he appears as a saviour and always as a bright and interesting figure who brings meaning into their existence. Amongst ancient legends the story of Perseus and Andromeda is typical: having achieved his quest by cutting off the head of Medusa, Perseus is on his way home to

Seriphos when he spies a young woman chained to a rock near the coast of Philistia. This is Andromeda who has been left as a sacrifice to a sea monster sent by Poseidon to ravage the land. Poseidon was annoyed because Andromeda's mother had boasted that she was more beautiful than the sea nymphs, and it is Andromeda's own parents who have decided that the sacrifice of their daughter might appease the god. Andromeda is thus completely helpless – abandoned by her parents, chained to a rock and threatened by a monster. In his retelling of the story Compton Mackenzie adds the titillating detail that she was 'naked except for a gem-studded necklace' (Mackenzie 1972: 35). Perseus decides to rescue and marry her and, given her situation, Andromeda has no choice but to accept his offer.

The helpless and threatened female who is rescued from great danger became a cliché in hero stories. In an exact replication of the Perseus and Andromeda legend Saint George rescues a princess who is about to be devoured by a dragon. In Malory various damsels are rescued by noble knights from oppression and imprisonment at the hands of a variety of tyrants and malefactors, and at the climax of the story Lancelot rescues Queen Guinevere from the fire to which Arthur has sorrowfully condemned her for her unfaithfulness. The motif is seen at its most ludicrous in Gordon Stables' *Stanley Grahame* in which the intrepid African adventurer rescues the beautiful Ida from wicked natives who have enslaved her and imprisoned her with her aged father on an island in the middle of a lake. Stanley and his friends overcome the 'savages' with consummate ease:

> The savages made no further resistance at present. They retreated to the shelter of the rocks.
>
> In a few moments more Ida, half fainting, was clasped in Stanley's arms.
>
> 'I thank you dear boy,' said old Captain Ross, with the tears streaming from his eyes, 'and I thank the dear God who sent you. My little girl and I never quite lost hope; we but prayed and prayed the more; and the Lord has heard us. Ever blessed be His name!'
>
> 'But you are wounded, Stanley,' said Ida with alarm.
>
> 'No,' said Stanley; 'it is a mere scratch on the shoulder . . .'
>
> (Stables, n.d.: 331)

The perfect example of female passivity is Beauty in the tale of 'The Sleeping Beauty'. She has lain supine for a hundred years; life does not exist for her until the prince arrives. Her relationships with her parents and everyone else who has surrounded her in her childhood, her interests, her very awareness of being – all are suspended until his coming. The spell of the bad fairy, placed upon her in her cradle, was death, but the good fairy's modification was, in effect, a condemnation to the archetypal role of the female. As soon as the prince appears she offers herself to him without hesitation, as though she has no right to choice or refusal. In the Grimm version she 'greeted him with smiles' (Grimm 1994: 241), and the wedding was announced immediately. Perrault, more archly, says that she awoke and 'bestowed upon him a look more tender than a first glance might seem to warrant' (Perrault [1697] 1969: 13). He suggests that she had been dreaming of him for a hundred years and so had prepared herself for the moment. He does not suggest, however, that she had ever considered refusing him. Refusal is not an option for the bride. She is chosen, and to be chosen is all that she can ask.

Rapunzel, who has been imprisoned all her life in a tower by the witch who took her away from her parents, is visited by a prince who has overheard the witch saying 'Rapunzel, Rapunzel, let down your hair' and so learned how to gain entry into the tower. He is uninvited. Rapunzel has never seen him before. When he appears and asks her to take him as a husband she thinks: '"Anyone may have me rather than the old woman"' (Grimm 1994: 82). She has no more control over her life than Andromeda or Beauty, and no choice but to accept the prince. His forcible entry into her secluded tower could be read as a story of violation, of a powerful, free agent taking advantage of an utterly powerless and completely inexperienced woman, but the closure of the story requires the reader to accept this as a fortunate turn of events in Rapunzel's life, for we are told they lived 'long, contented and happy' (p. 83). Bettelheim expresses the unexamined male response to this story when he describes 'Rapunzel' as: 'the story of a pubertal girl, and of a jealous mother who tries to prevent her from gaining independence – a typical adolescent problem, which finds a happy solution when Rapunzel becomes united with her prince' (Bettelheim 1976: 16–17). He has no doubt that the arrival of any old prince intent on sexual congress must be a happy solution for an over-protected girl.

The hero story naturalizes the powerlessness of women and their domination by men, and presents this as a desirable state of affairs for women as well as for men! It suggests to young women who may be dissatisfied with their circumscribed lives that all will be well when, inevitably, their prince appears – no matter who he may be. It functions to divert the energy which women's dissatisfaction might create away from efforts to change their lives, away from political action, into passive dreaming about a future when everything will be transformed because of the arrival of a man. The interim between puberty and the prince's arrival is filled with attempts to achieve the requisite style and standard of beauty. Thus the story serves the purposes of patriarchal hegemony as well as the fashion and cosmetics industries.

In this context we can see why it is that the Grimm version of 'Little Red Riding Hood', in which a hunter kills the wolf and rescues Red Riding Hood and her grandmother, became the established version of the tale. At one level of significance the wolf represents male predatoriness; his dangerous presence in the world 'proves' it is unwise for women to walk alone, to attempt to act independently. But, if the story ends, as Perrault's version does, with the eating up of Red Riding Hood, it leaves male power in a bad light, appearing as naked and ruthless dominance rather than as something natural, benevolent and essential. Hence the popularity of the hunter who demonstrates that, while there are evil men abroad in the world, women can, nevertheless, rely on men in general to protect them, and must do so, for they are too weak to protect themselves. Men's sexual predation is shown as 'wild', a basic instinct which they cannot be expected to control; yet at the same time men are depicted as strong, resourceful and benevolent, the natural protectors of female virtue. Both these attitudes are adolescent fantasies, but the story presents them as valid images of adult masculinity, images which are internalized by young readers.

While the passive, gentle, golden-haired brides of hero stories have contributed powerfully to the ideology of female subordination and submission, their function at the structural level of the story is identical with that of the Golden Fleece, the hoard of pirate gold or the gold medals awarded to victors at the Olympic games. They are trophies, indicators of the hero's success. At this level they do not need to be convincing representations of human beings. In fact the more implausibly perfect they are, the more effectively they function as symbols. If we consider their significance in terms of the theories of Chodorow, Ortner and Kristeva it is apparent that they are also idealized symbols of the domestic sphere, the space between the public culture which men dominate, and the disorder and chaos of 'nature'. In the public, political world of male culture, emotion is denied and energy is directed outward to the suppression of nature which the hero perceives as dangerous – violent, uncontrolled, overwhelming, a threat to his masculinity, his rationality, his power. But this leaves him incomplete. In order to be fulfilled as well as safe he needs to assimilate into himself the gentle emotions, the perfect love of the domestic sphere, and his marriage to the golden bride symbolizes this assimilation. She is an event in the psychic history of the hero.

Campbell, in *The Hero With a Thousand Faces*, sees marriage to the ethereally beautiful princess as emblematic of the male child's longing for reunion with the mother who nourished him, for the elixir of life, the ever-flowing milk which the heroes and gods consume in heaven in Greek, Scandinavian, Irish, Persian, Jewish and Japanese myths (Campbell 1968: 176–9). At the same time, in his view, it represents spiritual enlightenment, the understanding which is the real object of all human yearning: 'The ineffable teaching of the beatitude beyond imagination comes to us clothed, necessarily, in figures reminiscent of the imagined beatitude of infancy; hence the deceptive childishness of the tales. Hence, too, the inadequacy of any merely psychological reading' (Campbell 1968: 178). This seems a generous interpretation of a motif which carries such powerful suggestions of dominance and control. It is only if one is able to read these stories, as Campbell does, entirely from the hero's point of view, ignoring all other perspectives, that it is possible to construct such meanings from them. For female readers, whose responses Campbell does not consider, the meaning of the closure can only be that their lives are utterly subordinate to the lives of men.

At the surface level of the story this closure has other troubling features. Often the taking of the imprisoned, chained, sleeping or enchanted heroine seems close to fantasized rape. The hero does not know his bride. He makes no attempt to get to know her. It is as though it is too difficult to conceive any relationship with a woman beyond simple, physical possession. Bettelheim points out that in an earlier version of 'Sleeping Beauty', a story called 'Sun, Moon and Talia' in Basile's *Pentamerone*, the hero is unable to wake the princess, so 'falling in love with her beauty, he cohabited with her; then he left and forgot the whole affair' (Bettelheim 1976: 227). This is rape, pure and simple. The dressing up of the extremes of masculine dominance and female passivity as something glamorous and romantic has made 'Sleeping Beauty' one of the most popular of all fairy tales; clearly it appeals to some widely held fantasies. Apart from Beauty's extreme passivity the most significant thing about the marriage which is imminent at the conclusion of this story (and many similar marriages in other hero tales) is that it is merely potential. The future relationship exists only in the non-reality outside the text, for a hero cannot be a hero if he settles down. The effect of this formula is to dismiss this central human relationship as something of little interest or importance.

## RELATIONSHIPS

The women in the hero's story are rarely shown as involved in any kind of relationship with each other, and where a relationship between women, especially between mother and daughter, is featured it is almost invariably hostile and destructive. The story permits no solidarity amongst the oppressed. In the legend of Jason, Medea, consumed by jealousy, murders both his new bride and her own children. The witch in 'Rapunzel', a substitute mother, keeps Rapunzel imprisoned in a tower and is furious when she learns of the prince's visits. The stepmother in 'Hansel and Gretel' insists that both Gretel and Hansel be left in the forest to starve. In 'The Goose Girl' the maidservant terrorizes the true princess and urges her death. In Perrault's version of 'The Sleeping Beauty', which continues after the marriage of the prince and princess, Beauty's mother-in-law has ogrish instincts and is prevented from devouring her two children only by the efforts of compassionate servants. Two of the most famous fairy tales of all, 'Cinderella' and 'Snow White', are primarily concerned with hatred and rivalry between women, with the role of the princely hero being relatively marginal.

Marina Warner suggests (1994: 218–29) that much of the recurrent antagonism between daughters and stepmothers in fairy tales may be a reflection of the legal and social constraints which newly married brides encountered in earlier centuries. She points out that in English 'mother-in-law' meant stepmother until the mid-nineteenth century, leading to confusion between the two terms. A young bride would normally leave her home to live with her husband in his parents' house, and Warner argues that this motif:

> may stand for the dark time that can follow the first encounter between the older woman and her new daughter-in-law, the period when the young woman can do nothing, take charge of nothing, but suffer the sorcery and the authority – perhaps the hostility – of the woman whose house she has entered, whose daughter she has become.
>
> (Warner 1994: 220)

She suggests that the mother-in-law would often have seen the bride as a competitor for her son's allegiance which was important to her because of her own dependency upon the males in her family. It would become especially important if she were widowed, when her very livelihood would depend upon her son's continuing support. In these circumstances she might well come to regard her daughter-in-law as an enemy. Most of the storytellers were women who would remember such an experience of hostility towards them when they were young, and would be likely to weave it into the stories they told.

This is persuasive up to a point and may well be part of the explanation for the frequent depiction of inter-generational strife between women in fairy tales. But the major reason for strife between women is the nature of patriarchy itself, and it is this which is inscribed in the stories. The most obvious reason for such strife is the competition imposed upon women by their powerlessness. Where status, comfort and security, perhaps survival itself, depend upon being chosen and valued by men, women's natural enemies are each other. We can see the despair of the ageing woman who fears her beauty and power are fading in Snow White's stepmother anxiously interrogating her mirror each day. 'Cinderella' depicts the desperate struggle of young women to secure an appropriate husband. The stepsisters hate Cinderella because she is a rival, and in the Grimm version of this story one of the stepsisters cuts off her toe and the other part of her heel in order to fit into Cinderella's tiny slipper so they can claim to have been the mysterious beauty at the ball, the prince's chosen one. First one, then the other is revealed as false when the blood from their wounds soaks through their stockings and trickles from their shoes. This is a vivid metaphor for the psychological and emotional mutilation many women voluntarily inflicted upon themselves in their quest for a husband. It is an echo of Medea's terrible action when Jason puts her aside to take a new wife and she kills her own children, believing that she and they have now lost everything.

But patriarchy poisons women's relationships with each other, especially those of mother and daughter, in a more profound way than this. When a mother has had to bend and deform her own nature to please men she is likely to try to shape her daughter in the same way, partly because she genuinely believes this is necessary if her daughter is to secure a husband and partly because, somewhere in the darker corners of her being, she feels that, as she has had to suffer, all females should suffer likewise, even her own daughter. So Chinese women of the Ming dynasty, unable to walk properly themselves on their tiny, mutilated 'lotus' feet, bound the feet of their small daughters, causing them agony and robbing them of their freedom. How could such daughters not resent their mothers, or hate them, or pretend that they were only stepmothers? And how could the mothers not feel guilt for what they did, and resent their daughters as the cause of that guilt? And how could the daughters, sensing their mothers' unhappiness, not feel guilty at being its cause? And so on – resentment and guilt, like two mirrors endlessly reflecting each other.

Even if a passive, subservient mother does manage to avoid passing on her own psychological deformities to her daughters, how can those daughters not despise her for her weakness? And how can they not feel guilt for despising her, knowing that she loves them? Shere Hite records the testimony of thousands of contemporary young women determined not to grow up to be like their mothers: 'The basic reason most women give for not wanting to be like their mothers is, "She let my father treat her so badly, so condescendingly," "She didn't fight back enough," "She didn't have enough pride," "She was a wimp"' (Hite [1994] 1995: 140).

Gretel pushes her witch/mother into the oven, but Gretels are rare in fairy tales and hero stories. In most of these stories the women have no relationships with each other at all. As Shere Hite says:

> The relationship most crucial to disrupt and destroy in patriarchy is that between mother and daughter. Any natural feelings of physical closeness or desire, love, must be stamped out, forbidden, lest women become too strong through their belief and trust in each other.
>
> Patriarchal ideology is emphatic on this point.
>
> (Hite [1994] 1995: 137)

But it is good to be able to end this chapter by noting that Hite records a change in the last twenty years. In the 1970s a large number of the young women she surveyed said they absolutely despised their mothers, whereas in the 1990s the majority 'describe positive feelings for and experiences with their mother' (p. 138). Perhaps the women who became mothers in the 1960s and 1970s were strengthened by emergent feminism and so do not appear to be such 'wimps' as the mothers of earlier generations, perhaps they have been able to love their daughters without resenting their freedom, and perhaps the daughters have learnt to value other qualities besides male strength. Perhaps now the stories have begun to change.

# 5

# REWRITING THE STORY

The popularity of the linear adventure story is unlikely to decline. The pleasure it provides – repeated arousal and satisfaction of the desire to know what will happen next – is primitive and powerful. But if the traditional patriarchal values of Western culture are to be modified to allow the development of more genuinely humane attitudes we need different hero stories, stories which do not assert the natural mastery of the European patriarchy over all other living things. As Val Plumwood points out the inevitable final stage of the culture of mastery is the global Rational Economy and the assimilation of all planetary life to the needs of the masters (Plumwood 1993: 192–6). In this ultimate scenario all the remaining space on earth is gradually appropriated to the needs of the economy according to the dictates of Platonic and Cartesian 'reason' which sees nature as the inferior opposite of civilization, a resource to be exploited. Resources are increasingly withdrawn from those who refuse to be incorporated into the Rational Economy. Thus biodiversity dwindles and indigenous cultures are destroyed. Within the dominant culture space for love, friendship, contemplation, art, the development of psychic wholeness, is sacrificed to the needs of economic rationalism. Those who cannot conform to the demands of economic rationalism – the poor, the disabled and the old – are increasingly marginalized, and women, the irreducibly 'other', are either suborned or alienated. The final result, the last triumph of the hero, can only be the collapse of the culture of mastery, since nature is not an endlessly exploitable resource. We urgently need hero stories which, while retaining action and excitement, subvert the traditional dualisms and so do not impose the values of the culture of mastery upon the reader.

In recent years there has been a publishing boom in parodies of traditional stories which have sought to undermine the male/female dualism by inverting the stereotypes. Babette Cole has produced several amusingly illustrated stories of this kind including *Prince Cinders* [1987] and *Princess Smarty Pants* [1986]. In *Prince Cinders* the put-upon sibling who is forced to stay at home while the others go to the disco is a male – small, weedy, passive Cinders who is bullied by his large hairy brothers, but ends up marrying the Princess Lovelypenny simply because he does not fit the big hairy pattern of masculinity. *Princess*

*Smarty Pants* features an independent-minded girl who wants to remain single and have fun with her collection of bad-tempered and ferocious animals, so she sets every princely suitor an impossible task to perform. All fail until the annoyingly dashing and competent Swashbuckle appears on the scene. He performs every task with ease and Smarty Pants seems doomed to dwindle into a wife, but she has one defence left: she kisses the triumphant Swashbuckle and turns him into a toad.

Admirers of Cole's work enjoy the intertextual jokes and the vigour of her attacks on the gender stereotypes. John Stephens remarks on the grotesque nature of the illustrations of the hairy brothers and of the transformed Cinders who becomes an ape in a swimsuit. He concludes that, when the brothers are finally turned into house fairies who have to do the housework for ever and ever, the image of 'big hairy' masculinity is made 'utterly ridiculous and finally unrecuperable' (Stephens 1992: 144). But the jokes in these stories are not simply intertextual: the stories are parodies, and, like all parodies, they are parasitic upon the originals. That is, their humour depends upon the reader's having assimilated the originals and accepted the stereotypes. Cinders, the hairy brothers and the incompetent princes in *Princess Smarty Pants* seem absurd only to those who know what heroes and princes 'should' be like. Interestingly some teachers have reported that young readers of *Princess Smarty Pants* simply do not register the significance of the conclusion, but assume that Swashbuckle will turn back into a prince and marry Smarty Pants. For such readers the power of the original remains undimmed, and parodies generally have life only so long as the host originals remain strong, for it is the originals which provide their *raison d'être*. In a sense parodies increase the power of the originals by directing attention to them. (There are some rare instances of parodies which have overgrown the originals and acquired an autonomous life. For example Lewis Carroll's rhyme 'How doth the little crocodile/Improve his shining tail' has become more famous than the original 'How doth the little busy bee/Improve each shining hour'.)

A recent picture book in the style of Cole's parodies is Jean Hood's *The Dragon of Brog* [1994], illustrated by Peter Kavanagh. Its target is not a single story, but the whole genre of tales about dragon-slaying knights. Princess Lisa is a tomboyish girl who wears ragged clothes, carries a sword, and has no desire to marry a knight. Therefore she is pleased when each knight who attempts to win her hand by slaying the dragon of Brog fails dismally. These knights have punning names: Sir Prize, Sir Cumference, Sir Render and Sir Vuright and the drawings make them appear appropriately ridiculous. Eventually the dragon grows tired of being harassed by these incompetents and resolves to leave Brog, but Princess Lisa persuades him to remain and turns him into a tourist attraction, thus solving her father's financial problems and ensuring her own continuing independence. Just as Cole's stories lampoon the stereotypes of large hairy masculinity and the swashbuckling hero who overcomes all difficulties, so Hood's story ridicules the figure of the brave knight in armour whose profession is mayhem, and appreciation of the joke likewise depends upon familiarity with the originals.

These stories certainly raise the issue of gender, and provide effective discussion-starters for teachers. As Stephens says of *Prince Cinders*: 'that abjection, humility and passivity now become deficiencies poses the question of why they should be virtues for the female' (Stephens 1992: 140). But there are problems with these works that go beyond their parodic dependence upon the originals. Their ridicule of the gender stereotypes is ultimately nihilistic for they offer no alternative, positive models of behaviour for either males or females. There are no admirable male figures against whom to measure the exploded stereotypes, and the attitudes of the princesses Smarty Pants and Lisa suggest that all males are contemptible nuisances. While this might amuse some girls because it is such a neat inversion of the dismissal of females in so many stories, it offers nothing except a sense of pay-back. Smarty Pants and Lisa themselves are little more than the old male stereotypes in drag: they are arrogant, self-centred know-alls with no empathy for others – hardly positive embodiments of the female. The trouble with a dualism is that if you simply turn it on its head it is still a dualism. Inversion is not the same as subversion. As Val Plumwood puts it:

> In feminist and liberation theory, the misty, forbidding passes of the Mountains of Dualism have swallowed many an unwary traveller in their mazes and chasms. In these mountains a well-trodden path leads through a steep defile to the Cavern of Reversal, where travellers fall into an upside-down world which strangely resembles the one they seek to escape.
>
> (Plumwood 1993: 3)

Further, these stories fail to engage with the material they deride. Despite the patriarchal values inscribed in traditional hero tales the fields of folk tale, legend and romance are rich with potent symbols that work at many levels. They have great imaginative and emotional power as is evident in, for example, the continuing appeal of the Arthurian material and of archetypal images such as dragons. The figure of Sir Lancelot in Malory's romance – noble, passionate, flawed, torn by conflicting devotions, driven by a belief in the complex ideals of chivalry but also deeply humanistic, doomed – exerts a fascination on all readers (even those who question many of the values implicit in the work) which is unlikely to be touched by the cheap shots of *The Dragon of Brog*. Likewise the idea of the strength and fire, the primal force of the dragon remains powerful despite innumerable parodies. The Arthurian stories, like many heroic legends, also imply the nobility of altruism and selfless devotion to a cause: however bloodless and priggish Galahad may seem he does symbolize a significant stage in the evolution of moral thinking. The traditional material can be reworked to inscribe other values without sacrificing its richness, as Ursula Le Guin's treatment of the dragon motif shows (see below), but stories like *Princess Smarty Pants* and *The Dragon of Brog* are merely graffiti on its surface.

Of course these stories do have an ideological content. They are celebrations of self-interest, of ruthless, unconsidered individualism. The behaviour of Smarty Pants and Lisa, who both want to be able to do exactly as they like all the time, exemplifies the strident selfishness of the extremists who give feminism a bad name. *The Dragon of Brog* makes its values especially clear: there is no place for idealism; what matters is money and the freedom to get hold of as much of it for oneself as possible. What is the use of dragons (fairy penguins, coral reefs, beaches, waterfalls, gorillas . . .)? Why, to bring in the tourists and the dollars. In each of these stories, but especially in *The Dragon of Brog*, the narrative voice is that of a cynical and knowing adult inviting child readers to share the arid pragmatism which constitutes its point of view. These are stories for the age of economic rationalism, and perhaps some contemporary readers will find them just the thing. But those who seek stories which encourage acceptance of human diversity, respect for others, caring and compassion, sensitivity to the environment, the quest for understanding, which have humour that is creative without being cruel, will need to look elsewhere.

However, there are hero stories which subvert or shatter one or more of the dualisms and construct alternative values to replace them. They include some of the best-loved classics of children's literature and some very popular later works, some of which have been recognized by internationally acknowledged awards. The popularity of these stories suggests that children are responsive to alternative values when they are presented to them.

## SUBVERTING THE DUALISMS: GENDER

There are now many excellent children's stories with female protagonists who combine strength with qualities such as sensitivity and compassion, but the hero story, especially the fantasy hero story, presents a particular problem because of the gendered nature of the protagonist's role, and because it is this story structure which inscribes and naturalizes the ancillary roles of females. Stories in which a conventional heroic role is played by a woman do little to modify these meanings. The inference readers are likely to draw from such a story is that, if they wish their lives and deeds to be worthy of notice, women must strive to behave as much like men as possible. Nor do such stories pose any challenge to the heroic definition of ideal manhood, for the women display the same courage, prowess, arid rationalism and rigid sense of purpose. Retellings of the lives of female war leaders such as Boadicea and Joan of Arc in fact doubly devalue women, first by focusing on spheres of male action and thus implying the superior importance of men and their doings, and second by obliterating the women's specifically female qualities and reconstructing them as merely imperfect males. But there are some stories which tell of the adventures of women and girls who negotiate fantastic wildernesses in quite different ways from those employed by conventional heroes with sword or gun in hand and mastery in mind. One of them is perhaps the best known work in the entire field of children's literature.

Lewis Carroll's Alice stories have steadily increased in popularity from the first appearance of *Alice's Adventures in Wonderland* in 1864, and they have always been enjoyed by adults as well as by children – perhaps more so. They are not usually included in the category of hero tales for the very reason that they subvert the heroic values, but in fact they fit precisely the traditional pattern of the journey into the wilderness where the hero encounters a range of bizarre creatures and finally returns to the security of home. However, Alice does not resemble Odysseus or Max or any of their kind, nor does she assume a pseudo masculinity as Joan of Arc assumes her suit of armour. She is unequivocally both a child and a girl, but her sense, benevolence and self-possession make her a worthy representative of humankind despite her youth and her femininity. As Humphrey Carpenter puts it 'Alice is Everyman' (Carpenter 1985: 62). He does not seem to realize the remarkableness of this statement: here, for the first time in Western literature, a small female child functions as an emblem of all humanity confronting the absurdities of existence – and doing remarkably well without fighting or killing anyone!

Alice occupies the subject position in the stories; we perceive Wonderland as she perceives it, and the male characters, all seen through her eyes, appear, in various ways, eccentric and inadequate. There are no 'normal' males against whom Alice herself can be measured and found wanting. Carroll, whose own attitude to rigid Victorian gender divisions was equivocal, simply dissolves the standard concept of masculinity, and in the White Knight, who appears in *Through the Looking Glass* [1872], the traditional hero is reduced to a figure of mournful ineptitude who cannot remain seated on his horse and has no clear understanding of why he does anything, least of all fighting. More amusing, perhaps, is the treatment of the hero in 'Jabberwocky', the poem written in mirror image which can only be read when it is held up to a looking-glass, a metaphor for the absurdity of the heroic code inscribed in its story of the 'beamish boy' whose vorpal blade went snicker-snack as he cut off the jabberwock's head. The language of the poem, a mixture of bombast and nonsense, further undercuts the pretensions of the hero whose purpose in life is to find something – anything – to kill. But this deconstruction of traditional masculinity does not lead to the nihilism of stories like *The Dragon of Brog* and *Princess Smarty Pants* because Alice herself is a positive model for both males and females.

We are born without conscious volition and begin life with no clear goals in mind. Likewise Alice sets out on her journey accidentally, by falling down a rabbit hole, and at one point she tells the Cheshire Cat that she doesn't mind where she goes so long as she gets 'somewhere' (Carroll [1865, 1872] 1982: 57). She is interested in everything she experiences, and is content to take things as they come. There is no insistent forward momentum to her story; the incidents follow one another without causal connection, like incidents in a dream sequence. Unlike male heroes, from Odysseus to Sendak's Max, Alice fails to impose her will upon the creatures she meets who constantly order her about and refuse to give logical answers to her questions. Throughout her journey she is disoriented and her sense of identity is weakened. Things happen and transformations occur for no apparent reason, as when the Duchess's baby turns into a pig. Neither the material nor the moral norms of the real world prevail: the croquet mallets are flamingos, the Duchess sings a lullaby about beating her baby and the Queen orders beheadings with alacrity. The didactic verses which Alice knows by heart turn into nonsense rhymes when she recites them in Wonderland, so that she wonders whether she is still the same little girl or whether she has been turned into Mabel who 'knows such a very little' (p. 18). Perhaps most disturbingly of all for child readers, whose own bodies are growing, she constantly changes size with an alarming lack of control over the extent and speed of the process. In fact, she exhibits all the insecurities common to real children of both sexes, but Alice is allowed to express them while male heroes, and, too often, male children in real life, are required to display confidence and courage whether they feel them or not.

Despite this lack of control over both herself and her environment Alice is not especially distressed, and she suffers no damage. Indeed, by the time she reaches the final chapter of *Alice in Wonderland* she has gained considerably in confidence: she is able to criticize the courtroom proceedings, contradict the Queen, and defy the whole assembly of Wonderland creatures by telling them they are nothing but a pack of cards. She is able to cope with uncertainty and, although she finally stands up to the Wonderland creatures, refusing to let them bully her anymore, she feels no compulsion to dominate them. Her character does not generate the quest story. As she is not driven by destiny and ambition towards a goal she does not define the beings she encounters on the way as impediments to her purpose, and so she does not demonize them. Having created no monsters she does not need to overcome them; there are no heroic struggles and no triumphs in her story.

Carroll tells us that the visit to Wonderland was a dream ('"Oh, I've had such a curious dream!" said Alice.' (p. 110)) and therefore it represents, in a general way, a journey through Alice's unconscious. Certainly the description of her fall down the rabbit hole, during which she passes through levels furnished domestically with cupboards, bookshelves, maps and pictures, then into anonymous space, to arrive finally upon 'a heap of sticks and dry leaves' (p. 11) resembles Jung's dream, recorded in *Memories, Dreams and Reflections* (O'Connor 1985: 19–20), in which he descends through various levels of his house from a rococo salon, through mediaeval rooms and Roman cellars to a cave in the rocks containing broken pottery and disintegrating human skulls. Jung interpreted this dream as an image of the psyche with the first-floor salon representing daylight consciousness, the lower storeys the various levels of the unconscious, and the cave suggesting the primitive collective unconscious.

Carroll's story suggests that Alice is relatively at ease with her unconscious: she finds her experiences 'curious' and she is disoriented, but she is not afraid. The strange creatures interest, entertain, and even amuse her; at times she finds them tiresome, but never threatening. Although she is a rather prim child, particular about good manners and with a respect for knowledge, she is not alienated from her imagination, so the stories impose no rigorous preference for rationality upon the reader, and the reason for their enduring popularity with children and adults, of both sexes, is perhaps that they license this gentle playfulness.

The French feminist critic Hélène Cixous argues in 'The Laugh of the Medusa' [1976] that almost all writing has been male writing (for most women learn to write like men), inscribing male values in both its content and its 'codes' (Cixous [1976] 1981: 249). She says that it would be impossible to 'define a feminine practice of writing . . . for this practice can never be theorized, enclosed, coded – which doesn't mean that it doesn't exist' (p. 253). Because such writing (which need not be produced only by women) would dismantle the codes, including especially the code of binary oppositions which inscribe the dualisms that underlie patriarchal values, it would be in a sense bisexual writing, obliterating the oppositional definition of gender. Toril Moi links Cixous' concept of feminine writing to what Derrida called *différance*, the free play of the signifier (Moi 1985: 105–7), the recognition that meaning is shifting and unstable. While it is not clear what the range of such 'feminine' texts might include (Cixous admits only Colette, Marguerite Duras and Jean Genet from twentieth-century French literature) the Alice stories, with their deconstruction of the conventional hero story and of traditional logic, their subversion of the male/female dualism and their joyousness, must surely have an honoured place.

However, there are few other hero stories, especially amongst those written by men, which so happily dismantle the 'codes' and which contain female protagonists whose authenticity and autonomy approach those of the self-possessed Alice. Certainly not L. Frank Baum's *The Wonderful Wizard of Oz* [1900] whose whining Dorothy spends her entire time in Oz wanting to get back to Kansas and her Aunty Em. *The Wonderful Wizard of Oz* might seem to challenge gender stereotypes by making the protagonist a girl but in fact it reinforces them and establishes an essentially American variant of the basic pattern: the girl-woman of Hollywood. This perhaps accounts for the continuing popularity of this banal and mechanistic story which is written in flat, impoverished prose. It is difficult not to agree with the critic who wrote of the 1939 MGM film version: 'As for the light touch of fantasy, it weighs like a pound of fruitcake soaking wet' (quoted in Halliwell 1981: 1109). The division of Oz into four parts each dominated by a different colour – blue, green, yellow and red – and each associated with a different witch, with Dorothy in white moving across the landscape towards the Emerald City at the centre, irresistibly recalls a game of Chinese checkers and is just as contrived and predictable. (On the other hand *Alice's Adventures Through the Looking Glass* is *intended* to relate to a game of chess, but the fantasy is so rich, subtle and amusing that most readers lose sight of the parallels.)

Baum's declared intention was to write 'a series of new "wonder tales"' (Baum [1900] 1973: vii) which eliminated traditional dwarves and fairies and other 'horrible and blood-curdling' elements, apparently because such things would be out of place in a fantasy which is a projection of America as a new and innocent nation, free of European complexities. But in the course of this spring cleaning imaginative and emotional resonance have also been eliminated. Where this work does achieve a probably unintended depth is in the figure of Dorothy, and this is intensified in the film version where the child Dorothy is played by the clearly post-pubescent Judy Garland in a pinafore and bobby socks. While Dorothy's male companions, the Scarecrow, the Tin Woodman and the Lion, gain the qualities they seek as a result of the journey (brains, feeling and courage) thus becoming mature adults, Dorothy herself learns nothing from her adventures. She returns to Aunty Em the same little girl she was when she went away, simply glad to be home again. This sentimental valuing of childhood above maturity and experience sets up the child-woman as the female ideal: shallowness, ignorance and naivety are her characteristic attributes. Dorothy is the precursor of the American cult of youth, of the innocent, vulnerable but sexually enticing screen sirens, of Lolita. The male/female dualism is heavily reinforced by this story, and it is not until the second half of this century that more idiosyncratic and autonomous girls, such as Kit Tyler in Elizabeth Speare's *The Witch of Blackbird Pond* (1958) begin to make their appearance in American children's adventure stories.

Challenges to the conventional construction of male gender have been rather more numerous and successful. Innocent, gentle and essentially well-meaning young men with no ambitions to kill or conquer and no troublesome excesses of courage or prowess have wandered the wilderness from time to time and found it at least as absurd as Alice found Wonderland. Voltaire's *Candide* [1758] is perhaps the best known and most influential of them. The wilderness through which he journeys is eighteenth-century Europe, more or less, with all its suffering and injustice, compounded by accidental horrors such as the Lisbon earthquake in which many thousands of people died. But he also passes some time in a kingdom ruled by Reason, as eighteenth-century philosophers conceived it, an El Dorado in which neither crime nor war exist. While he recognizes this as certainly the best of all possible worlds it is ultimately unsatisfying because it lacks passion. He longs for the Lady Cunégonde, and so he leaves the earthly paradise to continue his search for her, but when he finds her she too is disappointing. Recognizing that suffering is the common lot of humanity and that neither reason nor passion provide lasting satisfaction, Candide falls back on quietude and work: he and his small group of friends withdraw from the world to cultivate their garden. Throughout his travels Candide harms no one and retains both vitality and compassion. Voltaire's tale uses the pattern of the hero's journey to inscribe quite different values including a radical deconstruction of heroic masculinity.

Douglas Adams' extraordinarily popular science fiction satire *The Hitch-hiker's Guide to the Galaxy* (1979) and its sequels *The Restaurant at the End of the Universe* (1980) and *Life, the Universe and Everything* (1982) are in many ways a modern version of *Candide*. They also – all texts being intertextual – inevitably contain elements of *Alice*. The protagonist, Arthur Dent, resembles Candide in his innocence, decency, lack of belligerence and buoyancy of spirit. He wanders not the world but the galaxy in the company of a small group of friends – the chief of whom is Ford Prefect who hails from a small planet somewhere in the vicinity of Betelgeuse and who has been engaged, for the last fifteen years, in compiling the Earth entry for *The Hitch-hiker's Guide* – but the targets of the satire are, of course, the ways of the world we know. This is signalled at the outset when the attempt of a local government department to bulldoze Arthur's house to make way for a bypass is reflected in the alien Vogons' demolition of the Earth because it is in the way of an inter-galactic bypass. Arthur finds vanity, venality and stupidity to be, quite literally, universal failings. More fundamentally, however, he finds the universe to be absurd. This is manifested partly in the eccentric behaviour of many of the beings he encounters, partly in the irritating pointlessness of the various tech-nological marvels, and partly in the sheer irrationality of the events which occur. The normal processes of cause and effect pertain no more than they do in *Alice in Wonderland*: just as the Duchess's baby turns into a pig for no detectable reason so Arthur and Ford are rescued from certain death in outer space by a passing space ship powered by the Infinite Improbability Drive (Adams 1979: 63–8). This occurs because 'Reason was in fact out to lunch' (p. 63), and other equally improbable events continue to occur.

While *Candide* ridicules the concept of a beneficent god who has created the best of all possible worlds, *The Hitch-hiker's Guide to the Galaxy* ridicules the idea that there is any sense in existence at all, and calls into question the very notion of Reason itself. Like Alice, Arthur and Ford plunge from one surreal sit-uation to another without any understanding or control of the process. In such a world logic does not apply as appropriate conclusions fail to follow from their premises. This effect is achieved by intermixing different logical systems, most strikingly in the incident where the great computer Deep Thought, after having cogitated for seven and a half million years, at last delivers the answer to the question: what is the meaning of life, the universe and everything? The answer is 'forty-two' (Adams 1979: 135). Frustration with this prompts Frankie Mouse (one of those who have been pursuing the inquiry) to comment:

> Well, I mean *yes* idealism, *yes* the dignity of pure research, *yes* the pur-suit of truth in all its forms, but there comes a point I'm afraid where you begin to suspect that if there's any *real* truth, it's that the entire multi-dimensional infinity of the Universe is almost certainly being

run by a bunch of maniacs. And if it comes to a choice between spending yet another ten million years finding that out, and on the other hand just taking the money and running, then I for one could do with the exercise.

(Adams 1979: 149)

Like *Alice in Wonderland*, *The Hitch-hiker's Guide* consists of a series of random incidents which follow one another without logical causation. In both cases the structure of the conventional hero story has been adapted to further the effect of inherent absurdity and the linear journey becomes a directionless and unpredictable progress towards no particular end. In this absurd universe there is no role for a traditional hero. Mastery is both impossible and meaningless where there are no clearly defined binary opposites and instability is the only constant. To avoid inflicting harm on others as far as that is possible is perhaps the only intelligible moral position, and Arthur remains throughout entirely harmless. At the same time he avoids Frankie Mouse's cynicism and venality.

*Candide*'s solution to the problem of how to live in such a world without succumbing to despair is also the one offered by *The Hitch-hiker's Guide*. The advice of the old Turkish farmer in *Candide* who says that only work can bring contentment (Voltaire [1758] 1947: 143) is echoed by the gentle Slartibartfast, a designer of coastlines, who lives on the planet of Megrathea. He has long ago decided that the effort to understand things is futile:

'I always think that the chances of finding out what is really going on are so absurdly remote that the only thing to do is to say hang the sense of it and just keep yourself occupied. Look at me: I design coastlines. I got an award for Norway.'

(Adams 1979: 143)

Although neither Candide nor Arthur find life amusing, humour is a major ingredient in both works; the narrative point of view in each case is witty and urbane, and the implication is that one should cultivate one's sense of humour as well as one's garden. Humour is an element in which conventional heroes cannot thrive, for their gendered grandiosities need to be taken seriously.

Amongst the heroes of twentieth-century realism perhaps the best known innocent idealist who is appalled by the world he wanders through is Holden Caulfield in J.D. Salinger's *The Catcher in the Rye* [1951]. He represents a significant mutation in the nature of the hero, and this work has influenced much of the later 'young adult' literature which features troubled adolescent protagonists who struggle to come to terms with the society in which they must live, rather than dominating it in the traditional manner by determination, courage and prowess. Holden, Salinger's first-person teenage narrator, is the emotionally damaged son of wealthy New York parents and inhabits a world of social privilege, but the text defines this as an impediment to his attainment of self-realization rather than a condition of such development as it is in *David Copperfield*. *The Catcher in the Rye* explicitly invites comparison with Dickens' work at the outset when Holden declares that he is not going to go into his parents' background and 'all that David Copperfield kind of crap' (Salinger [1951] 1958: 5).

Childhood innocence is a dominant motif in this novel as it frequently is in Dickens, and in both cases childhood is used as a foil for the sordid pragmatism, cynicism and guilt of the adult world. Innocent children, especially his sister Phoebe, are the only beings Holden can allow himself to love, and his unrealizable aim is to prevent them from growing up, to 'catch' them so they cannot fall into the corruption of adulthood. He sees most adults as ineluctably 'phoney' – shallow, egocentric and pretentious – and he measures them against the memory of his adored younger brother Allie who died of leukaemia at the age of 11, before the corrupting touch of maturity reached him. Although the reader comes to realize that it is the inevitability of death, as much as the loss of innocence, which appals him about growing up, the text does not question the essential truth of his vision of the 'phoniness' of New York society which is thrown into relief by the imagined purity of the children. New York is the wilderness through which Holden wanders for several days after he has run away from school, and like Candide wandering through Europe he finds nothing to admire and nothing to give him hope. The people he meets – such as the pathetic prostitute and her thuggish pimp, the three vapid blondes looking for movie stars in the Lavender Room, the pretentious drinkers at Ernie's bar – lead lives of empty self-deception. Holden's despair about the state of his world is further validated by an incident in which another schoolboy, James Castle, jumps out of a window to his death, unable either to resist or surrender to the bullying of a group of arrogant social superiors.

In *David Copperfield* the existence of Agnes, who is beautiful, intelligent and good, serves as a balance to the range of flawed and inadequate characters David encounters on his journey through life. His eventual marriage to her crowns his existence with success and provides an affirmative closure to the work, signifying, like all such happy endings to the hero's quest, the possibility and the worth of victory. But Agnes' counterpart in *The Catcher in the Rye* is an insubstantial and perhaps illusory figure. Holden has an idealized memory of a girl called Jane Gallagher and at several points in the novel, when he is most depressed, he makes up his mind to ring her, but each time refrains from actually doing so, perhaps afraid to discover that she too is a phoney. So in this text the existence of uncorrupted goodness in the adult world remains no more than a wavering possibility.

Unlike David Copperfield, Holden is in no way concerned with worldly success. He is lost in a moral wilderness and, like the inhabitants of Eliot's *Waste Land*, he searches for moral coherence but attains no more than the most fleeting glimpses of what he seeks. His efforts to impress the denizens of

New York with his sophistication is a gauche attempt to discover a way to live in this world rather than an attempt at mastery. Although he manages, finally, to relinquish the dream of keeping his sister Phoebe safe from death and corruption by keeping her safe from life, imprisoned in perpetual childhood, he cannot come to terms with the moral and spiritual aridity of his world, and so there is no affirming closure to his story. The real nature of Jane Gallagher remains unknown. We cannot tell whether or not Phoebe will remain uncorrupted; symbolically Holden allows her to take the risk of reaching for the gold ring on the carousel, but realizes she could fall (Salinger [1951] 1958: 218). At the conclusion of the book Holden himself is a temporary inmate of a psychiatric hospital facing an uncertain future.

A major pre-text which influences the way stories about growing up, like *David Copperfield* and *The Catcher in the Rye*, are read is the biblical account of the expulsion from paradise, the 'fall' from protected innocence and ignorance into sexual awareness and the need to cope on one's own initiative in a hard world. The paradox of the biblical story is that, although the fall is viewed as tragic and the cause of all humankind's sufferings, it is also the essential basis for their development of understanding including their understanding of God's glory and mercy. Likewise, in *David Copperfield* David feels the loss of his early childhood happiness with his mother as a piercing sorrow, but it is his suffering at the hands of Murdstone and his expulsion into the difficult world of work and struggle which enables him to become the mature adult who can appreciate the satisfactions of his work as a writer and the joy of Agnes' love.

*The Catcher in the Rye* invites this conventional reading in so far as Holden comes to accept the necessity of leaving childhood behind. That he sees this as a 'fall' into corruption is indicated by a number of symbolic images: his vision of himself standing in a field of rye *catching* small children as they run towards the edge of 'some crazy cliff' (Salinger [1951] 1958: 179–80), the words 'fuck you' graffitied on the school wall where the children would see it (Salinger [1951] 1958: 207), his fear that Phoebe might fall from the horse on the carousel. The advance towards maturity that he makes in the novel is to accept that it is impossible to remain in the secluded world of childhood: he abandons his plan to run away to the west and pretend to be a deaf mute so as to avoid the need for interaction with the adult world, and he lets Phoebe reach for the gold ring despite the danger. But he can see no possibility of moving forward in the adult world, of gaining wisdom or finding satisfaction. To Holden that world is entirely worthless and corrupt, and it is this dilemma which precipitates his fall into psychological breakdown, and at this point the possibility of reading the work in the conventional, *David Copperfield* way also breaks down.

The text proffers an answer to the problem which is not dissimilar to the answers provided by *Candide* and *The Hitch-hiker's Guide*, but leaves open the question of whether it is a sufficient answer. In this case the older adviser is Mr

Antolini, Holden's former English teacher, who tells Holden that if he applies himself to study he will discover that he is not alone in being 'sickened by human behaviour. . . . Many, many men have been just as troubled morally and spiritually as you are right now. Happily, some of them kept records of their troubles. You'll learn from them – if you want to' (Salinger [1951] 1958: 196). While this is unexceptionable (apart from its incidental sexism) it makes little impact on Holden at the time, partly because he believes Mr Antolini is drunk. It is further undercut by Holden's fear that Mr Antolini is about to make an unwelcome homosexual advance to him, an action which would reduce his words to a stage in the process of seduction. More fundamentally the speech seems conventional and platitudinous compared to the vivid colloquial style of Holden's narrative which creates a powerful effect of authenticity. It is as though a bookish cliché is being offered as a counterbalance to lived experience. In the final brief chapter Holden says that he thinks he is going to apply himself to study when he goes back to school, but cannot really know. This is a much more open ending than that of *Candide*. Holden's prognosis remains uncertain and the reader, likewise, remains uncertain of the adequacy of Mr Antolini's advice. The possibility that there is no satisfactory way of living in modern capitalist society remains an available interpretation.

In this way the novel functions as a criticism of the values of post-war American patriarchal capitalism and especially of the empty pretensions and hypocrisies of the social elite, and Holden himself is the antithesis of the traditional hero: the qualities the reader admires in him are his gentleness, compassion, self-deprecation and penchant for metaphysical inquiry. Although it was not written for children *The Catcher in the Rye* has had a significant impact on later children's literature, especially in the United States where writers such as Robert Cormier, Paul Zindel and Betsy Byars have produced starkly realistic fiction for young people. In their hero stories the protagonists are often from poor or dysfunctional families, and adults are depicted as flawed and limited human beings. The heroes are ordinary children who struggle to do the best they can in a difficult world, and usually try to avoid inflicting harm on others. Often the stories avoid closure, implying at best an uncertain future. Though male protagonists predominate in the work of each of these writers the images of masculinity they construct are radically different from the conventional hero.

A recent fantasy quest tale for younger readers which successfully challenges stereotyped conceptions of gender is Emily Rodda's *Rowan of Rin* [1993] which won the Children's Book Council of Australia's award for Book of the Year for Younger Readers in 1994. This story suggests that there are no human qualities or skills which belong exclusively to one sex or the other. In the imaginary village of Rin both men and women are physically strong, active and brave, women perhaps more so than men, and both perform the full range of manual work: a woman, Bronden, is a furniture maker; Val, another woman, is a miller as is her twin brother Ellis. On the other hand the most imaginative and creative person in the village is a man, Allun the baker, while Rowan, the protagonist, is a gentle, intuitive and timid boy. The qualities which the story valorizes are empathy, affection, humility and imagination. These qualities, which Rowan possesses, enable him to succeed in the quest to discover why the stream of fresh water on which the village depends has stopped flowing from the top of the mountain, whereas the physically stronger and more respected companions with whom he sets out fail one by one because physical strength and courage are not enough. Except for Allun, who suffered when young for being different from his peers, Rowan's companions have not had to develop mental endurance and adaptability because their physical prowess has protected them from challenge and self-doubt. Therefore, when tested by situations which require mental toughness and vision they fail. In this way the work implies the essential immaturity of the conventional hero.

Because it is intended for younger readers the book lacks the richness of detail which makes fantasies such as Le Guin's Earthsea stories so vivid and the story is somewhat rigid and predictable as the adventurers move from one point on their map, and one challenge, to the next, with little information provided about the spaces in between. Nevertheless it stimulates the desire to know what will happen next; its linearity manages to produce the serial pleasures of the genre without any fighting or slaughter of either animals or humans. This is emphasized when, at the climax of the story, Rowan confronts a dragon. In a deliberate reversal of the usual heroic action he does not kill it but relieves its pain and rage by removing a bone which had become stuck in its throat. Although this is somewhat contrived it makes its point effectively, and the superiority of Rowan's gentleness to the usual heroic aggression is established, because it is the dragon's fiery heat which melts the mountain ice and makes the stream flow. Had Rowan killed it the village would have been doomed.

## SUBVERTING THE DUALISMS: PUBLIC AND PRIVATE SPACE

The Alice stories subvert the traditional male/female duality and call reason and logic into hilarious question, but leave the concepts of home and wilderness and public and private spaces more or less in place. A much loved work of children's literature which turns the home/wilderness opposition upside down, forcing us to see our ordered, rational society as potentially oppressive and threatening, is Beatrix Potter's *The Tale of Peter Rabbit* (1902). Like the White Rabbit which Alice pursues at the beginning of *Wonderland*, Peter Rabbit wears human clothes on the upper part of his body, but his predatory expedition into Mr McGregor's garden and his passion for lettuce and radishes make him seem far more like a wild rabbit than the White Rabbit whose primary concern is that he will be late for the Duchess's party. By clothing her animals Potter signifies their liminality and so denies the human/nature duality, and the story focuses on the relationship between animals and human beings. The semi-anthropomorphized rabbits suggest the continuum between animal and human, a continuum which has traditionally been denied in Western thinking. Just as Plato denied that animals possessed either soul or reason the Genesis story inscribed a rigid division between humans and all other living things which has been integral to Christian values:

> And God said let us make man in our image, after our likeness; and let them have dominion over the fish of the sea, and over the fowl of the air, and over the cattle, and over all the earth, and over every creeping thing that creepeth upon the earth.
>
> (Genesis 1: 26)

It is this perception which enables the slaughter of animals for 'sport' as well as for food. But small children do not make this division, as can be seen by their readiness to accept stories in which animals speak and behave like human beings; it is a learned, not a natural perception. While the ability to categorize reality is an essential stage in a child's cognitive development the traditional categories of Western thought are culturally determined, not intrinsic, and may sometimes impede rather than facilitate understanding. The habit of placing human beings in a totally separate category from animals has blinded Westerners to our close links to other life forms and our dependence upon biodiversity for our own survival. The feeling of kinship with Peter Rabbit, and therefore with all animal life, which is evoked by Potter's story is likely to produce a more accurate sense of our place in the planet's biosphere than the fantasy of separateness and superiority implied in adventure stories about the exploits of great hunters shooting lions and grizzly bears.

Peter Rabbit's home is a burrow in a sand-bank where Mrs Rabbit cares for her four children, Flopsy, Mopsy, Cottontail and Peter. Potter's illustrations show it to be a comforting and ordered domestic space. Pots and pans hang neatly on the wall, there is a cosy fire and a kitchen bench where food is prepared. Mrs Rabbit is a plump, homely figure in her blue gown and voluminous white apron. The children are well-cared for: neatly dressed, generously fed and dosed with camomile tea when necessary. It is a site of the primary human virtues of love and caring, but from the normal human perspective, of course, rabbits are wild creatures and their home is in the wilderness. Opposed to the rabbit home is Mr McGregor's garden, a space where human effort has subdued the wild and vegetables are grown in carefully laid out beds. But for Peter this is a dangerous space, a 'wilderness', which he enters in defiance of his mother's orders, squeezing under the symbolic barrier of the gate. Earlier his father had been caught and killed there, and Mr McGregor who pursues Peter, calling out 'Stop thief!' and waving a rake with murderous intent, is an ogre from the world of fairy tales.

Like Jack in 'Jack and the Beanstalk' Peter is a young and irresponsible hero whose behaviour sometimes tries his mother's patience, but the reader enjoys his energy and initiative, and is positioned to share his perspective because he is the focalizing character of the story. Like most heroes he is aided by assistants who appear in his moment of greatest need – friendly sparrows who urge him to fresh efforts when he is caught in a gooseberry net. These are representatives of nature enlisted on his side against the dour Mr McGregor. So our neat, civilized world is perceived as dangerous and antithetical to nature and thus to life and joy, and the home/wilderness opposition is subverted.

The rabbits belong partly to nature and partly to the sphere of private human domesticity, but they are excluded from the public world of power and work which is dominated by reason and by men. All that we know of Potter's life before her marriage in 1913 at the age of 47 suggests that she found the structure of English middle-class society, with its rigid division between private and public life, oppressive. Like most women of her class she remained within the private world, living at home with her parents until her late marriage, and subject to her father's rule despite her maturity, her talents and the success of her books. Life at 2 Bolton Gardens was constrained by a stuffy and unvarying domestic routine focusing upon silent, formal meals and allowing no scope for spontaneous or creative action (Carpenter 1985: 139–40). By his escapade Peter, Potter's *alter ego*, challenges the dominance of the public world and the oppressive rules and routines which flow from it. His journey is not from civilization into the wilderness and back again, but rather from the point at which nature and culture intersect, and from which human consciousness and civilization develop – the private domain of women and children – into the life-denying formality of the public sector which he temporarily upsets by his cheekiness and daring, then back to security and love. Like the young protestors who scale the fences surrounding secret nuclear installations he is an unsuccessful revolutionary, but an endearing one. *The Tale of Peter Rabbit* recognizes the division in our culture between the domestic sphere and the public world where power is situated, just as it recognizes the perceived division between humans and animals but, unlike most hero tales, it values the private world above the public and denies the imagined boundary between humanity and nature.

A similarly popular but more recent hero story which likewise depicts the public world of the Western patriarchy as a dangerous wilderness is the 1982 Steven Spielberg film, *E.T.* E.T. journeys from a distant planet – from the human perspective the farthest possible wilderness – to the wealthiest and most technologically advanced nation of our world, but his experiences there show the power of the structured, public domain of the United States to be oppressive, insensitive and life-denying. His retreat, after he has at last managed to 'phone home', is an escape to a culture which, by implication, is more ethical and more attuned to life than the blinkered and arid rationalism of Western civilization where the overriding concern is the preservation of the existing power structure.

In this story the focalizing character is not E.T. himself, but Elliott, a human child who discovers and protects him, and this structural device aligns E.T., like Peter Rabbit, with the domestic world of children and women. It also provides the viewer with a subject position sympathetic to E.T. and opposed to the forces of the CIA or FBI who want to capture and analyse him in the name of national security. The brutal power of the federal agents is symbolized by their guns, boots and uniforms while the gentleness and powerlessness of the children's world is emphasized by their toys and bicycles, and the domestic settings. E.T. resembles the children's teddy bears and soft toys, further underlining his alignment with their world, and suggesting his innocence and benevolence. Relationships in this world are structured by affection, not enforced by power. It is affection alone which links E.T. and Elliott; their devotion to each other is voluntary. But the government agents who gain control of E.T. impose their will by force.

As his role as a Christ-figure becomes clear E.T.'s association with the children and the powerless, and his persecution by the state, take on additional significance. His apparent death on an operating table in a government institution, surrounded by state-controlled scientific and medical apparatus, is a symbolic crucifixion suggesting that the only reaction our culture is capable of when faced by innocents who come amongst us to challenge our preconceptions and our addiction to power is to destroy them, and the children's grief echoes the grief of those who wept at the foot of Christ's cross. But this dark meaning is modified for the viewer by the joy of E.T.'s resurrection when he contacts his own people and is taken home, ascending symbolically into the heavens. Thus the closure of the story implies that the gentle virtues of the private sphere, love and care for others, will triumph despite the brutalities of power. It is far more of a fairy tale ending than the somewhat wry conclusion of *Peter Rabbit*, but in both stories the world of patriarchal power is depicted as a place from which it is necessary to escape, a place where truly human values are denied.

*Peter Rabbit* is one of the best known and most widely read of all children's books, and Peter has achieved iconic status. His china image adorns the shelves of many children's rooms and he appears on wallpaper, friezes, cups and plates. *E.T.* is one of the most popular films ever made. Neither Peter nor E.T. possesses prowess or power, nor do they have any desire to fight their enemies. They are daring but completely lack aggression. Their stories are full of the excitement of exploration, not the struggle for dominance. It seems likely that part of the extraordinary appeal of these stories for children, and for adults, stems from their valorization of the interpersonal, of friendship, family relationships and affection, above the public world of regulations and power, which demands from children, as the price of entry, the abandonment of love and joy.

## SUBVERTING THE DUALISMS: CIVILIZATION AND WILDERNESS

Increasing awareness of environmental issues has had a significant impact on recent children's literature, suggesting that the loop between patriarchal attitudes and the literature which inscribes and naturalizes them can be broken.

In even the most straightforward contemporary children's adventure stories the wilderness is now rarely depicted as merely a field for the hero's domination, and in some outstanding works the relationship between human civilization and the wilderness which nourishes it and is threatened by it, is explored with insight and sensitivity.

Gary Paulsen's *Hatchet*, a 1988 Newbery Honor Book very popular with primary school readers, is a direct descendant of *Robinson Crusoe*, an exciting survival story which nevertheless manages to avoid most of the ideological imperatives of its progenitor. Although, like many books of its kind, it fails to avoid the male/female dualism, implying the inferiority of the female by simple omission, it treats the concepts of civilization and wilderness with some sophistication and shows the hero growing in strength and wisdom as his understanding of the wilderness increases. The hero is a 13-year-old city boy, Brian Robeson, who finds himself alone in the Canadian wilderness when the pilot of the small Cessna in which he is the only passenger has a heart attack, just as the pilot in Ivan Southall's *To the Wild Sky* did twenty years earlier. Whereas the children's efforts to survive are dealt with only perfunctorily in the last section of Southall's book, Brian's encounter with the wilderness occupies most of Paulsen's comparatively brief text.

Brian crash lands the Cessna in a lake so that everything in the plane is inaccessible to him. Unlike Crusoe he has no wreck to provide him with the basic resources of civilization; his only tool is a small hatchet which was attached to his belt at the time of the crash. He survives by becoming sensitive to the wilderness, observing it patiently and learning to adapt to it, not by imposing the learned attitudes of civilization upon it. For instance he is for a long time unable to catch any of the many birds which nest in the undergrowth because he does not see them until he is so close that he scares them off. Eventually he realizes that he had been looking for their colour rather than noticing the shapes of the undergrowth, and when he concentrates on the shapes he can see them everywhere and catch them with comparative ease: 'It was like turning on a television. Suddenly he could see things he never saw before. In just moments it seemed he saw three birds before they flew' (Paulsen 1994: 112). As he becomes increasingly attuned to his environment he discovers solutions to many of the difficulties which beset him and he grows in self-confidence and emotional equanimity at the same time as he becomes physically tougher and more adept. Despite the swiftness with which the story moves it conveys a sense of the richness and subtlety of the wilderness, and the inner growth Brian achieves as he learns its ways is convincing.

Amongst the increasing number of hero stories for young people which show the hero learning to respect the wilderness in this way Jean Craighead George's *Julie of the Wolves* [1972], which won the Newbery Medal in 1973, remains outstanding. While adhering precisely to the story pattern of the hero's journey from civilization into the wilderness and confrontation with the wild things, this tale subverts most of the patriarchal values inscribed in the traditional tales.

The major binary oppositions in this story are:

| | | |
|---|---|---|
| civilization | – | wilderness |
| humans | – | wolves |
| Americans | – | Eskimos (Inuit) |
| reason | – | empathy |
| technology | – | nature |
| male | – | female |

The male/female duality is questioned throughout because the protagonist who survives in the wilderness is a girl, and she survives because of her sensitivity and empathy, traditionally 'feminine' attributes. Likewise it is the 'wilderness . . . nature' side of the inter-linked oppositions which is valorized. Readers are invited to see the wilderness, the Alaskan tundra, as beautiful and fragile, and its increasing domination by civilization as tragic: the wasteful destruction of something supremely valuable. An oil drum on the snow which Julie recognizes as 'the beginning of civilization and the end of the wilderness' (George [1972] 1976: 123) functions as a sign of cultural as well as physical contamination. The wild things which inhabit this wilderness, a wolf pack with a noble black leader whom Julie calls Amaroq, become her friends, adopting and nourishing her when she is lost on the tundra. Far from dominating them she survives only by learning their ways and adapting to them. The 'savages', the Inuit, or Eskimo, people are shown as having evolved a culture that enabled them to live in harmony with their environment which is now being destroyed by the depredations of the civilized Americans.

The depiction of the wolf pack is based upon careful and detailed zoological observation of the behaviour of actual wolves in their natural habitat, and highlights the inaccuracies of the traditional image of the wolf in folk tales and popular literature. They are shown as intelligent, affectionate and highly social animals who take exemplary care of their young. They do not attack human beings, and their adoption of Julie accords with the many documented cases of wolves nurturing lost human children. Apart from survival, affection for each other is shown to be the wolves' primary motivation, and this is in accordance with a deduction Mary Midgley makes from reports of ethologists' observations of wolf behaviour:

> Cub care is *important* to wolves. So is affection for their friends and companions. (Indeed the two things go together; the gestures by which adults show affection are drawn from cub-rearing.) Affection is a prevailing motive. Powerful general motives like this can easily make them delay gratification of immediate desires like hunger or sleepiness. The whole pack is bound together by affection. But this affection is not

> 'blind impulse'; it has a *backbone*, a structure that keeps it steady through variations of mood.
>
> (Midgley 1995: 279)

She goes on to argue that, because they operate as a group, it is this affection for each other which ensures the wolves' survival so their affectionate behaviour is also intelligent, and the affection and the intelligence have developed in concert and operate interdependently.

The behaviour of the human beings in *Julie of the Wolves* is, by contrast, shown to be frequently neither intelligent nor affectionate, as in the drunkenness of Naka, a friend of Julie's father. Julie's father himself has abandoned the traditional ways of the Eskimo hunter he once was and acts as a guide and pilot for American hunters, thus colluding in the destruction of the environment and the culture he loved. These Eskimo men have lost their way under the influence of American civilization, but it is the behaviour of the American hunters themselves which seems most alienated and bizarre. When they shoot Amaroq from a plane and leave him dead on the snow Julie thinks at first that they have done it for money, for the government bounty, but when they do not even bother to collect his carcase she is completely at a loss to understand their behaviour. The wolves themselves are predators but they are an integral part of the ecology of the region and they kill for food. Julie recalls her father saying:

> When the wolves are gone there will be too many caribou grazing the grass and the lemmings will starve. Without the lemmings the foxes and birds and weasels will die. Their passing will end smaller lives upon which even man depends, whether he knows it or not, and the top of the world will pass into silence.
>
> (George [1972] 1976: 123)

The American hunters kill for neither food nor money nor fear; they kill for amusement and the cruelty and irrationality of their behaviour suggests that the values of their civilization have become distorted.

The related oppositional pairs in the story are symbolized by Julie's double name: Miyax, the Eskimo name she was given at birth, and Julie, the name she was given when, at the age of 9, she left her father, Kapugen, who had taught her Eskimo lore, to be educated in the American way. It is as Julie that, at the age of 13, she runs away from her arranged marriage to go to her American pen-friend in San Francisco, dreaming of the luxuries of the American way of life. When she becomes lost on the tundra she recalls the Eskimo survival skills her father taught her and gradually comes to think of herself as Miyax again as she learns to live in harmony with the environment. Her ability to survive in this way fills her with a sense of profound well-being which surpasses any pleasure she gained from her American education. After the killing of Amaroq she feels nothing but horror for American civilization, and decides that she will live as an Eskimo in the traditional way. However, when she rediscovers her father and finds that even he has married a Gussak, a white woman, and adapted to the American way, she realizes her dream is impossible. Amaroq's death is the symbol of the future: 'the hour of the wolf and the Eskimo is over' (George [1972] 1976: 155). So she becomes Julie again and resigns herself to living with her Americanized father.

Julie's quest, then, ends in failure: all that she most values is doomed. But it is triumph, of a kind, for the patriarchy: they are subduing the wilderness, destroying the wild things, and civilizing the savages. Because Julie is the focalizing character the reader sees their triumph as tragedy. Or at least the attentive reader does. In eliciting responses to this story from young readers I have noticed that many, familiar with the happy ending of traditional hero tales, simply do not register the significance of the final sentence: 'Julie pointed her boots towards Kapugen'. They believe she is going off to live happily as an Eskimo. The meaning that inheres in the shape of the hero story is deeply embedded in our consciousness, and perhaps this is why, for all its excitement and interest, *Julie of the Wolves* seems to be less popular with book-sellers and the public than the author's earlier work, *My Side of the Mountain* [1959] the story of a boy who runs away from his home in New York to live in a tree house in the Catskill Mountains for a year. His story ends happily when his family joins him in the mountains. This work has been made into a film, and appears to be always in print, whereas *Julie of the Wolves* is often difficult to obtain.

A more recent book which also addresses the gap between actual wolves and their mythical image is Gillian Cross's Carnegie Medal-winning *Wolf* [1990]. Aimed at young adult readers this work transposes 'Little Red Riding Hood' from the forest to the urban wilderness of modern London, and canvasses a number of contemporary social issues including IRA terrorism. It investigates human behaviour as well as the legendary behaviour of wolves and bears out Mary Midgley's view (Midgley 1995: 31) that human beings have always tried to deflect attention from the extreme ferocity of which they are themselves capable by exaggerating the ferocity of animals, especially wolves.

Little Red Riding Hood is 12-year-old Cassy who lives an ordered life with her grandmother in her meticulously neat flat, except when she is despatched without explanation to stay with her mother, Goldie, a gentle hippy who lives in the jungle of London squats and bed-sits. Her grandmother sends her away because her son, Cassy's father, a hunted member of the IRA, of whose existence Cassy is unaware, has turned up secretly over night to take refuge with his mother. Hidden in the basket her grandmother packs for her is a yellow substance which looks like butter but is actually some plastic explosive her father needs to dispose of. Cassy's father has the qualities traditionally attributed to wolves: he is cunning, predatory, ruthless and irrational in his obsessiveness. Cassy, like Little Red Riding Hood, is innocent, well-meaning and unaware of the dangers which surround her. She finds her mother living in a bizarrely decorated squat with her black lover, Lyall, and his son, Robert, performance artists who tour schools putting on educational entertainments for children. They are currently preparing a project on wolves, and as Cassy becomes involved in the background research and group discussions the differences between the mythical image of wolves and their actual nature is highlighted. They also visit real wolves at the zoo to observe their behaviour, underlining the harmlessness of these animals compared to the human terrorist on the loose. Concurrently Cassy comes to realize that her original fears of Lyall and Robert are unfounded: although they are black and different from the people she has known in her protected life with her grandmother, they are not wolves. Cassy's neat, respectable grandmother has always been contemptuous of Goldie because of her impractical romanticism, her untidiness, her disorganized life and what the grandmother sees as her total lack of responsibility, especially towards her child. But it is the grandmother's shielding of her son which puts Cassy in real danger and Goldie who ultimately takes the decisive, courageous action that saves her. The story thus interrogates conventional judgements of human behaviour at the same time as it exposes the fallacy of the conventional view of wolves.

Because Cassy is the focalizing character the reader shares her uncertainties about the real nature of the various characters. At first she is as much deceived about them as the original Little Red Riding Hood who mistakes a wolf for her grandmother, but gradually she realizes that simple black and white, dualistic judgements are inadequate. Cassy's changing perceptions of the people around her and the twists of the plot make this a very exciting story which nevertheless endorses tolerance and gentleness, and depicts the 'heroic' use of force and violence in support of a cause as a dangerous anachronism in our crowded modern world. Unlike such facile inversions of traditional fairy tales as *Princess Smarty Pants* and *The Dragon of Brog*, Cross's story uses the fairy-tale framework to explore the themes dramatized by the original story of 'Little Red Riding Hood': aggression and the danger it represents for women, and the deceptiveness of surface appearances, especially the seeming safety of home compared with the uncertainties of the wider world. The adaptation of the story to a contemporary political and social context encourages young readers to look beyond conventional dualistic analyses of current issues.

## DENYING DUALISM

In some recent popular children's books the subversion of duality has itself become a primary theme. Bob Graham's *Rose Meets Mr Wintergarten* [1992], which won the Children's Book Council of Australia Picture Book of the Year award in 1993, uses a range of obvious visual and verbal symbols, decodable by very young readers, to set up a complex of linked dualities for the purpose of knocking them down. Mr Wintergarten is a grumpy recluse who lives alone in an imposing grey house on which the sun never shines. It is surrounded by a spiky cactus garden and a high fence, and protected by a savage dog. The Summers family of mildly hippy parents, children and animals moves into the small house next door. They plant flowers in the sunshine and have fun. When Rose Summers kicks her football over the fence she invades Mr Wintergarten's sunless domain, bearing a gift of fairy cakes – a small hero entering the terrifying wilderness with a gift rather than a weapon and seeking not domination but friendship. Despite an initial surly response Mr Wintergarten's moroseness is thawed and he comes out to join the fun. The fence and the cacti go, his house is repainted in light colours and the sun shines on it. The story suggests that the difference between Rose and Mr Wintergarten is illusory, that dualism is not the universal structural principle, that human beings do not fall into separate and opposing categories: good and bad, happy and gloomy, friendly and antagonistic, us and them, that beneath their external oddities they are much the same.

A more profound challenge to traditional dualistic thinking is achieved in Ursula Le Guin's trilogy *A Wizard of Earthsea*, a rich fantasy full of invention, excitement and suspense, which uses the conventional shape of the hero story to construct a fable concerned with harmony rather than mastery, in which the hero, Ged, is engaged on a quest for enlightenment, not dominance. Ged's progress from gifted but arrogant, wilful and egocentric youth to maturity, wisdom and responsibility, and finally to the voluntary surrender of self to the whole, is rendered with at least as much colour and visceral excitement as the best stories of pirates, savages and hidden treasure, and with considerably more intellectual interest. Typical of the touches which combine cerebral and imaginative appeal is the Immanent Grove where the lore of wizards is taught, and which constantly shifts its position as the uninitiated attempt to enter it, being reachable only by those who are ready for what may be learned there, a motif far more memorable than the treasure chamber under the mountain in *King Solomon's Mines*, guarded by a series of laboured and mundane contrivances.

The universe of this text is one in which everything, from the elemental rocks to the minds of the greatest wizards, is part of a fragile and perpetually shifting balance, so that finally, in moments of true insight, it is impossible to tell the dancer from the dance. Le Guin eventually came to see that the trilogy did restate the male/female dualism, and the later work in the series, *Tehanu* [1990], was written in part to redress this:

> I look back and see that I was writing partly by the rules, as an artificial man, and partly against the rules, as an inadvertent revolutionary.
>
> (Le Guin 1993a: 7)

> The fourth book, *Tehanu*, takes up where the trilogy left off, in the same hierarchic, male-dominated society; but now, instead of using the pseudo-genderless male viewpoint of the heroic tradition, the world is seen through a woman's eyes.
>
> (Le Guin 1993a: 12)

But the male/female opposition is the only traditional dualism which survives unchallenged in the first three Earthsea books. Some were consciously undermined by Le Guin in a deliberate attempt to push against contemporary prejudices: she made Ged and the other 'good guys' brown or black and the villains white: 'I saw myself as luring white readers to identify with the hero, to get inside his skin and only then find it was a dark skin. I meant this as a strike against racial bigotry' (1993a: 8). In the first book, as we have seen, Ged comes finally to accept the Shadow against which he has struggled as part of himself and so achieves psychic wholeness, and this use of Jungian archetypes was also consciously undertaken (1993a: 5–6). It is an image which denies the Platonic-Cartesian exaltation of reason above all other mental functions, suggesting the need to integrate the conscious and the unconscious and the cognitive and affective aspects of the self.

But some of Le Guin's subversions were perhaps, as she has said, 'inadvertent'. As Peter Hollindale points out there are several levels of ideology in any text (Hollindale 1988: 19–24) and the more powerful are those of which the author is not wholly conscious: his or her own unexamined assumptions, the fundamental perspectives of the contemporary society, and the values embedded in the language itself, some of which escape even the most determined critical scrutiny. Probably the trilogy's most profound challenge to patriarchal values inheres in the attitude to the natural world implied by the narrative point of view, an attitude which ultimately entails a denial of the very notion of mastery. Ged slowly learns this attitude of acceptance, love and humility in the first story which deals with his journey to maturity, his attainment of the status of mage – 'wizard' or wise man. It is inscribed in the text in a variety of ways. It is shown to be the basis of the teachings of the great wizards, especially the wisest of all, Ged's first master, Ogion, who, despite his great power, elected to live the simplest possible life in a small house on the mountainside where he gathered herbs and studied the ways of nature. He tried to cultivate this understanding in the adolescent Ged:

> When you know the fourfoil in all its seasons, root and leaf and flower, by sight and scent and seed, then you may learn its true name, knowing its being: which is more than its use. What, after all, is the use of you? or of myself?
>
> (Le Guin [1968] 1971: 29)

Ged, however, is young, impatient and proud, and he cannot recognize the truths to which Ogion, in the way of a Zen master, can only point. He seeks power, suffers disaster when he releases the Shadow, and learns humility and respect slowly and with difficulty. He comes to understand something of what Ogion tried to teach him when, as a young wizard, he overstrains his powers attempting to save the life of a child and is left in a trance, or a coma, from which he is called back to life only by his pet otak, a small, cat-like animal that patiently licks his insensible form until he responds instinctively to its touch:

> It was only the dumb instinctive wisdom of the beast who licks his hurt companion to comfort him, and yet in that wisdom Ged saw something akin to his own power, something that went as deep as wizardry. From that time forth he believed that the wise man is one who never sets himself apart from other living things, whether they have speech or not, and in later years he strove to learn what can be learned, in silence, from the eyes of animals, the flight of birds, the great slow gestures of trees.
>
> (Le Guin [1968] 1971: 96–7)

He learns more about nature from his encounter with the great dragon, Yevaud, whose majestic size and power suggest the forces of the volcano and the tempest, and are complementary to the otak's small benevolent warmth. The dragon's rage and power are terrible but in no sense evil; Yevaud is not a Christian symbol, like the dragon confronted by Saint George, but an embodiment of the creative and destructive forces of nature which demand humanity's awed respect. In the final volume of the trilogy and in the later *Tehanu* a similar dragon, Kalessin, is depicted as possessing an elemental wisdom which is the natural corollary of its power. Le Guin herself said of this dragon who is genderless:

> So the dragon is subversion, revolution, change – a going beyond the old order in which men were taught to own and dominate and women were taught to collude with them: the order of oppression. It is the wildness of the spirit and of the earth, uprising against misrule.
>
> (Le Guin 1993a: 23–4)

This attitude to nature probably owes something to the beginnings of the modern environmental movement which had begun to affect Western thinking in the years when these books were being written, but it is more fundamentally an expression of the system of values underlying the trilogy, which seems more Taoist than Christian. The Christian conception of a world set between heaven and hell, beset by the opposing forces of good and evil, and consisting of separately created things, is replaced by the vision of a universe which is 'a seamless web of unbroken movement and change, filled with undulations, waves, patterns of ripples and temporary "standing waves" like a river' (Rawson and Legeza 1973: 10), in which there are no oppositions and no hierarchies. Ged achieves his first moment of Taoist insight when he arrives at the school for wizards on Roke Island and waits in the courtyard to meet the archmage:

> As their eyes met, a bird sang aloud in the branches of the tree. In that moment Ged understood the singing of the bird, and the language of the water falling in the basin of the fountain, and the shape of the

> clouds, and the beginning and end of the wind that stirred the leaves: it seemed to him that he himself was a word spoken by the sunlight.
> (Le Guin [1968] 1971: 47)

This is convincing as a glimpse of the Taoist web, the Heraclitean flow, the physicist's dance of the molecules, because the natural phenomena described are all in movement – notes of bird song, falling water, wind, moving clouds and leaves – and because Ged feels himself to be equally insubstantial, so that the observer is not separate from what he observes. Consciousness itself is one with the dance: Ged is a *word* spoken by sunlight.

Although the world of Earthsea is not technologically advanced this vision of a universe in equilibrium hints at the dangers of scientific interference with the natural balance, especially the dangers inherent in nuclear fission, and raises a contemporary issue in a way which compels attention. One of Ged's teachers says to him:

> To change this rock into a jewel, you must change its true name. And to do that, my son, even to so small a scrap of the world, is to change the world. It can be done. Indeed it can be done. It is the art of the Master Changer, and you will learn it, when you are ready to learn it. But you must not change one thing, one pebble, one grain of sand, until you know what good and evil will follow on the act. The world is in balance, in Equilibrium. A wizard's power of Changing and of Summoning can shake the balance of the world. It is dangerous that power. It is most perilous.
> (Le Guin [1968] 1971: 56)

According to this view everything has its place and must be respected as part of the whole, even things which appear to human observers to be terrifying or repulsive, and the third volume of the trilogy, *The Farthest Shore* [1973], is concerned with the place of death as an integral part of the whole: in trying to defy death a misguided wizard has damaged the Equilibrium and Ged, now the archmage and responsible for the wellbeing of all Earthsea, is forced to exhaust his powers to restore the balance. He realizes that without death life is impossible, and he knows that death means absorption into the whole to become part of 'the earth and sunlight, the leaves of trees, the eagle's flight' (Le Guin 1993b: 462). Dualistic thinking is impossible in the context of such a conception of the nature of things, and domination and mastery have no meaning. The traditional hero's enterprises become simply evidence of inadequate insight. The object of the universal quest can only be enlightenment.

## CHANGING THE POINT OF VIEW

In a 1992 lecture, *Earthsea Revisioned*, Ursula Le Guin told how she came to see that her Earthsea trilogy had been written from within the heroic tradition in which stories were concerned with the validation of manhood, women were subsidiary, and the anonymous narrative point of view supposedly transcended gender, but in reality implied that the universal norm was male. Two books of the trilogy have no major female characters, in all three the protagonist is male (Ged, the hero) and it is he who initiates action. Further, power in Earthsea belongs to communities of men, in particular to the cloister-like community of wizards on Roke Island, learned men who have no sexual contact with women. Women are devalued; at best they are village witches whose magic is weak and confused. The most significant female figure is Tenar, a major character in the second volume, *The Tombs of Atuan* [1972], but she is the priestess of an enclosed, female order whose holy place is a huge subterranean temple and from early childhood she has known only this suffocating underground world where she is given a form of respect but denied freedom. Her situation is thus an effective metaphor for the limitations and frustrations traditionally imposed on women. She is able to escape only with Ged's assistance, and this further underlines the dependence and subordination of women.

By the early 1970s, however, when the third volume of the trilogy had been published, definitions of gender were in question and, as Le Guin says: 'women readers were asking how come all the wise guys on the Isle of the Wise were guys. The artist who was above gender had been exposed as a man hiding in a raincoat' (Le Guin 1993a: 11). It took her sixteen years before she was able to write *Tehanu* which came from her own emerging perceptions of the nature of Western society, rather than from the heroic tradition on which it is possible to 'ride':

> If you refuse to ride, you have to stumble along on your own two feet; if you try to speak your own wisdom, you lose that wonderful fluency. You feel like a foreigner in your own country, amazed and troubled by the things you see, not sure of the way, not able to speak with authority.
> (Le Guin 1993a: 10)

She manages to speak her own wisdom by changing the narrative point of view and making her focalizing character a woman: Tenar, now a middle-aged widow with two grown-up children. The heroic society and the men who have power in it are thus depicted from the point of view of one who is essentially an outsider, who does not benefit from their rule or their system of values, and who therefore does not feel the status quo to be 'natural' or inevitable. From her position on the margins Tenar sees the contradictions and weaknesses in the heroic system and notes them with an attitude that varies from wry amusement to anger.

We learn that, after her escape from Atuan, she spent some time as pupil of the great mage, Ogion, but finally elected to live as an ordinary woman, a farmer's wife, turning her back on learning and power in an attempt to find herself. She did discover in herself the traditional female qualities of patience and compassion, and she also learnt the nature of passion. But the only role for women in Earthsea is a circumscribed and subservient one, and Tenar did not quite fit this, despite her voluntary submission. Thus at the beginning of the story, after her husband's death, she is alone and wondering what her future will be: she is ready to embark on her own quest, an attempt not only to discover a new role for herself now that her years as wife and mother are over, but also to achieve some understanding of the world in which, perforce, she lives – a world in which power is in the hands of men, and women and children are often the victims of their casual violence.

Her first significant action in her new life is to adopt a small girl child who had been raped, beaten and burned by a group of men, including her own father. They had left her for dead in the fire, but she survived although horribly disfigured and traumatized. There is no power which can heal her mutilation or reverse her trauma, but Tenar's love and care restores her physical health and provides her with a small space of peace and security within her continuing fear that the men might return. Just as Tenar's quest symbolizes the task which faces all women in the second half of their lives, so this child, whom Tenar calls Therru, is symbolic of the damage our male-dominated society has inflicted on girls: partially blinded, disfigured and disabled, she cannot see the world clearly, she will never be what she might have been, and her central awareness is of what men can do to her. Because there is no cure for Therru she must go forward. As Tenar is bitterly aware, her disfigurement means that she will not be able to follow the traditional female path of marriage and children, so she must find a new and transforming way to be. As Le Guin says Therru is the key to the book (Le Guin 1993a: 19) because *Tehanu* is about the emergence of new ways from the old, about the birth of a different Western society after the long and painful labour of race and gender reassessment, a society which we cannot yet see clearly because, like Therru, our sight is damaged, but one which is surely ahead of us.

Tenar is summoned by the old mage, Ogion, who is dying, and, accompanied by Therru, she travels, rather fearfully, along roads infested by bands of dubious men, to be with her old teacher. Unlike traditional male heroes she seeks to avoid rather than dominate the dangers on the way, and her aim is not to achieve mastery but simply to create some security for herself and those she loves so that their connectedness might grow. The casual harassment that she and Therru experience on their journey suggests the dark side of the heroic society. However, in his last moments Ogion has a vision of a new, emerging world: "'All changed! – Changed, Tenar!'" (Le Guin 1993b: 502) He realizes that Therru will be essential to this change, seeing in her the power of the dragon: the fiery energy which can burn away the old stultifying and cruel ways so that the new may become possible. And it is because of her suffering that she has this energy; it has sharpened her vision and given her a profound will to change things. The story hints that she may well be the next archmage of Earthsea. Because Ged, the former archmage, had exhausted his magic powers at the end of *The Farthest Shore* a search for a new archmage is in progress but has been so far unsuccessful. The only guidance the mage masters on Roke have is a prophecy which to them seems very cryptic: 'A woman on Gont'. Because they cannot conceive of a female archmage they assume there must be a Gontish woman who will guide them to the right man for the job, but Tenar realizes that the words may well mean simply what they seem to mean.

However, this is left as no more than a possibility. The nature of Therru's future remains uncertain because she will have to make that future. The closure of the traditional hero story which asserts the hero's mastery and the continuing dominance of the European patriarchy, the absence of change, is replaced by a symbol of overwhelming change. At the end of the book when Ged and Tenar face the corrupted defenders of the old tradition, 'the pure malevolence of institutionalized power' (Le Guin 1993a: 19) they are saved by the intervention of the dragon Kalessin who has been summoned by Therru. Kalessin's fire and brightness burn the would-be murderers to ashes, leaving Tenar, Ged and Therru free to find a new way to live. This conclusion has been criticized as too pat, the dragon seen as a convenient *deus ex machina* (Stephens 1992: 42), but in fact its function is the opposite to that of the *deus ex machina* who appeared in order to restate or symbolize the established social values of the classical world, the edicts of Olympus. The dragon's appearance symbolizes the end of Olympian power, but leaves the task of imagining the future to the reader.

The use of Tenar as the focalizing character has several significant effects: the domestic world of home, women and children is foregrounded and so the definition of what is 'important' is brought into question; men and the public world of male action are seen from outside, through a woman's eyes; relationships between women are acknowledged and in fact assume a larger role in the women's lives than their relationships with men, although these remain important. The focus on the domestic world – life at Tenar's farm and in Ogion's cottage at Re Albi – where there is food to be prepared, dishes to be washed, floors to be scrubbed, vegetables to be weeded, clothes to be made and mended, draws attention to the texture of daily existence which fills the larger part of most people's lives, making them what they are, and providing, or denying, most of their joy in being. The story shows us how the smallest of our actions matters, for ourselves and others. Thus the new dress which Tenar makes for Therru affirms the child's worth, expresses Tenar's love, and defies the cruelty of the men who raped and disfigured her.

Because, as Le Guin says, this story is not carried along by the sweep and style of the heroic tradition the language is much plainer, stumbling on its own two feet, and this gives weight to the simple actions described, especially the sharing of food and drink which assumes its significance as communion – the expression of mutual need and caring. Even the journalistic 'issue' of sharing the washing-up is invested with real meaning in this context: to clean and put away the bowl from which one has eaten appears the natural completion of the shared meal, no less important than any other part of the ritual. Ged does it without thinking: 'Then he too got up and brought his dish to the sink, and finished clearing the table' (Le Guin 1993b: 536). The contrasting behaviour of Tenar's son who comes home to claim the farm his mother has run and expects her to wait upon him and wash his dishes seems not merely ill-mannered, but literally ungracious – the breaking of a sacrament. One of the meanings which emerges from this close-up focus is that social and cultural change must be embedded in domestic life and relationships: political action alone is not enough.

Political action is seen from without and seen to matter because it helps shape the context of people's lives, but it is not central. The reforms of the young king who has recently come to the throne with Ged's help will reduce some of the worst abuses of the old system – piracy, local government corruption, the suborning of the representatives of justice – but will not by themselves transform the nature of society. Le Guin argues that the myths of gender are crucial to such a transformation:

> The deepest foundation of the order of oppression is gendering, which names the male normal, dominant, active, and the female other, subject, passive. To begin to imagine freedom, the myths of gender, like the myths of race, have to be exploded and discarded.
>
> (Le Guin 1993a: 24)

One of the ways this text addresses the myths of gender is by foregrounding relationships between women and girls. In traditional hero stories, as we have seen, these relationships are suppressed. Women are depicted only in relation to men. Where they do relate to other women it is always in the context of an overriding relationship to a man, for whose favour they are competing or whose needs they serve. In *Tehanu* the friendships between Tenar and Lark, and Tenar and the village witch, Aunty Moss, are completely independent of any links with men, and are in themselves satisfying and sustaining. Tenar's relationships with her daughter, Apple, and her adopted daughter, Therru, are central to her existence; only her relationship with Ged comes near them in importance to her. Her life is seen to take place within a web of female friendship which exists for its own sake.

The love of Tenar and Ged, which reaches a late fruition in this book, suggests that in the new society which is emerging relationships between men and women will be entered into freely, not as a matter of social conformity or a means of self-definition or assertion. Having lost his role as the archmage, a position of the greatest importance in the public, political world, Ged passes through a painful period of reassessment, and realizes finally with 'goat wisdom' (Le Guin 1993b: 666) that such functions are only one part of life, worth no more than other ways of being, so that what he gives to Tenar is not his power or his position but only himself. And she, having long ago abandoned the possibility of power, has only herself to offer. That being so, perhaps they will achieve a new kind of relationship in the small cottage on the mountainside at Re Albi. The closure leaves that, like Therru's future, as a potentiality for the reader to imagine.

## CONCLUSIONS

The tale of the hero and his quest has been the master story of Western civilization, and it has been especially ubiquitous in children's literature. It may once have inscribed the struggle of early human communities to achieve a sense of identity and establish a regime of order to support that identity in the face of the vast chaos of the unknown world, but it has always glorified the patriarchy. Now it is a disabling story, naturalizing the exploitation of the environment, the domination of non-European peoples, the marginalization and subordination of women, the wanton slaughter of animals for use and amusement, and the use of force and violence to achieve these ends. It depicts this behaviour as natural, rational and good, as the struggle of the morally and culturally superior to achieve appropriate mastery.

The story is powerfully entrenched in Western consciousness, and it is the basis of the most popular and commercially successful products of the entertainment industry. It provides readers and viewers with primitive pleasure, repeatedly arousing and satisfying the desire to know what will happen next, while boosting their sense of self-worth with images of alien and inferior 'others' who may be despised or hated, and blamed for whatever problems afflict them. Its final message is always a comforting reassurance that, despite intermittent threats, the superiority of the West, and in particular of Western men, is as it should be and will remain – a happy ending which encourages complacency. But if the destruction of other cultures is to be halted, if our own culture is to survive, if women are to achieve real equality, and if environmental disaster is to be averted, we must change our entrenched perceptions, and that involves changing the story which articulates and reinforces them.

The stories discussed in this chapter show that it is possible to retain the linear pattern of the hero tale with its succession of exciting incidents without reaffirming the traditional dualisms that have shaped our thinking. In these stories the protagonists are not fanatical men of action, noted for their outstanding prowess and courage, guided by single-minded devotion to their goals, struggling against opponents whom they condemn as evil, and determinedly asserting their mastery. They are not constrained by an arid rationalism and they do not deny or distrust their emotions. They are not invulnerable to doubt, disappointment and defeat. They are not superheroes. They are like all the rest of us, and they include females, non-Europeans and other outsiders. They are impelled by the urge to survive, by love, and by curiosity – the desire to learn and to understand themselves and the world about them better. Because their sensitivities are not shut off by prior certainties they do observe and learn, and this process is at least as interesting and exciting for the reader as the traditional tales' accounts of hairbreadth escapes and fights with dragons and other enemies, the outcomes of which are always predetermined.

The endings of these stories are somewhat problematic. There is no thunderclap from Zeus or hot supper from Mother to signify approval of the hero's deeds, the significance of the conclusion is often somewhat equivocal, and what will happen in the future is by no means certain. These stories do not imply that there are any final solutions to life's difficulties; they do not evoke the 'happy ever after' heaven outside the text. The reader is left to wonder what Julie's life will be like with her Americanized father and to wonder about the chances of survival for the wolves of the American north. Holden Caulfield's future remains deeply problematic. Brian Robeson has been strengthened and matured by his experiences in the Canadian wilderness, but the reader must decide whether this will help him cope with his parents' impending divorce and his own future. It is impossible to predict the futures of Tenar, Therru and Ged, but the one thing that is clear to the reader is that all will be changed utterly.

By adopting a narrative point of view which is not that of the patriarchal establishment, stories such as *Tehanu*, *Julie of the Wolves*, *E.T.*, *The Catcher in the Rye* and *Peter Rabbit* imply the partial and relative nature of all perceptions of truth. It is quite clear to the reader that the perspectives of Tenar, of Julie, of E.T.'s friend, Elliott, of Holden Caulfield, of Peter, are outsiders' perspectives, for they are constructed in opposition to the implied viewpoints of the powerful men at the centre of those societies – the Lord of Re Albi whose minions seek to destroy Tenar and Ged, Julie's father and the American hunters who kill the noble wolf Amaroq, the FBI and the CIA who hunt down E.T., the New York establishment which defines Holden as a failure, Mr McGregor who tries to impale Peter on a rake. They are perspectives which judge and condemn these other, traditional view-points, but do not deny their existence. Unlike conventional hero tales these stories do not claim absoluteness for their point of view, they do not pretend to exemplify '*what-goes-without-saying*' (Barthes [1957] 1973: 11), to become myths themselves. Nor do they imply that their point of view is the inevitable outcome of reason. Some, such as *Alice* and *The Hitch-hiker's Guide*, question the very possibility of using reason to understand the nature of existence; all acknowledge doubt and confusion.

These stories demand active participation by readers and viewers. They demand interpretation and the re-examination of received opinions. They demand the acceptance of uncertainty. But they reward their readers with intellectual, emotional and imaginative stimulation, with humour, with subtleties of insight, with opportunities to explore the perspectives of people different from themselves. At the same time they legitimize the perspectives and affirm the value of readers who are not members of the European patriarchy. It is not necessary to adopt the point of view of a white, establishment male while reading them. Some of these stories – *Alice, Peter Rabbit, E.T., The Hitch-hiker's Guide* – are more popular than most conventional hero tales, suggesting that, given the opportunity, young readers and viewers prefer works which do not impose the rigid, patriarchal world view upon them. The future of our culture and our planet depends upon today's young readers. It is vital to present them with stories which discourage the quest for domination and the use of force and violence to achieve it, and encourage a respect for the environment and for men and women of all cultural backgrounds.

# BIBLIOGRAPHY

Adams, Douglas (1979) *The Hitch-hiker's Guide to the Galaxy*, London and Sydney: Pan Books.
—— (1980) *The Restaurant at the End of the Universe*, London: Pan.
—— (1982) *Life, the Universe and Everything*, London: Pan.
Antonio, Diane (1995) 'Of wolves and women' in Adams, Carol J. and Donovan, Josephine (eds) *Animals and Women: Feminist Theoretical Explorations*, Durham and London: Duke University Press, pp. 213–30.
Apollonius of Rhodes, *Jason and the Golden Fleece* (*The Argonautica*), translated by Richard Hunter (1995) The World's Classics, Oxford: Oxford University Press.
Ardizzone, Edward [1936] (1995) *Little Tim and the Brave Sea Captain*, 2nd edn, New York: Scholastic Book Services.
Aristotle, *Politics*, translated by Benjamin Jowett (1905), London: Oxford University Press.
Arrian, *Life of Alexander the Great*, translated by Aubrey de Sélincourt (1958), Harmondsworth: Penguin.
Atwood, Margaret [1973] (1979) *Surfacing*, London: Virago.
Baillie, Allan (1985) *Little Brother*, Melbourne: Thomas Nelson Australia.
Ballantyne, R.M. [1857] (1953) *The Coral Island*, London and Glasgow: Collins.
—— (no date given), *The Dog Crusoe and his Master*, London: Juvenile Productions.
Barrie, J.M. [1904] (1942) *Peter Pan* in Wilson A.E. (ed.) *The Plays of J.M. Barrie*, revised edn, London: Hodder and Stoughton.
Barthes, Roland [1957] (1973) *Mythologies*, Paladin edn, St Albans: Paladin.
—— (1976) *The Pleasure of the Text* (*Le Plaisir du texte*) translated by Richard Miller, London: Cape.
Barwell, Ismay (1993) 'Feminist perspectives and narrative points of view' in Hein, Hilde and Korsmeyer, Carolyn (eds) *Aesthetics in Feminist Perspective*, Bloomington and Indianapolis: Indiana University Press.
Baum, L. Frank [1900] (1973) *The Wonderful Wizard of Oz*, London: Dent.
Beardsley, Aubrey, Drawings, reproduced in Walker, R.A. (ed.) (1983) *The Best of Beardsley*, London: Chancellor Press.
Belsey, Catherine [1980] (1988) *Critical Practice*, London: Routledge.
*Beowulf: A New Translation by David Wright* (1957), Harmondsworth: Penguin.
Bettelheim, Bruno (1976) *The Uses of Enchantment: The Meaning and Importance of Fairy Tales*, London: Thames & Hudson.
Blake, William [1794] (1913) 'Songs of Innocence and Experience' in *The Poetical Works of William Blake*, London: Oxford.
Bradbrook, M.C. [1951] (1977) 'The Sources of *Macbeth*', reprinted in Muir, K. and Edwards, P. (eds) *Aspects of Macbeth*, Cambridge: Cambridge University Press, pp. 12–25.

Bristow, Joseph (ed.) (1995) *The Oxford Book of Adventure Stories*, Oxford and New York: Oxford University Press.
Bronowski, J. and Mazlish, Bruce (1963) *The Western Intellectual Tradition: From Leonardo to Hegel*, Harmondsworth: Penguin.
Brown, Marcia (1950) *Dick Whittington and His Cat*, London: Scribner.
Bunyan, John [1678] (1954) *The Pilgrim's Progress*, Everyman edn, London: J.M. Dent & Sons.
Burnett, Frances Hodgson [1911] (1951) *The Secret Garden*, Puffin edn, Harmondsworth: Penguin.
Byars, Betsy [1973] (1976) *The Eighteenth Emergency*, Puffin edn, Harmondsworth: Penguin.
—— [1978] (1981) *The Cartoonist*, Puffin edn, Harmondsworth: Penguin.
Byatt, A.S. [1978] (1981) *The Virgin in the Garden*, Harmondsworth: Penguin.
Campbell, James (1995) 'And we moved!', *The Times Literary Supplement* No. 4822, 1 September, pp. 22–3.
Campbell, Joseph [1949] (1968) *The Hero with a Thousand Faces*, 2nd edn, Princeton, New Jersey: Princeton University Press.
Carpenter, Humphrey (1985) *Secret Gardens: The Golden Age of Children's Literature*, Boston: Houghton Mifflin Company.
Carroll, Lewis [1865 and 1872] (1982) *Alice's Adventures in Wonderland and Through the Looking Glass*, World's Classics edn, Oxford: Oxford University Press.
Chodorow, Nancy (1974) 'Family structure and feminine personality' in Rosaldo, M.Z. and Lamphere, L. (eds) *Woman, Culture and Society*, Stanford: Stanford University Press, pp. 43–66.
Christie, Agatha [1934] (1959) *Murder on the Orient Express*, Fontana edn, London: Fontana/Collins.
Cixous, Hélène [1976] (1981) 'The Laugh of the Medusa' reprinted in Marks, E. and de Courtrivon, I. (eds) *New French Feminisms: An Anthology*, Brighton: Harvester.
Cole, Babette [1986] (1988) *Princess Smarty Pants*, Collins Picture Lions edn, London: HarperCollins.
—— (1987) *Prince Cinders*, London: Hamish Hamilton.
Coleridge, Samuel Taylor [1798] (1906) 'The Rime of the Ancient Mariner' in *The Golden Book of Coleridge*, Everyman edn, London: J.M. Dent & Sons.
Cooper, Susan [1973] (1976) *The Dark is Rising*, Puffin edn, Harmondsworth: Penguin.
—— [1977] (1979) *Silver on the Tree*, Puffin edn, Harmondsworth: Penguin.
Copper, Basil (1977) *The Werewolf in Legend, Fact and Art*, New York: St Martin's Press.
Coyle, William (ed.) (1986), *Aspects of Fantasy, Selected Essays From the Second International Conference on the Fantastic in Literature and Film*, Westport, Connecticut: Greenwood Press.
Cranny-Francis, Anne (1992) *Engendered Fictions: Analysing Gender in the Production and Reception of Texts*, Kensington NSW: New South Wales University Press.
Cross, Gillian [1990] (1992) *Wolf*, Puffin edn, London: Penguin.
Culler, Jonathan [1982] (1983) *On Deconstruction: Theory and Criticism after Structuralism*, Ithaca, New York: Cornell University Press.
Cullinan, Bernice E. (1989) *Literature and the Child*, San Diego, California: Harcourt, Brace, Jovanovich.
Dante Alighieri [*c.* 1307–21] *The Divine Comedy; 1 Hell (l'Inferno)*, translated by Dorothy L. Sayers (1949), Harmondsworth: Penguin.
Darnton, Robert (1984) 'The Meaning of Mother Goose', *New York Review of Books* Vol. xxxi No. 1, 2 February, pp. 41–7.
Davis, D.M. (1963) 'A conversation with William Golding', *The New Republic*, 4 May.
Davis, Gerry (1974) *Doctor Who and the Cybermen*, London: W.H. Allen & Co.
De Brunhoff, Jean [1934] (1955) *The Story of Babar the Little Elephant*, London: Methuen & Co.

—— [1935] (1953) *Babar's Travels*, London: Methuen & Co.

—— [1938] (1954) *Babar at Home*, London: Methuen & Co.

Defoe, Daniel [1719] (1981) *The Life and Surprizing Strange Adventures of Robinson Crusoe*, World's Classics edn, Oxford: Oxford University Press.

Dickens, Charles [1850] (No date given) *David Copperfield*, Library of Classics edn, London and Glasgow: Collins.

—— [1860–61] (1963) *Great Expectations*, Penguin edn, Harmondsworth: Penguin.

*Doctor Who Magazine*, Issue 227 (July 1995), London: Marvel Comics.

Donne, John [1635] (1971) 'The Relic', in Smith, A.J. (ed.) *John Donne: The Complete English Poems*, Harmondsworth: Penguin, pp. 75–6.

Dorfman, Ariel (1983) *The Empire's Old Clothes: What the Lone Ranger, Babar and other Innocent Heroes do to our minds . . .*, London: Pluto Press.

Douglas, Adam (1992) *The Beast Within*, London: Chapmans.

Doyle, Sir Arthur Conan (1987) *Sherlock Holmes: The Complete Illustrated Novels*, London: Chancellor Press. *A Study in Scarlet* [1887], *The Sign of Four* [1890], *The Hound of the Baskervilles* [1901–2], *The Valley of Fear* [1914–15].

Eagleton, Terry (1978) *Criticism and Ideology: A Study in Marxist Literary Theory*, Verso edn, London: Verso.

—— (1983) *Literary Theory: An Introduction*, London: Basil Blackwell.

Eliot, T.S. (1922) *The Waste Land* in *Collected Poems 1909 – 1935* (1936), London: Faber & Faber.

Ende, Michael (1984) [First published in German 1979. First published in English 1983] *The Neverending Story*, Harmondsworth: Penguin.

Euripides, *Medea*, translated by R.C. Trevelyan (1949), in Robinson, C.A. (ed.), *An Anthology of Greek Drama*, New York: Rhinehart & Co., pp. 141–8.

Everman, Welch (1993) *Cult Horror Films*, New York: Carol Publishing Group.

Fiennes, Richard (1976) *The Order of Wolves*, London: Hamish Hamilton.

Fleming, Ian (1954) *Casino Royale*, New York: Macmillan.

Fordham, Freida (1966) *An Introduction to Jung's Psychology*, Penguin edn, Harmondsworth: Penguin.

Fowles, John [1969] (1971) *The French Lieutenant's Woman*, London: Panther Books.

Fox, Michael W. (1978) 'Man, wolf and dog' in Hall, Roberta L. and Sharp, Henry S. (eds) *Wolf and Man: Evolution in Parallel*, New York: Academic Press, pp. 25–30.

French, Marilyn (1992) *The War Against Women*, London: Hamish Hamilton.

Frye, Northrop (1966) 'The archetypes of literature', in Vickery, J.B. (ed.) *Myth and Literature: Contemporary Theory and Practice*, Lincoln: University of Nebraska Press.

—— (1983) *The Great Code: The Bible and Literature*, London: Ark Paperbacks.

Genette, Gérard [1972] (1980) *Narrative Discourse*, translated by Jane E. Lewin, Oxford: Basil Blackwell.

George, Jean Craighead [1959] (1975) *My Side of the Mountain*, New York: Dutton.

—— [1972] (1976) *Julie of the Wolves*, Harmondsworth: Penguin.

Golding, William [1954] (1962) *Lord of the Flies*, Educational Edn, London: Faber.

Gould, Stephen Jay (1988) *Time's Arrow, Time's Cycle: Myth and Metaphor in the Discovery of Geological Time*, Pelican edn, Harmondsworth: Penguin.

Graham, Bob [1992] (1994) *Rose Meets Mr Wintergarten*, Puffin edn, Ringwood, Victoria: Penguin.

Green, Roger Lancelyn (1956) *The Adventures of Robin Hood*, Harmondsworth: Penguin.

Grimm, The Brothers (1986) *Hansel and Gretel*, illustrated by Anthony Browne, London: Magnet.

—— [Grimm, Jacob and Grimm, Wilhelm] (1994) *The Complete Illustrated Works of the Brothers Grimm*, 1853 text, London: Chancellor Press.

Haggard, H. Rider [1885] (1958) *King Solomon's Mines*, Puffin edn, Harmondsworth: Penguin.
—— [1889] (1995) 'A Tale of Three Lions' in Bristow, Joseph (ed.) *The Oxford Book of Adventure Stories*, Oxford, New York: Oxford University Press, pp. 51–77.
Hall, Roberta L. and Sharp, Henry S. (eds) (1978) *Wolf and Man: Evolution in Parallel*, New York: Academic Press.
Halliwell, Leslie (1981) *Halliwell's Film Guide*, third edn, London: Granada.
Hart, Josephine [1991] (1992) *Damage*, London: Arrow Books.
Hein, Hilde (1993) 'Refining feminist theory: lessons from aesthetics' in Hein, Hilde and Korsmeyer, Carolyn (eds) *Aesthetics in Feminist Perspective*, Bloomington and Indianapolis: Indiana University Press, pp. 3–18.
Hein, Hilde and Korsmeyer, Carolyn (eds) (1993) *Aesthetics in Feminist Perspective*, Bloomington and Indianapolis: Indiana University Press.
Henderson, Joseph L. (1964) 'Ancient myths and modern man' in Jung, Carl G. *et al.*, *Man and His Symbols*, Laurel edn, New York: Dell Publishing.
Henty, G.A. [1894] (1995) 'The Man-Eater of the Terai' in Bristow, Joseph (ed.) *The Oxford Book of Adventure Stories*, Oxford, New York: Oxford University Press, pp. 97–107.
Herbert, Frank [1966] (1984) *Dune*, London: New English Library.
Heseltine, Harry (ed.) (1972) *The Penguin Book of Australian Verse*, Harmondsworth: Penguin.
Hite, Shere [1994] (1995) *The Hite Report on the Family: Growing Up Under Patriarchy*, paperback edn, London: Hodder and Stoughton.
Holbrook, David (1973) 'The problem of C.S. Lewis' in *Children's Literature in Education* 10, March, pp. 3–25.
Hollindale, Peter (1988) 'Ideology and the children's book', *Signal* No. 55, January, pp. 11–30.
Holm, Anne [1963] (1980) *I am David*, Magnet edn, London: Methuen.
Holt, J.C. (1982) *Robin Hood*, London: Thames & Hudson.
*Holy Bible* (No date given), King James version, Oxford: Oxford University Press.
Homer, *The Odyssey*, translated by E.V. Rieu (1946), Harmondsworth: Penguin.
—— *The Iliad*, translated by E.V. Rieu (1950), Harmondsworth: Penguin.
*Homilies* [1574] (1850) edited by G.E. Corrie, London: Cambridge University Press.
Hood, Jean [1994] (1996) *The Dragon of Brog*, illustrated by Peter Kavanagh, Oxford Paperback edn, Oxford: Oxford University Press.
Huck, Charlotte S., Hepler, Susan and Hickman, Janet (1987) *Children's Literature in the Elementary School*, 4th edn, Fort Worth, Texas: Holt, Rinehart & Winston.
Hunt, Peter (1991) *Criticism, Theory and Children's Literature*, Oxford: Blackwell.
—— (1994) *An Introduction to Children's Literature*, Oxford: Oxford University Press.
Isaacs, Neil D. and Zimbardo, Rose A. (eds) (1968) *Tolkien and the Critics: Essays on J.R.R. Tolkien's 'The Lord of the Rings'*, Notre Dame, Indiana: University of Notre Dame Press.
Iser, Wolfgang (1980) *The Act of Reading: A Theory of Aesthetic Response*, London: Johns Hopkins University Press.
Jackson, Steve and Livingstone, Jan (1982) *The Warlock of Firetop Mountain*, Puffin Books, Harmondsworth: Penguin.
James, P.D. (1982) *The Skull Beneath the Skin*, London: Sphere Books.
Joyce, James [1916] (1952) *A Portrait of the Artist as a Young Man*, London: Jonathan Cape.
Jung, C.G. (1959) *Collected Works*, Vol. 9, Part 1, London: Routledge & Kegan Paul.
—— [1964] (1968) 'Approaching the unconscious' in Jung, Carl G. *et al.*, *Man and His Symbols*, Laurel edn, New York: Dell Publishing, pp. 1–94.

Jung, Carl G., von Franz, M.L., Henderson, Joseph, L., Jacobi, Jolande, Jaffé, Aniela, (1968) *Man and His Symbols*, Laurel edn, New York: Dell Publishing.
Keats, John (no date given) *Letters*, London: Thomas Nelson & Sons.
—— [1819] (1995) 'La Belle Dame Sans Merci', reprinted in *Selected Poems*, Everyman edn, London: J.M. Dent.
Keenan, Hugh T. (1968), 'The appeal of *The Lord of the Rings*: A struggle for life' in Isaacs, N.D. and Zimbardo, R.A. (eds) *Tolkien and the Critics*, London: University of Notre Dame Press.
Kennedy, E.B. (1889) *Blacks and Bushrangers: Adventures in Queensland*, London: Sampson, Low, Marston & Co.
Kerenyi, Carl (1958) *The Gods of the Greeks*, Harmondsworth: Penguin.
Kermode, Frank (1964) Introduction to *The Tempest*, Arden Shakespeare Series, London: Methuen & Co.
—— (1966) *The Sense of an Ending: Studies in the Theory of Fiction*, London: Oxford University Press.
Kerouac, Jack [1957] (1972) *On the Road*, Harmondsworth: Penguin.
Kingston, W.H.G. (no date given) *True Blue*, London: Griffith Farran Browne & Co.
Kipling, Rudyard [1901] (1946) *Kim*, Melbourne: Macmillan.
Kristeva, Julia (1986) 'A question of subjectivity – an interview' in *Women's Review* No. 12, reprinted in Rice, P. and Waugh, P. (eds) (1989) *Modern Literary Theory: A Reader*, pp. 128–34, London: Edward Arnold.
Lawson, Henry [1892] (1986) 'The Drover's Wife', reprinted in J. Barnes (ed.) *The Penguin Henry Lawson Short Stories*, Ringwood, Victoria: Penguin.
Leach, Edmund (1970) *Levi-Strauss*, London: Fontana.
Le Guin, Ursula [1968] (1971) *A Wizard of Earthsea*, Puffin edn, Harmondsworth: Penguin.
—— (1975) 'This fear of dragons' in Blishen, Edward (ed.) *The Thorny Paradise*, London: Kestrel.
—— (1993a) *Earthsea Revisioned*, Cambridge: Children's Literature New England in association with Green Bay Publications.
—— (1993b) *The Earthsea Quartet* (*A Wizard of Earthsea* [1968], *The Tombs of Atuan* [1972], *The Farthest Shore* [1973], *Tehanu* [1990]), Puffin, one-volume edn, London: Penguin.
Leser, David (1995) 'Gender mender', *Good Weekend*, 7 October, Sydney: John Fairfax Publications, pp. 24–30.
Lethbridge, T.C. (1962) *Witches*, London: Routledge & Kegan Paul.
Lewis, C.S. [1950] (1959) *The Lion, the Witch and the Wardrobe*, Puffin edn, Harmondsworth: Penguin.
—— [1954] (1965) *The Horse and his Boy*, Puffin edn, Harmondsworth: Penguin.
—— [1955] (1963) *The Magician's Nephew*, Puffin edn, Harmondsworth: Penguin.
—— (1955) 'The dethronement of power', *Time and Tide*, 22 October, reprinted in Isaacs, N.D. and Zimbardo, R.A. (eds) (1968) *Tolkien and the Critics*, London: University of Notre Dame Press, pp. 12–16.
—— [1956] (1964) *The Last Battle*, Puffin edn, Harmondsworth: Penguin.
Livingstone, Ian (1983) *The Forest of Doom*, Puffin Books, Harmondsworth: Penguin.
Lodge, David (ed.) (1988) *Modern Criticism and Theory*, London: Longman.
Lodge, Louis (1987) 'Tales of adventure' in Saxby, M. and Winch, G. (eds) *Give Them Wings: The Experience of Children's Literature*, South Melbourne: Macmillan.
London, Jack [1903] (1967) *The Call of the Wild*, Masterpiece Library edn, New York: Magnum Books.
Lopez, Barry H. (1978) *Of Wolves and Men*, London, Toronto, Melbourne: J.M. Dent & Sons.

McCaughey, Patrick (1984) 'Picasso: innovator and image-maker' in *Picasso*, Melbourne: Cultural Corporation of Australia.
McCaughrean, Geraldine and Palin, Nicki (illustrator), [1989] (1994) *Saint George and the Dragon*, paperback edn, Oxford: Oxford University Press.
Mackenzie, Compton (1972) *Perseus*, Golden Tales of Greece Series, New York: World Publishing.
Mahy, Margaret (1995) *The Man whose Mother was a Pirate*, illustrated by Margaret Chamberlain, Puffin edn, London: Penguin.
Malory, Sir Thomas [1485] (1906) *Le Morte d'Arthur*, Everyman edn (two vols), London: Dent.
Malouf, David (1993) *Remembering Babylon*, Sydney: Random House Australia.
Marks, Elaine and de Courtivron, Isabelle (eds) (1981) *New French Feminisms: An Anthology*, Brighton: Harvester.
Marlowe, Christopher [*c*.1604] (1909) *Dr Faustus* in *Christopher Marlowe: Plays*, Everyman edn, London: J.M. Dent & Sons, pp. 120–58.
Marryat, Captain (no date given) *The Settlers in Canada*, London: Juvenile Productions.
Mason, Gay (1995) 'Deconstructing masculinity: body politics, organisations, and strategies for social change', a paper delivered at the National Conference on the Effect of Organisational Culture on Women in Universities: *Women, Culture and Universities: A Chilly Climate*, University of Technology, Sydney, 19 and 20 April.
Midgley, Mary (1995) *Beast and Man: The Roots of Human Nature*, revised edn, London: Routledge.
Miles, Rosalind (1989) *The Women's History of the World*, London: Paladin.
Moi, Toril (1985) *Sexual Textual Politics*, London: Methuen.
Montaigne, Michel de [1603] (1965) *Essays*, translated by John Florio, Everyman edn, London: J.M. Dent & Sons.
Moseley, Ann (1988) 'The journey through the "space in the text" to *Where the Wild Things Are*', *Children's Literature in Education*, Vol. 19, No. 2, pp. 86–93.
Noyes, Alfred [1910] (1981) *The Highwayman*, illustrated by Charles Keeping, Oxford: Oxford University Press.
O'Connor, Peter (1985) *Understanding Jung: Understanding Yourself*, North Ryde, NSW: Methuen Haynes.
Opie, Iona and Opie, Peter (1974) *The Classic Fairy Tales*, London: Oxford University Press.
Ortner, Sherry B. (1974) 'Is male to female as nature is to culture?' in Rosaldo, M.Z. and Lamphere, L. (eds) *Woman, Culture & Society*, Stanford: Stanford University Press, pp. 67–87.
Otten, Charlotte F. (ed.) (1986) *A Lycanthoropy Reader: Werewolves in Western Culture*, Syracuse, New York: Syracuse University Press.
Owen, Wilfred (1933) *The Poems of Wilfred Owen*, London: Chatto & Windus.
Park, Ruth [1974] (1977) *Callie's Castle*, paperback edn, London and Sydney: Angus & Robertson.
Paterson, Andrew Barton [1895] (1972) 'The Man from Snowy River' in Heseltine, Harry (ed.) *The Penguin Book of Australian Verse*, Harmondsworth: Penguin, pp. 78–82.
Paterson, Katherine [1978] (1980) *Bridge to Terabithia*, Puffin edn, Harmondsworth: Penguin.
—— [1978] (1981) *The Great Gilly Hopkins*, Puffin edn, Harmondsworth: Penguin.
Paulsen, Garry (1994) *Hatchet*, Macmillan Children's Books, London: Macmillan.
Pearce, Philippa [1958] (1976) *Tom's Midnight Garden*, Puffin edn, Harmondsworth: Penguin.
Pearson, Carol and Pope, Katherine (1981) *The Female Hero in British and American Literature*, New York and London: R.R. Bowker.

Perrault, Charles [1697] (1969) *Fairy Tales*, translated by A.E. Johnson, New York: Dover Publications.
Plato, *The Republic*, translated by F.M. Cornford (1941), Oxford, Clarendon Press.
—— *Phaedo* in *The Last Days of Socrates*, translated by Hugh Tredennick (1954), Harmondsworth: Penguin.
Plumwood, Val (1993) *Feminism and the Mastery of Nature*, London and New York: Routledge.
Poe, Edgar Allan [1844] (1985) 'The purloined letter' reprinted in *The Norton Anthology of American Literature*, Vol. 1, 2nd edn, New York, London: Norton.
Potter, Beatrix (1902) *The Tale of Peter Rabbit*, London: Frederick Warne.
Praz, Mario (1960) *The Romantic Agony*, translated by Angus Davidson, London: Fontana Library.
Prescott, William H. [1847] (1908) *History of the Conquest of Peru*, Everyman edn, London: J.M. Dent & Sons.
Rawson, Philip and Legeza, Laszlo (1973) *Tao: the Chinese Philosophy of Time and Change*, London: Thames & Hudson.
Rees, David (1980) *The Marble in the Water: Essays on contemporary writers of fiction for children and young adults*, Boston: Horn Book.
Renault, Mary (1984) *The Alexander Trilogy* (*Fire From Heaven* [1970], *The Persian Boy* [1972], *Funeral Games* [1981]), Harmondsworth: Penguin.
Rice, Philip and Waugh, Patricia (1989) *Modern Literary Theory: A Reader*, London: Edward Arnold.
Rodda, Emily (1993) *Rowan of Rin*, Sydney: Omnibus Books, Ashton Scholastic.
Rosaldo, Michelle Zimbalist and Lamphere, Louise (eds) (1974) *Women, Culture and Society*, Stanford, California: Stanford University Press.
Rose, H.J. (1958) *A Handbook of Greek Mythology*, London: Methuen.
Ryan, John [1976] (1995) *Pugwash and the Sea Monster*, Puffin edn, London: Penguin.
Said, Edward [1978] (1995) *Orientalism: Western Conceptions of the Orient*, Harmondsworth: Penguin.
—— [1993] (1994) *Culture and Imperialism*, London: Vintage.
Salinger, J.D. [1951] (1958) *The Catcher in the Rye*, Harmondsworth: Penguin.
Sandars, N.K. (translator) (1960) *The Epic of Gilgamesh*, Harmondsworth: Penguin.
de Saussure, Ferdinand [1915] (1985) 'The Linguistic Sign', reprinted in Innis, R.E. (ed.) *Semiotics*, Bloomington: Indiana University Press.
—— [1915] (1974) *Course in General Linguistics*, London: Fontana/Collins.
Saxby, H.M. (1969) *A History of Australian Children's Literature 1841 – 1941*, Sydney: Wentworth Books.
—— (1990) *The Great Deeds of Heroic Women*, illustrated by Robert Ingpen, Newtown, NSW: Millenium Books.
—— (1993) *The Proof of the Puddin': Australian Children's Literature 1970 – 1990*, Gosford: Ashton Scholastic.
Sayers, Dorothy [1937] (1974) *Busman's Honeymoon*, NEL paperback edn, London: New English Library.
Schefold, Karl (1966) *Myth and Legend in Early Greek Art*, London: Thames & Hudson.
Selden, Raman (1986) *A Reader's Guide to Contemporary Literary Theory*, Lexington: University Press of Kentucky.
Sendak, Maurice [1963] (1967) *Where the Wild Things Are*, London: Bodley Head.
Shakespeare, William (*c.* 1602) *Hamlet*, New Penguin Shakespeare edn (1980), Harmondsworth: Penguin.
—— (*c.* 1602) *Troilus and Cressida*, New Penguin Shakespeare edn (1986), Harmondsworth: Penguin.
—— (*c.* 1604) *Othello*, Arden edn (1965), London: Methuen & Co.

—— (*c*. 1605) *King Lear*, Arden edn (1972), London: Methuen & Co.
—— (*c*. 1611) *The Tempest*, Arden edn (1964), London: Methuen & Co.
Sharp, Henry S. (1978) 'Comparative ethnology of the wolf and the Chipeweyan' in Hall, Roberta L. and Sharp, Henry S. (eds) *Wolf and Man: Evolution in Parallel*, New York: Academic Press, pp. 163–8.
Shelley, Percy Bysshe [1819] (1970) 'On the Medusa of Leonardo da Vinci' in *Poetical Works*, edited by Thomas Hutchinson (1970), London, Oxford, New York: Oxford University Press.
Showalter, Elaine [1979] (1989) 'Towards a feminist poetics' in Rice, P. and Waugh, P. (eds) *Modern Literary Theory: A Reader*, London: Edward Arnold.
Southall, Ivan [1967] (1971) *To the Wild Sky*, Puffin edn, Harmondsworth: Penguin.
Spacks, Patricia Meyer (1968) 'Power and meaning in *The Lord of the Rings*' in Isaacs, Neil D. and Zimbardo, Rose A. (eds) *Tolkien and the Critics: Essays on J.R.R. Tolkien's 'The Lord of the Rings'*, Notre Dame, Indiana: University of Notre Dame Press.
Speare, Elizabeth George (1958) *The Witch of Blackbird Pond*, Boston: Houghton Mifflin.
Stables, Gordon (no date given) *Stanley Grahame: Boy and Man: A Tale of the Dark Continent*, London: Henry Frowde, Hodder & Stoughton.
Stephens, John (1992) *Language and Ideology in Children's Fiction*, London and New York: Longman.
Stevenson, Robert Louis [1883] (1946) *Treasure Island*, Puffin edn, Harmondsworth: Puffin Books.
—— [1886] (1925) *Kidnapped* in *Treasure Island and Kidnapped*, Everyman edn, London: J.M. Dent & Sons.
Sturrock, John (1986) *Structuralism*, London: Paladin.
Sutcliff, Rosemary [1954] (1977) *The Eagle of the Ninth*, Puffin edn, Harmondsworth: Penguin.
—— [1958] (1976) *Warrior Scarlet*, Puffin edn, Harmondsworth: Penguin.
—— [1959] (1972) *The Lantern Bearers*, London: Oxford University Press.
—— [1960] (1965) *Rudyard Kipling*, London: Bodley Head.
—— [1961] (1982) *Dawn Wind*, Puffin edn, Harmondsworth: Penguin.
—— [1961] (1966) *Dragon Slayer; The Story of Beowulf*, Puffin edn, Harmondsworth: Penguin.
—— [1964] (1965) *Sword at Sunset*, Peacock edn, Harmondsworth: Penguin.
—— (1974) Interview with Emma Fisher in Wintle, Justin and Fisher, Emma (eds), *The Pied Pipers: Interviews with the Influential Creators of Children's Literature*, London: Paddington Press.
—— [1977] (1982) *Sun Horse, Moon Horse*, Knight Books edn, London: Hodder & Stoughton.
—— [1978] (1980) *Song for a Dark Queen*, Knight Books edn, London: Hodder & Stoughton.
Swinburne, A.C. [1887] (1919) 'Dolores', reprinted in *Selections from A.C. Swinburne*, edited by Edmund Gosse and Thomas James Wise, London: William Heinemann.
Taylor, Theodore [1969] (1973) *The Cay*, Puffin edn, Harmondsworth: Penguin.
Tennyson, Alfred [1842] (1971) 'Ulysses' reprinted in *Poems and Plays*, London, Oxford, New York: Oxford University Press.
Thompson, Jon (1993) *Fiction, Crime and Empire: Clues to Modernity and Postmodernism*, Urbana and Chicago: University of Illinois Press.
Todorov, Tzvetan [1970] (1975) *The Fantastic; A Structural Approach to a Literary Genre*, translated by Richard Howard, Ithaca, New York: Cornell University Press.
Tolkien, J.R.R. [1937] (1966) *The Hobbit*, paperback edn, London: Allen & Unwin.
—— (1954) *The Fellowship of the Ring*, London: Allen & Unwin.
—— [1954] (1981) *The Two Towers*, 4th edn, London: Allen & Unwin.

—— (1955) *The Return of the King*, London: Allen & Unwin.
—— (1964) *Tree and Leaf*, London: Unwin Books.
Townsend, John Rowe [1965] (1976) *Written for Children*, Harmondsworth: Penguin.
Trease, Geoffrey (1977) *Bows Against the Barons*, revised edn, London: Hodder & Stoughton.
Treece, Henry [1955] (1967a) *Viking's Dawn*, Puffin edn, Harmondsworth: Penguin.
—— [1957] (1967b) *The Road to Miklagard*, Puffin edn, Harmondsworth: Penguin.
—— [1960] (1967c) *Viking's Sunset*, Puffin edn, Harmondsworth: Penguin.
Tunstall, Gillian (1992) *The Image of Mothers in Contemporary Children's Picture Books*, Kuring-Gai Studies in Children's Literature No. 4, School of Teacher Education: University of Technology, Sydney.
Untermeyer, Bryna and Untermeyer, Louis (1973) *Stories and Poems for the Very Young*, New York: Golden Press.
Vickery, John B. (ed.) (1966) *Myth and Literature: Contemporary Theory and Practice*, Lincoln: University of Nebraska Press.
Voltaire [1758] (1947) *Candide or Optimism*, translated by John Butt, Harmondsworth: Penguin.
Wagner, Jenny [1977] (1979) *John Brown, Rose and the Midnight Cat*, illustrated by Ron Brooks, Puffin edn, Harmondsworth: Penguin.
Warner, Marina (1994) *From the Beast to the Blonde: On Fairy Tales and their Tellers*, London: Chatto & Windus.
Webster, John [1623] (1956) *The Duchess of Malfi* in *John Webster and Cyril Tourneur (Four Plays)*, A Mermaid Dramabook, New York: Hill and Wang.
Webster, Roger (1990) *Studying Literary Theory*, London: Edward Arnold.
Welch, Ronald [1954] (1970) *Knight Crusader*, London: Oxford University Press.
Weston, Jessie L. [1920] (1957) *From Ritual to Romance*, New York: Doubleday Anchor Books.
White, Patrick [1957] (1960) *Voss*, Harmondsworth: Penguin.
White, Richard (1995) 'The Man from Snowy River', *The Australian*, 17 October, p. 15.
Wilde, Oscar [1894] (1954) *Salome* in *Penguin Plays: Oscar Wilde*, Harmondsworth: Penguin.
Wintle, Justin and Fisher, Emma (eds) (1974) *The Pied Pipers: Interviews with the Influential Creators of Children's Literature*, London: Paddington Press.
Wrightson, Patricia [1973] (1975) *The Nargun and the Stars*, Ringwood, Victoria: Penguin.
Yeats, W.B. [1933] (1950) 'Byzantium', reprinted in *The Collected Poems*, 2nd edn, London: Macmillan.
Zipes, Jack (1979) *Breaking the Magic Spell: Radical Theories of Folk and Fairy Tales*, London: Heinemann.

## FILMS CITED

*Alien* (1979), Director: Ridley Scott. TCF.
*Apocalypse Now* (1979), Director: Francis Coppola. Omni Zoetrope.
*Blood Orgy of the She Devils* (1973), Director: Ted Mikels. Geneni Film Distributing Company.
*The Curse of the Werewolf* (1961), Director: Terence Fisher. U-I/Hammer.
*Daughters of Darkness* (1971), Director: Harvey Kumel. Geneni.
*E.T.* (1982), Director: Steven Spielberg. Universal.
*Fatal Attraction* (1987), Director: Adrian Lyne. Paramount.
*The Howling* (1981), Director: Joe Dante. Avco Embassy/International Film Distributors.
*I Was a Teenage Werewolf* (1957), Director: Gene Fowler jnr. AIP.
*Jaws* (1975), Director: Steven Spielberg. Universal.

*Lady Frankenstein* (1971), Director: Mel Welles. New World Pictures.
*Legend of the Wolf Woman* (1977), Director: Rino di Silvestro. Dimension Pictures.
*The Lion King* (1996), Walt Disney Home Video, The Walt Disney Company.
*The Neverending Story* (1983), Director: Wolfgang Petersen. Roadshow Distributors.
*One Hundred and One Dalmatians* (1960), Director: Wolfgang Reitherman. Walt Disney.
*Presumed Innocent* (1990), Director: Alan J. Pakula. Warner.
*Snow White and the Seven Dwarves* (1937), Director: David Hand. Walt Disney.
*Star Wars* (1977), Director: George Lucas. TCF/Lucasfilm.
*The Werewolf* (1956), Director: Fred F. Sears. Columbia/Clover.
*The Werewolf of London* (1935), Director: Stuart Walker. Universal.
*Werewolf of Washington* (1973), Director: Milton Ginsberg. Diplomat Pictures.
*The Wizard of Oz* (1939), Director: Victor Fleming. MGM.
*The Wolf Man* (1940), Director: George Waggner. Universal.
*Working Girl* (1988), Director: Mike Nichols. Fox.

# INDEX

LaVergne, TN USA
15 September 2010
197202LV00002B/15/A